INNOVATIVE GROWTH

PRAISE FOR INNOVATIVE GROWTH

"At last, a book that demystifies innovation with a toolkit that everyone can follow to accelerate growth."

—**Eduardo Gomez,** Chief of Strategy and Business Development, LRN.com, USA

"Nowadays, in order to maintain a sustained business, a company needs to gather customer insights and develop a balanced innovation strategy. Here you will really learn how to make it happen."

—**Caroline Matti,** Head of Rates Sales, HSBC Continental Europe, France

"If you are a mid-sized business looking to match your technology to market needs, this book tells you how. Innovative Growth might not be easy but in this book you'll find practical ways to make it possible."

—**Dr Matthias Seiler,** CEO, BFI, Germany

"Distils key essentials for entrepreneurial growth, so that senior teams can tackle the knotty problem of protecting today's business while building innovation for tomorrow."

—**Professor Andrew Burke,** Dean of Trinity Business School, Ireland

"For me, customer insights have always been the most crucial element of innovation and so it's good to see a book that puts the voice of the customer centre-stage."

—**Tove Weigel,** Technology Development, SKF, Sweden

"Illustrates that behind great innovations are diverse people who collaborate brilliantly and that behind great businesses are innovative cultures."

—**Tara Foley,** CEO, AXA Retail, UK

PRAISE FOR INNOVATIVE GROWTH

"Truly understanding people's needs and then meeting those needs better than everyone else, determines success. This continuous cycle of exploring, testing and adapting requires a coherent set of innovation disciplines which are found in this book."

—**Kelly Solomon,** Global Chief Marketing Officer, KIND Snacks, USA

"Multinationals scale for many reasons; but the innovation of subsidiary teams should not be underestimated – whether that be in product, processes or practices. Innovative Growth recognizes this and offers a turbo charge to local SBU leadership teams."

—**Gareth Lambe,** VP International Business and Head of Meta, Ireland

"Innovation is synonymous with technology; however, it is engaged teams with different skillsets and mindsets that drive innovation. This book charts how to develop a sustainable growth organization."

—**Professor Amanda Shantz,** MBA Director, University of St Gallen, Switzerland

"Developing disruptive, digital business models requires managing many moving parts. The lessons here are imperative for senior teams seeking to rapidly scale and sustain performance."

—**Dr Shahram Famorzadeh,** Senior VP Engineering, DrChrono, USA

"The management of innovation is essential to sustainable growth. The journey to higher innovation is demanding. This insightful book provides a valuable map to complete it successfully. Leaders and teams will be better equipped after reading it."

—**Paschal Donohoe,** Minister for Finance, Ireland, and President of the Eurogroup

INNOVATIVE GROWTH
ISBN 978-91-87791-32-1
First edition, first print run

© Keith Goffin and Ian Kierans 2023
All rights reserved. No Reproduction, copy or transmission of this publication may be made without written permission.

DESIGN: Victor Mingovits
EDITOR: Allison McKechnie
AUTHOR PHOTOS: Smiles Photography
PRINTER: Bulls Graphics AB

Nordic Swan Ecolabel, printed matter, 3041 0984

PUBLISHER:
Rheologica Publishing
www.rheologica.com

KEITH GOFFIN AND **IAN KIERANS**

INNOVATIVE GROWTH

THE JOURNEY FROM A TO B WHILE BUILDING C

*Inspired by the managers and innovators
who keep the wheels of progress turning.*

CONTENTS

Preface .... **xiii**
Online resources .... **xv**
Case studies .... **xvi**
About the authors .... **xviii**
Motivation for this book .... **xxi**
Acknowledgements .... **xxiii**
Copyright material .... **xxvi**

Introduction: The innovation journey
    Introduction **3**
    Innovative growth **12**
    Components of innovation management **21**
    Phases of the innovation journey................................. **24**
    Format of this book... **27**
    Summary **29**

Phase 1: Shaping innovation strategy
    Introduction **33**
    Essential background **37**
    Aligning business and innovation strategy **50**
    Scanning the innovation landscape.............................. **52**
    Declaring innovation intent **73**
    Mindset matters... **77**
    Summary **79**

Phase 2: Organizing the journey
Introduction 83
Essential background 86
Mechanisms for the innovation journey 97
Forming innovation governance 98
Designing innovation structure 108
Designing innovation teams 112
Mindset matters 121
Summary 125

Phase 3: Generating deep insights and novel solutions
Introduction 129
Essential background 133
Planning insight generation 143
Identifying customer needs—Data collection 145
Identifying customer needs—Data analysis 163
Creating novel solutions—Ideation 185
Mindset matters 191
Summary 193

Phase 4: Selecting projects for implementation
Introduction 197
Essential background 202
Defining selection criteria 205
Reviewing the whole portfolio 214
Managing portfolio meetings 221
Mindset matters 227
Summary 229

Phase 5: Getting innovations to market

Introduction **233**
Essential background **237**
Managing incremental projects **245**
Driving breakthrough and radical projects **251**
Developing new markets **265**
Mindset matters **273**
Summary **275**

Phase 6: Building a dynamic innovation capability

Introduction **279**
Essential background **282**
Step 1—Reviewing innovation projects **290**
Step 2—Diagnosing the journey **293**
Step 3—Learning from outside **296**
Step 4—Preparing for the next journey **311**
Mindset matters (in conclusion) **317**
Summary **319**

References and notes **321**
Index **337**

PREFACE

There are many books on innovation management. Maybe too many. So, why write another one? Quite simply because the majority of existing innovation books are written either for start-ups or for large corporates. Nothing previously focused exactly on mid-sized businesses (MSBs) and strategic business units (SBUs) that want to achieve growth through business-wide innovation. Such businesses face unique challenges and opportunities and so we have written this book for them. It is a practical guide for their journey to innovative growth that addresses four issues.

First, so much has been written on the topic of innovation that MSB and SBU managers face an information tsunami, a myriad of 'hot' innovation topics and tools on top of proven classics. Managers do not have the time to wade through all of these. So, we provide a carefully selected set of tools and techniques that can be applied in an integrative way to drive innovative growth.

Second, globalization, digitalization and newly emerged environmental and social consciousness have created not only opportunities but also challenges for MSBs and SBUs. This creates a pressing need for business-wide innovation—new products, services, experiences, channels, processes and entire business models. Nowadays, innovation must address the needs of multiple stakeholders: from customers, employees and partners to the wider community and of course investors. So, in this book, we consider innovation in its broadest sense and with a broad set of stakeholders.

Third, although senior managers have the autonomy and responsibility to create new growth, their mindsets tend to focus on operational efficiency and incremental innovation. Other books concentrate on innovation processes but do not tell you about the mindsets—the mix of thoughts, feelings and behaviours you and your fellow travellers will experience. These will include moments of doubt and moments of elation. Remember that processes make innovation possible, but people make it happen.

Fourth, achieving innovative growth is like going on a journey; a journey that will be distinct for each and every business. Making the journey a success requires you to understand your starting point 'A', to declare the desired destination, point 'B', and to develop the innovation capabilities 'C' needed to get there. We clearly map out the phases of this innovation journey, providing a no-nonsense guide for not only senior managers but also the employees and other external collaborators who will be making this journey.

This guidebook takes you through five phases. Phase 1 helps you shape your innovation strategy and Phase 2 will organize the journey by balancing both the hard and soft mechanisms required to go the distance. Phase 3 will develop deep customer insights and novel solutions, to address market needs. Next, Phase 4 will enable you to select the optimum portfolio of projects to implement and to achieve your strategy. Phase 5 supports you in tailoring your processes to get innovations to market. The end of the first innovation journey marks the transition to the next journey. Therefore, we explain the importance of taking the time to reflect in Phase 6, focusing on enhancing your capability to innovate, time and time again.

We deliberately present the journey from 'A' to 'B' while developing 'C' as a set of distinct phases, which is simple for MSBs and SBUs to follow. We're not saying that everything about the journey will be easy, but it will be worthwhile. Innovation requires energy, determination and patience. We've accompanied numerous managers and teams on their innovation journeys and we have learnt from them just how satisfying it is to launch successful innovations. Many of the managers and teams we've worked with have contributed directly to this book. So, it is ideas from managers and innovators working at the leading edge that we share in this book.

ONLINE RESOURCES

Extensive resources are available at www.innovativegrowth.com

- Downloadable copies of key tools included in this book.
- Supplementary tools.
- A statement about fair use of tools / copyright.
- Instructions on how to connect and share your stories of making the innovation journey.

CASE STUDIES

Innovation is a very practical subject and so we include 24 cases based on our experience with businesses. The cases bring to life the phases of the innovation journey. They originate from ten different countries and are a mix of mid-sized businesses (MSBs) and strategic business units (SBUs), which span B2B and B2C and products and services. A few cases of start-ups, small sized businesses and corporates have also been included.

CHAPTER TITLE	NAME & ORIGIN	INDUSTRY	BUSINESS TYPE	REVENUE	EMPLOYEES
Introduction **The innovation journey**	I-1 Svensson Sweden (1887)	Textiles	MSB: B2B Product	€80M	420
	I-2 Shotgun France (2014)	Live Events	Start-up: B2C & B2B Digital Platform Services	€30M	30
	I-3 Heitkamp & Thumann Germany (1978)	Precision Components	MSB: B2B Products & Services	€508M	2,312
Phase 1 **Shaping innovation strategy**	1-1 "X"	Technical OEM services	MSB: B2B Services	€90M	2,000
	1-2 Coillte Ireland (1989)	Forestry, Wood Products, Land Services	MSB: B2B Products & Services	€327M	1,100
	1-3 Fashion Power Netherlands (1897)	Textiles	MSB: B2C to B2B Products & Services	N/A	100
	1-4 Diageo EU Beer Ireland (1759)	FMCG Alcohol	SBU: Beer Products	N/A	1,000
Phase 2 **Organizing the journey**	2-1 Red Ventures USA (2000)	Internet Media and Marketing Services	MSB: B2C & B2B Digital Services	$2B	3,500
	2-2 DCC Ireland (1976)	Energy, Healthcare & Technology	Corporate: B2C & B2B Products & Services	£14.8B	13,000
	2-3 Bank of Ireland Ireland (1783)	Financial Services (Retail Ireland)	SBU: B2C Services	€2.12B (Group)	9,782 (Group)

xvi   CASE STUDIES

CHAPTER TITLE	NAME & ORIGIN	INDUSTRY	BUSINESS TYPE	REVENUE	EMPLOYEES
Phase 3 Generating deep insights and novel solutions	3-1 Red Ventures USA (2000)	Internet Media and Marketing Services	MSB: B2C & B2B Digital Services	$2B	3,500
	3-2 Altro UK (1919)	Construction Products	MSB: B2B Products	£143M	800
	3-3 BASF Germany (1865)	Chemicals	SBU: B2B Products & Services	€59B (Group)	110,300 (Group)
	3-4 Climb On USA (2000)	Skin Products	SSB: B2C Products	N/A	3
Phase 4 Selecting projects for implementation	4-1 Richardson Sheffield UK (1839)	Consumer Goods (Kitchenware)	SBU: B2C Products	€66M (Amefa)	195 (Amefa)
	4-2 Softbank Robotics France (2005)	AI / Robotics	SBU: B2B Products & Services	N/A	500
	4-3 VMT Vision Power Germany (1995)	Image Processing	SBU: B2B Products & Services	€25M	130
Phase 5 Getting innovations to market	5-1 Mölnlycke Sweden (1849)	Medical Devices	MSB: B2B Products & Services	€1.45B	7,000
	5-2 Eurocaps UK (1994)	Health & Beauty Products	SBU: B2B Products & Services	£45M	270
	5-3 Nuesoft USA (1993)	Software / SaaS	MSB: B2B Software Services	$16M	200
Phase 6 Building a dynamic innovation capability	6-1 Patagonia USA (1973)	Textiles	MSB: B2C Products & Services	$1B	2,300
	6-2 Pinarello Italy (1952)	Sports Bicycles	SBU: B2B & B2C Products	€50M	45
	6-3 Cranfield Foundry Macedonia (2014)	Manufacturing Metal Components	MSB: B2B Products	N/A	150
	6-4 Alltech USA (1980)	Agricultural Products	MSB: B2B & B2C Products & Services	$3B	5,000

ABOUT THE AUTHORS

Keith Goffin (BSc, MSc, PhD) trained as a medical physicist and then worked on product and market management at Hewlett-Packard Medical Products Group, where he later studied part-time for his PhD. He is an Emeritus Professor at Cranfield School of Management, UK, and a Research Professor at Stockholm School of Economics. Keith has published over 50 academic papers and three books. His textbook, *Innovation Management: Effective Strategy and Implementation* (3rd edition 2017) is used in many universities and business schools. He is a world leader in techniques for identifying customers' hidden needs and linking these to innovation strategy. Currently, he teaches on several MBA programmes and is a consultant to leading organizations, supporting their successful implementation of innovation strategy.

Ian Kierans (BA, MA, MBA, PhD) trained as an organization psychologist, before becoming a management consultant at Accenture (Atlanta) and Diamond Technology Partners (New York), helping businesses shape and implement strategies for a digital era. In 2005 he co-founded Advanced Organisation—a consultancy and capability development firm specializing in strategy, innovation, and change. His PhD, at Cranfield School of Management, focused on a crucial topic: how established businesses can succeed at business model innovation. In his consultancy work, Ian helps businesses develop new strategies and market innovations, dynamic capabilities and to overcome mindset issues. He is an award-winning adjunct Professor at Trinity Business School and Mannheim Business School.

THE MOTIVATION FOR THE BOOK

How did two people from such different backgrounds come to collaborate on a book? Keith's background is the medical electronics industry, where he worked in technical and marketing functions before joining academia to research and teach innovation—this led him to a strong process and technology perspective on innovation. Ian's background is organizational psychology and business consultancy focusing on business change—this led him to a strategic and people perspective on innovation. Keith initially thought that Ian's perspective focused only on 'soft and holistic factors' and lacked precision. Ian initially thought that Keith's perspective was simply too 'process-driven' and lacked inspiration. Working together allowed them to agree that they were both wrong!

Before writing this book, Keith and Ian had cooperated on several consultancy projects. These helped established businesses navigate their innovation journeys, towards renewed success. Keith and Ian instinctively applied different approaches, which gave the client the benefit of understanding the strategic, technical, process and the people aspects of managing innovative growth. This created a novel, joint perspective on what matters in innovation. From this, they started to research appropriate tools and techniques, spanning strategic management, innovation management, and change management. All of the selected tools and techniques can help businesses achieve innovative growth, but it was the need to integrate them into a coherent set that was the motivation for this book.

Keith and Ian have worked with a wide range of MSBs and SBUs in very different industries. They've been party to the ups and downs these businesses have experienced, as certain approaches have worked while others disappointed. In addition, they have taught thousands of senior managers at top business schools. The ongoing interaction with senior managers highlighted two common problems. First, the responsibility for innovation is most often closely tied to one function, such as R&D or marketing, rather than being a fully cross-functional (business-wide) affair. That is why we guide the whole of the senior management team and all business functions. Innovation is a dynamic capability, not a function. The second common problem is that businesses become fixed on incremental innovation; here we show how to bring breakthrough and radical ideas to current and new markets.

Our motivation for this book was to help mid-sized businesses and strategic business units achieve innovative growth. We provide the key tools and techniques, presented in a way that will enable you to drive tangible results and build an innovation capability that can sustain your business for many years to come.

ACKNOWLEDGEMENTS

A book aimed at people working on innovation projects requires regular contact with companies. We are lucky enough to have been invited over recent years to work, long-term, with a significant number of mid-sized businesses, including some family-owned companies and strategic business units of larger corporations. Their projects, many of which are described in the case studies, are fascinating. It is this constant interaction with industry that has honed our views on how to manage innovation.

Many people have given up precious time to help us with the case studies or have provided material and ideas through being regular guest speakers at our lectures and in our client work. In addition, many colleagues at universities and institutes provided useful recommendations and have continually invited us to 'road-test' this work on their executive programmes. We are grateful to the following (in alphabetical order):

- Professor Pär Åhlström (Stockholm School of Economics)
- Massoud Alibakhsh (CEO, Xeba Technologies)
- Carlos Angrisano (President, Head of Digital Labs, Red Ventures)
- Paul Armstrong (European Supply Chain Director, Diageo)
- Dawn Bailey (Head of Financial Wellbeing, Bank of Ireland)
- Robert Behan (CEO, Olleco)
- Aleksei Beznosov (CEO TripleJump consultants)
- Lucy Bilotto (Marketing Manager, Altro Ltd.)
- Ciaran Black (Group Innovation Director, Coillte, now Innovation Consultant, Alltech)
- Andrew Bowen (Head of Mid-Market Enterprises HSBC Ireland)

- Professor Louis Brennan (Trinity College Dublin)
- Louise Brierley-Ingham (PR Manager, Patagonia EMEA)
- Gerard Britchfield (CFO & COO, Coillte)
- Charles Broussaudier (VP, CIO, SoftBank Robotics)
- Dr Giulio Buciuni (Assistant Professor, Trinity College Dublin)
- Professor David Coghlan (Emeritus, Trinity College Dublin)
- Hallie Cornetta (Head of Human Capital, Red Ventures)
- Brian Corr (Senior Corporate Finance Specialist, Dept. of Finance, Ireland)
- Grégory Couture (Global Product Manager, AB Ludvig Svensson)
- Dr Ed Delany (Strategy Consultant)
- Kieran Donoghue (Global Head of Strategy, Public Policy and International Financial Services IDA)
- Evelyn Doyle (Director of HR, Patagonia EMEA, APAC, LATAM)
- Romain Dugier (CRO—Chief Revenue Officer, Shotgun)
- Dr Loren Duffy (Leadership Consultant)
- Dariusz Dziuba (CEO, Cranfield Foundry)
- Dr Shahram Famorzadeh (VP engineering, DrChrono)
- Marion Ehscheid (Program Manager Executive MBA Mannheim Business School)
- Clive Fitzharris (MD Exertis International, DCC Group)
- Rob Flanaghan (Group Strategy, DCC Group)
- Sabrina Fox (Director of Customer Delivery, Bank of Ireland)
- Professor Stefano Gatti (SDA Bocconi University)
- Lucas Gerard (CTO, Shotgun)
- Paul Gilbride (Head of Emerging Technologies, Eir Evo)
- Polly Glasse (President, SKINourishment Inc.)
- Colin Goffin (MSc student)
- Yannick Griveau (Head of Cereal Crop Systems, BASF)
- David Gunning (CEO, Coillte 2006-2013, CEO, NPHDB)
- Per Holgerson (R&D Manager, AB Ludvig Svensson)
- David Keeley (Senior Executive Innovation, Enterprise Ireland)
- Sean Kennedy (Digital Transformation Director, Auxilion)
- Dr-Ing. Michael Kleinkes (CEO, Vision Power)
- Edouard Lagrue (Strategic Innovation Director, SoftBank Robotics)
- Tristan Le Corre (CEO, Shotgun)
- Antonio Lourenco (Global Product Manager – Transport, Altro Ltd.)
- Anders Ludvigson (CEO, AB Ludvig Svensson)
- Laura Lynch (Group Chief Marketing Officer, Bank of Ireland)
- Dr Mark Lyons (CEO, Alltech)
- Siobhan McAleer (Commercial Director, Irish Management Institute)
- Dr Claire McBride (Senior Lecturer, TU Dublin)
- Frédéric Merck (Program Manager Executive MBA, Mannheim Business School)
- Maeve McGrath (Head of Healthcare Innovation, Roche Ireland)
- Professor Rick Mitchell (Cambridge University)

- Dr Ed Molloy (Management Consultant)
- Maxim Nelemans (COO, FashionPower B.V.)
- Reg Nelemans (Managing Director, FashionPower B.V.)
- Ronald Nelemans (Commercial Director, FashionPower B.V.)
- Eoghan Nolan (VP of Engineering, Red Ventures)
- John Nugent (Head of Premier and Private Banking, Bank of Ireland)
- Jim O'Brien (Consulting Partner, Signium)
- Thor O'Brien (Director, Designbank MBD)
- Seán Ó Murchú (Director of Wealth Management, Bank of Ireland)
- Professor Charles O'Reilly III (Stanford Graduate School of Business)
- Alexander Osterwalder (Co-Founder Strategyzer)
- Professor Federica Pazzaglia (University College Dublin)
- Fausto Pinarello (founding Partner and Chairman, Cicli Pinarello)
- Daryl Regan (Programme Manager, Leadership and Scaling, Enterprise Ireland)
- Donal Prior (Head of Learner Experience, Diageo)
- Jennifer Rech (Head of Crop Management, BASF)
- Damian Reid (Talent and Engagement Manager, Irish Management Institute)
- Carol Ryan (Operations and Innovation Manager, Coillte)
- Gerry Scullion (CEO, The Human Centered Design Network)
- Dr Matthias Seiler (Executive Director Innovation Management Heitkamp & Thumann Group, now CEO, VDEh-BFI GmbH)
- Brid Seymour (HR Director, Laya Healthcare)
- Dr Marc Sniukas (Innovation Consultant and Strategy Advisor Deloitte)
- Brett Tomlin (Managing Director, Euro Caps Ltd.)
- Lesley Tully (CEO and Founder, Penny Financial Services)
- Tove Weigel (Mölnlycke Health Care, now Head R&D, SKF)
- David Williams (R&D Manager, Richardson Sheffield)

Last but definitely not least, we must express our huge gratitude to our families! Writing a book takes time and effort and this would never have been possible without their support and patience. Keith thanks both his wife Sonja and their son Colin. Ian thanks his wife Olga, who has taken the lead with their two children—Ava and Ellen—who arrived during the book's creation. And a special thanks to their older brother Kaine for all his help.

Keith Goffin and Ian Kierans
Kirchheim Teck, Germany and Dublin, Ireland: January 2023

COPYRIGHT MATERIAL

The authors and publishers are grateful to the following organizations for permission to reproduce and adapt copyright material:

INTRODUCTORY CHAPTER

DIAGRAM 1-4: The Pentathlon Framework
Anglo-German Foundation for permission to reproduce with significant adaptations.

CHAPTER 1

DIAGRAM 1-2: THE BUILDING BLOCKS OF STRATEGY
Top right of diagram representing the GE-McKinsey Matrix is excerpted from: Enduring Ideas: The GE-McKinsey nine-box matrix, September (2008), McKinsey Quarterly, www.mckinsey.com. Copyright © 2022 McKinsey & Company. All rights reserved. Reprinted by permission.

DIAGRAM 1-3: THE BUSINESS MODEL CANVAS
John Wiley & Sons - Books, for permission to reproduce and adapt: 'The Business Model Canvas', from Business model generation, by Osterwalder, A. & Pigneur, Y. (2010); permission conveyed through Copyright Clearance Center, Inc.

DIAGRAM 1-11: INNOVATION STRATEGY MATRIX
Harvard Business Review, for permission to reproduce and adapt: 'The Innovation Ambition Matrix', from Managing your innovation portfolio, by Nagji, B. & Tuff, G. (May 2012). Copyright © 2012 by the Harvard Business School Publishing Corporation; all rights reserved.

CHAPTER 2

DIAGRAM 2-3: ORGANIZATIONAL CULTURE-SCHEIN'S 3 LEVELS
John Wiley & Sons - Books, for permission to reproduce and adapt: 'The Levels of Culture' from Organizational culture and leadership. 3rd ed., by Schein, E. H. (2004); permission conveyed through Copyright Clearance Center, Inc.

CHAPTER 3

DIAGRAM 3-2: DOUBLE DIAMOND OF DESIGN
Design Council, for permission to reproduce and adapt: 'The Double Diamond', from Framework for Innovation: Design Council's evolved Double Diamond (2019), by the design council www.designcouncil.org.uk Copyright © Design Council.

CASE STUDY 3.2: ALTRO LTD. CASE STUDY
Taylor & Francis Group, LLC. for permission to reproduce: 'Altro Ltd. Case' from Countering commoditization through innovation. Challenges for European B2B companies, Research-Technology Management, by Goffin, K. et al (2021). Copyright © 2021 Goffin, K., Beznosov, A. & Seiler, M.

DIAGRAM 3-13: EMPATHY MAP
O'Reilly Media, Inc., for permission to reproduce and adapt: 'Empathy Map', from Gamestorming, by Gray, D., Brown, S. & Macanufo, J. (2010); permission conveyed through Copyright Clearance Center, Inc.

DIAGRAM 3-18: KANO MODEL OF PRODUCT FEATURES

Kano Quality Research Office (KQRO) and Dr. Noriaki Kano (with additional thanks to Secretary Ms Narie Morita), for permission to reproduce and adapt: 'Matrix for Allocating Product Features to their Kano Categories', from Attractive quality and must-be quality, Hinshitsu – Journal of Japanese Society for Quality Control, by Kano, N. et al (1984). Copyright © 1984 Dr. Noriaki Kano.

CHAPTER 5

DIAGRAM 5-3: THE STAGE GATE™ APPROACH TO PRODUCT DEVELOPMENT
Hachette Books Group, for permission to reproduce and adapt: 'The Typical Stage-Gate Model—From Discovery to Launch' (Figure 5.4), from Winning at new products. 3rd ed., by Cooper, R.G. (2001); permission conveyed through Copyright Clearance Center, Inc.

DIAGRAM 5-4: SPIRAL DEVELOPMENT PROCESS FOR BREAKTHROUGH AND RADICAL PROJECTS
IEEE for permission to reproduce and adapt: 'Spiral model of the software process' (Figure 2), from A spiral model of software development and enhancement, Computer, by Boehm, B.W. (1988). Copyright © 1988 IEEE.

DIAGRAM 5-5: ADOPTION LIFE CYCLE
Simon & Schuster contacted in May 2022 for permission to reproduce and adapt: 'Adopter Categorization' (Figure 7-3) from, The diffusion of innovations. 5th ed., by Rogers, E. M. (2003). Copyright © 2003 Simon & Schuster. The same diagram is indicated to be in the public domain by Wikipedia (see https://en.wikipedia.org/wiki/Diffusion_of_innovations#/media/File:Diffusion_of_ideas.svg [Accessed 30th August 2022].

TABLE 5-5: RWW SCREENING QUESTIONS
Harvard Business Review, for permission to reproduce and adapt: 'RWW Screening Questions' from Is It Real? Can We Win? Is It Worth Doing?: Managing Risk and Reward in an Innovation Portfolio by George Day (December 2007). Copyright © 2007 by the Harvard Business School Publishing Corporation; all rights reserved.

TABLE 5-7: WILLINGNESS TO PAY QUESTIONS
John Wiley & Sons - Books, for permission to reproduce and adapt: 'Willingness to pay, direct questions' (p. 45), from Monetizing innovation, by Ramanujan, M. & Tacke, G. (2016); permission conveyed through Copyright Clearance Center, Inc.

CHAPTER 6

DIAGRAM 6-4: DIGITAL BUSINESS MODEL FRAMEWORK
Harvard Business Review, for permission to reproduce: 'The Digital Business Model Framework', from What's Your Digital Business Model? Six Questions to Help You Build the Next Generation Enterprise, by Weill. P & Woerner, S.L. Copyright © 2018 by the Harvard Business School Publishing Corporation; all rights reserved.

If any copyright issues have been inadvertently overlooked the authors will make the necessary arrangements at the first opportunity.

Introduction
The innovation journey

The innovation journey

INTRODUCTION

Mid-sized businesses (MSBs) play a major role in the economies of many nations. Economists view mid-sized businesses as having revenues in the range of €10M to €1B (approximately $12M to $1.2B) and employing anything from around 100 to several thousand people. In the US, such businesses are "the unsung heroes of America's economy".[1] Although there are over half a million MSBs worldwide, which employ a staggering 208 million people, these companies are often overlooked by governments.[2]

There are over 70,000 MSBs in the EU. In Germany they are known as the *Mittelstand*, and while few of these companies are household names, they're strong exporters, often called "hidden champions". Mid-sized businesses are also crucial in the UK[3,4], Sweden, France and Finland.[5] Table I-1 shows that MSBs in Europe typically employ over 20% of the workforce and often generate about 30% of a country's gross national product (GNP).

In many European countries, MSBs have been neglected as most government policies focus on start-ups and corporates.[6] The reason for this neglect is that only 1–2% of all companies are MSBs, and their capability for growth is often underestimated[7]—MSBs simply don't get the level of attention they deserve.

TABLE I-1: MID-SIZED BUSINESSES IN EUROPE[8]

COUNTRY	NUMBER OF MSBs	EMPLOYMENT	TURNOVER
Germany	19,000	23%	32%
France	14,000	25%	30%
UK	9,500	21%	20%
Sweden	2,600	29%	33%
Finland	1,250	26%	32%
Ireland[9]	1,000	30%	35%

Mid-sized businesses, including many family-owned businesses, are resilient, stable, have high growth potential and can boost employment.[10] Their advantages are based on their fast decision-making, long-term thinking, technological capabilities, strong local connections, a focus on exports, and a clear understanding of customer needs. In response to increasing global competition, 85% of MSBs are placing "the same or greater emphasis on investing in innovation"[11]—to develop more new products, new services, new processes, and new business models. This book is focused on *how* an MSB can become more innovative.

This book is equally relevant for *Strategic Business Units* (SBUs) in larger corporations, which have a high degree of autonomy. For example, an SBU in a federated group structure, or an SBU with responsibility for a product-market and freedom to decide how to achieve growth. Large corporates usually prescribe how their SBUs should approach innovation, with strictly defined processes, and don't allow the degree of autonomy required to apply the ideas we cover. However, any ambitious SBU management team can and should apply the approaches recommended here.

Throughout this book, we will refer to MSBs and SBUs as 'businesses'.[12] Such organizations are established and are of a manageable size for growth. However, their current business models and capabilities may constrain their ability to grow. These organizations will have a single senior management team responsible for shaping and implementing business strategy but their mindsets often focus on current business rather than innovative growth. Similarly, as businesses, they may have a narrow, incremental view of innovation, rather than recognizing the value of business-wide innovation. Businesses that can overcome such constraints will grow successfully.

Most of the vast literature on innovation management is aimed at either start-ups or large corporates. For start-ups, the recommendations are about entrepreneurial thinking, creating value, obtaining funding, and constantly changing their business model. For corporates, numerous books and articles describe how to develop major initiatives to boost innovation. These include corporate *hackathons*, intensive idea generation sessions, and founding a corporate innovation lab where extensive experimentation can take place. Such initiatives require significant resources and management time—both of which are at a premium in businesses. So, many of the books on innovation management don't take account of the unique challenges that MSBs and SBUs face, including their restrained resources.

TOPICS AND TOOLS

There is significant hype around innovation management and 'hot topics' are quickly turned into new books. Bestsellers in the corporate world, such as *Blue Ocean Strategy*[13] and *Business Model Generation*,[14] mean that many managers are reading about the same ideas. The danger is that managers will apply the ideas in superficial and similar ways to their competitors. Such books include important concepts, many of which we have included, but these concepts need to be applied carefully, systematically and not superficially.

Even if it's the 'very latest', a single tool or technique will not address all the innovation management issues your business faces. However, applying too many tools and techniques will sow confusion and so you need a carefully selected set of innovation tools and techniques. In terms of Pareto, applying 20% of the innovation tools and techniques available will probably give you

80% of the results. The big question is: which 20% of the tools and techniques should you apply?

Both the CEO of an MSB and the director of an SBU have a wide range of responsibilities. So, when they decide to focus on innovation, they don't have the time to read about all the innovation tools available, in order to select the most appropriate. Furthermore, in a business world where artificial intelligence and digitization and *Industry 4.0* (connected intelligent devices and robotics) were already presenting businesses with significant challenges, the stakes have been raised by the global pandemic plus pressing environmental issues. Consequently, it's more crucial than ever for MSBs to manage innovation in a relatively simple, fast and pragmatic way. Therefore, we: make sense of innovation; give practical recommendations for managers and employees; and describe how to apply key tools and techniques.

Tools and techniques take time to learn and tenacity to apply. Without making things over-complex, we believe there is real advantage in a systematic analysis of the commercial viability of market offerings. Our view is also backed by research, which shows that businesses with a better understanding of their customers are more successful at innovation. This means you'll need to put more effort into managing innovation than your competitors. Remember 'no pain, no innovation gain'. Put another way, if everything about innovation was that easy, then you wouldn't be able to gain a competitive advantage from it.

THE INNOVATION JOURNEY

Over the last 20 years we've collected data on the ways different businesses have achieved innovative growth[15] and these form the basis for our integrated approach. Building a more innovative business is like going on a difficult journey for the first time—a journey from Point 'A' to Point 'B'. This journey will take time, effort and determination. It'll also demand the ability to deal with uncertainty, as success is rarely linear. And it will take discipline to plan and not just rush on. Before the innovation journey can begin, managers need to be clear where they are starting from—their current *business context*, or situation. This is Point 'A'. Based on this, managers must define their desired competitive position. This is Point 'B'.

A word of caution about the journey: the Wikipedia entry for 'innovation management' says it's "a combination of the management of innovation processes, and change management… [and] is the subject of ISO 56000 [The International Organization for Standardization] series standards".[16] This could be seen as implying that there is a single, standard process for managing innovation; the same route for all businesses. Be careful here, because innovation management depends heavily on the business context. Whether you operate in a B2B (*business-to-business*) or B2C (*business-to-consumer*) market, producing products or delivering services, your current business context 'A' and your intended performance 'B' will determine the type of innovation journey you face. There is no standard process for businesses and ISO 56000 is a broad approach rather than a strict process to follow.

The starting point for a family business we are currently supporting was a requirement for more innovative products and services to counter Asian competition, which is causing commoditization in their markets. So, the intent of innovation can be to fight off competition but, equally, it can be the pursuit of growth. Similarly, a B2B manufacturer has told us that its unique technology has generated over 80% market share in a specific niche. Consequently, growth must now come from radical innovation, moving them into new markets. After 20 years relying on one technology and one market for growth, the manufacturer knows it faces a real challenge as it hasn't innovated for a such a long time.

INNOVATION CAPABILITY

The innovation journey is more than moving from 'A' to 'B'. To develop successful innovation, businesses require *innovation capabilities* 'C'. These capabilities include having appropriate business processes—the 'system'—to drive innovation, and having skilled, experienced people to apply them. To move from 'A' to 'B', businesses must complement existing capabilities with new ones. In short, the innovation journey is moving: *from 'A' to 'B', while building 'C'*.

One fundamental innovation capability is being able to understand customer needs. This is referred to as listening to the *voice of the customer* (VOC). This work is often based on customer interviews but, in this book, we place strong emphasis on using more sophisticated tools and techniques to understand customer needs. This is because a business that has the capability to generate deep customer insights will have a long-term competitive advantage. Another crucial capability is being able to select the most promising innovation projects from the many ideas generated. Similarly, for some of the innovation projects selected, the capability to develop new and emerging markets will be crucial.

A problem for many businesses is that their innovation capabilities aren't strong enough to deliver their growth plans. Although senior management teams say they want more innovation, they struggle to free up the resources—particularly the time—needed for innovation (including the time they themselves must spend driving innovation). Similarly, although employees in MSBs and SBUs are highly motivated to participate in innovation projects, their ability to take the time needed for innovation is often hampered by day-to-day priorities. Thus, it is essential that a specific person—an *Innovation Manager*, be given the responsibility for making the journey a success. Of course, the innovation manager does not work alone but in collaboration across the business.

Time and time again, we meet managers who have set or have been assigned ambitious growth goals. Typically, these are financial goals to double market share, revenue or margin within a few years. Setting such financial goals is easy, achieving them is harder. When we ask managers how they intend to achieve their goals, their responses invariably include two approaches. First and foremost, managers want to *exploit* existing markets, making incremental changes to existing products and services (based on existing capabilities). This approach is often accompanied with slogans like 'win market share', or 'beat the competition'. The second approach to growth is to *explore* adjacent and new markets, creating innovative new products, services, processes and business models that bring competitive advantage. This ambition is often accompanied by phrases like 'breakthroughs', 'game-changers' and 'disruption'.

Although managers mention both approaches to growth, few realize how profoundly different they are. Based on their past successes, businesses will be so wedded to exploitation that they must rebuild their capability to explore.

Being good at both is called *Ambidextrous Innovation*[17]—a real advantage in turbulent times. Ambidextrous innovation requires managers to have a flexible mindset, allowing them to perform outside their comfort zone.

INNOVATION MINDSET

Mindsets determine how individuals and, collectively, organizations think, feel and behave. Typical mindset issues that emerge during the innovation journey are blinkered thinking, people staying in their comfort zone, and decision-making that is unknowingly influenced by feelings. To succeed at innovation, the mindset required is very much that of an explorer who plans a journey knowing that not everything can be foreseen, and so unexpected things are certain to happen. Case Study I-1 explains the innovation challenges facing the mid-sized Swedish manufacturer Svensson and the capabilities and commitment needed.

Surprisingly, innovation management books tend to talk about passion and playfulness during idea generation but do not mention feelings in the implementation and other phases. Yet, the field of behavioural economics has found that the way people make decisions is not based on purely rational thought but rather on unconscious, learnt patterns of thinking and feelings, which lead to biased decisions and habitual behaviours. Therefore, it's vital to consider mindset matters and not only formal management processes. So, as we explain the innovation journey, we'll make managers, teams and employees aware of how they will think, feel and behave along the way.

Building innovation capabilities requires sustained effort, and during this time there can be periods of frustration when managers feel impatient for growth. This is because appropriate, unfamiliar tools and techniques must be learnt, and it takes practice to become proficient with them. Therefore, you, your senior management team, and your employees, will find parts of the innovation journey reassuring (as some approaches work) and other parts disheartening (when results don't meet expectations). Dealing with the latter situation requires management to be patient and show belief that innovations will succeed—remember, building new markets and gaining market acceptance for radically new products typically takes longer than expected. The emotional 'ups and downs' that management, project teams and individual employees encounter on the innovation journey are vital to understand, as they directly impact progress.

The rest of this chapter discusses innovative growth; the key components of innovation management; and the main phases of the innovation journey for businesses.

CASE STUDY I-1: AB LUDVIG SVENSSON SCREENING PRODUCTS[18]

Svensson AB is a family-owned business based near Gothenburg that was founded in 1887. It has 420 employees, a turnover in excess of €80M and sells its products in 130 countries. Its factory is in an area of Sweden that is well known for textiles. Svensson has a successful interior textiles business, producing attractive designs based on robust materials, for window shades, curtains and seat coverings used in buses, trains and cruise ships.

What is now the company's largest business unit was founded in the 1970s. It arose from a search to find a use for waste from curtain manufacturing. Different ideas for the tonnes of offcuts were considered, including a way of strengthening lawn turf. Discussions with horticultural experts showed that the idea for lawn turf was not viable but one expert suggested 'curtains' for greenhouses, and the idea of climate control screens was born. These screens can be pulled out under the glass roof of a greenhouse to maintain temperature and then folded back when they are not needed. In the energy crisis of the 1970s, the screens gave greenhouse growers in countries like Holland a way to reduce heating costs and, subsequently, ways to increase crop yields. Svensson received its first patent for a knitted climate screen in 1980 and today's products are a complex, knitted mix of aluminium and plastic. Modern greenhouse screens have the capability to control sunlight, maintain crops at the right temperature, reduce heating costs, and regulate humidity levels (preventing crop-damaging condensation).

Over 30 years Svensson has built a large market share but, increasingly, competitors have introduced copycat products. Anders Ludvigson became CEO in 2015 and quickly realized that, although Svensson had a proud history of innovation, *"We were too cautious and did not have enough ideas for new products from sales and marketing."* Similar to many other family businesses, Svensson's drive for innovation came from a new generation taking the helm (Anders is fourth generation): *"To counter the competition, we had to change our way of thinking and focus on the voice of the customer—VOC"*, says Anders.

Two of the principal functions in any organization involved in innovation are R&D and product management. At Svensson, R&D is led by Per Holgerson and product management by Grégory Couture. Per says: *"You have to remember that in a small company like ours, getting better at innovation is a long journey. This is because everyone is very busy, wears many 'hats' and does not only work on innovation. There is a lot of capacity for innovation but it is spread out. An appropriate structure is needed to connect the individuals, who are our 'islands of innovation'."* He and Grégory have together created a task-focused structure, where cross-functional teams (including sales, R&D, marketing, technical and horticultural specialists) conduct VOC work. Teams are brought together for defined periods to focus on innovation. The teams' time is first spent visiting customers, observing their challenges first-hand, and generating deep insights. Then, team time is spent developing innovative solutions. *"VOC leads to much more customer contact. Even people who normally would not visit customers now do. And because everyone meets customers, their buy-in to the process is immediate,"* says Per.

Focusing on VOC has both long-term and short-term impacts. From an R&D perspective Per says, *"For the longer-term, our whole future product portfolio is based on ideas from our insight work, so the impact of our VOC work is exciting"*. In the shorter term, VOC has also generated ideas for improving current products and radically changed Svensson's approach to marketing. From a product management perspective Grégory says, *"One of the main impacts of VOC is you get a full understanding of local issues.*

This means you can match global innovation initiatives with specific local requirements. VOC has also helped us identify important segments that we had not recognized before. Through differentiated products, specific packaging, the right pricing, and an optimal sales approach, we have successfully created new segments in the market!"

Svensson's innovation journey is far from finished. Per and Grégory think that the structure, involvement and commitment that's so essential to innovation has been built. But, as CEO, Anders has a healthy impatience when it comes to innovation. He has ambitious growth plans and isn't yet satisfied with the outcomes: *"We need to become more effective in implementing our VOC ideas"* he says, *"Although we have learnt a lot and have an excellent product pipeline, our challenge now is to make each idea into a big market success. And even when that has been achieved, our innovation journey will still need to continue."*

INNOVATIVE GROWTH

As businesses grow, they pass through different stages in their life cycle. At their inception, they will have developed a business idea, dealt with funding and development issues, and built a business around a unique value proposition (for example, product or service). Growth comes with much change and the need for more formal business processes.

BUSINESS LIFE CYCLES

Back in 1965, the management researcher Theodor Levitt developed a concept that we will call the *business life cycle*.[19] Since then extensive research[20] has identified the four stages of development shown in Diagram I-1. The horizontal axis is time and the vertical axis is performance (for example, revenue or margin growth). The first two stages are *start-up* and *scale* representing the *entrepreneurial* stages of a business. The next two stages: *success* and *decline* represent the *established* stages. We use shading to represent the shift from white-space—new, poorly defined markets without

DIAGRAM I-1: BUSINESS LIFE CYCLE

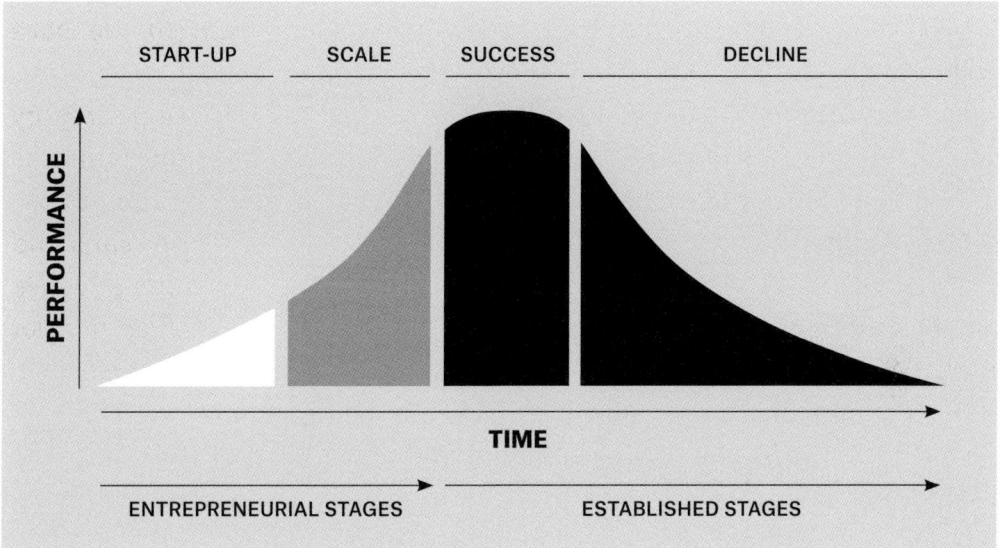

established business models—to *black-space*—existing core markets with established business models.[21] Between the black and the white is *grey-space*—where markets and business models are emerging.

Start-up and scale (entrepreneurial stages)

Businesses at the start-up stage are focused on discovering a *value proposition* that will attract customers. It's about knowing what customers need, and designing suitable products and services. Start-ups may target a white-space and create new markets with innovative value propositions, or they can offer novel value propositions in existing markets. Either way, the level of knowledge about what will succeed is low and the number of assumptions is high. Thus, an exploratory and innovative mindset is vital because market insights will be fuzzy and taking advantage of them will require creativity and the willingness to learn through experimentation. Entrepreneurs make up for their lack of resources through resourcefulness and tenacity, which enables them to transition from start-up to scale.

During the scale stage, a founder's intent is to survive and grow the business significantly. This involves designing, testing and refining the business model. The entrepreneurial stages are treacherous, and many businesses fail. Research shows that businesses that survive are good at *pivoting*—when major changes in the value proposition and/or the business model are necessary because the original business idea isn't delivering the desired success. For example, Shotgun, a Parisian start-up, pivoted five times from start-up to scale and then had to respond to the wholesale impact of Covid-19 on their business (see Case Study I-2).

Success and Decline (Established Stages)
During the success stage the business is thriving, a strong market position has been established, and healthy profits are being generated. The typical aims are to optimize the business model and stay ahead of the competition. To achieve this, businesses tend to focus internally, concentrating on order fulfilment, operational efficiency, and fine-tuning the business model for the current market. During success, when revenues and margins are high, businesses should invest in innovation for long-term growth. However, most successful businesses become so focused on operational efficiency that they lose their capability to innovate. This is the *success trap*[22]—where businesses become inward-looking and overlook market signals.

The early signs of decline are stalling growth; new entrants gaining market share; and a business failing to register changes in customer needs. When sales start to fall, the business has already entered decline and innovation is urgently needed. Ironically, decline means there is less cash available to invest in innovation projects. In addition, competitors will have established themselves in your market with better alternatives. As pressure builds, the danger is senior managers will focus on the current business (within their comfort zone), pursuing lean objectives rather than bringing much-needed innovations to market. Even in the face of significant threats to current markets, most managers direct investments towards exploitation and don't invest enough time and resources in exploration (outside their comfort zone). Decline is accelerated by a 'red pen mentality', which regards innovation investments as too risky.

DIAGRAM I-2: RENEWAL IN THE BUSINESS LIFE CYCLE

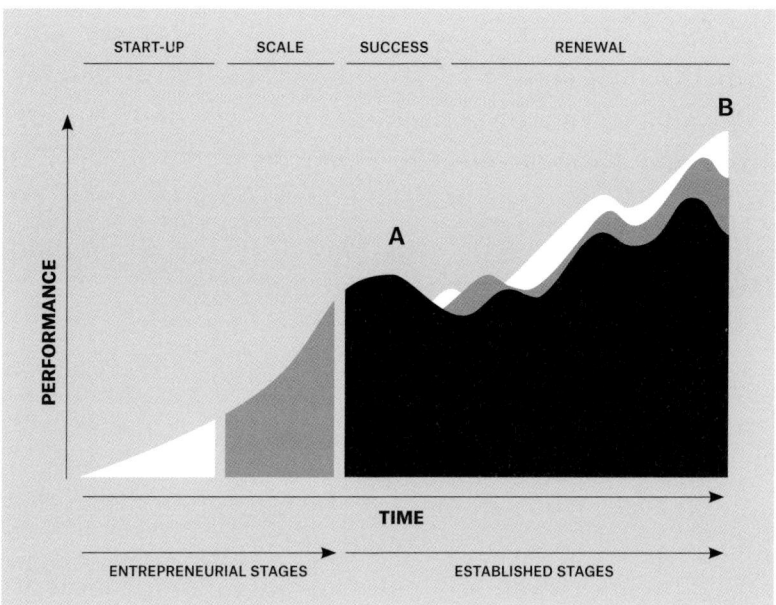

Renewal

For a business to avoid or break out of decline, it must enter a *renewal* stage and achieve a new cycle of growth. There are three growth categories which can be pursued (see Diagram I-2), in moving business performance from 'A' to 'B'. Businesses naturally want to defend their core markets. Growth in the *core business* (black-space) focuses on increasing customer demand through incremental product or service innovation and optimizing operational efficiency (for example, lean management, automation and digitization). Incremental innovation does not presuppose incremental payback; on the contrary incremental innovation can generate fast and significant returns. The main caveat with core markets is they may diminish over time.

Emerging business requires new capabilities to grow in adjacent or early stage markets (grey-space). To be successful here, businesses must generate deep insights into customer needs and experiment with the breakthrough innovation they will offer (pivoting is likely). Customers may be slower than expected to adopt breakthrough innovations and emerging markets can often take time to mature. So, managers must be patient and avoid knee-jerk decisions removing resources from such projects.

New business, or white-space, is where longer-term and potentially significant growth can be generated. It explores new-to-world innovations and business models that can create entirely new markets, or disrupt existing ones. It may combine new technologies (for example, the internet of things) with social trends (for example, the gig economy). For every successful disruptive innovation there are countless failures. Therefore, the senior managers must make 'small bets', testing assumptions early and often.

Every renewal strategy must consider the three business growth categories and the role of innovation in each of them. Top businesses can simultaneously balance exploiting their core business and exploring emerging and new business through breakthrough and radical innovation.[23] This requires senior managers who can manage the tension between these different categories and have the appropriate mindset for each.

Table I-2 specifies seven attributes of the different growth categories. It can be seen that for the core business (black-space) business models are clear and established and customer needs are known. Growth in this space is exploitation and is normally based on incremental product innovation by the market incumbents. Established businesses will strive to improve their manufacturing or service processes (termed *process innovation*). Typically, the only breakthrough innovation in black-space is by new entrants, who may offer distinctly different value propositions and business models. This will out-manoeuvre established businesses that are caught in the success trap. It's important to note that truly breakthrough propositions can revolutionize existing markets and so there's a strong argument for 're-exploring' your existing markets. What do we mean by this? Re-exploring existing markets is taking a fresh, unbiased look at customer needs that your competitors have not seen.

Table I-2 also shows that grey-space and white-space involves evolving and poorly defined markets that lack proven business models. Customer needs are either unknown or hidden (needs which customers themselves have not yet recognized). To explore grey- and white-space and create breakthrough and radical innovations, new capabilities are required and these will be at the limits of or outside the senior team's comfort zone.

Overall, Table I-2 allows the senior teams at MSBs and SBUs to consider where their businesses are on the business life cycle. This prompts them to start thinking about what attributes their businesses have and what capabilities will be needed for innovative growth. It is important to note that ambidextrous innovation addresses all three business growth categories.

TABLE I-2: BUSINESS GROWTH CATEGORIES AND INNOVATION[24]

	ATTRIBUTES	BUSINESS GROWTH CATEGORIES		
		CORE BUSINESS BLACK-SPACE	**EMERGING BUSINESS** GREY-SPACE	**NEW BUSINESS** WHITE-SPACE
1	Market characteristics	Existing core markets with clear and established business models. Focused on the short term.	Adjacent or emerging markets where business models are evolving.	New, poorly defined markets without established business models. Focused on the long term.
2	Customer needs	Known.	Unknown or hidden needs.	Unknown or hidden needs.
3	Exploitation or exploration	Exploitation.	Exploration.	Exploration.
4	Typical innovations	Incremental and process.	Breakthrough innovation.	Radical innovation.
5	Capabilities	Existing.	Existing and new.	New.
6	Metrics	Financial measures such as ROI, NPV.	Financial such as sales and qualitative such as learning from market experimentation.	Learning measures such as depth of customer insights and novel market points of view.
7	Mindset matters	Within senior team's comfort zone. Also within innovation teams' comfort zones.	At the limits of senior team's comfort zone. At the limits of innovation teams' comfort zones.	Outside senior team's comfort zone. Outside innovation teams' comfort zones.

CASE STUDY I-2: SHOTGUN
TIME TO PIVOT (AGAIN AND AGAIN)[25]

France, 2014. Inspired by the explosive growth of Uber, Instagram and Tinder, Tristan Le Corre, Romain Dugier and Lucas Gerard were eager to found a mobile service of their own. They knew that millennials like themselves were always looking for good apps, but what service should they offer and would they need to pivot? The first idea was to create a marketplace to exchange unwanted items. They developed an app, naming it 'Shotgun'. Like Tinder, each item was shown as a 'screen card' and the first person to swipe right (who 'shotguns' it) had the right to buy it directly from the seller. But after four months of trials with family and friends, nobody was supplying new items to sell on the app. It was time to pivot. (See Diagram I-3.)

The next idea was to create an app marketing the offerings of independent retailers, restaurants, bars and coffee shops. Shotgun offered discounted products and services from over 200 suppliers, including a handful of nightclubs. However, for the next 18 months user purchasing was low. It was time to pivot (again).

Over the 2015 Christmas holidays, the three reflected on their lacklustre growth. They noted that some 'new organic users' (people beyond friends and family) were buying nightclub offerings. Eager to know more, they contacted them via Facebook. Most gave suggestions and some even became 'Shotgun Ambassadors'; advocates who maintained close contact with the founders. *"We found it was the nightclub offers that users cared about. So much so, that they would wade through offers of shoes and skateboards just to find a nightclub deal"* says CEO, Tristan Le Corre. Users appreciated the ability to buy an experience that included tickets and some products (for example food and drinks), plus convenience (for example queue avoidance). The mobile generation was arranging their nights out using different apps for travel, food and partying. Traditional event organizers were simply overlooking such needs. It was time to pivot (again).

Early in 2016, the three founders decided to focus exclusively on nightlife and drop retail. They recruited more nightclubs, by convincing club and event owners (called 'clients') that Shotgun would increase their ticket sales. Although just one of several channels that drove customer traffic to event organizers (Facebook was the primary channel), Shotgun grew rapidly in 2016. Every night, the founders would engage with users and non-users in 'darkly lit' clubs. Every morning, the founders would 'huddle' to share their insights. These led not only to incremental innovations such as 'search' and 'calendar' functions but also the invention of 'swipe digital tickets' that solved the bottleneck of scanning admissions to enter an event. *"By the end of 2016 we had 20,000 users, almost 100 event organizers and we were capturing a percentage of every ticket and product sale. We had a business model that could 'just about wash its face' but we needed growth,"* says Tristan. It was time to pivot (slightly).

Roman, Lucas and Tristan had also noted from their interactions with users that some were passionate about organizing their own events. These users now became clients by organizing DJs, artists, locations and

DIAGRAM I-3: SHOTGUN'S BUSINESS LIFE CYCLE TO DATE

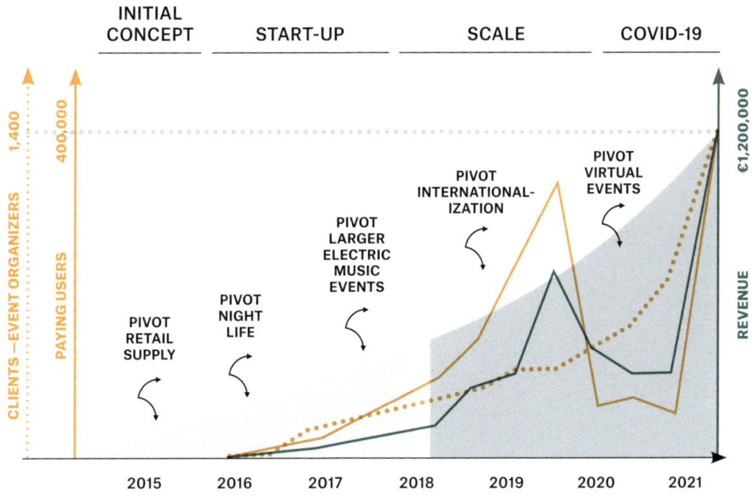

equipment, with Shotgun managing sales. For event organizers the aim is to sell out, yet only 20% achieve this. Shotgun could now guide own event organizers on what is popular. Larger event organizers such as festivals and large club owners, however, were reluctant to work exclusively with Shotgun. Such clients wanted to manage their pricing and promotion in real-time and needed specific digital tools for seamless omnichannel promotion. It was time to pivot (again, slightly).

As the volume of live electronic music events had grown exponentially, in September 2017 the Shotgun founders secured €1M funding to develop a full software solution for event management. This enabled event organizers to understand, control and de-risk their sales. The 'per use' fee structure was transparent and popular with event organizers.

Shotgun's B2B market grew as they could help clients with 'booster ads' that are much more effective than normal campaigns and avoid last-minute discounting. Shotgun also developed a solution for the re-sale market that prevents speculation but allows users to be reimbursed when their plans change. With an additional €2M of venture funding they had over 400 clients in Paris, Nantes, Marseille, Bordeaux and Lyon and 500,000 users with 70% repeat purchasing. It was time to scale internationally.

But then came Covid-19. So, it was time to pivot (again). As the events industry struggled with restrictions, Shotgun concentrated on not only optimizing their platform for when real events could restart but also creating an exciting virtual service. While other providers have gone for streamed events, Shotgun have focused on creating unique, temporal events. As Tristan says, *"Streaming appeared to be a simple solution but it wasn't. The uniqueness of an event is its temporality: the excitement it generates in the days beforehand; the sense of urgency it provokes on the actual day; having someone 'tear' your ticket in half before entering the arena; and then the event itself—each step, each glance at the DJ and the feeling of the music will be unique for every member of the audience. And when the lights come up, the frantic search for an afterparty starts. To be memorable, an event has to be temporary and live: you can pause a stream; you can't pause an event."*

Based on these insights, Shotgun's 'Disdancing' interactive streaming platform hosts big acts 'live only' from unique locations like the top floor of the Pompidou Centre. And Disdancing imparts far more of the energy of an event, even down to the experience of someone tearing your ticket.

During Covid-19 new event organizers continued to sign up to Shotgun. Now all these event organizers need support to ensure that, as events restart, they are sold out. Also, with a generation even more hungry for real events, Shotgun can help their users to get out to dance and party with both old friends and new. Shotgun is fully back in business with €30m per year in generated merchandise value (total volume of transactions on the Shotgun platform) and is scaling internationally in Brazil and Iberia. It's just opened a New York office as well.

COMPONENTS OF INNOVATION MANAGEMENT

A huge amount has been published on 'innovation management' and Google lists over 14.8 million items, including many analysis tools and techniques, and recommended business processes. Faced with this information tsunami, it's hard for managers to gain an overview of the most important actions for driving innovation. This is further complicated by the cross-functional nature of innovation, and the very different interventions required, spanning technology management and human resource management.

PENTATHLON FRAMEWORK

In a project in the 1990s, we found that managers were striving to bring together different aspects of innovation management in a logical way. The research led to the *Pentathlon Framework* (see Diagram I-4), which views innovation management as consisting of five main components.[26]

The five components are: deciding on the right innovation strategy for your business; creating ideas for innovations that meet customer needs; selecting the right projects; implementing innovations; and building an organization with a culture of innovation. A business needs to have a balance of performance across the five components. Just like the Olympic Pentathlon event, successful innovation is not about being exceptional in one or two disciplines—top performance in all five is essential.

Diagram I-4 shows the five components that make up the *internal context*—the way an organization manages innovation internally. For example, it can be seen that a pipeline of black-, grey- and white-space innovation options are generated, selected and implemented. An organization operates in a broader business situation, the *external context*, and so market forces (customers, competitors, suppliers, and technology) have an influence. The output of the internal processes are new products, new processes, new services, and new business models, all of which are launched onto the external market. Case Study I-3 illustrates how Heitkamp & Thumann Group tackled the different issues that the Pentathlon identifies.

DIAGRAM I-4: THE PENTATHLON FRAMEWORK

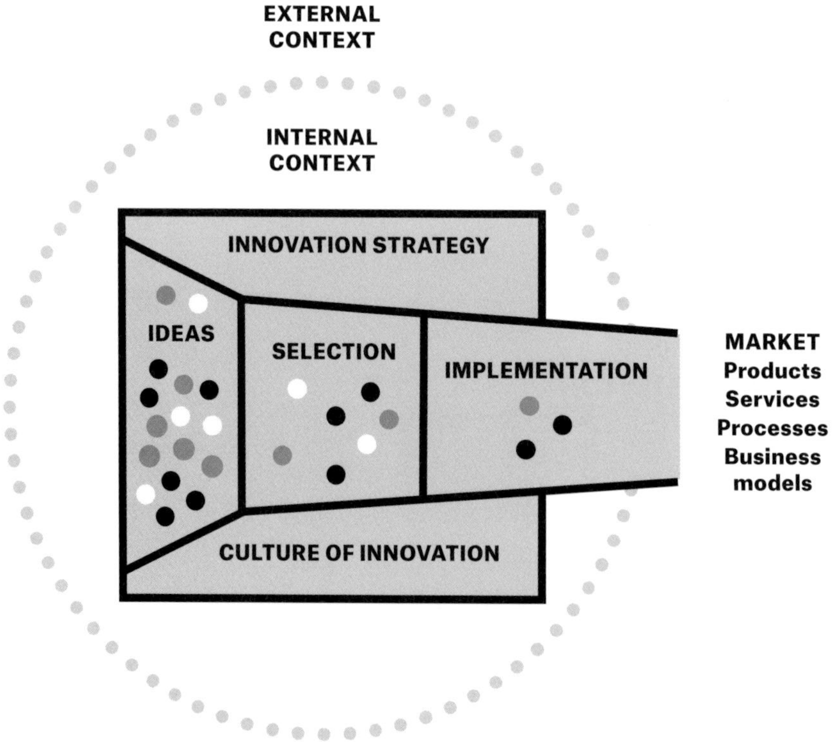

CASE STUDY I-3: HEITKAMP & THUMANN GROUP COMPONENTS OF LEARNING[27]

The Heitkamp & Thumann Group is a family-owned global group of companies, founded nearly 40 years ago and with its headquarters in Düsseldorf, Germany. The Group consists of 16 companies organized into two divisions and four business units, employing about 2,000 people. From the beginning, the Group has strategically focused on niche products for high-volume markets, with the aim of becoming the leader in selected markets. For example, H&T Battery Components Division produces components for the consumer battery industry and the fast-growing e-mobility market. Similarly, H&T Presspart leads in the manufacture of highly specialized metal and plastic components for the pharmaceutical industry. The Group has a strong track record of process innovation and has the capability to develop equipment, tooling, and manufacturing systems.

For the Heitkamp & Thumann Group, innovation is an extremely important group-wide initiative that's always been at the centre of its corporate philosophy and entrepreneurial activities. A recent innovation brochure stressed that an employee-driven culture of innovation is being created, built on the strengths of the different divisions and business units. A range of new products have been developed and launched.

Over five years, a systematic innovation management process has been implemented and an 'innovation management toolbox' has been developed to support the development of breakthrough products with a sustainable competitive advantage. This toolbox includes different techniques to analyse and develop markets and teams have been trained in these techniques, including how to identify customers' hidden needs. The Heitkamp & Thumann Group believes that it has learnt the following three key lessons from its innovation activities:

First, deriving a solid understanding of customer requirements using hidden needs techniques such as repertory grid analysis or ethnographic studies is key to developing differentiated B2B products. Especially deriving a meaningful Diffusion of Innovations and Kano analysis is not possible without interviewing all of the stakeholders in the customer's decision-making unit based on a systematic repertory grid analysis.

Second, if a B2B company aiming to develop breakthrough products does not manage to finish its project-related interviews to identify customers' hidden needs right at the front end of its development pipeline or, in other words, prior to allocating substantial resources for product development, it will end up in the incremental product trap. Having an advanced innovation toolbox for the development of breakthrough products isn't sufficient if these tools are applied too late during the product development process. The moment a project team focuses on preparing for the first sales pitch of a newly developed product it's too late and too costly to start identifying and addressing customers' hidden needs. This is why the timing of applying a suitable innovation toolbox is crucial for the successful development of breakthrough products. Most innovation tools must be applied during the first stages of a product development process and must adequately support the prototyping and learning efforts.

Third, modifying a project management toolbox by integrating methods to identify customers' hidden needs and applying these innovation tools systematically throughout a company is a major change process especially for profitable companies. The process takes at least five years, requires ambidextrous leadership and a healthy company culture that encourages organizational learning and a continuous effort to strengthen the key attributes of a 'culture of innovation'.

PHASES OF THE INNOVATION JOURNEY

As mentioned, the journey from 'A' to 'B' requires a range of innovation capabilities 'C' to be applied, in effect taking you through the five phases of the journey, which correspond to the five components of the Pentathlon. Diagram I-5 shows the five phases and should be read from the bottom-left, mirroring how innovative growth raises performance from 'A' to 'B'. The five phases are aligned to specific chapters, each of which has an assigned colour, to aid in navigating within this book. After the five phases, Phase 6 reflects on how well your innovation capabilities functioned and how to enhance them for the future. In discussing the journey, we always refer to 'phases', as we want to stress that there is some overlap and iteration between them. It can be seen from the diagram that Phases 1-5 each have three sub-phases that represent the key actions to take.

Phase 1: Shaping innovation strategy (Chapter 1) consists of strategic analysis that is mainly the responsibility of the senior team. They must first align innovation with the business strategy. Then they must 'scan' the innovation landscape—considering where innovation can generate business opportunities in both existing and potential markets. After the opportunities have been identified, growth goals (innovation intent) can be declared. This defines Point 'B', the destination of the innovation journey.

Phase 2: Organizing the journey (Chapter 2). It consists of the governance (for example planning and allocation of resources); locating innovation responsibilities in the organizational structure; and designing and developing innovation teams. Businesses must plan their innovation journey carefully, rather than blindly rushing on.

Phase 3: Generating deep insights and novel solutions (Chapter 3) is about insights teams investigating promising markets. This phase requires dedicated teams to identify customers' needs *before* coming up with novel solutions. The output of Phase 3 will be a number of ideas for potential innovation projects for the senior team to consider, in existing, emerging, or new markets.

Phase 4: Selecting projects for implementation (Chapter 4) consists of defining selection criteria for assessing innovation projects and then reviewing the whole portfolio. Managing innovation portfolio meetings leads to decisions on which projects will be funded. Although Phase 4 is simpler than the earlier phases, its impact on success should not be underestimated and the senior team needs to be fully engaged. Their decisions on which projects will be implemented are strategic. The output of Phase 4 is a balanced set of projects, from black- to white-space, chosen for implementation.

Phase 5: Getting innovations to market (Chapter 5) is process-driven. One process is needed for incremental projects, whereas a more agile approach will be needed for breakthrough and radical projects. As some innovations

DIAGRAM I-5: SIX PHASES OF THE INNOVATION JOURNEY

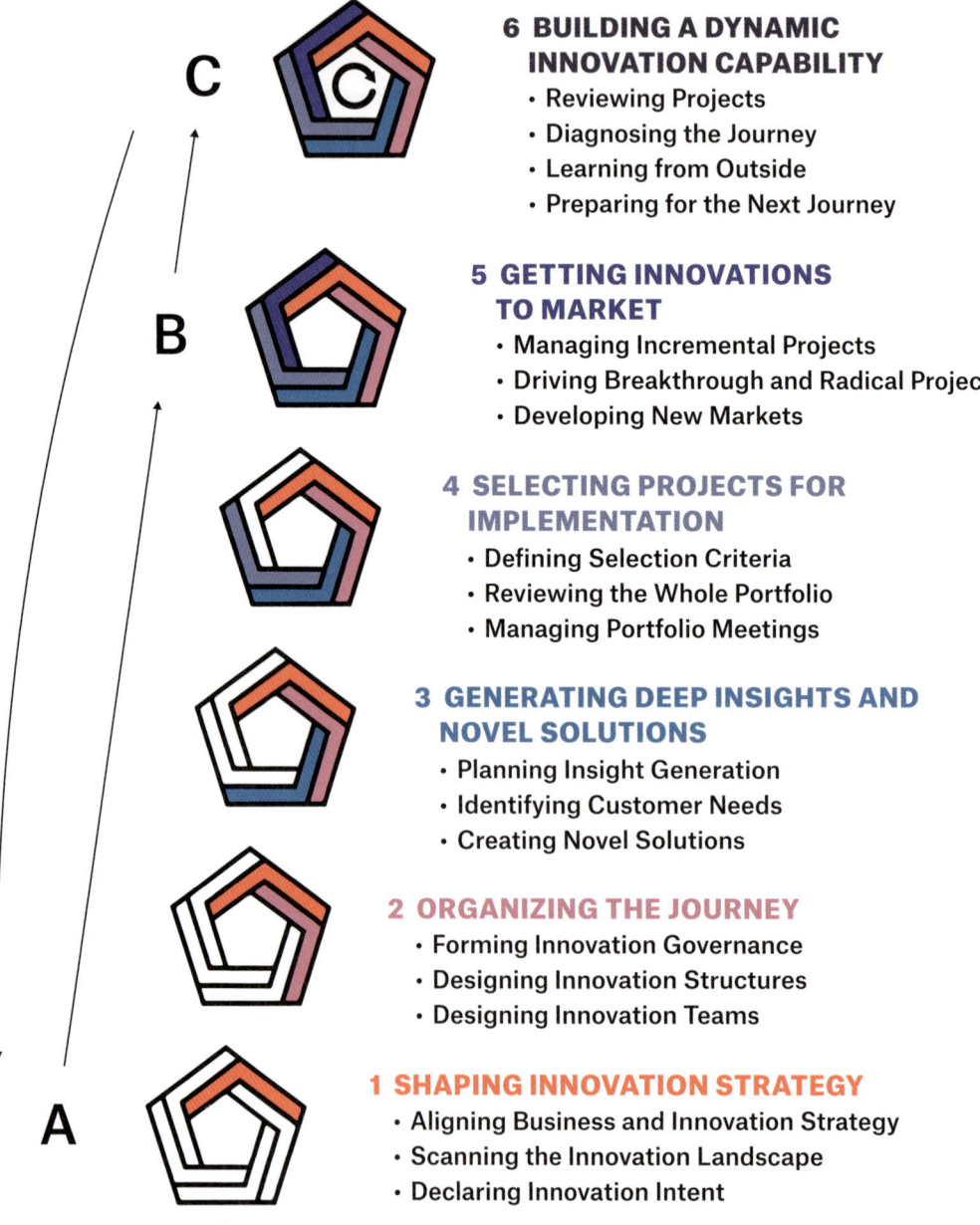

6 BUILDING A DYNAMIC INNOVATION CAPABILITY
- Reviewing Projects
- Diagnosing the Journey
- Learning from Outside
- Preparing for the Next Journey

5 GETTING INNOVATIONS TO MARKET
- Managing Incremental Projects
- Driving Breakthrough and Radical Projects
- Developing New Markets

4 SELECTING PROJECTS FOR IMPLEMENTATION
- Defining Selection Criteria
- Reviewing the Whole Portfolio
- Managing Portfolio Meetings

3 GENERATING DEEP INSIGHTS AND NOVEL SOLUTIONS
- Planning Insight Generation
- Identifying Customer Needs
- Creating Novel Solutions

2 ORGANIZING THE JOURNEY
- Forming Innovation Governance
- Designing Innovation Structures
- Designing Innovation Teams

1 SHAPING INNOVATION STRATEGY
- Aligning Business and Innovation Strategy
- Scanning the Innovation Landscape
- Declaring Innovation Intent

will be launched in emerging or new markets, this phase must also include market development. This is often overlooked by businesses concentrating on the new product or service. For new and emerging markets, it's crucial to conduct market development in parallel to new product (or new service) development. The output of Phase 5 will be products, services and new business models launched onto the market and, in some cases, new processes launched internally (not directly onto the market).

Phase 6: Building a dynamic innovation capability (Chapter 6) consists of four steps. It reviews project performance and then conducts a diagnosis of the journey (assessing whether the intended destination 'B' was reached and whether suitable capabilities 'C' were developed). Next it aims to learn from external businesses before looking to ensure that good innovation capabilities are embedded in your own organizational culture for future innovation journeys. The output of Phase 6 will be an organization that has the dynamic capability to innovate time and time again in changing markets.

Before embarking on the journey, it's worth reflecting that it will involve risk and uncertainty, which senior managers need to be prepared for. As an innovation manager at a European company recently told us, *"In setting strategic direction, the senior management team needs to be aware that it is switching from exploitation, with few assumptions, to the high assumption world of exploration. In my experience, this is clearly outside the comfort zone of most senior managers. And so, the senior management team need to accept that developing the first breakthrough and radical products can take significant time and is extremely risky. If they do not accept this, then innovation is not for them."* Readers should note that an effective way to prepare the senior management team for the innovation journey is to discuss the implications of Table I-2 for your business.

FORMAT OF THIS BOOK

STYLE AND CONTENTS

This book is based on our experience working with a wide range of MSBs and SBUs in very different industries. As we have worked with each business for several years, this has allowed us to be present on the different phases of the journey. We've been party to the ups and downs encountered, as certain approaches have worked while others have disappointed. Comparing the businesses' experiences and identifying best practice led us to the journey metaphor and to the set of tools and techniques we recommend and present in an integrated way.

Each chapter is directly aligned with the phases of the journey (Diagram I-5) and, as mentioned earlier, each chapter has a dedicated colour indicated by tabs and headings. In each chapter, we include a short history on how management approaches have developed. Managers have told us that this background is essential, as it enables them to place their own knowledge in context and understand why certain approaches are recommended, whereas others are not. Tools and techniques are explained carefully, in order to make them easy to understand and apply. These key tools are available digitally on our Online Appendix (www.innovativegrowth.com). We've found that managers and employees want to learn how other businesses have used tools and techniques, and how other businesses have dealt with the emotional rollercoaster of innovation. Therefore, throughout this book we include short case studies (in colour shaded boxes), to provide detailed, practical insights from businesses. In a sense, this book was co-written by practitioners at different phases of the journey, as many of the managers mentioned in the cases gave comments on early drafts of the book.

Each chapter also has a table of key themes that acts as a phase checklist. This includes: actions (or steps) to take; tools and concepts to be applied; people responsible; mindset matters for everyone involved; and the key outputs. Mindset matters are rarely mentioned in innovation management books, but they are vital for the multiple stakeholders to understand, so they are suitably engaged to make the journey a success. For every chapter we provide a summary, similar to the one shown at the end of this chapter.

INTENDED AUDIENCE

The intended audience for this book is not just the senior management team. It's a guidebook for everyone on the journey. Innovation is a cross-functional activity that spans business hierarchy and, therefore, everyone should understand not only their own roles but also those of others. Certain chapters and Phases are more relevant to the senior managers, such as Chapters 1 and 2 on strategy and organization and Chapter 6 on developing a dynamic capability. However, it will help employees in innovation teams to better understand the senior team's role if they also read these chapters. Similarly, the teams conducting market investigations should study Chapter 3 but it will help the senior team to understand how the market research will be conducted if they also review this chapter.

In any event, having all the issues in one book means that you can quickly learn what each phase of the journey entails, become familiar with the key tools and techniques to apply, and know the tasks that others will be working on. That said, the book is probably best treated like a travel guidebook, to be regularly consulted during the innovation journey.

SUMMARY

- Mid-sized businesses tend to be overlooked by government policy and management books, although such businesses can drive economic growth through innovation.
- Similarly, strategic business units that have high levels of autonomy can and should focus on innovative growth.
- Business life cycle studies show the importance of established businesses using three categories to renew growth—core (black-space), emerging (grey-space) and new (white-space).
- There is a plethora of tools and techniques for managing innovation and a set of the most relevant tools is presented in this book.
- Long-term innovation success requires a business to define its current position 'A' and move to a more competitive position 'B', at the same time as building innovation capabilities 'C'.
- Becoming proficient at innovation is a journey with six phases, and the next chapter focuses on Phase 1, Shaping innovation strategy.

Phase 1
Shaping innovation strategy

Shaping innovation strategy

INTRODUCTION

It's unanimous. Both managers and scholars agree that innovative businesses thrive. Compared to more conservative businesses, they create and capture superior value over sustained timeframes[1], and in times of crisis innovative businesses are more likely to survive. However, successful innovation is still the exception rather than the rule, as there are multiple barriers to innovation in *Mid-Sized Businesses* (MSBs) and similarly in a *Strategic Business Unit* (SBU). This chapter concentrates on overcoming a very common barrier—the lack of a clear and coherent innovation strategy. Therefore, Phase 1 shapes the innovation strategy and launches the entire journey, as shown in Diagram 1-1.

DIAGRAM 1-1: PHASE 1 IN THE INNOVATION JOURNEY

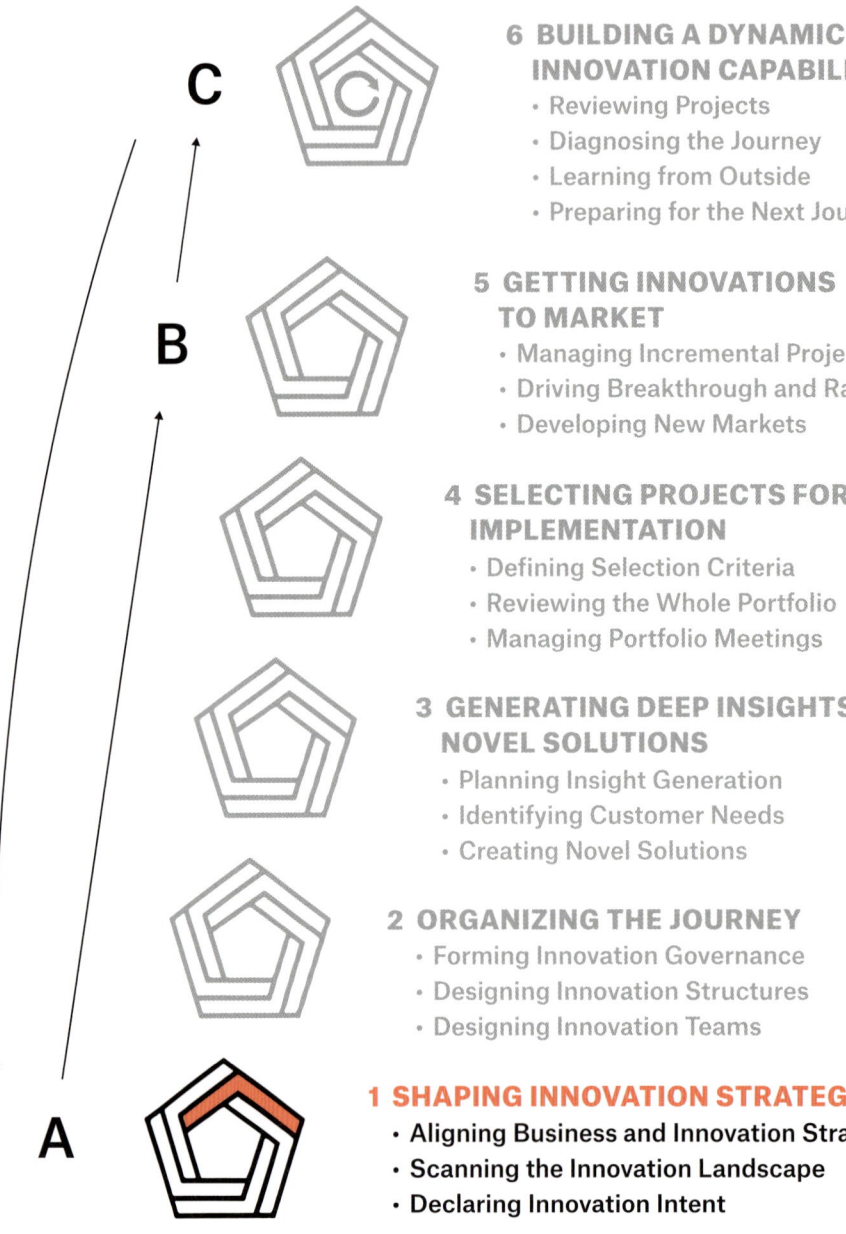

6 BUILDING A DYNAMIC INNOVATION CAPABILITY
- Reviewing Projects
- Diagnosing the Journey
- Learning from Outside
- Preparing for the Next Journey

5 GETTING INNOVATIONS TO MARKET
- Managing Incremental Projects
- Driving Breakthrough and Radical Projects
- Developing New Markets

4 SELECTING PROJECTS FOR IMPLEMENTATION
- Defining Selection Criteria
- Reviewing the Whole Portfolio
- Managing Portfolio Meetings

3 GENERATING DEEP INSIGHTS AND NOVEL SOLUTIONS
- Planning Insight Generation
- Identifying Customer Needs
- Creating Novel Solutions

2 ORGANIZING THE JOURNEY
- Forming Innovation Governance
- Designing Innovation Structures
- Designing Innovation Teams

1 SHAPING INNOVATION STRATEGY
- Aligning Business and Innovation Strategy
- Scanning the Innovation Landscape
- Declaring Innovation Intent

The desire for growth has elevated the role of innovation in businesses, particularly since 2000. While R&D was once a largely 'behind-the-scenes' activity in product businesses, innovation has now moved centre stage in all types of businesses. *Business-wide innovation* should involve all functional areas including marketing, information technology, finance and human resources. However, businesses typically take a 'scattergun' approach to innovation, with each functional area focusing on what they think will help. For example, the IT function might want to digitize processes, whereas HR might commission design thinking workshops to spark creativity. While well intentioned, such ad hoc approaches generate short-lived momentum and provide little or no return. What's worse, uncoordinated attempts at innovation can lead to a debilitating climate where employees think, *'We tried innovation but it didn't work'*.

Managers need to be aware of the important distinction between *business strategy* and *innovation strategy*. Business strategy sets direction at the highest level; it should be developed in advance and cover three things. Firstly, it assesses your business *context*—the dynamics of your markets and how effective your business model is, now and into the future, in these markets. Secondly, it sets out your company's vision with long-term goals and a range of *strategic options*—where to compete and how to be successful in these markets. It should be noted that strategic options are typically based on geographical expansion, or increasing market share, process efficiency (lean management), mergers and acquisitions, or innovation. Thirdly, business strategy must *organize* how a company's limited resources will be allocated to implement strategic options.

Most businesses select innovation as their means to achieve growth. However, saying *'Our strategy is innovation'* isn't enough. You must know where innovation can bring growth and *how* innovation can deliver that growth. Therefore, whenever innovation is part of your business strategy, you must develop a separate innovation strategy[2]. This will scan the business landscape to identify what we call *Innovation Strategic Options* (ISOs). We refer to them frequently in this book. They designate where to innovate and give preliminary ideas on how to innovate in these markets. Innovation strategy also sets goals and organizes how resources are allocated and managed.

Table 1-1 summarizes the key themes covered in Phase 1. There are three actions to take: review the current business strategy; scan the innovation landscape for ISOs; and declare the innovation intent of your business, including the ISOs to take forward. Five main tools are needed in shaping innovation strategy: a *Financial Growth Check; Innovation Landscape Boundary Check;* the *Strategic Roadmap; Innovation Capability Audit;* and the *Innovation Strategy Matrix.*

The people involved in Phase 1 are the senior management team supported by an innovation manager and strategic roadmapping teams for each ISO. The most prevalent mindset issue is the senior team sticks only to what it knows (that is, it remains within its comfort zone), because this has worked to date. This results in business strategies that sound ambitious yet are basically more of the same. Every business should exploit what works, so long

TABLE 1-1: PHASE 1—KEY THEMES AND CHECKLIST

THEMES	DETAILS
Actions to take	☐ Review your business strategy ☐ Scan the landscape for ISOs ☐ Declare your innovation intent
Tools and concepts	☐ Financial growth check ☐ Innovation landscape boundary check ☐ Strategic roadmap ☐ Innovation capability audit ☐ Innovation strategy matrix
People responsible	☐ Senior management team ☐ Innovation manager ☐ Innovation specialists ☐ Strategic roadmapping teams for each ISO
Mindset matters	☐ Ability to drive core (black-), emerging and new business (grey-/white-space) ☐ Senior management's comfort zone
Key outputs	☐ On-board and energized senior management team ☐ Clear and measurable innovation goals ☐ ISOs are selected for Phase 3

as it provides acceptable and sustainable profits but, at the same time, a business must not overlook other opportunities or threats. Innovation, by its very nature, involves exploring new and better things and this requires an explorer's mindset. The senior team in top companies has the capability to simultaneously exploit the core business and explore new business opportunities. This means they have to be closely involved in the innovation journey and not think that they can delegate everything to the innovation manager.

The key outputs of Phase 1 are: the senior team is on-board and energized to lead the innovation journey; clear measurable goals for innovation are set; and the ISOs to pursue are identified.

ESSENTIAL BACKGROUND

Strategy is primarily a task for senior management—deciding how to succeed today and in the future. The best approaches to strategic management have been vigorously debated for years but innovation is now considered as the pre-eminent way to achieve growth. This has led the fields of strategic management and innovation management to converge. Understanding the origins of strategic management and how they relate to business-wide innovation helps managers make informed, balanced decisions.

HISTORY OF STRATEGIC MANAGEMENT

The word 'strategy' stems from the Greek *Strategos*—meaning to lead widely dispersed resources—and it arose from military leadership. The famous Chinese strategist Sun Tzu (4th Century BC) maintained that military success is based not only on external insights about the enemy but also internal insights on your own army's strengths and morale (motivation). He also said that strategy (long-term goals and ways to achieve them) must be complemented by tactics (short-term actions to move forward).[3]

For over 70 years, scholars have been interested in business strategy. Many theories and tools for strategic management have been developed and these tend to mirror the prevalent business challenges of their times. This brief history identifies the thought leaders and concepts that are relevant to businesses pursuing innovative growth.

The 1950s and 1960s—Building Blocks

In the 1950s, *long-term planning* arose as a way for large companies to manage resources and achieve growth. Peter Drucker's 1954 book *The practice of management*[4] contended that a business exists to serve the customer, who decides what is of value and ultimately funds the business. Senior managers must define long-term *strategic goals* (the ends, collectively called *vision*) and then figure out how to achieve them (the means). Both Drucker and later Theodore Levitt[5] argued that senior managers must frequently ask a question of scope: *What business are we in?* The answer to this question equates to a company's purpose (*mission*). Drucker recommended a second question: *What should our business be?* Asking this question can, for example, help a company recognize that it is in the transport business rather than the railway business (which is a too narrow, product-centric view).

DIAGRAM 1-2: THE BUILDING BLOCKS OF STRATEGY

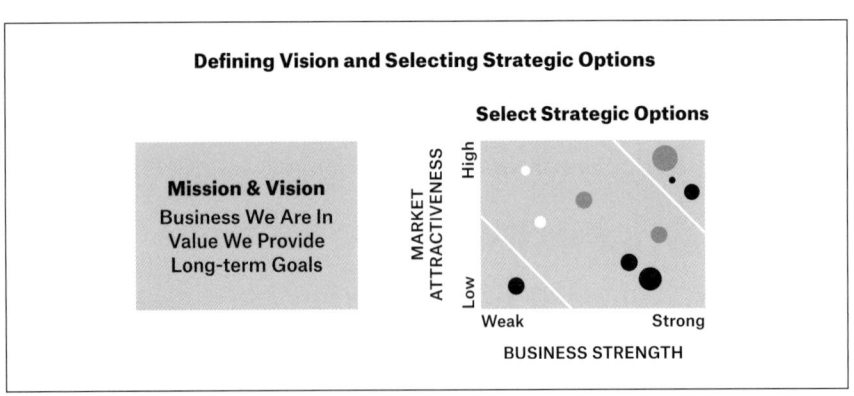

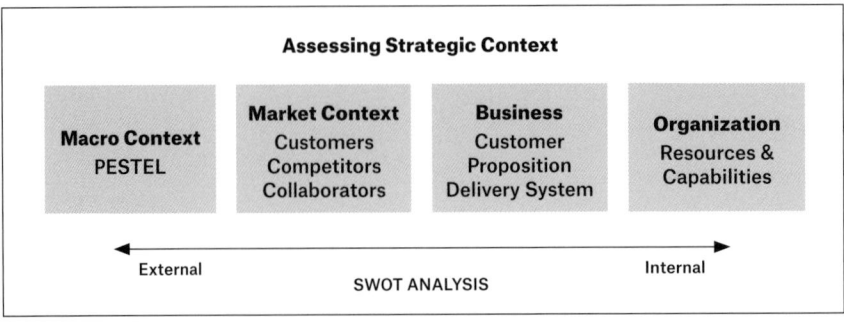

In 1958, James March and Herbert Simon found that, when shaping strategy, managers neither make fully rational decisions, nor consider all the information available.[6] Managers have *bounded rationality*—they can only consciously process a certain level of complexity. In complex situations like strategic decision-making, managers prioritize the information that they believe is most important and don't get immersed in the detail.

During the 1960s, several analysis tools emerged to help managers make sense of complex businesses contexts and set long-term strategic goals. *SWOT Analysis* was developed to assess a company's internal Strengths and Weaknesses, plus external Opportunities and Threats[7] (reflecting Sun Tzu's ideas on insights). Internal strengths and weaknesses should be assessed vis-à-vis competitors. The assessment should consider the customer value proposition and delivery system; and the required organizational configuration of *resources* (things that you own, for example patents, facilities) and capabilities (things that you do, for example manufacturing activities). External opportunities and threats are influenced by many factors. Consequently, the *PESTEL* tool was first developed to assesses the *macro context* for Political, Economic, Socio-cultural, Technological, Environmental, and Legal trends.[8] In addition, the external context must consider the company's *market context*—customers, competitors, and collaborators.

During the 1960s, a consensus on the building blocks of strategic management emerged that is still valid today (see Diagram 1-2). The bottom of the diagram shows four blocks for *Assessing Strategic Context*: these consider the *external* (*macro* and *market*) *context* and *internal context* (business and organization). The external and internal contexts can be assessed using PESTEL and SWOT. Then, as shown on top of Diagram 1-2, *Defining Vision and Selecting Strategic Options* consists of two blocks, defining the mission and vision including long-term goals and selecting which strategic options (opportunities) to invest in for growth.

The late 1960s was marked by the proliferation of 2x2 matrices, to help businesses select strategic options in changing contexts. Igor Ansoff's diversification matrix from 1965[9] considered whether strategic options involved entering *new markets* and/or developing *new products*. It emphasized that the further a business moves from its current markets and products, the greater the risk. Another well-known matrix, the *Boston Box*, emphasized opportunity and assessed different strategic options by comparing *market growth* and *relative market share*.

The *McKinsey-GE Matrix* (see top-right of Diagram 1-2) was, arguably, the most effective tool for assessing and selecting strategic options and it looked at two aspects. The first was *market attractiveness* (related to market opportunities), which amalgamated a combination of factors such as industry growth, geography, and customer segments, etc. The second was current *business strength* (relative to competitors) in the potential market area. On the McKinsey-GE Matrix, each strategic option is denoted by a circle, the size of which relates to the potential returns (profit or revenues).[10] For example, on Diagram 1-2 the circles indicate that 10 strategic options are considered. These are shaded to denote if the options address current (black-), emerging (grey-), or new (white-) spaces. The bottom-left option is not attractive, whereas options in the upper-middle and top-right of the matrix merit closer examination.

Different matrices have associated advantages and limitations, as would be expected of tools that simplify complex situations. One problem is when a matrix's dimensions are analysed superficially. In such cases, the comparison of strategic options is based on poor data leading to poor strategic decisions (for example overly conservative judgements).

The 1970s and 1980s—Market-based View

The 1970s saw increased levels of change with the oil crisis and the rise of business schools. Strategy scholars investigated why certain industries and businesses were more profitable than others. This led to an ongoing quest to identify sources of *competitive advantage*—measured by superior and sustainable profits.

The 1980s were the era of Michael Porter and the *Market-based View* (MBV) of success. Here a *competitive strategy* consists of choosing an attractive market area (industry and segment) to play in and choosing a business strategy that employs specific activities to create superior customer value and capture superior economic value. Thus, the market-based view uses two interrelated questions.[11]

The first is: *Where to play?* Porter's *Five Forces* tool helps managers assess how attractive a business's chosen (or potential) market area is by analysing: rivalry among existing competitors; the threat of new entrants; the bargaining power of suppliers; the bargaining power of buyers; and the threat of substitute products.

The second question is: *How to win?* This is the distinct choice for each activity (for example product attributes, supply sources and pricing) that encompass a winning strategy. Porter proposes choosing a *generic strategy* to win. These concentrate on mass or niche markets and cheaper or differentiated products. Each generic strategy in a given industry segment has what are commonly referred to as *key success factors*. Generic strategies are criticized because they can be easily copied. For example, Ryanair and EasyJet carry almost 30% of Europe's air passengers and have similar low-cost strategies. However, it is the distinct choices and linkages between market areas and business activities that currently gives Ryanair a competitive advantage over EasyJet (for example more destinations, single plane type and ultra-low, absolutely no-frills prices).

To assess the distinct choices that provide a competitive advantage for a business in a given industry, Porter followed up with the *value chain*—a linear set of primary activities from inputs (for example acquiring raw materials) to innovation (for example developing new products in R&D), to production (for example manufacturing or service delivery), to marketing and distribution (for example sales) that add value to the customer product and allow the business to profit. These primary activities are enabled by supporting activities (for example functions such as technology and human resources). Most businesses are part of a wider *value system* (commonly referred to as the industry value chain) that links different businesses (e.g. suppliers, channels) to produce a product or service for a customer market. A competitive business aspires to dominate its market and can grow by expanding up the value chain (for example by producing its own components), or down the value chain (for example becoming involved in retail). Understanding competitive advantage depends on understanding a business's own value chain and how it fits in the value system. Porter's work remains relevant today; however, it stems from a more stable, physical product dominated era and the value chain is considered too linear for a more dynamic and networked business world.

The 1990s and 2000s—Resource-based View and Dynamic Capabilities View

The 1990s were marked by the *Resource-based View* (RBV), which takes an internal and learning perspective to explain why certain companies win. The resource-based view emphasizes *organizational capabilities* as the main source of competitive advantage.[12] Also called *core competencies*, these are the unique resources and capabilities that underpin business activities. Organizational capabilities are hard to identify as they are embedded in the day-to-day routines, processes, and company culture. Consequently, this makes them hard to copy and allows a company to sustain its competitive advantage. For example, Apple's product-based competitive advantage stems not only from being a world-class industrial design group but also from design being embedded in the company culture.

Jay Barney developed the *VRIO* tool in 1991, to help managers identify important organizational capabilities.[13] It assessed them in terms of their: Value to customers; Rarity; Inimitability (that is hard-to-copy); and Organizational support, such as the structures and processes needed to deploy them. Building on this, around 1994 Gary Hamel and C.K. Prahalad argued that, as markets change, it is a business's organizational capabilities that enable strategic moves. For example, organizational capabilities can expand the scope of a business, enabling it to boldly enter new markets. Therefore, companies' visions and goals—their *Strategic Intent*—should be ambitious (for example Canon's goal was not only to develop a photocopier but also to beat Xerox), and then should be broken down into tactics.[14]

The market-based view helps identify a winning market position and the resource-based view explains how to sustain it. Going further, the *Dynamic Capabilities View* (DCV) explains how a company can manage the *renewal stage* of the business life cycle (Introductory Chapter, Diagram I-1). Ideas on dynamic capabilities were developed by David Teece and colleagues around 1997 and, as the name implies, this view enables managers to sense the opportunities that change brings (for example new technological possibilities, or unmet customer needs) and seize them to establish a stronger market position. This means reconfiguring your capabilities and those of collaborating companies in your value system quicker than competitors.[15]

It was Henry Mintzberg in 1998 who found that strategy is often not implemented in the way it's envisaged.[16] Research showed that more than 70% of a company's realized strategy emerges during the implementation phase, when middle managers' ideas and actions have a strong influence. Based on this, Mintzberg said that strategic management must include two distinct but inter-related phases. The first is *formulation*, where the senior team assess the context, define their goals and select options. The second is *formation*, where resources are allocated, performance measures defined, and structures designed for implementing the strategy. Thus, organizing specifically for strategy implementation is imperative (and will be covered in Phase 2, Chapter 2).

In 1997 Clayton Christensen found that most managers gravitate towards incremental innovation, as it's more predictable. This can cause them to be blind to *Disruptive Innovation*—a technology and/or business model that brings disorder to existing markets[17] (for example Netflix's disruption of movie rental, TV and film, and gaming). Every technology evolves from the laboratory to commercial applications, to a time when it becomes obsolete and vulnerable to being disrupted by a new technology. Christensen also found that disruptive business models can create new markets by meeting customer needs in easier and cheaper ways. Such businesses, for example eBay, orchestrate a network that creates the value. Such value networks are typically referred to as *value ecosystems* today.[18] In contrast to traditional, linear value chains, ecosystems link multiple players on both the supply and demand sides, to create new customer value.

An impressive body of research led by Charles O'Reilly III and Michael Tushman started around 1996 and has focused on *Ambidextrous Innovation*—the capability of a company to exploit existing business opportunities (with incremental innovation) and explore new opportunities (with breakthrough or radical innovation) at the same time.[19] Longitudinal studies show that top companies are good at simultaneously exploiting and exploring, over the short, medium and long term.[20] This requires senior managers to have a flexible mindset and to develop the right capabilities such as structures, processes, and culture to support ambidextrous innovation.

The 2010s and 2020s—Dealing with Relentless Change

In recent years, strategy researchers have concentrated on the increasingly unpredictable contexts in which businesses operate. Prevalent concepts are: *VUCA* (macro contexts that are Volatile, Uncertain, Complex and Ambiguous); *Hypercompetition* (highly contested, rapidly changing markets with low entry barriers); and *Industry 4.0* (the trend towards automation and data exchange including the Internet of Things and Artificial Intelligence). To deal with relentless change, companies must constantly adapt. This means they must proactively invest in the capabilities they consider critical to future success.[21] This requires strategy processes to be *geared* to different types of change (for example short-term, incremental innovation and long-term disruptive innovation). The way a business creates and delivers value to its customers cannot be viewed as static, so it's worrying that recent research shows that 75% of companies develop their strategy based on tools unsuited to the dynamic, networked contexts that span traditional industry value chains.[22]

The 2010 book by Alexander Osterwalder and Yves Pigneur on business models (*Business Model Generation*) has made this aspect of strategy development more accessible. Although the business model isn't an entirely new concept, Osterwalder's simple but effective *Business Model Canvas* tool has had a major influence on business strategy, and we describe it in detail below.

BUSINESS MODEL CANVAS

A business model shows how a company *creates* customer value, *delivers* that value, and *captures* the economic value. Diagram 1-3 shows the canvas, so-called because it allows managers to 'paint' (or 'design') their business model. Designing a business model must consider four components, as shown in the diagram in the order: who, what, how and how much.[23]

The first component, 'who?', at the top right of Diagram 1-3, refers to customer segments—the people or entities to be targeted and whose needs must be satisfied. Needs are customers' desired outcomes, often called their *jobs to be done*.[24] Customer needs are not just functional (for example 'I'm hungry'), but also social (for example 'I enjoy eating with others') and emotional (for example 'I want to feel comforted').

The second component to consider is 'what' customer value is created and consists of three elements. The *value proposition* should explain how the company will fulfil customers' needs more effectively than its competitors; the customer relationships (for example mass or personalized engagement, brand) should indicate how the company empathizes with its customers; and the channels (for example physical, digital, or omnichannel) will define the means by which customers can access the proposition. Of course, the value created for customers drives business revenues, as can be seen lower down on the canvas.

The third component, 'how', is the value delivery system, represents the operational engine of the business and has three elements. It entails the configuration of key resources (for example manufacturing operations; databases; or technologies) and key activities (for example processes such as recruiting and data analysis) that produce and deliver customer value. These organizational capabilities may belong to the company, or to key collaborators such as suppliers and alliances in the value ecosystem.

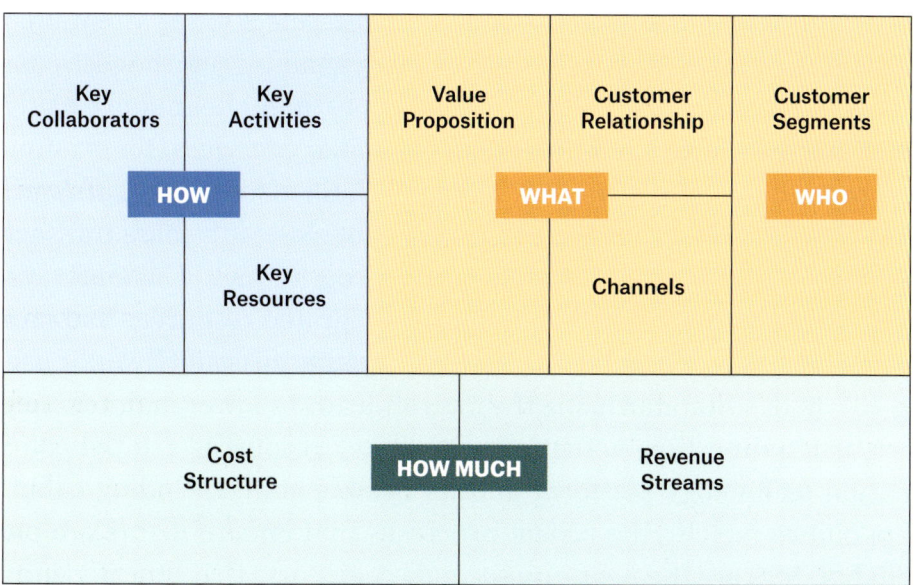

DIAGRAM 1-3: THE BUSINESS MODEL CANVAS

The fourth component, 'how much', identifies cost drivers and how economic value is captured by a business. Key activities, resources and collaboration involved in producing and delivering value all have an associated cost structure with fixed and variable costs. The revenue streams element identifies the way the customer pays. Revenues often stem from traditional product or service sales. However, other approaches such as leasing, cheap products and more expensive accessories, or pay-per-result charges should be considered as alternatives. For example, Rolls-Royce charges 'power by the hour' for airlines using its jet engines, rather than a traditional product sale. It's crucial to consider how value is priced. The difference between revenue and costs leads to the margin captured by a business. A well-known example ('razor and blades' business model), is the success of Nespresso's low-priced coffee machines and relatively expensive, highly profitable pod sales.

The business model canvas gives managers a high-level perspective on how their business operates. It can be used to better understand an existing business model, comparing it with competitors' business models and those of successful companies in other sectors. Looking at different business models stimulates ideas on how to improve an existing business model or create an entirely new one.[25]

Again, Ryanair's 'no-frills business model' gets a lot of attention, and it does provide a useful perspective on strategy. Ryanair targets the cost-conscious traveller with the value proposition of regular, on-time, cheap short-haul flights to many European cities, with the option of ancillary services (for example food and beverages, hotels and hire cars). The sales channel for flights, cars and hotels is digital. The relationship with customers is not close; it is mass transactional, as opposed to traditional airlines' loyalty programmes. Customer value is delivered through a configuration of tightly integrated resources that minimize operating costs. A key resource is a fleet of the same aircraft (Ryanair uses only Boeing 737-800s). Standardizing the aircraft leads to lower maintenance costs and fast turnaround (key activities). Other key resources are the company's information technology platform and its flexible staff, including cabin crew. Key capabilities include the robust processes that ensure flights are on time. Key collaborators are the near-city secondary airports that incentivize airlines to bring tourists to their regions with cheap landing rights. Ryanair keeps its operating costs very low and maximizes revenues through demand pricing, aircraft utilization, and high passenger loading.

Ryanair is also at the centre of a wider tourism value ecosystem that supports hotels and restaurants, entertainment and property, etc. Not content with his successful airline business model, Ryanair's CEO Michael O'Leary recently announced his strategic intent to be the 'Amazon of travel' and "to disintermediate all the disintermediators" (for example TripAdvisor). Since then, Ryanair has hired hundreds of information technologists, organized them into an innovation function called 'Ryanair Labs' and tasked them with building a comprehensive digital travel platform.[26]

STRATEGY AS A PROCESS (4+4+4)

No single tool or theory can manage the complexity of short-, medium- and long-term success. Businesses require an appropriate combination of tools based on insights from research. Therefore, we give clear recommendations on the tools MSBs and SBUs should apply for managing strategy.

The market-based view helps identify strategic options, whereas the resource-based view emphasizes the organizational capabilities needed to achieve and sustain competitive advantage. And dynamic capabilities are crucial, in order to seize growth opportunities. In simple terms, strategy is the process of moving from 'A' (the current position) to 'B' (the intended position). To move from 'A' to 'B', businesses must leverage existing and new organizational capabilities 'C'. As we say repeatedly, an effective strategy can be expressed as *From 'A' to 'B', while building 'C'*.

Diagram 1-4 shows the three steps of strategic management, each of which is based on four blocks, giving a '4+4+4 process'. The first step at the bottom is *Assessing Business Context* ('A') covering the four blocks: macro context (analysed using PESTEL and SWOT); market context and business model (analysed using SWOT, Five Forces and BM Canvas); and organizational capabilities (analysed using VRIO).

The second step is *Defining Vision and Selecting Options*, describing where you envisage your business to be in the future 'B'. The four blocks here cover: mission and values; vision including long-term goals; selected strategic options; and how current capabilities can be complemented with new ones.

DIAGRAM 1-4: THE THREE-STEP PROCESS OF STRATEGIC MANAGEMENT (4+4+4 BLOCKS)

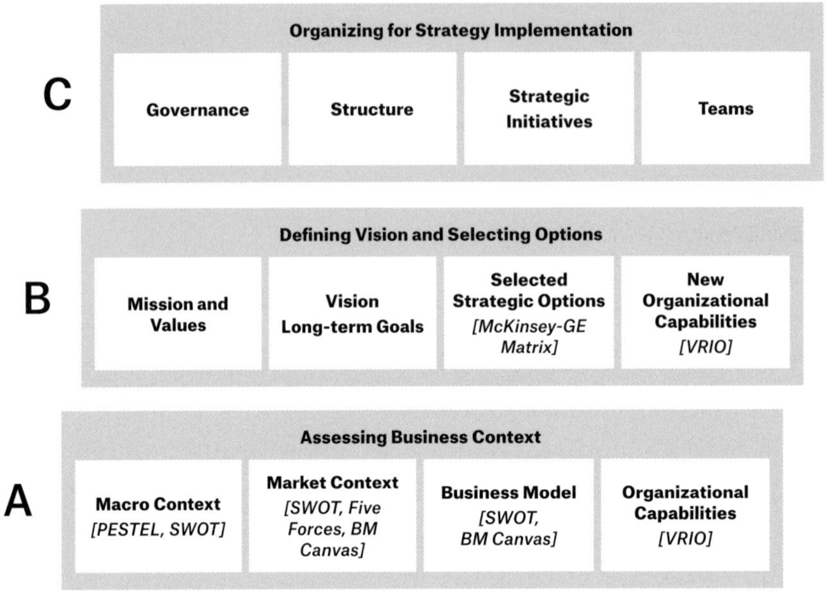

C — Organizing for Strategy Implementation
- Governance
- Structure
- Strategic Initiatives
- Teams

B — Defining Vision and Selecting Options
- Mission and Values
- Vision Long-term Goals
- Selected Strategic Options [McKinsey-GE Matrix]
- New Organizational Capabilities [VRIO]

A — Assessing Business Context
- Macro Context [PESTEL, SWOT]
- Market Context [SWOT, Five Forces, BM Canvas]
- Business Model [SWOT, BM Canvas]
- Organizational Capabilities [VRIO]

The third step, *Organizing for Strategy Implementation*, ensures the strategy is achieved, that is the move from 'A' to 'B' is accomplished through specific organization mechanisms such as governance (for example performance measures); structure (for example project office); strategic initiatives; and project teams. When there is a significant change of strategy, this is commonly called transformation. While these steps are sequential, subsequent choices within each step and between steps cause necessary iterations. SBUs must also consider their corporate parent as an additional dimension throughout the strategy process.

There are three common limitations in the way businesses strategize: 1) Business strategy is not really documented (for example only in PowerPoint slides) and not effectively communicated (as it resides largely in the heads of the senior team); 2) The business strategy articulates bold growth goals but is light on how (that is, the strategic options) to achieve them and; 3) The strategic options identified are too narrow, based entirely on today's offering and limited by the biases of the senior team.

Diagram 1-4 enables companies to check that their business strategy has been based on an appropriate level of analysis and has avoided bias. Case Study 1-1 explains how some of the tools were applied at a service company in the B2B sector.

CASE STUDY 1-1:
COMPANY X: B2B SERVICES[27]

One of the companies we have supported with its strategy process is an international B2B service provider. Its technical services are used in verifying both product quality and manufacturing process efficacy. As its strategic moves are obviously confidential, we'll refer to it as 'Company X'. It is family-owned, employs 2,000 people and has a 50-year history of providing technical tests, to automotive original equipment manufacturers (OEMs) and medical companies, often based on its unique technology.

Company X's strategy had mainly been decided by the owners and was largely undocumented. To strengthen the strategy, four tools were applied to assess its business context ('A'). The PESTEL analysis revealed trends such as increasing international competition, technological advances which could make new tests possible, and increasing market regulations for testing. The SWOT analysis showed the company had strong technological capabilities but was weaker at operations—the processes needed to deliver services in a fast and consistent, repeatable manner. The business model canvas demonstrated that the 'pay per test' model was prevalent in the industry. Furthermore, the VRIO analysis showed that Company X's testing capabilities and technology had all been copied by competitors.

The main perceived threat was Asian competitors, with increasing technological capabilities and efficient service delivery. So, the senior management team decided on a two-pronged five-year strategy. The mission was defined as: *"To provide unique testing capabilities and efficient service delivery for automotive and medical OEMs, in ways competitors cannot match"*. The vision pushed by the CEO was to add new annual revenues of €2.6M by 2025. This growth was to be based on regaining technological leadership; and identifying where customer segments required new, innovative services.

In two senior management team half-day meetings, four strategic options were identified. First, an emerging segment in the automotive OEM sector was identified where existing software testing services could be offered. Second, a growth opportunity in Poland was recognized. Third, an emerging need for testing cell therapies was identified. Fourth, components based on 3-D printing need stringent quality testing but robust test procedures are not yet available. Here, the senior team could even imagine a product-based solution, rather than a service.

Once the strategic options were identified, the CEO, R&D manager and marketing manager agreed that the R&D manager should take the lead as 'innovation manager' but the other two would remain closely involved.

ALIGNING BUSINESS AND INNOVATION STRATEGY

INNOVATION ROLES AND RESPONSIBILITIES

It's vital to have one person responsible for navigating the innovation journey and, consequently, businesses need an *innovation manager*. We advise choosing someone with strategic and creative skills; the ability to stimulate business-wide innovation (not only innovation in R&D); and the confidence to challenge the senior team's thinking (Phase 2, Chapter 2 discusses this in more detail).

Nominating an innovation manager doesn't mean that the senior team can delegate all responsibility; successful innovation demands their active involvement. If this isn't the case, employees will be quick to interpret this as showing that the senior team is not serious about innovation. The senior team must consider the company's position on its business life cycle (Introductory Chapter, Diagram I-1), reflecting on the need for innovation in core and emerging businesses. This brings the senior team 'on-board'; recognizing the imperative for business-wide innovation and comprehending what the journey entails. It is best for senior team members to reserve a percentage of their time for innovation, to be used in the most appropriate way. For example, they can help identify potential markets, identify the organizational capabilities needed, and later act as project sponsors.

Most senior teams have significant experience and tenure but this can be a double-edged sword. On the one hand, their expertise is invaluable for the current business. On the other hand, the senior team may discard opportunities that are outside their typical field of vision. Consequently, fresh and diverse minds must be engaged. We therefore recommend that, in addition to the innovation manager, two or three experienced employees and a trusted external innovation advisor should be involved. We will refer to them as the *innovation specialists*. They need the ability to think strategically about the business's current and potential markets. One advantage of an external advisor is that they can assist with the innovation journey, bringing an outside perspective and pointing out when the senior team's thinking is biased.

INNOVATION STRATEGY DEVELOPMENT PROCESS (3+3+3)

Innovation strategy stems from the business strategy. A business strategy identifies high-level goals and strategic options to achieve them. For example, Company X's business strategy (Case Study 1-1) contained the following goals connected to strategic options:

1. Become market leader in automotive software testing services, an emerging segment, offering the most efficient and reliable service (€0.6M).
2. Double annual revenue in Poland, using a sales and test centre to support expansion (€0.5M).
3. Design innovative testing methods for cell therapy and generate €1M annual revenues by 2025.
4. Develop an innovative, automated procedure for testing 3-D printed components and generate €0.5M annual revenues by 2025.

Three of the above strategic options are dependent on innovation. The first requires process innovation for existing procedures (for example optimized service delivery with digitized activities). The second, Company X's expansion in Poland, does not need innovation and so only the revenue it can deliver must be considered in the innovation strategy. The third requires significant innovation: investigating the cell therapy market, identifying customer needs, and designing a distinctive value proposition. The fourth strategic option requires innovative ways to test 3-D components to be developed.

Strategic Options 1, 3 and 4 all specifically depend on innovation, and so they are what we call *Innovation Strategic Options* (ISOs). Consequently, an innovation strategy must define each ISO, delineating where to innovate and how to innovate.

The innovation strategy process help progress the business *From 'A' to 'B', while building 'C'* and consists of three steps: Scanning the Innovation Landscape; Declaring Innovation Intent; and Organizing the Journey, as illustrated in Diagram 1-5. This makes the innovation strategy a 3+3+3 block process. Note that the recommended tools for each block are shown in italics. Again, although the process is depicted as sequential from the bottom-up, inevitably some iteration will be necessary. Chapter 2 explains Phase 2, Organizing the journey, through three mechanisms: form governance, design structure, and design teams. The rest of this chapter will explain the first two steps, what we call Phase 1.

SCANNING THE INNOVATION LANDSCAPE

This step checks whether the current strategic options and ISOs can generate sufficient revenue to meet growth goals. Then, it checks that opportunities are not overlooked (when companies fail to look beyond their current markets). This pushes the boundaries of what we call the *Innovation Landscape*, which includes all possible opportunities.

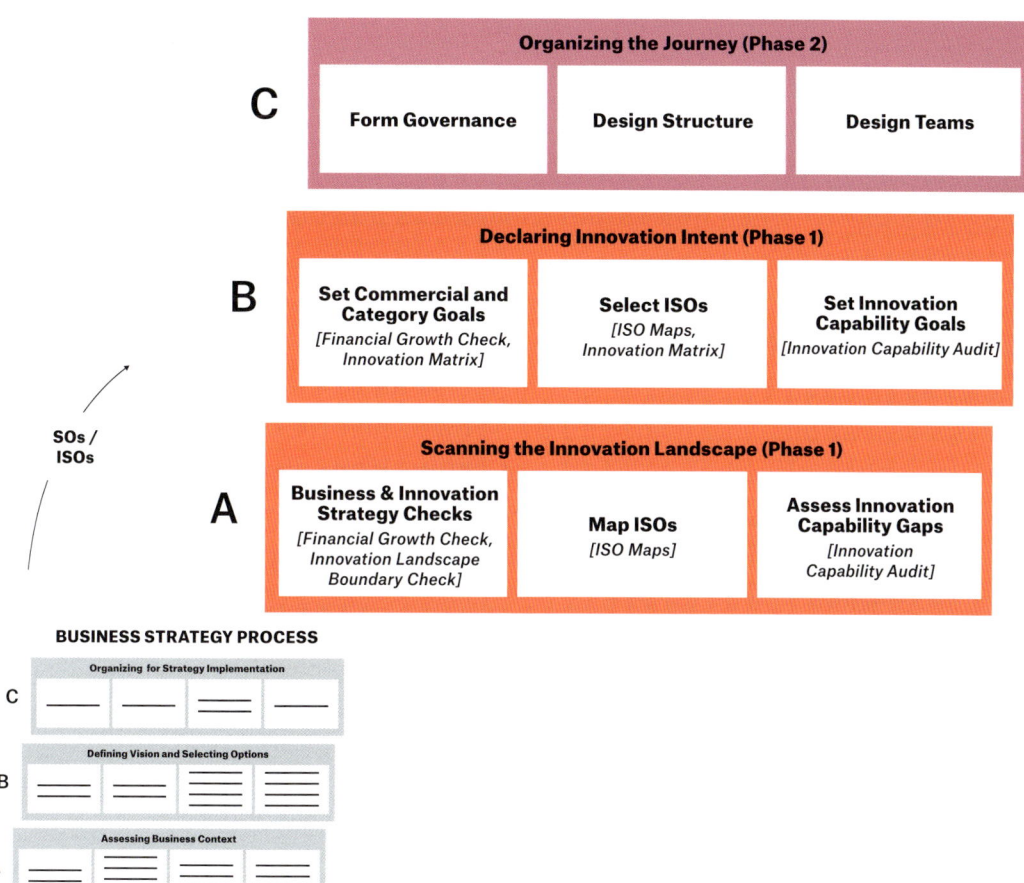

DIAGRAM 1-5: THE THREE-STEP INNOVATION STRATEGY PROCESS (3+3+3 BLOCKS)

BUSINESS AND INNOVATION STRATEGY CHECKS

The best way to kick-off the innovation strategy process is for the innovation manager to organize a one-day workshop (*Workshop 1*) with the senior team and any innovation specialists. This will review all existing strategy documentation, 'on-board' everyone and create the momentum necessary for innovation strategy work. To get the most out of such workshops, innovation managers must ensure a clear agenda is set and necessary preparation is conducted (for example, financial data will be needed). The aim of *Workshop 1* should be:

1. To check that the intended financial growth will be delivered by the strategic options identified.
2. To push the boundaries of the innovation landscape, identifying further ISOs.
3. To identify which innovation capabilities must be developed.

Financial Growth Check

The simple *Financial Growth Check* looks for a gap between the senior team's five-year financial goals and the growth that the core business and the strategic options (including ISOs) can bring. If the financial growth check shows a gap, then more ISOs need to be identified. Note that grey- and white-space revenue growth is typically slow at first and the probability of success (or failure) should be factored in.[28]

Case Study 1-2 explains the results of a financial growth check at an Irish company and shows the importance of having a budget and a team responsible for innovation. This might seem obvious but many businesses have neither the funds reserved for innovation nor people assigned for the journey. If the allocation of funding and people isn't decided in advance, progress will be severely hindered.

CASE STUDY 1-2: COILLTE
MIND (AND CLOSE) THE GAP[29]

Coillte, a commercial company established in 1988, is owned by the Irish State and has about 1,000 employees. It owns about 7% of the land area in Ireland and has three divisions. Coillte Forest operates in commercial

DIAGRAM 1-6: FINANCIAL GROWTH CHECK AT COILLTE

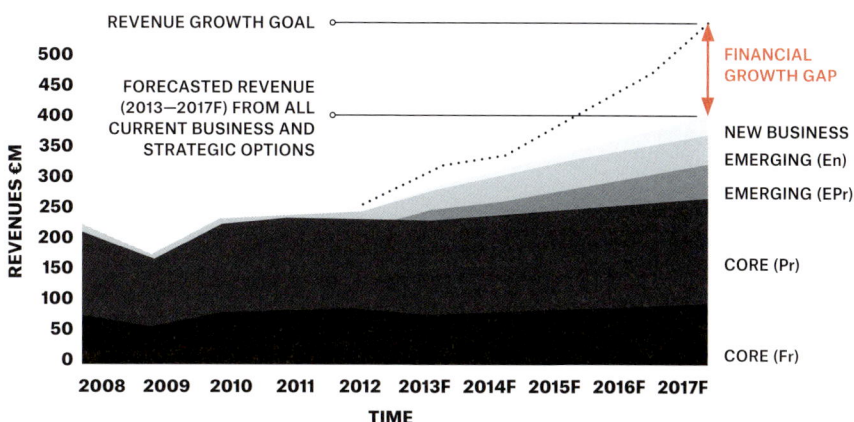

forestry and public recreation; Coillte Panel Products manufactures and distributes wood products (for example chipboard); and Coillte Enterprise manages a collection of diverse businesses that leverage the land and forest resources (for example wind energy and biomass energy).

In 2012, the CEO David Gunning initiated a business strategy process for 2013–2017. The emphasis was on cost reduction in the core forestry business plus growth from new markets, value propositions and business models. As an exercise to stretch their thinking, the senior team set a proxy revenue goal of €500M by the end of 2017 (up from €262M in 2012). Diagram 1-6 shows their core business and strategic options forecasts (2013F to 2017F) categorized by: core forest (Fr); core wood products (Pr); emerging wood products (EPr); the early-stage wind energy business (En); and new business. As can be seen from the diagram, the financial growth check highlighted a revenue gap of €100M in 2017. This led Coillte to launch an innovation strategy process, to identify more breakthrough and disruptive innovation strategic options to close the gap.

The company had accumulated a smattering of ideas for growth over recent years but as it had neither an innovation budget nor innovation team none of the radical ideas achieved traction. Now, driven by the revenue gap, coordinated workshops were launched to encourage fresh thinking, unconstrained by divisional boundaries, and to consider longer timeframes. Revisiting previous ideas and gathering new ones led to a total of 40 opportunities. These were organized into possible innovation strategic options (which Coillte called 'fields') and categorized as black-, grey- or white-space.

The senior team used three criteria to select the most promising innovation strategic options:

1. High market attractiveness. Defined as innovation strategic options which are: based on radically new and potentially scalable business models (generating >€5M cash); are differentiated from current business; show international potential; and require minor capital investment.
2. Strategic fit. innovation strategic options which align with Coillte's core purpose, identified markets, resources and capabilities.
3. Breakthrough and disruptive: Opportunities that might remain unexplored within the divisional structure and processes.

Four white-space innovation strategic options were selected by the senior team, based on the criteria, and assigned for deeper market research (insight teams). A newly appointed innovation director, Ciaran Black, and his division-based matrix team were assigned to drive the white-space ideas and given an appropriate budget and resources to explore the innovation strategic options.

Innovation Landscape Boundary Check

Whenever you have a financial growth gap, or when core markets are relentlessly changing, you must push the boundaries and look for more opportunities. Managers often subconsciously set boundaries to their business based on previous successes. It is therefore important to be able to consider whether significant changes are necessary (see Case Study 1-3 on how FashionPower reinvented its business and developed new capabilities).

CASE STUDY 1-3: FASHIONPOWER TRADITION WITH INNOVATION[30]

FashionPower is a traditional family business that has managed to become very innovative. How can tradition go together with innovation?

The company's heritage goes back to 1897 when Jan Nelemans founded a business in Zundert, Holland, established around his skills as a tailor. From the beginning, it was about the highest-quality clothing, selling directly to consumers. The business opened its first retail store in the Netherlands in 1949 and, over subsequent decades, the company built a large chain of shops, known for making quality clothing for the whole family, from socks to overcoats, to outdoor clothing. Four generations later, FashionPower focuses solely on performance clothing, for sports and outdoor activities. So, what happened to the tailoring and retail tradition of this family business?

Reg Nelemans and his brother Ronald are the fourth generation and decided to shift to new areas of market opportunity. They moved away from retail completely, and from B2C into B2B, establishing FashionPower as it is today. One reason for this sea-change was that they thought their company had many ideas on how to design better high-performance clothing. Another reason was that being in retail meant significant capital was engaged in keeping large stocks, reducing the amount available for investment in innovation. Thus, many creative ideas for products and production processes weren't being implemented. Reg felt that their company's capabilities could have more impact within the industry if they put more effort into innovation and finding new ways to make more sustainable products.

Maxim Nelemans, from the fifth generation, is responsible for buying and sourcing within the company and he manages the innovation process. In explaining the switch to B2B he explains, *"It was about treasuring and respecting what we had built over the last 120 years. But, at the same time, it was being open to re-invent the business. It was not about letting go of our company values but about how we could apply those values differently; as experts in clothing design and textiles we could create much more value by delivering our total solutions rather than managing retail stores."*

The scope of the company now spans in-house design and styling, own patternmaking, sustainable and responsible overseas production, fast logistics and online and offline marketing support for their retailers. This is all managed by their Dutch head office (still in Zundert), a German sales office, and a production office in China. FashionPower is well known among retailers but, in addition and harking back to its tradition, the company has invested in a B2C brand to enlarge their visibility and market presence. This is the Redmax® brand for activewear and for outdoor clothing.

The production of a cotton T-shirt requires about 3,000 litres of water and jeans about 8,000 litres, and textiles is the second most polluting industry in the world. Originally sportswear was based on cotton, but this has shifted to synthetic fibres such as polyester and polyamides. Consequently, many sports brands now use recycled synthetic fibres. However, for FashionPower, recycled fibres are only a small part of sustainability. Maxim relates his experience of *"buying a tracksuit from a famous US brand, advertised as 'recycled material', only for me to find that merely the pockets were made from recycled material!"* This and some other claims made by the fashion industry about sustainability have led FashionPower to guarantee it will be fully sustainable by 2030 and it will help develop not only better products but also enhanced production processes.

When clothing is intended for sports and outdoor activities, it's all about functionality and comfort based on the right materials, fitting and design. Most functional yarns are oil-based, which means they have a very negative ecological footprint. *"As textiles are not naturally functional, to add a particular functionality means chemical additives and additional waste water. Plus, after 20 washes, most of those chemicals are in your laundromat and water pipeline"* says Maxim. Although he studied international business and not textile science, Maxim has an enviable knowledge of natural materials and their functional impact. FashionPower has developed processes to add functionality by using coconut, bamboo and coffee charcoal. These natural constituents can improve moisture management, UV protection and odour control in textiles. For example, activated charcoal made from these materials is inserted using nano-technology and gives textiles unlimited functionality, even after repeated washing.

Another FashionPower innovation is the so-called 'dope dyed' process. In this process, dyeing takes place during the spinning of the fibre rather than afterwards. This means the entire fibre is dyed, increasing colour fastness. Compared to the conventional dyeing process, water usage is reduced by over 80%, pigments are used instead of chemicals, and energy consumption is reduced by over 60%. FashionPower is very keen to implement dope dyeing with all of their suppliers, and it hopes that such innovations will be widely adopted by the industry, so that the maximum environmental benefit can be gained.

FashionPower has changed track successfully, moving from fashion retail into sports- and outdoor wear and from a focus on product innovation to both product and process innovation. For other companies wanting to pivot in similar ways, Maxim's advice is: *"Try to focus on where you see the business in the future and not only today's sales figures. And do not only listen to what people tell you today, as you might not be able to envision what your company should be doing in the future."* Another piece of advice he would like to share is: *"When you want to move forward, you should realize that this can only be managed with the right partners. We have been working together with many of them for 20 years+ and this has certainly helped us in getting where we are today."*

The innovation manager must ensure that options that can deliver new growth are not overlooked. Table 1-2 is a tool to support this, the *Innovation Landscape Boundary Check*. It gives 10 questions to discuss, broadening perspectives and considering the medium and long term, in order to identify additional ISOs.

Once the boundary check has identified additional ISOs, the senior team must decide which to explore. We recommend a democratic decision where each senior team member rates each ISOs (scored on a scale of '5' [very attractive] to '1' [unattractive]). The scores can be tallied and decisions based on them.

TABLE 1-2: INNOVATION LANDSCAPE BOUNDARY CHECK

QUESTIONS TO DISCUSS	ADDITIONAL ISOs IDENTIFIED	POTENTIAL REVENUE
1 Which areas of market opportunity have we not considered?		
2 What biases are stopping us looking beyond the norm?		
3 What do we consider to be the key success factors for our market position in 20 years?		
4 What might new competitors (for example new entrants in current and emerging markets) see that we don't?		
5 What technological and other capabilities can we build on?		
6 What emerging technologies could potentially disrupt our markets and business model(s)?		
7 What new customer value propositions (for example adding services to products or vice versa) can we offer?		
8 What new business model(s) could we offer?		
9 What new collaborators could we work with to create new customer value propositions and business models?		
10 Where are our competitors expanding and what can we do to out-manoeuvre them?		

The total number of ISOs worth exploring depends on your growth goals and resources. As a rule of thumb, we suggest 2 to 4 ISOs from the strategy and 1 to 2 additional ones. Rejected ideas should be regarded as shelved, as they may become more interesting in the future (for example as new technology becomes available).

Once a set of ISOs has been selected there is 'homework' to be done; analysis of each ISO (showing *where* and how to innovate), which will need to be conducted between *Workshop 1* and *Workshop 2* (which will focus on the innovation intent).

MAP INNOVATION STRATEGIC OPTIONS

At this stage, innovation strategic options (ISOs) are still high-level, preliminary ideas that can bring growth in current and new markets. As ISOs may require significant investment, it's prudent to do some analysis based on the strategic roadmapping approach developed by Robert Phaal and associates at Cambridge University.[31]

Strategic Roadmaps and S-curves

The *Strategic Roadmap* shown in Diagram 1-7 highlights market drivers over time. The name 'roadmap' implies that the tool shows the direction in which markets are 'travelling' and the diagram consists of five 'swim-lanes', which should be filled in from left to right. The horizontal axis is time and we recommend considering the next 20 years in order to stretch thinking in how to move from black- to white-space. The strategic roadmap is a sophisticated tool that integrates strategic thinking, including the market-based view, the resource-based view, and the dynamic capabilities view, as we will see.

DIAGRAM 1-7: STRATEGIC ROADMAP

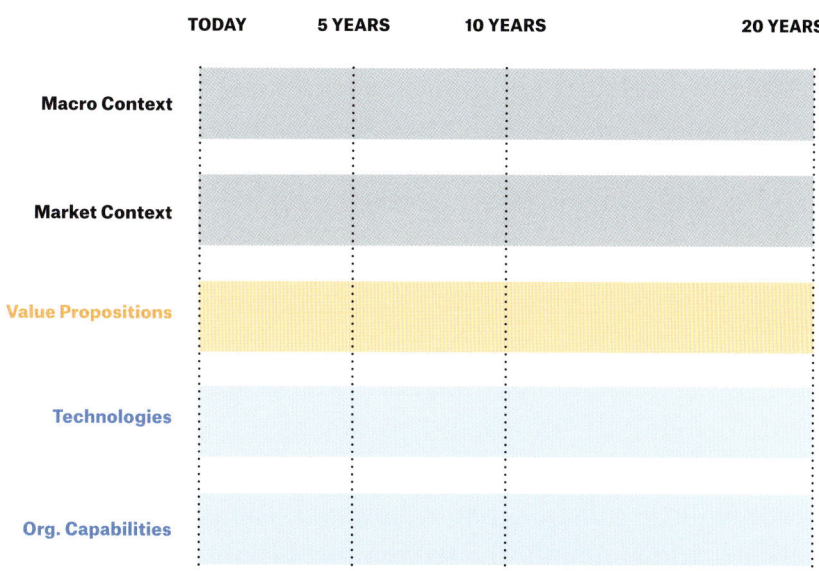

The top swim-lane is the *macro context*. The current situation needs to be added on the left (in the 'Today to 5 years' field) and the changing situation over the next 20 years (in the '5–10 years' and '10–20 years' fields). PESTEL can stimulate future thinking on the drivers of change, whereas VUCA can identify market dynamics.

The second swim-lane is used to capture the *market context*. SWOT is a useful tool to summarize insights into relevant competitors and collaborators. This can be supplemented with ideas from the business model canvas and five forces analysis. The top two swim-lanes take very much a market-based view.

The third swim-lane analyses *value propositions*. It looks at current products and services and the customer experience, and how these will change over the coming 20 years. Again, the business model canvas helps to prompt insights into how value propositions from today will change or be disrupted over time.

The fourth swim-lane identifies the *technologies* needed to support evolving products and services. Don't forget to consider the technologies used to manufacture and deliver products and services. It's important to identify the technologies used in the market and to decide how they will change. Be aware that companies tend to overestimate the impact of a new technology in the short run and underestimate it in the long run.[32] For example, many materials-based companies were quick to invest in graphene (the carbon-based material, with unique electrical and optical properties) but its commercial applications are slower to emerge than many had expected.

The technology *s-curve* can discern where a technology is in its development (Diagram 1-8). The vertical axis shows the performance of a key aspect of the technology. Typically, this equates to product attributes such as speed, accuracy, resolution and the like, that are important to the customer. The horizontal axis denotes the cumulative investment made in improving the performance. When a technology is at an early stage, its performance is low, the promise is high but the rate of improvement is relatively slow. At this early stage, development is best left to universities and research institutes, as commercialization will be difficult. Later, however, the rate of performance improvement climbs and suddenly the technology becomes commercially viable. Much later, the rate of performance improvement slows, then plateaus.

When a technology approaches this plateau, progress slows and investment becomes less and less productive. This leaves the technology prone to disruption—senior managers may not be aware that their products or services are built around technologies that are at the end of their s-curves.

DIAGRAM 1-8: THE TECHNOLOGY S-CURVE

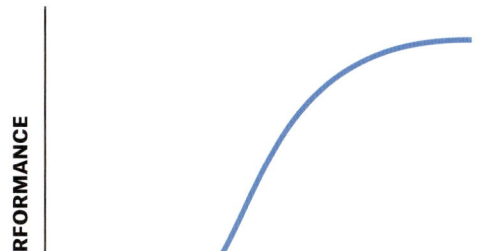

Referring again to Diagram 1-7, the bottom (fifth) swim-lane identifies the *organizational capabilities* that your business already possesses and what will be necessary in the future. Here VRIO analysis is particularly useful, as it identifies your unique capabilities. The bottom swim-lane takes a resource-based view and looks at how capabilities change (that is, a dynamic capabilities view). Thus, the strategic roadmap blends key perspectives of strategic management in one diagram, in a practical way.

In dynamic market conditions, it's important to sense opportunities and threats[33] and the roadmap approach takes a long-term (typically 20-year) view. Some managers say they can't predict things 20 years ahead, and we agree. However, considering what can happen over such a timescale challenges management thinking. For example, a few years ago we facilitated a roadmapping exercise with a manufacturer of exhaust pipes for large trucks. The management team initially wanted to draw a 10-year roadmap but were encouraged to consider 20 years instead. In drawing the 20-year roadmap, they recognized that the slowly emerging trend towards electric trucks would destroy most of their market in coming years. However, using the unique capabilities of the company identified in the bottom swim-lane, the management team created a transition plan to create components for electric trucks. The company's unique ability to create components that can withstand high temperatures and vibration led them to identify several products they can produce for electric trucks. A year later the company was sold and the strategic roadmap played an important role in the negotiations, convincing the buyer that the company had a viable long-term strategy.

Constructing a strategic roadmap is a time-consuming and demanding exercise. It's worth the effort, though, because it ensures that the senior team is presented with a systematic analysis of market opportunities—far removed from a strategy based on gut feelings. Strategic roadmapping will surface many issues connected with an ISO, including gaps in an organization's knowledge. Remember the aim is to generate a good understanding of an ISO. More comprehensive research will be conducted in Phase 3 generating deep insights and novel solutions for the ISOs that are selected.

Strategic Roadmapping Teams
Analysis tools are important but so are the people selected to apply them. They must consider complex contexts and envision future scenarios. With several ISOs where strategic roadmaps need to be prepared, time is at a premium. The innovation manager and innovation specialists should take overall responsibility and for each ISO we recommend a team of four people, including a member of the senior team. Where necessary, people with domain specific knowledge (for example of markets and technologies) can be asked to join or provide key inputs. Some preparatory work is necessary and then roadmapping each ISO will take the relevant team about a day's work in a spacious room with lots of wall space. If an innovation manager hasn't yet been appointed, roadmapping is an ideal opportunity to watch potential candidates apply their skills—more on this in Chapter 2.

Strategic Roadmapping Example
To demonstrate the value of strategic roadmapping and ISO's, we provide an actual example. This is Company X's (Case Study 1-1) recognition that cell

therapy is an emerging opportunity for the company. Diagram 1-9 is the roadmap, completed by a team of four from Company X, including a clinical expert.

The team used the *Brainwriting Technique* to facilitate the preparation of the map. In typical brainstorming, a group of people launches directly into discussion. In contrast, brainwriting is based on each individual taking a few minutes to write their ideas on post-its, before discussions commence. The big advantage of brainwriting is that all ideas are considered and not influenced by the first person to speak. Ideas can then be clustered, duplicates removed, timescales discussed, and Post-it® sticky notes applied to the roadmap.

As shown in Diagram 1-9, Company X's team analysed the *macro context*, based on PESTEL, across the 20 years of the top swim-lane. It can be seen that cell therapy (CT) is currently expensive and there are few products on the market, and therapy is complex and strictly regulated. Government support for both research and start-ups is widespread. An increase in clinical studies is expected and value-based (VB) healthcare is emerging. This changes reimbursement from a per-treatment payment into a pay-for-performance system and is expected to accelerate the acceptance of cell therapy. Some of the longer-term trends identified included increasing life expectancy but increasing rates of NCDs (non-communicable diseases, such as heart and lung disease, and cancer) with 60M deaths expected globally in 2040. However, cheaper and personalized cell therapy is expected to reduce this morbidity in 10–16 years' time.

The *market context* showed the current situation to be many start-ups with products in clinical trials for both state and private healthcare providers. The main barriers are the strict regulations and problems with the clinical process, 'cleanroom' manufacturing and logistics (as cell therapy requires cells from a specific patient to be taken, carefully cultured and then re-injected into the same patient). As cell therapy's benefits become known, it's expected that in about five years affluent individuals will be willing to pay for treatments that are not reimbursed. Longer-term, it's expected that 'big pharma' will acquire the successful start-ups, dominating the market, and cell therapy will become widely available in 'CT apothecaries' in 20 years' time. The main impacts of the macro context on the market context were added as downward arrows (for example, increasing life expectancy

DIAGRAM 1-9: STRATEGIC ROADMAP FOR THE CELL THERAPY MARKET[34]

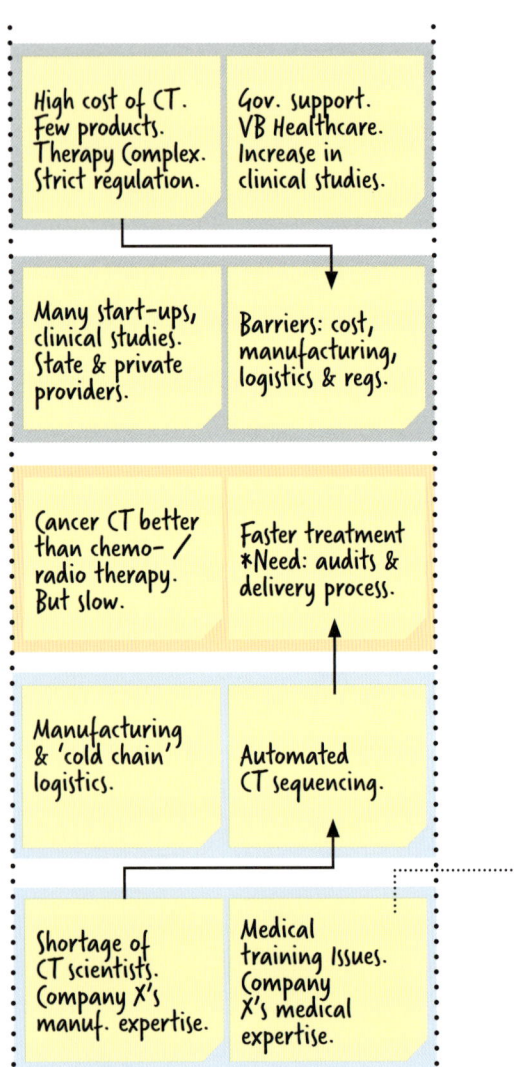

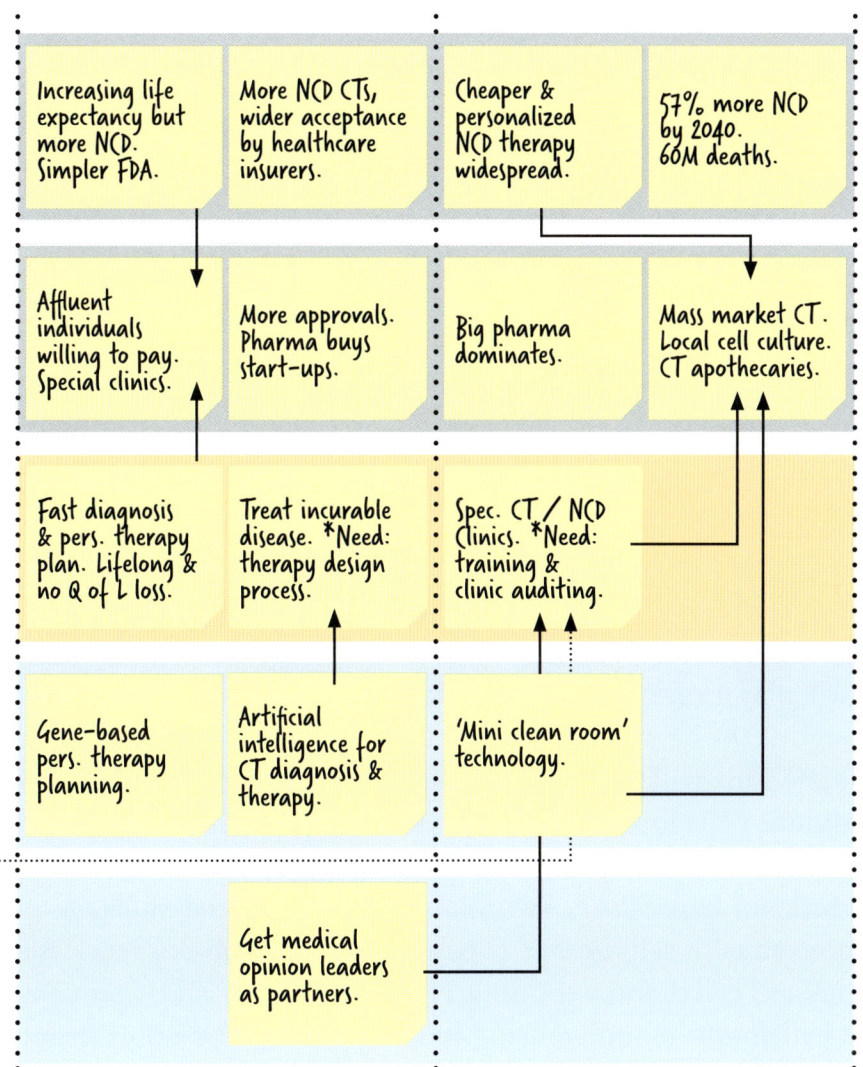

Dynamic Capabilities View

will mean that high-value individuals will be willing to pay for treatment in special clinics in just over five years' time).

The *value proposition* swim-lane showed there are few cell therapy products today but those in the market offer promising treatment for cancer, as they can be more effective than chemo- or radio therapy. In coming years, products will emerge that offer faster diagnosis and personalized therapy, enabling lifelong cures and no loss of 'Q of L' (quality of life) for the patient. Cell therapy will move to address currently uncurable diseases and specialist cell therapy clinics will become the norm in 10–15 years. In this swim-lane Company X could already not only identify the cell therapy products that would be on the market but also the need for new services that they could provide (shown by an * on Diagram 1-9). This included audits for the sequencing and delivery process of cells for individual patients, plus ways to audit the efficacy of individual therapy plans.

The *technology* swim-lane showed that various technologies will be needed to support the diffusion of cell therapy products. Currently, all the discussion is about automated manufacturing and the 'cold chain' needed for cell collection and delivery to specific patients. Automated, digital sequencing is also crucial. For the future, gene-based methods to plan personalized therapy are needed. Due to the complexity of treatment planning, artificial intelligence (AI) will play a key role. It was also identified that 'mini cleanroom' technology, although at the beginning of its s-curve, is expected to be available in the next ten years. This will enable 'local cell culture'—specialized clinics will be able to produce cells for specific patients—and will remove the need for cold chain logistics.

The *organizational capabilities* swim-lane highlighted the shortage of scientists and engineers with cell therapy experience and, in coming years, the need for specific medical cell therapy training. However, using VRIO, Company X identified that it had unique manufacturing and medical expertise, plus strong links to medical opinion leaders, all of which would support new services.

The completed strategic roadmap gave Company X a comprehensive understanding of the cell therapy market. Company X then reflected, as a provider of technical testing services, on the implications for their organization. Many new opportunities were identified within the ISO. For example, verifying manufacturing and sequencing; cold chain logistics; and therapy planning procedures. This also led to the key inter-relationships, which were added to the roadmap as arrows. These upward arrows indicated, for example, how Company X's medical expertise and contacts with opinion leaders could lead to appropriate training and auditing for specialized cell therapy clinics.

Roadmaps summarize strategic thinking and so it's essential that they are kept and digital copies produced. Strategic roadmaps will be used extensively in *Workshop 2*, where the most promising ISOs will be selected.

ASSESS CAPABILITY GAPS

Two kinds of capabilities ('C') must be built to progress the journey from 'A' to 'B'. The first kind are the *domain-specific capabilities* required for implementing each ISO, as indicated on the bottom swim-lanes of the strategic roadmap for an ISO. Typically, these include: expertise in specific technologies; capabilities in manufacturing or service delivery; and capabilities to reach new markets. Some of them will already exist in your business, whereas others will have to be developed and will require investment. At this initial point, prior to ISO selection, the aim is to gain an overview of the different capabilities needed. In *Workshop 1*, the senior team and innovation manager should conduct an initial audit of the capabilities needed, and whether they already exist, using the first three questions of Table 1-3.

The second kind are the *innovation management capabilities* required across several ISOs. By this, we mean the concepts, tools and techniques covered in this book, which allow businesses to dynamically innovate in black-, grey- and white-space.

At the end of *Workshop 1*, the senior team and innovation manager should complete the audit in Table 1-3, which compares your capabilities to the competition. The tool uses questions to highlight deficiencies and, in practice, it often shows that companies are poor at understanding customer needs. Managers from the senior team should note that a common pitfall is overconfidence in the organization's capabilities (and discounting pending threats). So, it's critical to candidly assess your innovation capabilities and provide evidence or state the assumptions behind your rating in the column for comments.

TABLE 1-3: INNOVATION CAPABILITY AUDIT

DOMAIN-SPECIFIC CAPABILITIES

		QUESTIONS TO DISCUSS	ASSESSMENT VERSUS COMPETITORS (BETTER/SIMILAR/WORSE)	COMMENTS / GOALS
	1	What specific capabilities are needed for the ISOs?		
	2	Are these existing capabilities, or do they need to be developed?		
	3	Which organizations already have these capabilities?		

INNOVATION MANAGEMENT CAPABILITIES

		QUESTIONS TO DISCUSS	ASSESSMENT VERSUS COMPETITORS (BETTER/SIMILAR/WORSE)	COMMENTS / GOALS
INCREMENTAL	4	How good are we at identifying customers' incremental needs?		
	5	How good are we at creating incremental solutions?		
	6	How good are we at developing incremental products and services?		
	7	How good are we at designing new business models?		
	8	How good are we at launching new products and services?		
	9	How can our existing capabilities be used to support additional growth?		
BREAKTHROUGH AND RADICAL	10	How good are we at identifying customers' emerging and hidden needs?		
	11	How good are we at creating breakthrough and radical solutions?		
	12	How good are we at developing breakthrough and radical products and services?		
	13	How good are we at designing breakthrough and radical new business models?		
	14	How good are we at launching breakthrough and radical new products and services?		
	15	How can our existing capabilities be used to support additional growth?		

Note that the audit should not only check for missing capabilities but also check (Questions #9 and #15) whether existing capabilities can be applied to generate additional growth—this is based on the resource-based view of strategy. Case 1-4 explains how the resource-based view helped the European Beer Supply business unit of Diageo, the drinks company.

CASE STUDY 1-4: DIAGEO EUROPEAN BEER FROM BLACK(-STUFF) TO WHITE(-SPACE)[35]

Diageo is a global leader in alcoholic beverages. It owns an outstanding collection of brands including spirits (for example Johnny Walker, Smirnoff and Baileys), and beers (for example Guinness—colloquially known as the 'black-stuff'). The company possesses world-class capabilities in: generating consumer insights; product development; brand building; and manufacturing. Diageo is organized into business units, responsible either for 'demand' (innovation, marketing and sales), or 'supply' (procurement, manufacturing, top quality, and distribution). 'Innovation' in the minds of most Diageo people means new drinks (for example line extensions of new flavours, seasonal brews), formats (for example ready to drink, packaging for new occasions) and marketing (for example iconic advertising, consumer outlet and visitor centre experiences).

In 2012, the business unit responsible for producing Guinness, European Beer Supply, was optimizing its business. The primary goal was efficient, quality beer supply with reduced cost of goods sold (COGS). To achieve this, the state-of-the-art 'Brewhouse No. 4' costing €169M was built. However, the European Beer Supply senior management team had the aspiration to create additional value for Diageo. They recognized that the global beer market now required craft and local beers and sustainable supply chains. They also knew that European Beer Supply possessed world-class technical and environmental capabilities. The question was could these capabilities generate additional growth for Diageo?

DIAGRAM 1-10: BUSINESS-WIDE SCOPE FOR INNOVATION AT DIAGEO'S EUROPEAN BEER SUPPLY

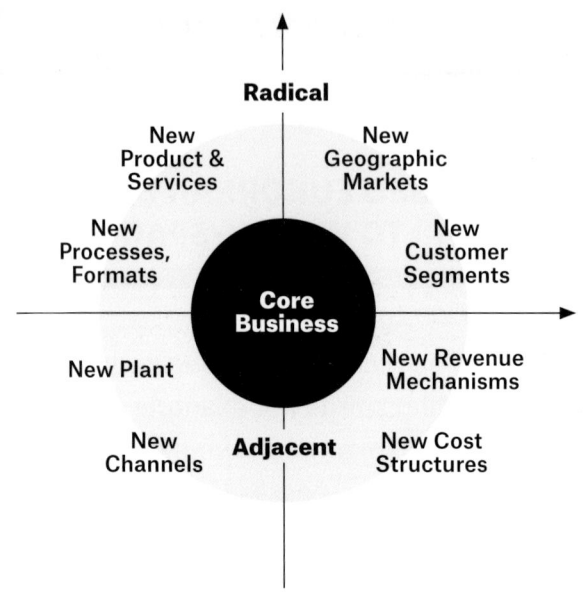

HR Director Donal Prior, with some consultant support, organized four innovation strategy workshops for management, run over a period of six months. These aimed to not only achieve a lower COGS but also to push boundaries. This led the management team to identify the full innovation landscape for European Beer Supply, as shown in Diagram 1-10. Presentations from the managing directors of similar supply SBUs (including Pepsi and Intel Ireland) stimulated the European Beer Supply team, by explaining their journey to generate corporate value well beyond their original mandates. This helped them to identify four 'themes': a Guinness Flavour Extract to allow Guinness to be manufactured around the world; value adding services to support global supply; closer relationships with the 'demand' SBUs in all markets; and breakthroughs in product and format innovation.

The next two workshops focused on exploring the themes, looking at global trends and the customer and competitor context (with 'demand' colleagues and invited specialists). Discussions based on the business model canvas led to several innovation strategic options (ISOs) being identified for each theme, which were mapped by sub-groups. Then, opportunities were discussed and evaluated, and the best ideas selected to be developed into 'stories', with clear statements on how they would create, deliver and add value to Diageo.

The final management workshop, dubbed the 'Kilmainham Gaol Strategy', focused on what resources would be needed to ensure the ISOs would be successful. These ISOs were shared with and strengthened by other local and global executives who were also considering similar opportunities. European Beer Supply Director Paul Armstrong said: *"This innovation strategy process helped stretch our long-term thinking. It encouraged us to explore opportunities beyond our primary business model focus of value delivery, into customer needs, customer value creation and even new revenue models."* Ultimately, the decision was made to sponsor investment in new beers, an adapted business model for craft brews, and a new Dublin-based whiskey business (Roe & Co.).

DECLARING INNOVATION INTENT

In the second step of innovation strategy, the senior team and innovation manager must declare their intent for the journey, specifying commercial, category and capability goals. Innovation intent should be defined at a second 1-day workshop involving the SMT, the innovation manager and innovation leads. The aims of *Workshop 2* should be:

1. To set commercial goals and category goals.
2. To present and discuss each ISO Roadmap with the senior team.
3. To select the ISOs to be investigated further.
4. To set capability goals.

In addition, innovation intent should consider different timeframes: short-term (1–2 years, usually tactical), medium-term (3–5 years, more strategic) and long-term (5+ years, strategic). These timeframes are commonly called the *three horizons*[36] and considering them helps the senior team ensure success today and in the future.

SET COMMERCIAL AND CATEGORY GOALS

Commercial Goals

In setting commercial goals, first and foremost, consider the financial gap. A big financial gap, as in the case of Coillte (see Diagram 1-6), can only be closed by substantial, realistic ISOs. Your innovation performance vis-à-vis competitors and your stage in the business life cycle can provide a reality check.

A typical goal would be: *'To generate €50M revenue from innovation in five years, with a pipeline to contribute €150M within ten years.'* Innovation financial goals can also be set as a percentage of a business financial goal, for example: *'30% of revenues in year x will come from innovation.'*

Category Goals and Innovation Strategy Matrix

Investment also needs to be planned. Unfortunately, many senior teams say to their people: *'Come with the ideas and we will find the money'*. Do not fall into this trap. In the absence of a predetermined innovation budget, progress will be very slow, as management struggles to find funds. The size of the innovation budget needs to be decided by the whole senior team and not only the financial director. Typically, anything other than 'safe bets' (ISOs with clear and predictable returns on investment) will lose out on investment. Return on investment calculations can be a restraint on innovation (and must be considered in Phase 4), and a category check is needed.

Category goals look for balance and are illustrated by the *Innovation Strategy Matrix*, shown in Diagram 1-11. The vertical axis addresses where to innovate and the full landscape covers current, adjacent or early-stage and new markets. The horizontal axis addresses how to innovate and covers the degree of innovation, from incremental to radical and any combination of innovation dimensions. Together, these axes delineate our familiar innovation categories of core (black-), emerging (grey-) and new market (white-space).

DIAGRAM 1-11: INNOVATION STRATEGY MATRIX

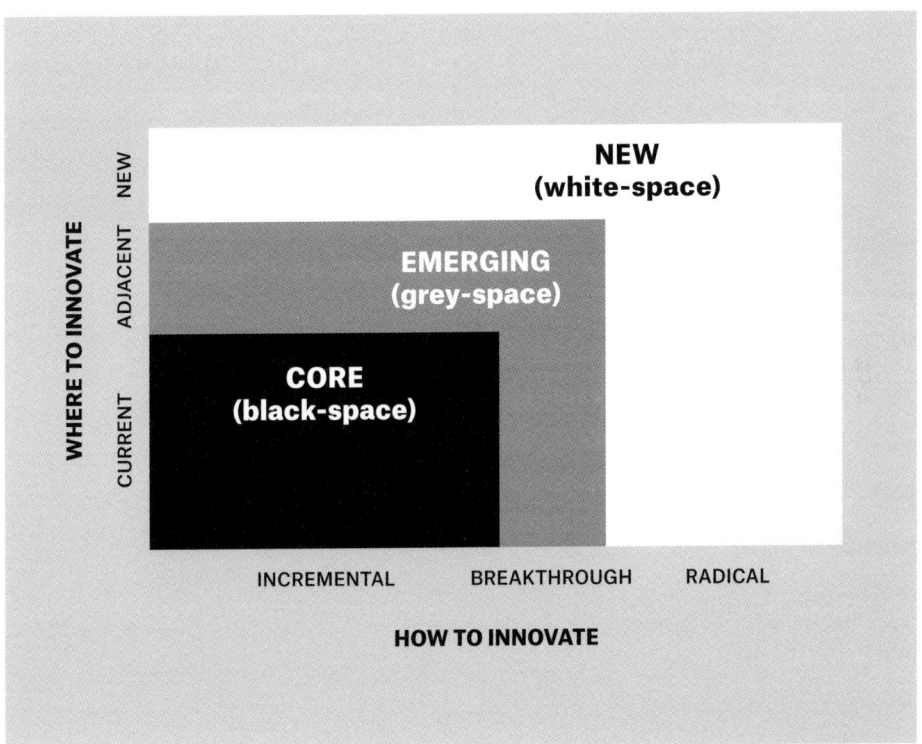

The matrix helps monitor the proportions of innovation investments and checks for ambidextrous innovation.

Managers often ask: *'What should the proportions be?'* Research has shown that the proportions 70:20:10 (black-space: grey-space: white-space) are often found in high-performing companies in various industries.[37] However, there is no magic formula and the senior team must carefully consider what makes sense for their business. Applying the matrix, one Swedish company found that the vast majority of investment was in incremental projects (the company had proportional investments of 98:2:0). The senior team then decided to set a goal of 80:15:5, which was appropriate for the family business concerned.

Research shows that investments in grey- and white-space typically bring higher returns. However, it should be remembered that new products and services in grey- and white-space are riskier. So, weighing the risks and returns of innovation projects is an evergreen task for senior managers and strong governance is required to maintain the proportions if some innovation strategic options don't yield the desired results. Further guidance is provided in Chapters 2 (Phase 2) and 4 (Phase 4).

With the commercial and category goals set, the senior team can now select the most promising ISOs.

Select Innovation Strategic Options

The innovation manager should discuss with the senior team how many ISOs to progress. The number will depend on your commercial goals, the time and resources available and the effort required. We suggest progressing a total of 2–6 opportunities in a given year.

Reviewing and selecting ISOs is where innovation strategy really starts to take shape. Most companies use standard PowerPoint presentations to review ISOs, but a more effective way is to have the teams print out poster-sized ISO Roadmaps and hang them on the walls of a large conference room. In 30-minute slots, each team lead can explain their ISO Roadmap and then take Q&A. In presenting their ISO roadmaps, the teams can bring the topic to life by telling a 'story' about the opportunity they have identified, potentially using graphics to illustrate customer needs and the value proposition.

In this early phase, the selection process should be simple and transparent. An effective way is a democratic decision where each senior manager rates each ISO on *attractiveness* (market opportunity) and *feasibility* (the ability to develop the ISO). Both attractiveness and feasibility should be rated on a scale of '5' [very attractive / very feasible] to '1' [unattractive / unfeasible]). The tally of scores should be discussed and everyone should say if and why they have a particular favourite and where they perceive risk. A favoured ISO or perceived risks are not necessarily good or bad, but open discussion allows the senior team to reach the best decisions. As ISOs are selected in *Workshop 2*, the innovation manager should first check that the investment proportions are 'roughly' on target (using Diagram 1-11).

SET INNOVATION CAPABILITY GOALS

With ISOs selected, the leadership team and innovation manager should reflect on the organizational capabilities needed to achieve them. Gaps in current capability should be identified and goals to close them defined, using the Innovation Capability Audit (Table 1-3). Check for similar capability requirements across the different ISOs, as this will influence how gaps are closed (for example by new hiring, collaborating, or acquiring specific capabilities such as emerging technologies).

WORKSHOP 2 OUTPUTS

As *Workshop 2* draws to a close, your business's innovation strategy will have taken shape. Now, the innovation manager must consolidate the documentation, as this knowledge will be indispensable on the journey ahead. For example, the strategic roadmap of each ISO should be passed to the insight teams who will investigate the market in Phase 3. Most encouragingly, you now have an engaged group consisting of the senior team, the innovation manager and the innovation specialists, all with a vested interest in making the innovation journey a success.

MINDSET MATTERS

For everyone involved in shaping innovation strategy, the process will be new and much about the ISOs being considered will also be new. With newness comes ambiguity but here the key message is: if you don't at times feel uncomfortable with the process, then something's probably wrong! As we stress often, everyone needs to adopt an explorer's mindset.

While strategy is often thought of as a purely rational process, the thinking and feelings of the senior managers involved have untold influence on what is considered, how decisions are made, and what is actually implemented. Remember managers have bounded rationality—they only have time to deal with a certain level of complexity. When senior teams are confronted with relentless change and many potential strategic options, it's no wonder that they tend to revert to what they know best. However, in considering the innovation landscape, managers must step outside their comfort zones. The 3+3+3 innovation strategy process provides a way for the senior team to stretch its thinking, question conventional wisdom, and consider the full innovation landscape. It's crucial to avoid the success trap, where a company focuses on exploiting the current business and fails to explore opportunities for the medium and long term. Here, the case studies of Coillte, FashionPower and Diageo European Beer Supply demonstrate that opportunities arose from the senior team's ability to question current thinking and markets.

The mindset of the finance function requires special mention in the context of ambidextrous innovation. For incremental innovation (black-space projects), the aim is to conduct them efficiently and a lean management, cost-focus is appropriate (using financial measures such as return on investment). However, for grey-space and white-space innovations, finance managers must take an 'investment perspective' (like a venture capitalist), viewing ISOs as options to be exercised, based on key learnings during successive implementation phases. Finance managers often find this ambiguity challenging. Typically, businesses that are very strong at process efficiency struggle with funding innovation. In one European company we know, innovation projects always have to compete for funding with lean management programmes; innovation projects are nearly always rejected as the board invariably looks for short-term returns.

In Phase 1, the innovation manager helps shape innovation strategy and this can sometimes mean challenging the thinking of the senior team. Here, a trusted external consultant can help, as they can challenge the senior team's thinking and use their experience to draw on examples of how other businesses reacted in similar situations. The innovation manager must also bring a lot of energy to this first phase of the innovation journey; they must show endless enthusiasm during the innovation strategy process. Similarly, the innovation specialists should bring fresh and diverse thinking to the process and they must challenge engrained thinking.

The first two steps of the innovation strategy process (Phase 1), scanning the landscape and declaring your intent, have been completed. In Chapter 2, we will provide clear guidelines on how to organize for the journey (Phase 2).

SUMMARY

- Strategic management is about succeeding today and winning tomorrow. It considers options to protect and grow a business. It typically focuses on protecting current strengths and predictable options.
- A separate but aligned innovation strategy is needed to give innovation the resolute focus that can create competitive advantages.
- The first step of innovation strategy is scanning the broader landscape over longer timeframes to identify innovation strategic options (ISOs). This requires new knowledge, fresh minds and tools to both research and imagine likely futures.
- The second step of innovation strategy is declaring a compelling intent for innovation that includes clear commercial, category and capability goals that will guide all information efforts.
- Even with the best intentions, innovation will go nowhere unless implementation is organized specifically. So, in the next chapter we will explain the third step of innovation strategy, which is Phase 2, Organizing the journey.

Phase 2
Organizing the journey

Organizing the journey

INTRODUCTION

Your innovation journey will be shaped by where you are today 'A' and your business's intended position 'B'. You will also need to build the capabilities 'C' that will be required on the journey. Moving from 'A' to 'B' while building 'C' might sound simple but it does involve some degree of transition from the familiar (black-space) into uncharted territory (grey- / white-space). It's surprising how many companies rush into this, without the necessary planning, or considering if they've the right culture for innovation. Diagram 2-1 shows how organizing the journey makes a direct link from the innovation strategy declared in Phase 1 to the rest of the journey (Phases 3–5). Phase 6 will concentrate on building the long-term innovation management capabilities of your business.

DIAGRAM 2-1: PHASE 2 IN THE INNOVATION JOURNEY

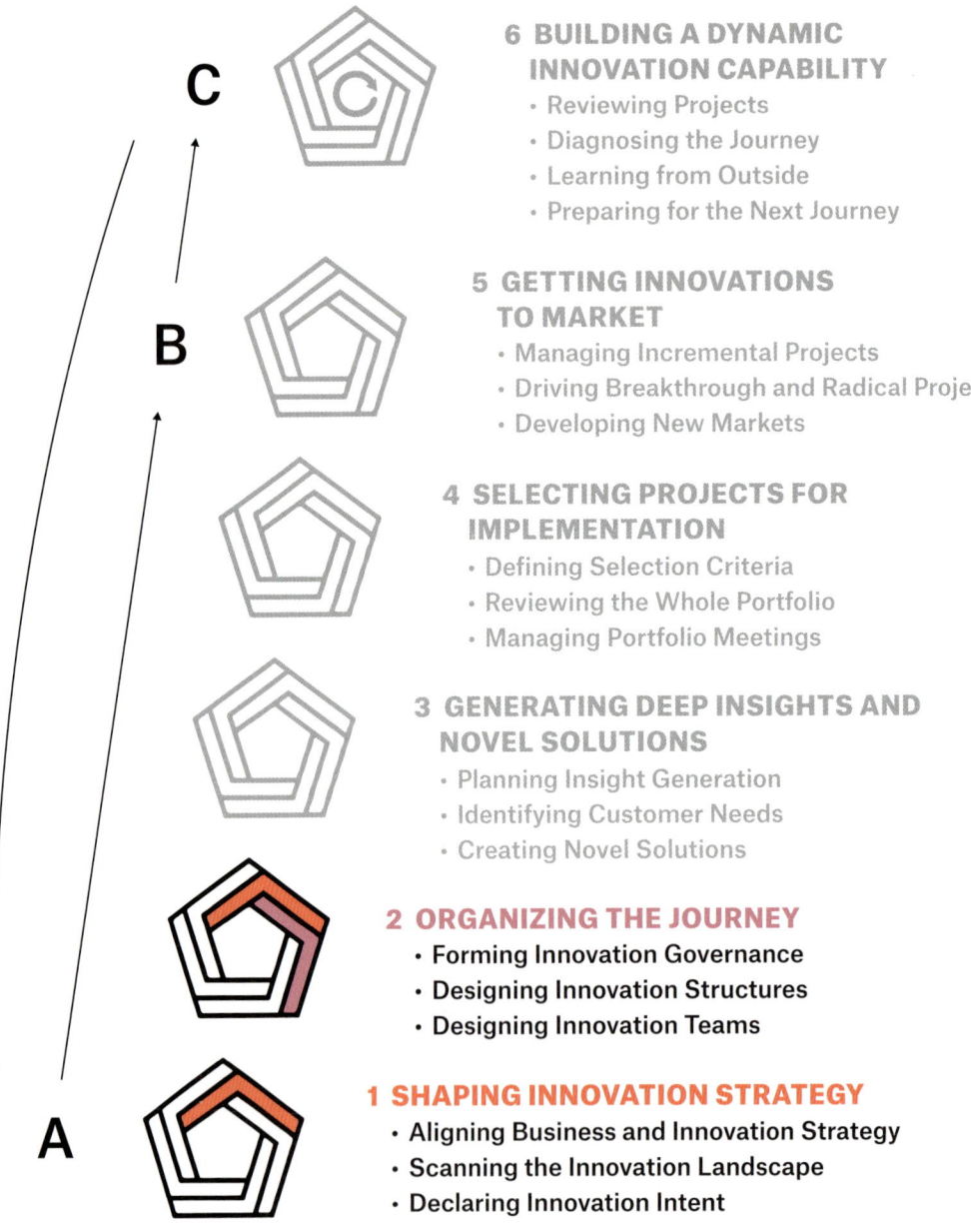

C

6 BUILDING A DYNAMIC INNOVATION CAPABILITY
- Reviewing Projects
- Diagnosing the Journey
- Learning from Outside
- Preparing for the Next Journey

B

5 GETTING INNOVATIONS TO MARKET
- Managing Incremental Projects
- Driving Breakthrough and Radical Projects
- Developing New Markets

4 SELECTING PROJECTS FOR IMPLEMENTATION
- Defining Selection Criteria
- Reviewing the Whole Portfolio
- Managing Portfolio Meetings

3 GENERATING DEEP INSIGHTS AND NOVEL SOLUTIONS
- Planning Insight Generation
- Identifying Customer Needs
- Creating Novel Solutions

2 ORGANIZING THE JOURNEY
- Forming Innovation Governance
- Designing Innovation Structures
- Designing Innovation Teams

A

1 SHAPING INNOVATION STRATEGY
- Aligning Business and Innovation Strategy
- Scanning the Innovation Landscape
- Declaring Innovation Intent

Senior management must invest a few days to organize the journey. This is to decide how to govern resources (people and money); agree on where to locate innovation in the organizational structure; and create teams for each of the innovation strategic options chosen in Phase 1. The term 'organizational structure' conjures up corporations and hierarchies, which have the resources to manage incremental innovation in the core business and set up separate structures for breakthrough / radical innovation. But innovative mid-sized businesses (MSBs) and strategic business units (SBUs) need simple, flexible structures. Most MSBs don't have the resources for full-time innovation teams, so 'ring-fencing' time for innovation is essential. With such limited resources, innovation capabilities have to be built by employees who are used to dealing with the current business. So, innovation must be infused into your organization prior to the journey,[1] using *hard* mechanisms (budgets, metrics, and structures) and *soft* mechanisms (how employees think, feel and behave).

Table 2-1 summarizes the key themes covered in this chapter. These are *form innovation governance*—resource allocation, performance measurement, values, and communications and engagement; *design innovation structure*—roles and reporting; and *design innovation teams*—capabilities, goals and team dynamics. Practical tools will be explained including the *Innovation Values Map*, *Innovation Performance Measures*, a *Business-wide Innovation Structure*, and an *Innovation Team Selection Matrix*.

Senior management and the innovation manager are responsible for Phase 2. They must be realistic about the resources required for the journey because innovation presents a decidedly different set of management problems compared to normal business.

Innovation involves changes to both customer offerings and internal ways of working. Trying to implement an innovative strategy with existing mindsets is ineffective, as people resist change based on fear of the unknown. An enabling organizational culture is needed. Employees must also be able to switch their thinking from incremental (black-) to breakthrough (grey-) / radical innovation (white-space). The output of Phase 2 is an organization that will implement your innovation strategy in Phases 3 to 5.

TABLE 2-1: PHASE 2—KEY THEMES AND CHECKLIST

THEMES	DETAILS
Actions to take	☐ Form innovation governance ☐ Design a business-wide innovation structure ☐ Design and develop innovation teams
Tools and concepts	☐ Innovation Values Map (Culture) ☐ Innovation Performance Measures ☐ Business-wide Innovation Structure ☐ Innovation Team Selection Matrix
People responsible	☐ Senior management team ☐ Innovation manager
Mindset matters	☐ Resistance to change and innovation ☐ Developing a collective innovation mindset
Outputs	☐ An organization that is ready for the journey ☐ The right governance, structure and teams

ESSENTIAL BACKGROUND

This section gives a historical perspective on how businesses organize for innovation and explains mindset matters and cultural issues. The word 'organization' stems from the Greek *organon*—meaning tool or instrument. An organization—two or more people—is set up to achieve specific goals that would not be accomplished otherwise.

THE HISTORY OF ORGANIZATION

Many of the ideas about organization evolved during the Industrial Revolution (1760–1860). At that time, agricultural workers gave up their relative autonomy to work in unskilled factory jobs. In 1776, economist Adam Smith lauded the *division of labour* and the power of machines to increase efficiency. During this time, Frederick the Great of Prussia (1740–1786) created an army from criminals, paupers and mercenaries. Inspired by the way the Romans organized their legions, he established a hierarchy based on fear and standardized everything from uniforms and weapons to language and training.[2]

Around 1905, the German scholar Max Weber established *bureaucratic theory*,[3] which emphasized defined roles, formal rules and centralized hierarchies. American engineer Frederick Taylor (1856–1915) established *scientific management* circa 1911, using time and motion studies to collect data on work performance and improve efficiency.[4] From Smith to Taylor, the focus was on dividing work into repetitive tasks, specialization, formal processes, centralized resource control and hierarchical decision-making. Henry Ford (1863–1947), creator of the Model-T production line, even said: "Nothing is particularly hard if you divide it into small jobs".

In 1933, Australian psychologist Elton Mayo recognized the shortcomings of trying to manage people using engineering-based thinking.[5] Mayo's thinking triggered the *Theory of Sociotechnical Systems*, which stressed the importance of not only the technical aspects of organizations (machines and processes) but also the social aspects (people and community). It also recognized that teams are vital for managing high-risk activities. This led to the concept of *Responsible Autonomy*, where teams take responsibility for agreed performance but are given the freedom to direct their own efforts.[6]

ORGANIZING FOR INNOVATION

In the 1960s, Alfred Chandler studied organizational structures at 50 corporations. He showed the advantages of dividing large companies into strategic business units (SBUs), closely linked to specific market segments. SBUs are guided by the corporate, in terms of goals and budgets, but have the autonomy to decide how to achieve them.

Later in the 1960s, Tom Burns and G. M. Stalker studied 150 MSBs, finding *mechanistic* and *organic structures*. The former are suitable for stable and efficiency-driven contexts (and require clear task definition and hierarchical control), whereas the latter are best in changing contexts (and require multidisciplinary teams, flexible tasks, and distributed control). However, most businesses persevere with one structure even as their business context changes, making the mistake of intending to change their strategy without reflecting on the necessary organizational structure.[7]

Building on these ideas, Michael Tushman and Charles O'Reilly III found that successful companies have one organization for incremental innovation (black-space) and another, parallel organization for breakthrough / radical innovation (grey- and white-space). Creating such an ambidextrous organization is difficult because of *Organizational Inertia*, with its technical and cultural aspects.[8] Technical inertia depends on company size and the complexity of governance systems, structures and processes. Cultural inertia stems from employees' ingrained mindsets, and resolving such softer issues is vital to innovative growth.

MINDSET MATTERS AND THEIR IMPACT

Individual mindsets are our preferred ways of thinking. For example: Are we open to learning? Do we have a positive or negative view of innovation? As shown in Diagram 2-2, contexts generate *inputs* (events and information) and these lead to *thoughts*, *feelings* and *behaviours*.[9] Thoughts are based on personal beliefs, assumptions, meaning and identity. Thoughts impact feelings, which are a mix of positive and negative emotions accompanied by distinct physical sensations, such as accelerating heart rate. Thoughts and feelings impact behaviour, leading to actions that influence outcomes. We might like to think that we are fully rational, thinking individuals but our thoughts and feelings mainly operate at the unconscious level. So, we mostly act instinctively, out of learnt habits, with similar inputs leading to similar outcomes.[10]

Our mindsets reflect our character and identity, affecting how others see us and how we see ourselves. Tried and tested mindsets work in stable contexts but can cause us to overlook new inputs and new ways of responding. Mindsets promote or hinder innovation at an individual level because of the biochemistry associated with the emotions that underpin our thoughts, feelings and behaviours.

Five negative emotions are primarily associated with promoting survival: *fear*, *anger*, *sadness*, *disgust* and *shame*. These trigger the release of cortisol, a hormone leading to feelings of stress. Fear overrides everything,

DIAGRAM 2-2: THE NATURE OF MINDSETS

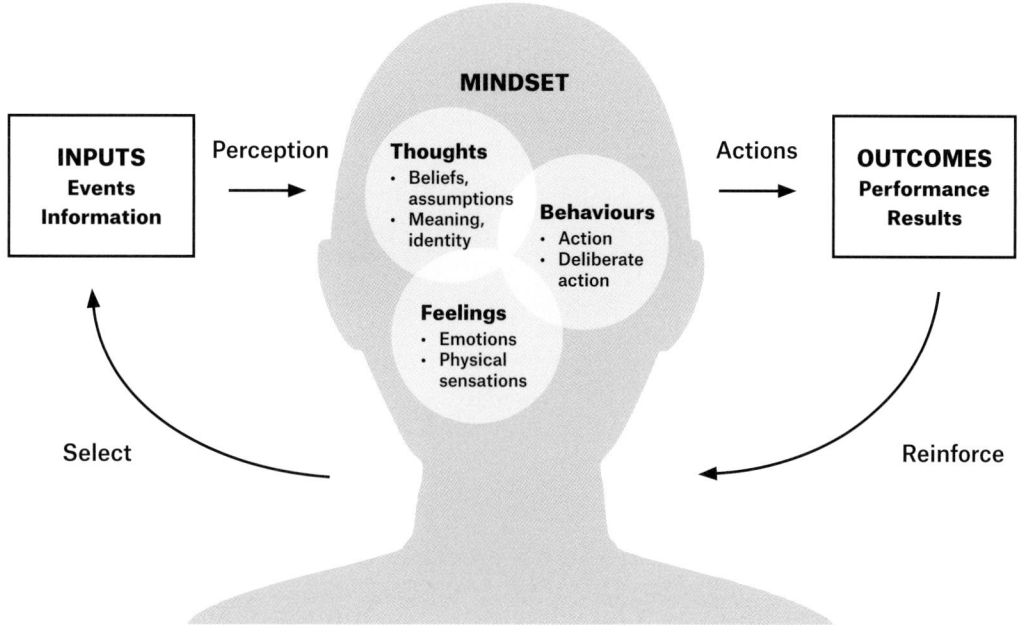

conserving energy to counter threats and releasing adrenaline, which triggers the 'flight or fight' response.

Three positive emotions, *surprise*, *excitement* and *trust*, enable us to thrive, in other words connect with others, learn and innovate. They release pleasurable hormones such as dopamine. Surprise acts in two ways depending on whether it's perceived positively (delight), or negatively (startled). Respectively, these lead to a 'connect and learn' response, or an 'avoid and escape' response.

When inputs generate a mix of positive and negative emotions, negative ones have the strongest influence. In short, many individuals are predisposed to avoid rather than to embrace innovation.[11] For example, some managers will feel more comfortable with incremental innovation, as it matches their mindset. For some employees, suddenly being assigned to an innovation team can induce discomfort or even fear, whereas others will be delighted to be assigned to an innovation team, and fully embrace the opportunity.

SHAPING MINDSETS

Individual mindsets are shaped by experience. Everything we think, feel and do is made possible by *neurons*, the basic unit of the brain. Up to 90 billion neurons receive and process information and communicate with the nervous system, inducing behaviour. Repetitive, positive outcomes cause neural connections to become stronger, or 'hard wired'. Humans are the only species where thoughts and feelings create new neural connections. In other words, we learn and form mindsets (patterns of thinking), which become habitual.

When we experience new things, we react to them based on our existing mindsets. This conflict between the new and familiar causes a neural process consuming so much energy that, literally, 'your brain hurts'. Outside our comfort zone we feel anxious about whether we'll be able to meet the new challenge.[12] Given this anxiety, it's no surprise that some people have a *fixed mindset* that's closed to learning while others have a *growth mindset* and enjoy learning and developing new capabilities.[13]

What's more, as shown in Diagram 2-2, mindsets are impacted by feedback loops. Positive outcomes reinforce our existing mindsets[14] and cause us to focus on (select) only certain inputs—taking an *inside* view. This behaviour can lead us to over-value our own experience and ignore reality; in other words, it causes personal bias.[15] Digital media exacerbates this problem, with algorithms presenting people with similar material to what they've already viewed, creating 'echo chambers', with repetition reinforcing polarized views. The inside view tends to be myopic, overconfident and error prone. To avoid it managers consciously need to adopt different perspectives and focus on evidence—the *outside view*.

Deeply held mindsets are hard to change because being right feels good and being wrong feels so bad. Recall an experience when you defended your beliefs and won. That righteous feeling was a potent mix of adrenaline (strength) and dopamine (satisfaction). When our mindset leads us to be wrong, it attacks our identity and and this is emotionally painful. This can lead to an overly emotional reaction that's out of all proportion.[16]

Fortunately, mindsets are not genetic and can be learnt and unlearnt. Also, we can have a fixed mindset that performs well in one context and an open mindset that performs well in a different context. An innovator's mindset overcomes an individual's fear of failure by the force of their desire not to miss opportunities.[17] Innovators consider multiple viewpoints (including the outside view); imagine multiple solutions and timeframes; and analytically evaluate the diverse range of options. Managers need to foster a climate where employees feel secure enough to explore, to challenge, even to fail—but to learn, and then succeed.[18]

SHARED MINDSETS AND ORGANIZATIONAL CULTURE

Innovation is a collective endeavour that thrives on creating and applying new knowledge. It's inherently collaborative and cross-functional, based on learning in multidisciplinary teams and networks. Individuals' mindsets are shaped by interaction, and this leads to shared mindsets at the team, function and organization levels. Shared mindsets have a big influence on whether an organization can achieve innovative growth.[19] *Organizational culture* (often called 'DNA') is the manifestation of shared mindsets at an organizational level, determining how the organization thinks, feels and behaves, and consequently influencing what it achieves.

Unfortunately, organizational culture is more often an inhibitor than an enabler of innovation. Therefore, interventions are needed to ensure that shared mindsets support innovation. Just telling people to 'think outside the box' is trite and insufficient. Direct mechanisms like governance, structures and processes must be combined with softer interventions, in order to mould an innovative culture.

Organization culture evolves as a business grows. In a start-up, everything is creative, informal and fast-moving. Since everyone works closely together, mindsets are constantly shared and values such as openness to ideas will be pervasive. Start-up culture is influenced by founders' mindsets and Peter Thiel, co-founder of PayPal, said that culture is the foundation on which all future innovation is based.[20]

As a business grows, it becomes more difficult to informally share values and senior managers must document and communicate the values they want their organization to share. Compounding the challenge, larger organizations tend to become focused on efficiency, with the consequence that innovation is neglected. So, communicating innovation as an organizational value becomes crucial. For example, when Netflix grew, management documented their culture in the now freely available 'Reference Guide on our Freedom & Responsibility Culture'.[21] This very detailed 128-slide deck emphasizes innovation, with a call to "challenge prevailing assumptions [and] create new ideas". Managers recognize the significance of organizational culture, as evidenced by over 20 million downloads of the Netflix slide deck.

Edgar Schein developed a model of organizational culture with three levels.[22] This is shown in black at the centre of Diagram 2-3. Understanding the levels enables managers to ensure their organizational culture will support their innovation journey.

At the top level, culture consists of *organizational artefacts*—the hard, visible aspects of culture such as a company's formal structure, its brand, the style of its facilities, and key business processes (such as the way projects are selected). However, these more formal aspects don't provide the full picture. At the middle level are the *espoused values*; what a business formally claims to excel at, and its strategy including its widely communicated mission and vision. These statements are intentional. For a sense of the actual culture, you must look deeper at the *underlying assumptions*—the softer, less visible values and shared mindsets. These are unconscious and taken-for-granted employees' views (mindset patterns) about what it takes to succeed as a business, and as an employee in that business. When the things employees feel, think, say and do are consistent (left of Diagram 2-3), this is the hallmark of a strong culture and usually a high-performing organization.[23] However, a strong culture which fails to adapt can be harmful.

Hard (technical), organizational artefacts such as the formal organization and statements of strategy are relatively easy to change, whereas the soft underlying assumptions are entrenched and make change harder. This is why large organizations which claim to have changed their corporate culture but have only modified their organizational structure don't really change. An example of this is the continuing debate around several big banks responsible for financial scandals and whether they have really changed their organizational culture.

DIAGRAM 2-3: ORGANIZATIONAL CULTURE AND INNOVATION

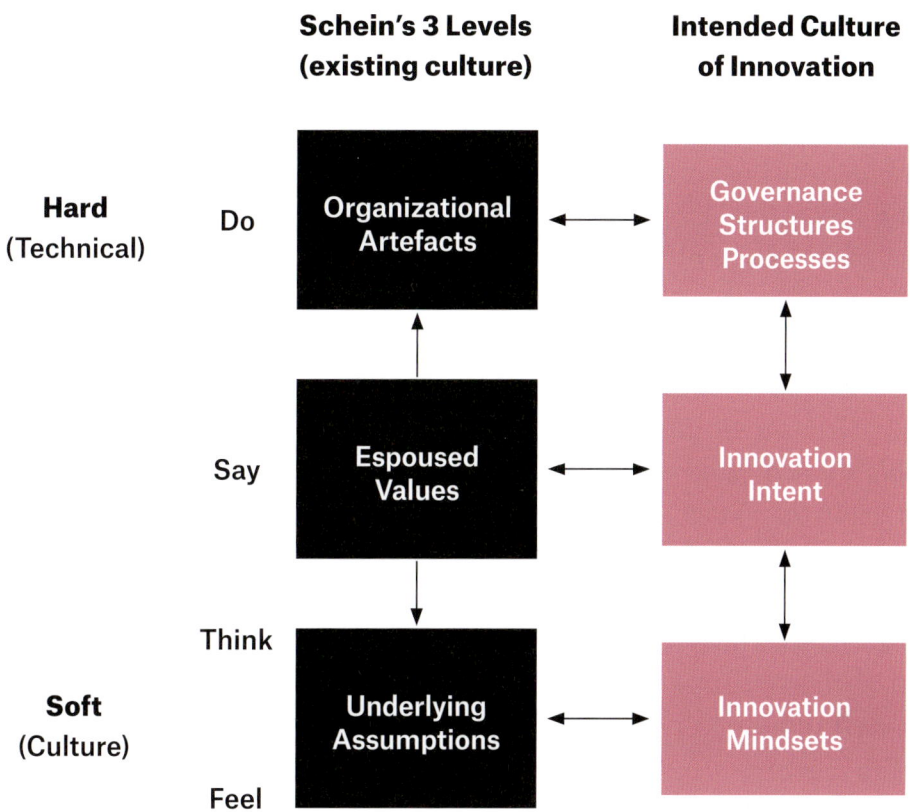

Discussing values and underlying assumptions tends to arouse cynicism, especially from technically and financially minded employees (who will say, 'that's just soft stuff'). Nevertheless, as it is often said: 'The soft stuff is the hard stuff to do' and so it must be tackled. This is demonstrated by the example of a European manufacturing company that had excelled at continuous improvement using six-sigma methods, cost control and process innovation for many years. The six-sigma programme was led by a manager with an ability to corner resources and drive projects successfully. Senior management then decided to shift the focus to developing innovative products for growth, and an experienced innovation manager was hired externally to manage this. This led to friction between the innovation manager, trying to gain support for innovation projects, and the finance department prioritizing six-sigma projects because of their demonstrable, fast return on investment. Clearly, innovation didn't fit with the prevalent culture and, after a couple of years, the company made the innovation manager redundant and dropped product innovation. This is a classic example of what can prevent a business becoming ambidextrous, and it illustrates the importance of tackling the 'softer' issues.

A real *Culture of Innovation* is achieved when the three levels of the existing business match with the intended culture of innovation (Diagram 2-3) and where conflicts with the underlying assumptions have been reconciled. Typical assumptions that hinder innovation[24] are epitomized by statements such as, *'This is a mature industry with no space for innovation'*, or *'Our industry is highly regulated and so innovation is pointless'*, or *'Our customers can't tell us what they need'*, and *'We have no access to end customers.'* To break free from such underlying assumptions, corporates often create a separate unit but most MSBs and SBUs must create a culture of innovation within the existing organization. This means some employees will have to switch mindsets for their part-time innovation role and then switch back to their normal day-to-day thinking. This makes it imperative to have clear mechanisms to guide the journey.

Case 2-1 discusses how innovation is aligned to organizational values at the MSB Red Ventures, and how resource allocation, and communications and engagement are carefully managed for consistency.

CASE STUDY 2-1: RED VENTURES
THE NEVER-ENDING INNOVATION VENTURE[25]

Red Ventures is a US-based technology and internet services company with over 3,500 employees distributed across more than 15 locations around the world. Over its 21-year history, the company has continually renewed and transformed itself. It has built a portfolio of influential brands, digital platforms, and strategic partnerships that work together to seamlessly connect millions of people with information and tools to help them 'discover and decide' on key aspects of their life. Red Ventures owns over a dozen brands that are household names in the US, such as TVGuide, CNET, Lonely Planet, The Points Guy and Bankrate.com. Another example is the widely used website NextAdvisor, which is operated under a partnership with Time Magazine.

On the Red Ventures website, they define themselves as a global company that behaves like a start-up and embraces change, that shares core beliefs such as 'running up escalators', 'getting better every day', and that 'everything is written in pencil'. These core beliefs are imbued with innovation rhetoric such as having 'growth mindsets', 'spirit of debate', 'improving the world', 'setting aspirational example', 'adaptability' and 'embracing differences'. After reviewing the culture with Head of Human Capital Hallie Cornetta and VP of Engineering Eoghan Nolan, it is obvious that the text on the Red Ventures' website is not just rhetoric but embedded in how RV'ers think, feel and behave. The following mechanisms epitomize how they 'walk the talk'.

Strategic Context is Critical: Red Ventures has many different business models in different industry groups. Everyone is supported by internal communications, their managers and colleagues, to understand how their business model works and what their role is in the development of that business as well as the bigger Red Ventures growth journey. A strategic shift, since 2015, has been from short cycles, where their B2B customers evaluate performance quarterly, to considering the lifetime needs of their own B2C customers across multiple verticals. Red Ventures maintains their short game mindset and manages longer, sustainable growth through portfolio management. Hallie says *"We see our portfolio like a large group of kids. Not everyone will be totally happy and healthy, or sick at the same time. This has been so evident during Covid-19, where some markets like credit cards have been hit and others like health care have taken off. However, our growing and evolving family is our strength."*

Structures and Processes Realize Intentions: Red Ventures balances stability and fluidity through its organizational structures. The stable part is that everyone works in small teams that focus on specific business areas with a common operating rhythm and structure. Co-founder Ric Elias used to keep a jar to collect a dollar every time someone said "I/You" instead of "We" as a small but powerful way to instil this founder mindset into the teams. The fluid part is maintained through flat structures, hiring and coaching flexible people and explicitly rewarding coachability and adaptability.

Red Ventures uses structure to drive innovation in three ways. First, core operation teams intentionally work under resource constraints. Paradoxically, this motivates people to continually find better ways of doing things. Second, they create new products and services that come from connecting the right brains in sprint teams to solve initiatives such as a new geography, customer proposition or business model. Managers and HR partners carefully design these teams to ensure they have the required composite talent and bandwidth. These teams are sponsored by a Senior Leader who works with them 20% of the time. Third, they create dedicated structures such as Digital Labs that act as an internal innovation engine for big opportunities and new capabilities that have the potential to impact multiple verticals. The labs work *with* and not *for* internal and external clients, meaning that from the outset the client owns the output and co-creates the process that they will soon fully operate.

Talent Thrives on Action and Feedback: What is palpable about Red Ventures is its approach to learning and talent development. When it comes to performance management Red Ventures rewards and recognizes inputs and actions consistent with their beliefs, not outputs such as hitting key performance indicators or growth targets. This bias for learning (inputs) and action drives teamwork and experimentation. In addition, candid feedback is the norm and it can come from anywhere to anyone. This helps teams move faster with the benefit of other people's knowledge and the trust that comes with knowing others are vested, not just watching on the side lines. Hallie says *"We have a high tolerance for failure and especially for innovations, but less so for repeated errors, so we are all responsible for helping each other out with constructive feedback".* There is also a formal 360-review process biannually that allows everyone to anonymously provide feedback to their manager.

Shared Leadership: Leadership means embodying the core beliefs—something which they screen for in recruiting. Looking forward, Hallie sees two big shifts for the next stage of their innovation journey. The first is towards more decentralization as business units get bigger, allowing more strategic autonomy. The second is that every leader is expected to develop the next generation to do what they do better and to renew the business. *"However, our DNA of learning, changing and innovating together will be our enduring bond."*

After six months at Red Ventures Eoghan had this to say about their innovation culture. *"I've been very fortunate to work at some great companies, like Google and eBay and scaling start-ups, with amazing products, cultures and teams. At RV, we are faithful to what we say as a people-first company and what happens on the ground. The foundation is trust, ambition and a constant drive to improve. Teams are free to leverage what they know and quickly act and get direct feedback from colleagues and partners to course correct or scale-up execution. There is a clear, real feeling that we are in the same boat and have each other's backs."*

MECHANISMS FOR THE INNOVATION JOURNEY

Table 2-2 provides three mechanisms to organize the innovation journey. Each has corresponding hard and soft aspects.

The first mechanism is *Forming Innovation Governance*, which consists of four points. These are the hard aspects resource allocation and performance measurement, plus soft aspects: innovation values, communications and engagement. *Designing Innovation Structure* deems where innovation 'will happen'. As it's likely to be a part-time activity for most employees, reporting lines for innovation tasks need to be simple, flat and flexible and they must

TABLE 2-2: MECHANISMS TO ORGANIZE THE INNOVATION JOURNEY

ASPECTS	THREE MECHANISMS FOR ORGANIZING THE JOURNEY		
	FORMING INNOVATION GOVERNANCE	**DESIGNING INNOVATION STRUCTURE**	**DESIGNING INNOVATION TEAMS**
Hard (technical)	• Resource allocation • Performance measurement	• Business-wide innovation	• Team design
Soft (cultural)	• Innovation values • Communications and engagement	• Selecting the innovation manager	• Team development for high performance

ensure time is strictly reserved for innovation (since time is often *the* key resource for innovation). *Designing Innovation Teams* ensures the right people are identified, carefully selected and prepared for the journey. The rest of this chapter explains the three mechanisms for organizing the journey in detail.

FORMING INNOVATION GOVERNANCE

Governance builds a direct link between the senior team's innovation intent and everyone involved with innovation. We will now give pragmatic recommendations for governance, starting with innovation values.

INNOVATION VALUES

The senior team must check that underlying values support innovation. *The Innovation Values Map*, shown in Diagram 2-4, is a tool for this. It is applied in two steps, which will be explained using the example of an energy company founded 30 years ago, with 2,000 employees and a focus on significant innovative growth.

The first step is for the innovation manager working with the senior team to draft an aspirational innovation value. This must directly relate to the innovation intent decided in Phase 1. Diagram 2-4 shows that the energy company, based on their ambitious financial intent ('*30% revenue growth based on new value propositions and markets*'), formulated the innovation value: '*We are brave, challenge the status quo and find new options for growth.*' Two questions were asked to check the innovation value was realistic. The first question (Q1.1) was: *For our innovation journey to succeed what mindsets are required?* As shown in Diagram 2-4, this led to the description of the mindset required as including an openness to diverse internal and external views, and five other bullet points. The second question (Q1.2) prompts specificity: *What does this mean in practical terms?* Here, the innovation manager facilitated the management team's discussions, probing for specific behaviours that would be required to 'live' the innovation value. This showed that the company needed to dedicate resources to business-wide innovation (across functional areas) and give people time for innovation, and so on. Discussing the practical level helped the energy company to really understand what innovation required.

The second step is to identify the current espoused and underlying values (assumptions), through discussions with the senior management and with employees; then reconcile them with the innovation value. Here, the energy company identified four things that it tries to excel at. These were being *customer-centric, operationally excellent, performance driven*, and *teamwork oriented*. As shown on the left of Diagram 2-4, each current espoused value should be probed using three questions (Q2.2–2.4). At the energy company this showed that its teamwork was associated with continuous improvement teams working within a function to save costs. The lack of established cross-functional teamwork was viewed as a hindrance to business-wide innovation. Therefore, cross-functional teamwork training was conducted. For the other three underlying values, steps were also taken to establish a match with innovation. For example, the annual customer feedback survey was seen as a key element of the customer-centricity but this only afforded contact with current customers and structured their feedback in a way that did not allow creative ideas to be collected. Therefore, an initiative was launched to understand potential customers and understand current ones more deeply.

DIAGRAM 2-4: INNOVATION VALUES MAP

	Innovation Intent: 30% revenue growth based on new value propositions and markets.			
1. Aspirational Innovation Values	**Innovation Value:** We are brave, challenge the status quo and find new options for growth.			
Q1.1 For our innovation journey to succeed what mindsets are required?	**1.1: Required mindset:**			
	Open to diverse internal and external views.		Not afraid to speak up, learn and fail.	
	Enjoy exploring new opportunities.		Focused on opportunities and solving problems that arise.	
	Actively build new and deeper customer relationships.		Want to challenge mediocrity.	
Q1.2 What does this mean in practical terms?	**1.2: This means we:**			
	Dedicate resources to business-wide opportunities.		Give people the time they need for innovation.	
	Empower people to work on projects beyond their functional role.		Do not give up at the first hurdle.	
2. Current Underlying Values				
Q2.1 What are our existing main 3-4 values?	Customer-centric.	Operationally excellent.	Performance driven.	Teamwork oriented.
Q2.2 How do we live these values day-to-day?	• Service-minded. • Regular contact. • Annual, customer feedback survey.	• Set processes. • Continuous improvement. • Functional.	• Fast response. • SLA driven. • Customer complaints.	• Continuous improvement teams compete on cost savings.
Q2.3 How will the current values impact innovation?	• Fixed feedback limits new ideas. • Missing potential new customers.	• Viewing a mature industry as not innovative. • Not thinking big.	• Only solving immediate priorities inhibits longer term thinking.	• The lack of cross-functional teams will hinder.
Q2.4 What do we need to do to match the current values with innovation?	• Find new ways to understand customers.	• Make clear what types of innovation are needed.	• Measures for day-to-day and longer-term performance.	• Train cross-functional teams.

COMMUNICATIONS AND ENGAGEMENT

The main reasons why strategies fail are poor communications and a lack of engagement (not enough listening, empathizing, and co-creating).[26] The innovation journey requires the support of various stakeholders such as the board, functional areas and external collaborators. In addition, you must inform other employees why an innovation initiative is being launched. Each stakeholder will have a different mindset and so your communications must create clarity and collective enthusiasm for innovation. It helps that innovation is often perceived positively, as creating value, in comparison to change management for example, which is more associated with downsizing.

There are three steps to communications and engagement.[27] The first is to talk to your groups of stakeholders. Consider each group's influence and potential impact on innovation; then consider whether each group will be broadly supportive, or not. Those with more influence require more attention but don't forget that engaging employees not directly involved in innovation is necessary to prevent them feeling 'excluded' and subtly sabotaging change.

The next step is to draft a narrative that can be used to fully explain the innovation intent and innovation journey. Here, much of what is documented in the Innovation Values Map will be directly relevant, and your earlier conversations with stakeholders helps to co-author the narrative. The perspective of customers (who are, of course, also stakeholders) will greatly strengthen the narrative. The narrative itself is likely to be summarized in a set of presentation slides and, potentially, a video. Whatever the medium chosen, the message must present a compelling case for growth through innovation; outline what the innovation intent will deliver; and explain how the programme will be managed.[28] For example, the Swedish ferry company Stena Line produced an engaging video in which many employees from different departments shared their views on the role of innovation and senior managers explained why innovation was mission critical.

The third step is to tailor and reinforce the message. The innovation narrative should be consistent yet tailored for each stakeholder group clarifying what it means for them. These messages need to be repeated in order to change existing mindsets. So, you must decide when and how to give regular updates and engage employees in a dialogue about the criticality and progress of your innovation journey. At the energy company discussed earlier, quarterly updates were supplemented by an annual innovation conference, where employees learnt about innovation projects and the overall progress of the innovation journey.

RESOURCE ALLOCATION

Resource allocation is often overlooked at this stage of the journey. In Phase 1, Shaping innovation strategy, the innovation intent specified the commercial, category and capability goals. Now, the allocation of money, time and people will determine whether you are backing your innovation intent sufficiently. Therefore, the role of the senior team and the innovation manager is to decide what funds need to be reserved. The resourcing of innovation initiatives must be on the agenda of senior managers' regular meetings.

There are three common mistakes to avoid with resource allocation. The first mistake is not reserving funds for innovation in advance. This means that any costs connected with, for example, insight generation, will lead to funds from operational budgets having to be diverted and this can be contentious. It's also demotivating for teams to have to wait for funds to be re-allocated. Therefore, senior management should estimate the costs of travel, people's time and anything else associated with Phase 3, Generating deep insights and novel solutions.

The second common mistake is not having an effective mechanism for choosing the best projects. Your current method for project selection will almost certainly be based on financial approaches, such as return on investment. Different approaches are needed, as explained in Phase 4, Choosing projects to implement. Therefore, senior management should now plan a regular forum—*Portfolio Management Meetings*—where innovation projects and their funding will be discussed.

The third common mistake is inaccurate estimation of project costs. As innovation projects are selected for commercialization, the required investments will climb quickly. Phase 5, Getting innovations to market describes the intricacies of bringing an innovation to market. Each project will need a level of funding that's consistent with the technical and market challenges that are being addressed. The more radical a project is, the more difficult it is to estimate the investment required for commercialization. Innovation teams may ask for extra resources believing this will increase their odds of success and pre-empt a lower offer from the senior team. This 'game' is common in budget negotiations but is exacerbated by the number of unknowns connected with innovation projects. Here, it helps to be open and call on innovation teams to give requests based on clear evidence at portfolio meetings. Case 2-2 explains how the Development Capital Corporation (DCC) manages to instil an entrepreneurial, growth mindset in its many strategic business units (SBUs), giving them autonomy backed by simple governance mechanisms.

In summary, senior management should consider the costs of insight generation work on specific ISOs; how project selection can be optimized; how many innovation projects can be funded; and how much should be invested in taking innovations to market. Discussion on these points must start now, so the innovation journey is not slowed later on.

CASE STUDY 2-2: DCC
OPPORTUNITY MINDSET AT THE CRUX OF GROWTH[29]

The Development Capital Corporation (DCC) was established by Jim Flavin in 1976, to help Irish start-ups and mid-sized businesses grow. Today DCC is an international sales, marketing, distribution and support services Group with 50 to 60 strategic business units (called businesses), operating mainly in the sectors of energy, healthcare and technology (called divisions). The businesses operate under their own or partner brands, depending on the market. For example, one healthcare business operates under the brand EuroCaps and supplies softgel capsules to the nutritional supplements industry (see Case Study 5.2). The Group listed on the stock market in 1994 and has had a continued compound annual growth rate of 14.5%. Now a FTSE 100 company, DCC generated £14.8B in revenues in 2020 and employs over 13,000 people. This performance reflects the growth mindset at the root of its culture that infuses every part of the organization.

The Group centre is comparatively small (less than 1% headcount), focusing primarily on financial reporting, risk & compliance, strategy and mergers and acquisitions. This is made possible through clear governance mechanisms that encourage and support growth. Rob Flanagan, Group Strategy Manager, summarizes the DCC approach as *"A growth focus is at the crux of everything. The businesses shape their local growth strategies. The Divisions identify opportunities for growth through market expansion. The growth is then supported from the centre through strong capital investment and M&A capability."*

The senior team of each business is responsible for its own strategy, its implementation, and the resulting profit and loss. The shared mindset between the Group and a business is founded on trust and transparency. As managers in each business have expertise in their markets and capabilities, the centre seeks to back most of their ideas. While an entrepreneurial spirit and innovation are made explicit under the Group values and strategic framework, there is no formal innovation unit at the centre. Rather, organic growth through innovation—whether it is operational breakthroughs, incremental services improvements that drive loyalty, new product offerings, better supply chains, or business model reinvention—is the remit of each business. Each business organizes for innovation to fit their specific context, yet there are two common threads. First, innovation is a continuous conversation among managers at each business. Second, innovation is not overly engineered; it is expected of everyone, and the role of senior managers is to ensure opportunities are vetted and progressed in a mode of learning and adaptation to reduce unnecessary risk.

Each business strategy and innovation process is supported by a small Divisional team comprising senior executives and specialists who support the regular performance and development of a business. Their approach is to get on the ground and collaborate closely with the business's senior team to both leverage capability and generate new growth options. For example, their French liquid petroleum gas business recently came up with an automated cylinder dispensing system that allows 24/7 access to cylinders, providing a digital customer experience and greater flexibility for retail partners. This innovation has been shared among similar businesses in the energy Division and is under trial in Ireland. Meanwhile, the Division is also looking for new geographies or sectors with similar characteristics to its existing footprint. They then identify the best paths, such as mergers and acquisitions, to enter that market.

Reflecting on his past three years at DCC, Rob offers three lessons for SBUs and MSBs embarking on an innovation journey. First, striking a balance between capital discipline and investment is key. This means rigorous management of cash and performance, while continuing to routinely deploy capital against growth opportunities. Second is recognizing that the first lesson cannot be achieved by one group of people for all strategic choices that arise. The growth focus needs to be embedded throughout different parts of the organization: for the business (SBU) organic growth through business-wide innovation, for the Divisions supporting the business's innovation strategy and looking at sector and geographic growth, and the centre managing the overall strategy and deployment of capital. Third, making all of this happen relies on a shared language and ways of working to drive the different growth categories, be they organic innovation or inorganic acquisitions. Here culture and strategy work in lock-step, with a growth culture promoting a consistent focus, and a consistent strategic framework ensuring that growth for a given opportunity is carefully described across 'where we play' and 'how we win'.

INNOVATION PERFORMANCE MEASUREMENT

The fourth governance mechanism is performance measurement. Measures should link directly to the *commercial, category* and *capability* goals from your innovation intent. For each phase of the journey, these measures will inform people how the journey is progressing and what they need to focus on. Research shows that performance measures must be aligned with strategic goals (in this case innovation intent), focus on what's measurable and

TABLE 2-3: INNOVATION PERFORMANCE MEASURES

	PHASE 3, GENERATING DEEP INSIGHTS AND NOVEL SOLUTIONS	**PHASE 4, SELECTING PROJECTS FOR IMPLEMENTATION**	**PHASE 5, GETTING INNOVATIONS TO MARKET**
JOURNEY LEVEL	• Commercial potential of the ISOs investigated • Total insight generation costs versus budget • Overall range and quality of insights and ideas generated • Time spent by senior managers understanding deep market insights and contributing ideas • Number of employees who are now skilled in customer insight methods	• Project portfolio matches the commercial goals of the innovation intent (including growth gap and category ratio) • Effectiveness of the portfolio selection process	• Actual performance (sales growth and costs versus estimates) • Category ratio achieved • Degree to which the company has built a capability for black-, grey- and white-space innovation
PROJECT LEVEL	• Number of insights generated • Quality of insights • Degree to which the team has the capability to generate deep customer insights and solutions	• Teams are clear on decision criteria • Clarity and coherence of teams' proposals	• Achievement of project's commercial goals • Time to market • Degree to which the team has developed the capability to get innovations to market and develop new markets

important, and be simple to understand. Table 2-3 provides a recommended set of performance measures at the journey (strategic) and project levels. The measures are a sample drawn from a larger pool derived from a careful review of the research literature and are given in the Online Appendix (www.innovativegrowth.com)

In Phase 3, Generating deep insights and novel solutions, insight teams are tasked with generating deep, novel insights on a specific innovation strategic option (ISO). Therefore, the journey-level measures relate to the potential commercial value of the ISOs investigated (that is, have we identified *significant* market opportunities?); the investment in insight generation work versus what was allocated; and the overall range and quality of ideas generated. Also, at a journey level, we recommend that the capabilities developed are measured using the time senior managers invest in supporting teams, and the number of employees who are now skilled in applying customer insight methods. At the project level, the measures are the number and quality of insights that each project team identifies (here the emphasis should be on measuring that teams have conducted a systematic analysis that has uncovered novel commercial opportunities). The project-level capability measure should gauge how effective each team is at generating deep customer insights and appropriate solutions.

The outputs of Phase 4, Selecting projects for implementation, are a well-designed process for project selection, plus a project portfolio that the senior team is confident will deliver their innovation intent. Therefore, the recommended journey measures are whether the project portfolio matches the commercial goals (including the financial growth gap and category goals) and that the selection process is efficient. At the project level, each team must understand the criteria used for project selection and be able to coherently propose their analysis of customer needs and a solution that will generate growth.

Phase 5, Getting innovations to market, is action-oriented and can range from weeks to years, depending on the complexity of projects. It brings the cumulative investments and potential commercial returns into sharp focus. Appropriate journey measures are actual performance (sales growth and costs versus estimates), and the category ratio achieved. Looking at capabilities, the degree to which the company can drive black-, grey- and white-space innovation (ambidextrous innovation) is a clear measure. Project measures are: achievement of commercial goals; time to market; and each team's capability to commercialize innovations and develop new markets.

DESIGNING INNOVATION STRUCTURE

Research has shown that even more than leadership, it's clearly defined structures and roles that have the greatest impact on employee motivation.[30] Therefore, it's important to check how innovation tasks align with your current organizational structure. The human resource function is typically less familiar with structures that support business-wide innovation, especially as most people involved in innovation will only ever be part-time. So, clarity of reporting is crucial for part-time innovation roles, which compete for their time with full-time functional roles. Therefore, innovation structure must delineate who's responsible for innovation activities and how much of their time is dedicated for these activities; who they report to; who makes which decisions; what level of autonomy will be given to the innovation teams; and who needs to work with whom. Organizational structure also makes innovation activities visible and understood within the wider organization and safeguards against functional silos.

BUSINESS-WIDE INNOVATION

Diagram 2-5 shows the typical functions of a business, from R&D to Finance, each reporting to the CEO and the senior management team. Innovation activities must be established parallel to the existing organization, as shown on the left of the diagram. This ensures that innovation work is given the necessary priority, and that time and resourcing conflicts are addressed. The people who will be responsible for innovation are: the nominated innovation manager (which should be a full-time role); senior sponsors (senior managers responsible for a team); innovation teams (insight generation teams and innovation project teams); innovation team leaders; and some specialists.

The innovation manager must coach multiple cross-functional teams, and navigate the innovation journey with the senior team. Consequently, the innovation manager's level of authority must be on par with the senior team. The innovation manager should report directly to the CEO and, may or may not be a formal director of the company (in legal terms). The innovation manager must communicate constantly with innovation teams, their sponsors, the CEO, and the senior team. This is a challenging role and, in many ways, more complex than a functional role, as it involves building long-term, cross-functional innovation capabilities.

A number of part-time innovation teams are required for the innovation journey, to investigate and develop innovations. These teams should report to both the innovation manager and their senior sponsor. Sometimes innovation specialists, be they internal or external, are required to temporarily support an innovation team. Specialists may be required to provide expertise related to a specific domain (for example a particular market or technology), or innovation management capabilities (for example innovation portfolio management techniques). Specialists must be able to share their knowledge in such a way that their teams can quickly apply it. Innovation teams and their team leaders must be carefully identified and selected, which we will discuss later in this chapter.

DIAGRAM 2-5: STRUCTURE FOR BUSINESS-WIDE INNOVATION

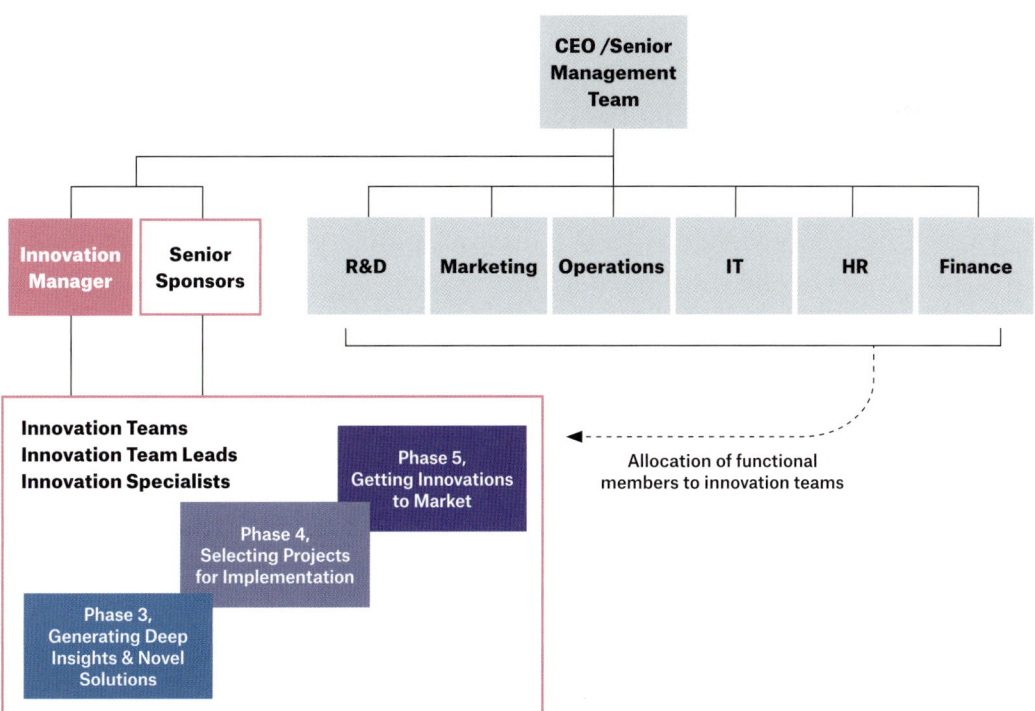

ORGANIZING THE JOURNEY   109

The innovation teams will be recruited from the functional areas (as shown by the dotted line on Diagram 2-5), and this can cause conflicts over the amount of time available for innovation activities. As most innovation team members will be working part-time, it really helps to assign a dedicated space to them for the duration of their work. This allows market, customer and other relevant data to be displayed and means that each time the team meets, they are immediately in a space that helps them switch their thinking to innovation work. A common mistake with teams is assigning part-time innovation responsibilities and expecting people to conduct these 'on top' of their normal role and at the 'side of their desk'. To be effective, at least 20% of their time must be diarized for innovation and one day a week is simply not as effective as a 4- to 5-day block per month.

For each innovation team, a senior sponsor from the senior management team should be nominated and these sponsors should be ultimately responsible for their team's performance. This brings an edge to the role that should mitigate the tendency of some senior managers to try to delegate the entire innovation process. Sponsors must provide direction and be willing to use their authority to make the tough decisions to keep innovation on track. Common issues they have to solve are convincing functional managers to allow some of their top people to be assigned to part-time innovation roles and ensuring that team members have enough time for innovation. Another common issue is that individuals and departments are reluctant to share pertinent knowledge with the teams. Sponsors should actively engage with the teams, discussing market information and innovation capabilities and the solutions being developed. The mindset required is openness and strategic breadth, but also able to challenge, focus and motivate the team.

The structure shown in Diagram 2-5 promotes business-wide innovation involving people from every function. This ensures that innovations are based on multiple, original perspectives and are not one-dimensional. In some manufacturing companies the mindset is that R&D is responsible for innovation. Diagram 2-5 deliberately shows innovation as coming from cross-functional activities collected together in the part-time teams with clear tasks. This has the advantage that innovation is not just perceived as 'R&D'. It also means that innovation will not be product-centric; a business-wide approach will ensure that product innovation is complemented by service, process and business model innovation. For example, Mölnlycke Health Case (Case Study 5-1) found that diverse insight generation teams (with members from several functions) developed very creative, novel solutions to customer problems.

Most service businesses don't have an R&D function. This means that innovation activities have probably been informally generated by marketing in the past. For service businesses, the structure in Diagram 2-5 clearly defines where innovation activities are located in the company. For example, the Swedish ferry company Stena Line found it was crucial to clarify what innovation means in a service context and how employees in every part of the business could participate. This led Stena Line to discover ways to innovate across all aspects of its business, including faster ways to load trucks and passengers onto their ferries, and ways to make the travel experience more enjoyable for all passengers.

SELECTING THE INNOVATION MANAGER

The innovation manager plays a crucial role in the structure, and therefore all the senior team should fully support the person appointed. Too often we've seen senior teams with a strong desire for growth but limited commitment to the innovation manager. Consequently, we've observed several innovation managers who have burnt out, been side-lined, or left within a few years.

Most businesses have a functional area that has been dominant in innovation in the past. In pharmaceuticals, R&D dominates and science expertise is king; in software companies, product development and coders rule. In B2B services, operations drive the service experience (process innovation) and have the most influence. The dilemma is: Do you select an innovation manager from the dominant functional area? If you want to build business-wide innovation, you require an innovation manager with deep functional expertise and broader management skills. Abilities honed solely in R&D, marketing or operations will not be sufficient for the role.

Finding the right person can be a tricky, soft process, and remember that up to 50% of outside hires fail.[31] To reduce this risk, take the time to check the skillset and mindset of candidates. It's best to invite several suitable people to demonstrate their interest in the role, as this will lead you to employees who are intrinsically motivated by innovation.[32] However, any candidate should be *T-shaped*—with a mix of both broad knowledge of business and deep knowledge of the most critical discipline, in this case innovation.[33] It's also essential to be able to take an initial idea and enhance it by mustering cross-functional (multidisciplinary) views. Suitable candidates will gain respect based on their expertise, but check that their past experience is relevant to the task of driving business-wide innovation. To make the decision on who should be innovation manager you can use formal HR assessments[34], but the ideal is to observe candidates in action. Here a simple but effective tip is to observe 2–3 candidates managing small teams making an initial assessment of an ISO using the strategic roadmap (see Diagram 1-7).

DESIGNING INNOVATION TEAMS

Before we could speak, humans had the ability to hunt and survive as teams. Today, teams are the norm in start-ups and large corporations, manufacturing and services, co-located and global organizations, physical and digital working. Therefore, we all know how to select, form and apply innovation teams… or do we?

Innovation teamwork differs from day-to-day, operational teamwork. Operational teams deal mostly with *knowns* and predictable, unambiguous data, where team performance is based on experience, scoping recognized problems, and established approaches. In contrast, innovation projects deal with *unknowns*—ambiguity, questioning assumptions about technical, market and commercial challenges that inevitably emerge. The speed of innovation projects is mainly determined by how quickly teams convert unknowns into knowns[35] (how quickly they climb *the learning curve*). Therefore, designing innovation teams is different to designing and developing operational ones. By *designing* we mean identifying the skillset and mindsets, matching the right people, and by *developing* we mean ensuring they are fully supported and engaged, so they can perform highly.

INNOVATION TEAM LEARNING

Diagram 2-6 shows the relationship between investment, return and learning for a breakthrough or radical innovation project. The horizontal axis is time. The key phases are shown at the top of the diagram. The left vertical axis is cumulative costs and returns, and the graph shows that in Phase 3 and Phase 5, investment increases (red curve) until launch, when revenues commence, leading to break-even and then profits (green curve).[36]

The right vertical axis indicates the amount of learning required during the phases, and there are typically three waves. In Phase 3, significant learning is necessary (with a steep learning curve, initially). This wave of learning has two peaks, as the insight teams must first learn how to collect deep,

DIAGRAM 2-6: INNOVATION INVESTMENT AND LEARNING

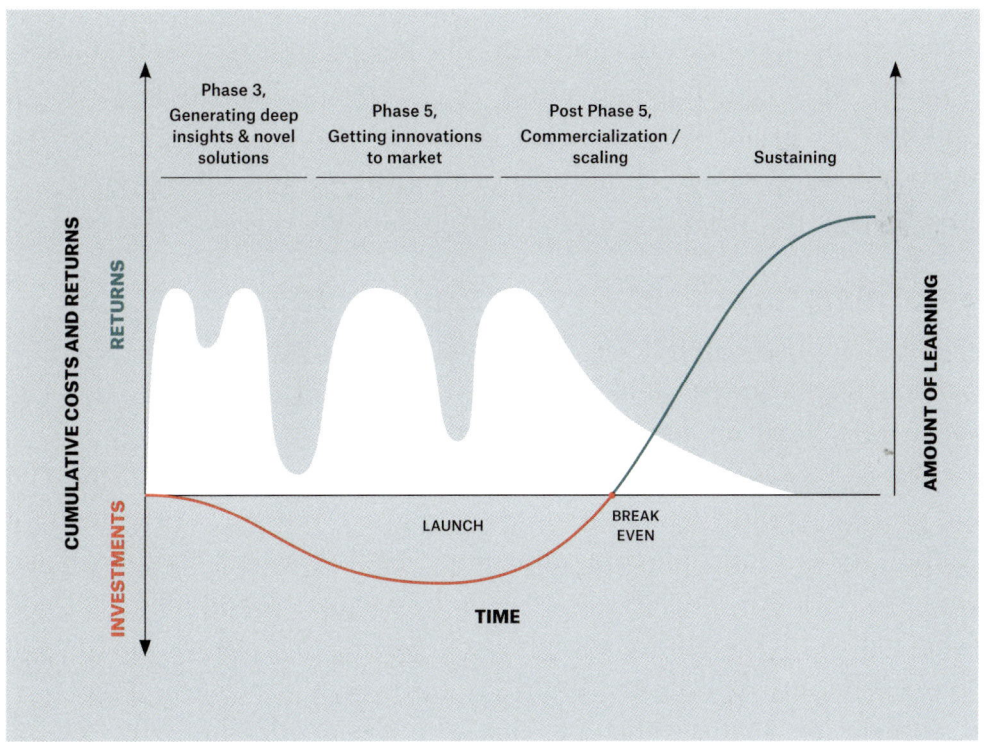

ORGANIZING THE JOURNEY 113

qualitative customer data and then learn how to identify customers' hidden needs and generate novel solutions. The second wave of learning is when teams develop solutions to customer needs and solve the technical challenges that arise. A third wave of learning occurs at the launch of an innovation; this is learning about markets. Incremental innovation addresses established markets and so there is less learning required. Breakthrough and radical innovations address grey- and white-space respectively, so a lot of learning is required to know how to develop these markets. The amount of learning required, and the time before sales take-off and break-even, are nearly always underestimated by management. As the innovation is scaled and reaches break-even, the amount of learning drops but even when the market is established (corresponding to black-space), some learning is still necessary.

Diagram 2-6 is conceptual in that it illustrates typical waves of learning associated with a typical innovation project rather than empirical, measured values. Similar but not identical waves of learning can be expected in any breakthrough or radical project. The key point to note is that learning is essential for successful innovation. As a project progresses, so the ratio of 'unknowns' to 'knowns' should decrease rapidly.[37] High-performing innovation teams excel at climbing learning curves and, consequently, time spent on designing, selecting and developing teams is time well spent.

CHARACTERISTICS OF HIGH-PERFORMING INNOVATION TEAMS

Innovation is a team sport! We now focus on two critical teams, the insight generation teams (often called scouting teams) and subsequent innovation project teams. Early on, teams are required to generate deep insights on each of the selected ISOs (typically 5–6 people per ISO, working part-time). Later in the process, project teams take innovations to market. These teams will typically have more people and, depending on the project complexity, some will need to work full-time. In some cases, the insight generation team that has investigated an ISO can move straight on to getting that innovation to market. However, different skillsets and mindsets are needed for Phases 3 and 5.

Innovation teams must be carefully designed. Here, it's useful to remember that when venture capitalists consider which projects to fund, they not only look at the business plan but also deliberate on the abilities of the team proposing it. Not every team has the capability to drive breakthrough and radical innovation and so you must find the right people to achieve high performance.

High-performing innovation teams have four characteristics: clear and challenging goals; appropriate skillsets and mindsets; agreed tailored processes; and positive team dynamics.[38] These characteristics have a hierarchical impact on performance. Reflecting this, most problems with teams are caused by: vague and uninspiring goals; a lack of capabilities; poorly suited processes; and negative team dynamics.

CLEAR AND CHALLENGING GOALS

Meaningful goals challenge convention, make it easier to identify market opportunities, and build capabilities. Each innovation team must have goals aligned to the innovation intent goals, and define success as measurable actions and results in a set timeframe. Clear goals define what is and isn't in scope for each innovation team at each phase. Early phase goals will be weighted to learning and later to commercial results. Moreover clear goals help identify the capabilities a team needs.

For insight generation teams, base the goals on the strategic roadmaps generated in Phase 1. The risks (unknowns) identified should be prioritized and then translated into 'research questions' to be solved. Insight teams face the challenge of many unknowns (for example customer needs; suitable solutions; and market size), whereas innovation commercialization teams must design solutions, and must frequently solve technical issues. Some teams face both market and technical challenges at an early stage. An example is the radical innovation team at the Irish wood products company Coillte that had to explore commercial opportunities for a patented bio resin. Coillte had an exclusive rights arrangement for this technology. The first big unknown was the market potential in core markets (such as 'green credential wood products') and adjacent markets. The second unknown was whether it was technically feasible to manufacture resin for these markets in volume. The team's priority was to clear up these unknowns.

TABLE 2-4: ATTRIBUTES OF INNOVATION TEAMS

		INCREMENTAL PROJECT TEAMS (BLACK-SPACE)	**BREAKTHROUGH/RADICAL PROJECT TEAMS** (GREY- AND WHITE-SPACE)
SKILLSETS	**MARKET KNOWLEDGE**	• **Single Functional/Discipline:** Depth in the main functional/discipline. • **Single Industry/Market:** Deep knowledge related to core market areas.	• **Multi-functional/Discipline:** Depth in several functions/disciplines. • **Multi-industry/Market:** Depth in multiple industries/markets beyond core.
	INNOVATION PROCESS KNOWLEDGE	• **Innovation Project Management:** Competent in the main innovation development processes. • **Commercial:** Ability to develop commercial ranges and key ratios (for example ROI).	• **Multiple Methods:** Competent in multiple innovation development processes for different dimensions, degrees and phases. • **Business-wide Innovation:** Understands several innovation dimensions and links.
MINDSETS	**THINK**	• **Researcher:** Diligent researcher of facts, figures; less comfortable with ambiguity. • **Customer Focus:** Customer oriented and driven to understand hidden needs.	• **Strategic:** Sees big picture, has a vision, comfortable with ambiguity. • **Reflective:** Reflective thinker, can be objective, analytical and questioning.
	FEEL	• **Creative and Insightful:** Creative, feels safe, unconstrained and shares intuition. • **Passionate:** Demonstrably passionate about ISO and gets stuck in when permitted.	• **Open and Challenging:** Open to new ideas, and naturally challenges assumptions. • **Entrepreneurial:** Independent minded, not waiting for permission, source of ideas.
	BEHAVE	• **Commit:** Prepares well and gives full attention when together. • **Teaming:** Inclusive, curious of and listens to others, practically shares their knowledge.	• **Leadership:** Drives progress, decisive as needed; engages team. • **Advocate:** Advocates, connects to others internally and externally for resources.

DESIGNING AND SELECTING INNOVATION TEAMS

Most managers can quickly name the people they want to have in an innovation team. Normally, they are people who are thought to have the 'right' skills, above all creativity. Our research with innovation teams found that, in addition to creativity, the 'right' skillset and a distinctive mindset are vital for team members.[39] This is summarized in Table 2-4, and it can be seen that the breakthrough/radical innovation projects require a number of skillset and mindset attributes, in addition to the ones identified for incremental projects. Table 2-4 is a useful starting point to design teams.

The *Innovation Team Design Matrix*, shown in Table 2-5, assists the design and selection of a high-performing innovation team. The table includes space to write the names and goals of the innovation team being considered and whether the team is responsible for incremental or breakthrough/radical innovation. As an example, we'll discuss the design and selection of a team to investigate the cell therapy market (featured in Chapter 1—see Diagram 1-9). An insight generation team consisting of a team leader and four members was required to investigate a white-space market.

The innovation manager and senior sponsor talked through and specified the composite skillsets and mindsets required for this insight generation team. These are shown in the column headed 'Required attributes' in Table 2-5. The next task was to identify a pool of potentially matching candidates, and from this they selected an initial team. They then assessed the team leader and each member against the required attributes for a match using high (H), medium (M), or low (L) ratings. For example, the potential team leader Sarah McNully had worked in different functional areas and so was assessed 'H' on these points, whereas she had very limited knowledge about technology. The aim is to check that the required attributes are available in the composite team, and it can be seen that three potential team members had particularly good technological knowledge (Peter Jones, Magnus Smith and John Tomlin). Sarah McNully was rated highly on nearly all points and so was perceived to be an ideal candidate, even though to date she had had relatively little opportunity to prove her leadership skills. She was, however, selected as she had helped prepare an ISO roadmap and her senior sponsor, who had experience with different types of innovation, agreed to coach her.

Other team members brought various strengths that were perceived, in aggregate, to constitute a strong team.

Overall, Tables 2-4 and 2-5 give the innovation manager and senior sponsors clear criteria with which they can design and select innovation teams. This is not only an issue for MSBs but also multinationals. For example, BASF knows that finding suitable innovation team leaders is difficult, as the combination of the right skillsets and mindsets is rare. We accept that designing a 'dream team' each time is unrealistic. However, we can clearly see the gaps in skills or mindsets that should close during team development.

For example, in Table 2-5 the team is perceived to lack mindsets for entrepreneurial activities, strategic decision-making and advocating resources. This gap must be managed by both the team lead and also senior sponsor through coaching and/or hands-on support from innovation specialists.

TAILORED PROCESSES

High-performing innovation teams need suitable processes to guide them. These should be geared to learning effectively (just like a low gear and high cadence gets a cyclist up a steep hill). Therefore, the next three chapters (Phases 3 to 5) give detailed, clear-cut processes for the innovation manager, innovation teams and senior sponsors to follow. They involve learning-by-doing, trial and error, validating assumptions and reducing unknowns. This will build the confidence to ultimately succeed.

While there are many different innovation development processes, they all stem from the same basic approach of diagnosing a problem (producing a problem statement); deciding how you intend to solve the problem; making trials, then reflecting, learning and moving on to the next most important problem (or assumption). So, innovation can be thought of as a set of action-oriented experiments to find ways to identify and solve market, customer and technical problems. Contrary to the stereotype of innovation being about unbridled creativity, innovation flourishes with disciplined project management suitably adapted for innovation. Remember, innovation isn't only about creativity and invention but also commercialization.

TABLE 2-5: INNOVATION TEAM DESIGN MATRIX

Innovation Team:	Cell Therapy Insight Generation Team
Team Goals:	Research the cell therapy market: 1) Determine customer needs; 2) Identify the sales process and decision-making unit; 3) Analyse competitors' offerings; Identify market opportunities and; 4) Estimate market size.
Type of Innovation:	White-space team.

ASSESSMENT OF A POTENTIAL INNOVATION TEAM

		REQUIRED ATTRIBUTES (SPECIFIED)	Leader: Sarah McNully			Member 1: Peter Jones			Member 2: Magnus Smith			Member 3: Gabi Möller			Member 4: John Tomlin		
SKILLSETS	**DOMAIN KNOWLEDGE**	Knowledge of several functions / disciplines?	H	M	L	H	**M**	L	H	**M**	L	H	M	L	H	M	L
		Knowledge of multiple industries / markets?	H	M	L	H	**M**	L	H	M	L	H	M	L	H	M	L
		Broad technological knowledge?	H	M	**L**	H	M	L	H	M	L	H	M	L	H	M	L
	PROCESS KNOWLEDGE	Competent at innovation development processes for different phases?	H	M	**L**	H	M	L	H	M	L	H	M	L	H	M	L
		Understands business-wide innovation?	H	M	L	H	M	L	H	M	L	H	M	L	H	M	L
MINDSETS	**THINK**	Understands the big picture and vision, comfortable with ambiguity?	H	M	L	H	M	L	H	M	L	H	M	L	H	M	L
		Reflective thinker, can be systematic, objective, analytical and questioning?	H	M	L	H	M	L	H	**M**	L	H	M	**L**	H	M	L
	FEEL	Open to new ideas, and naturally challenges assumptions?	H	M	L	H	**M**	L	H	M	L	H	M	L	H	M	L
		Entrepreneurial and independently minded, not waiting for permission, source of ideas?	H	M	L	H	**M**	L	H	M	**L**	H	M	**L**	H	**M**	L
	BEHAVE	Proven leader who drives progress, makes decisions and engages teams?	H	**M**	L	H	**M**	L	H	M	**L**	H	M	**L**	H	M	**L**
		Advocates and draws on internal and external resources?	H	M	L	H	**M**	L	H	M	**L**	H	M	**L**	H	M	**L**

INNOVATION TEAM DYNAMICS

Some companies' approach to team dynamics is to submit teams to 'know-thyself' assessments and awkward icebreaking exercises. We recommend you move beyond these approaches and run a highly motivating kick-off meeting, organized by the senior sponsor and the innovation manager. This should develop an innovation team charter covering: ownership of the goals; agreeing how to engage and work together; and project planning (see Online Appendix—*Innovation Team Charter* (www.innovativegrowth.com).

The team and sponsor should review the innovation intent and decide where the team's goals fit within it, their criticality to the business and specific performance measures. To get to know each other and focus on the task ahead, the team should also openly discuss the combined team's strengths and weaknesses (compared to the goals and ideal team design) and find ways to leverage and mitigate them. For a weakness, you might decide on specific training (for example commercialization), or a senior sponsor might coach the team leader.

With the goals and team composition clarified, a critical part of the kick-off meeting is to agree ways of working for the phase ahead. The innovation manager should set the scene by explaining the characteristics of high-performing innovation teams[40] and the tools and techniques that will be applied. Team members and the sponsor should decide how they can come together to make the team a high-performing one. Challenge is needed to transform good ideas into winning ones, so teams must have accepted ways to challenge assumptions, data, insights and ideas—but in a constructive way.

Finally, the team must plan their work. There will invariably be resource requirements to be discussed with the senior sponsor. These discussions will identify requirements from outside the team—for example, access to critical knowledge (reports or individuals), or for the sponsor to solve conflicts with team members' functional bosses. Set times should be decided, ideally in blocks of days, and specific places dedicated for innovation teamwork. Communication is crucial and the best teams develop ways to communicate frequently but in an effective, parsimonious way.[41]

MINDSET MATTERS

Throughout this chapter we've explained the concept of mindsets. At this point you may be thinking *'this is too complicated; we've innovated in the past so we'll be able to do it again'*. However, business-wide innovation isn't like riding a bike (something you never forget how to do). It's more like returning to competitive sport after a break. Not only has muscle atrophy set in, but as anyone who takes time out knows, the 'game' will also have moved on. So, don't underestimate the impact of mindset and other soft issues… they will make or break innovation efforts.

The top players in every industry are increasingly sophisticated in the ways they manage business-wide innovation. So learn from the examples of nimble start-ups and world-class innovators. But remember there's no silver bullet—no recipe for innovation that works in every organization. Blindly applying entrepreneurial methods[42] or shoehorning the mechanisms from large corporations[43] will not bring results in MSBs and SBUs. Your business and your people are unique, and so your innovation journey will be a largely unique experience (to enjoy!).

The Bank of Ireland (Case Study 2-3) describes how their retail business unit designed several customer insights teams. These teams generated many deep insights about different segments that have led to several innovations.

CASE STUDY 2-3: BANK OF IRELAND
TOWARDS A CUSTOMER-CENTRIC DIGITAL BANK[44]

Bank of Ireland (BOI) was established in 1783 and is the oldest and leading full-service bank in Ireland. The company is organized into retail, insurance, corporate banking and finance business units, and has an annual net interest income of €2.12B. In the past few years, CEO

Francesca McDonagh has been leading an organizational, cultural and digital transformation aimed at making it a customer-centric, agile and digital bank.

Within this context, BOI's Irish Retail Unit has been driving business-wide innovation through multidisciplinary teams that work with its different business areas. At the outset, a small team examined the ideas of the Fintech industry for threats and opportunities. They also initiated several programmes to unleash employee and external partner innovations. For example, the new FarmPro product provides a broad financial solution for farmers. It helps them both operate and develop their businesses, by joining up the accounting, software and banking offerings from three partners.

At the heart of BOI's innovation has been a focus on customer needs. Laura Lynch, then the Director of Customer Segments & Propositions, has embedded an internal capability to identify customers' needs and design unique propositions. Crucial was training employees in methods such as ethnography, repertory grid technique and journey mapping to unearth the hidden and unmet needs of segments such as 'youth', 'mass affluent' (also called 'premier customers') and business segments (for example farmers). Two big insights emerged. First, many life-stage decisions are dependent on financial services, yet customers are poorly served by a product-focused and siloed industry. For example, for those getting married or planning long-term financial well-being, the products and processes were complex, disjointed, and left customers wanting. Second, given BOI's extensive capabilities, the company is uniquely able to develop offerings that coherently address each segment's life-stage decisions, be they personal or business ones.

To leverage these customer insights, BOI's different retail business areas were engaged to collaborate on innovation. For example, Seán Ó Murchú, Director of Wealth Management, and John Nugent, Head of Premier and Private Banking, co-sponsored a team to design and develop a service called 'Life Planning'. The wealth management industry traditionally focuses on highly affluent customers with holistic, hands-on and high-commission private banking services. BOI had a proposition for mid-earners, but customer research showed it was perceived as short term, product-driven and focused on the individual and not the family. John also led the multidisciplinary Life Planning design team. This included people with expertise in proposition design, banking and wealth advice, financial planning software design, risk and service operations. Together, they designed an end-to-end process with a clear aim: to engage their premier customers in a trusting and holistic way; to address their life-stage issues; and provide them with a tailored, living financial plan to achieve their goals.

The team produced and tested an early prototype. With the full permission of a representative sample of customers, this involved shadowing, video recording and analysing advisor-customer meetings in customers' homes and bank branches. Customer feedback was very positive, and they enjoyed the interactive tools of the prototype that customers said made them "think deeper about their financial needs"; "focus on the big picture over time"; "pull everything together in one place"; and "prioritise". However, the process was heavily people-dependent, and it took a long time for customers to complete their Life Plan. The performance of the financial advisors was also mixed; some were 'naturals', others were less impactful. This led to the development of a specific 'learning scorecard', that helps advisors engage effectively with customers and develop life plans efficiently. After a few iterations of using this tool, customer engagement and requests for products have increased dramatically.

BOI's Life Planning services are now digitally enabled, and this makes it possible for customers to work through a series of 'what-if scenarios' based on their life goals. While the service leverages technology, it also deliberately allows for continued engagement with a Life Planning professional. The team explored the potential of 'robo-advisors' but John says, *"We are a long way from that, if ever. Customers' Life Plans are highly emotive, used to make once-in-a-lifetime decisions. So, if and when they want to engage with a qualified trusted professional, we have to be there for them."* Moreover, BOI has found that advisors really welcome the opportunity of working in deep, trusting relationships with customers. Due to the level of insights derived and the very positive customer reactions, BOI is now in the process of a full market launch of the Life Plan service that goes beyond their premier customer segment.

Customer-centricity, combined with the capability to generate deep insights, mobilize cross-functional teams and digitize processes, has propelled many other innovations. For example, Seán Ó Murchú also sponsored deep customer insight research into the 'senior customers segment' (aged 70 years and older), to look at how these people prepare for and transition into retirement. This work led to a rounded senior wealth management service. Based on his experiences, Seán has advice for managers embarking on customer-centric service innovation: *"I've been involved in many transformations. With this customer-centric one, there was a need to move slowly initially, in order to really clarify the unique problems and priorities of each customer segment, at life-stage moments. Don't try and rush because, for example, a quick survey will not surface the real issues. Later in a project, there is a need to go fast, acting rather than waiting for perfection. Even if the technology is not ready, there are ways to test and refine ideas with the customer before investing in scaling."*

SUMMARY

- To move from 'A' to 'B', organization of resources and capabilities 'C' for the journey is imperative. Organizing for innovation requires three coherent mechanisms.
- First, govern organizational behaviour through innovation values that are understood and believed through continuous communications and engagement. Reinforce innovation values with resource allocation and innovation performance measures.
- Second, design a business-wide innovation structure with clearly defined roles and fitting talent to drive the entire innovation journey.
- Third, design and develop diverse teams with clear goals, composite skillsets and mindsets, and suitably tailored innovation development processes, and develop the team dynamics to perform highly.
- With governance, structure and teams decided, you are now ready to get going. In the next chapter we explain Phase 3, Generating deep insights and novel solutions.

# Phase 3
Generating deep insights and novel solutions

Generating deep insights and novel solutions

INTRODUCTION

In Phase 1 of your innovation journey, the senior team will have developed its innovation strategy. This will have identified the *Innovation Strategic Options* (ISOs) and strategic roadmaps will have been drawn, which will have identified market opportunities and potential combinations of product, service and business model innovation to drive growth. In Phase 2, the senior team will also have selected the best people for their insight generation teams. So, everything is now ready to move from strategizing and organizing and to get going in Phase 3 (Diagram 3-1).

DIAGRAM 3-1: PHASE 3 IN THE INNOVATION JOURNEY

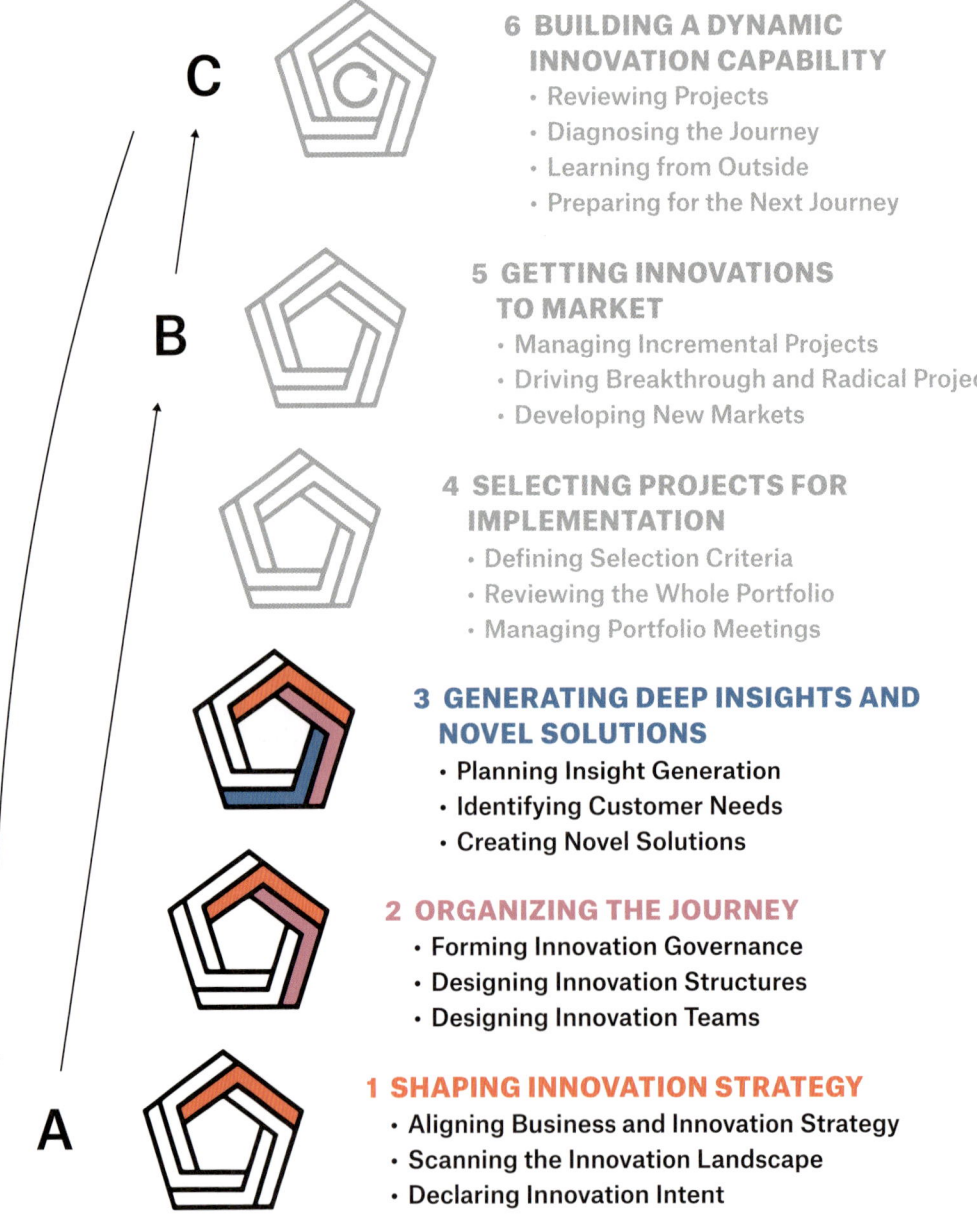

C

6 BUILDING A DYNAMIC INNOVATION CAPABILITY
- Reviewing Projects
- Diagnosing the Journey
- Learning from Outside
- Preparing for the Next Journey

5 GETTING INNOVATIONS TO MARKET
- Managing Incremental Projects
- Driving Breakthrough and Radical Projects
- Developing New Markets

B

4 SELECTING PROJECTS FOR IMPLEMENTATION
- Defining Selection Criteria
- Reviewing the Whole Portfolio
- Managing Portfolio Meetings

3 GENERATING DEEP INSIGHTS AND NOVEL SOLUTIONS
- Planning Insight Generation
- Identifying Customer Needs
- Creating Novel Solutions

2 ORGANIZING THE JOURNEY
- Forming Innovation Governance
- Designing Innovation Structures
- Designing Innovation Teams

A

1 SHAPING INNOVATION STRATEGY
- Aligning Business and Innovation Strategy
- Scanning the Innovation Landscape
- Declaring Innovation Intent

Traditionally, market research has been built on asking customers about their needs—so-called *Voice of the Customer* (VOC) work. Some managers believe good market research is simply asking customers what they want. Other managers will invoke Henry Ford's famous quote: "If I had asked people what they wanted, they would have said faster horses", to argue against market research.[1] We disagree with both views! Customer needs are neither obvious nor easy to elicit and successful innovation is rarely about following the same path as your competitors. Real innovation is about generating deep insights about your customers. By *deep insights* we mean understanding customers' needs, behaviours and emotions better than your competitors. Insights emerge from understanding exactly what customers are trying to achieve, and recognizing their motivations and frustrations with current products and services. Deep insights enable us to create novel solutions.

Recently, managers at an Irish business told us that they thought that a market research technique we had recommended was "*too much effort and an overkill*". We responded that their proposed use of simple, direct interviews would, at best, put them on a par with their competitors. We also asked if their product design technical work required a lot of effort. "*Yes, of course it does*", they answered. We then said that market research is as challenging as technical work and so it does require effort and systematic techniques. This convinced the company to put more effort into their insights work.

Table 3-1 summarizes the key themes of Phase 3. There are four actions to take: planning and preparing the teams for insight generation; collecting appropriate market data; analysing the data to find real customer insights; and creating novel solutions—new products, services and business models.

Again, we'll be introducing new tools and techniques. If your teams take the time and effort to learn them, then you'll be building an innovation capability that puts your business ahead of the competition. The tools include systematic ways to uncover customer needs, such as ethnographic market research, and ways of summarizing market data, such as the Kano Model.

Phase 3 is an exciting part of your innovation journey and it requires dedicated, highly motivated teams, with the full backing of the senior team. Such work is about exploring the unknown, and some individuals who like clear, unambiguous processes struggle with deep insights work. For others, insight generation is an exciting but demanding opportunity to learn new skills and become market experts. Members of the senior team will also be outside their comfort zone, as they are required to assimilate new and ambiguous market data. They should also be aware that the insight generation teams will look to them for encouragement. An excellent way for senior managers to encourage the teams is to ask to go along on a few of the customer visits. The CEO of a service company based in Germany decided that his active participation in some of the VOC work gave him useful insights as well as sending a strong message to the teams about the importance of innovation.

TABLE 3-1: PHASE 3—KEY THEMES AND CHECKLIST

THEMES	DETAILS
Actions to take	☐ Planning insight generation ☐ Collect appropriate data about different ISOs ☐ Analyse the customer data to identify customer needs ☐ Create novel solutions to meet customer needs

Tools and concepts	☐ The decision-making unit (DMU)
	 ☐ Techniques for identifying hidden needs
	   Repertory grid technique
	   Ethnographic market research
	   Lead user technique
	 ☐ Problem definition and brainwriting
	 ☐ Strategic roadmaps
	 ☐ Kano model

People responsible	☐ Insight generation teams and their team leaders ☐ Senior sponsor ☐ The innovation manager
Mindset matters	☐ Exploring the unknown is demanding ☐ Senior sponsors outside their comfort zone ☐ Insight generation teams must be fully supported
Outputs	☐ A comprehensive analysis of each of the ISOs ☐ Development of novel concepts for each of the ISOs

At the end of Phase 3, the insight teams will have made a comprehensive analysis of several ISOs. The ideas in the ISO maps will have been refined and, in the process, novel innovation concepts will have been defined. This is a huge step, as it paves the way for successful innovation.

One final comment to readers about to embark on this chapter: generating insights requires systematic techniques, there are quite a lot of tools and techniques to learn and so this is a relatively long chapter. Therefore, we recommend reading the sections up to and including 'Data Collection' together as a team, whereas the sections from 'Data Analysis' onwards should be read individually.

ESSENTIAL BACKGROUND

Businesses wanting to develop innovative products need to conduct *market research*. There are four outputs of great market research: a deep understanding of customer needs; an appreciation of expected buying behaviour; a good estimation of market size; and a clear grasp of competitors.

HISTORY OF MARKET RESEARCH

Putting customer needs at the centre of innovation projects is taken for granted today. However, this wasn't always the case and so we give an overview of market research here. The history of market research is inextricably linked to the use of surveys, interviewing techniques and focus groups.

Surveys and Direct Questions

Throughout history, there have been surveys and a *census*—a survey of the whole population—was conducted by the Romans at the time of Christ's birth. After invading England in 1066, William the Conqueror used a survey to determine land ownership and consolidate his power. Much later, as the social sciences emerged, surveys were used to study how ordinary people lived. In 1889, Charles Booth published a monumental 17-volume study of the life of people in London,[2] having attempted to collect data from every single Londoner!

Opinion polls for US presidential elections emerged in the early 20th century. For the 1936 election, the *Literary Digest* magazine surveyed two million (telephone-owning) households to predict the election results. The magazine's prediction was wrong and Franklin D. Roosevelt did become president. Telephone ownership was not widespread in 1936 and polling predictions rely on *representative samples*—getting answers from respondents typical of the wider population. Another 1936 poll used a much smaller but representative sample and made the right prediction, establishing the *Gallup Poll* methodology. Representative surveys quickly became adopted as a way to understand the impact of advertising, with B2C giants such as Procter and Gamble in the vanguard.

Indirect Questioning Emerges

Surveys use direct questions but psychoanalysts like Sigmund Freud (1856–1939) often found responses to direct questions unreliable. This led to methods for uncovering suppressed and unconscious thoughts, including *projection*—this technique prompts respondents to share their opinions of others.

Projection has been used in market research since the 1940s.[3] A famous study[4] used two shopping lists—one including 'instant coffee' and other 'non-instant coffee'. Housewives were asked to describe the typical shopper for each list. The shopping list with instant coffee was often identified as being from a 'lazy' housewife, whereas the one with non-instant coffee was from a 'thrifty' and 'good' housewife.[5] Adverts were developed to overcome this bias and instant coffee became a huge success. Projection techniques have since been used to investigate purchasing behaviour, packaging, and emotional responses to brands.[6]

Another indirect approach is *Repertory Grid Technique*, invented in the 1950s. It's a structured way to surface unconscious views. As it's very effective for generating insights, it will be fully explained in this chapter.

Focus Groups

These consist of small groups of customers discussing products, led by a facilitator. Focus groups originated in the 1930s and were used during World War II to understand how radio broadcasts affected morale. The name Focus

Group stems from the influential sociologist Robert K. Merton, who coined the term in 1956,[7] after which the technique was widely adopted. Today, focus groups are omnipresent and used to study consumer attitudes (or mindsets), consumer needs, views on advertising, and political trends.

Market Research for Product Design
Early market research focused on advertising and only later was it used in product design. In the shipyards in Kobe, Japan, in the 1980s, an emphasis on customer needs emerged and the phrase 'voice of the customer' was coined. The Japanese approach was to match each customer need with a suitable engineering solution. However, good product design emerged earlier with, for example, the German engineer Karl Kromer designing ergonomic products in the US around 1900.[8] Informally, however, ergonomics dates back to prehistoric stone tools. Human factor analysis emerged during World War II with aircraft designers analysing the interaction between the user and a device, in order to prevent incorrect usage. Following the war, the designer Chuck Mauro became famous for designing the NASA control room and the floor of the New York Stock Exchange (to match controllers' and traders' respective needs).

Ethnography
Unfortunately, traditional techniques such as surveys and focus groups generate incremental rather than breakthrough innovation.[9] Therefore, new techniques were required and the potential of ethnography was recognized for generating deep insights.

In colonial times, academics in Britain, France and other nations began studying tribes in Africa.[10] Bizarre as it seems today, these academics never visited the cultures they studied, instead conducting surveys from afar using a standardized questionnaire! This early research led to many misconceptions about tribal culture. However, in 1922, Bronislaw Malinowski lived with islanders for his famous study of Western Pacific culture.[11] Other researchers made extended trips to Africa, such as E. E. Evans-Prichard, who studied the Nuer tribe.[12] Around the same time, Chicago sociologists studied urban, 'street corner' society. The change from surveys to direct observation ('in the field') led to particular research techniques and a much more accurate understanding of both ethnic and urban culture.

The potential of ethnography was recognized in the US by people like Jane Fulton Suri, who championed speaking to and observing customers in their own settings. Ron Sears, an experimental psychologist, worked on designing easier-to-use photocopiers from 1979. Similarly, at Rank Xerox, anthropologist Lucy Suchman led a group investigating user behaviour. In the 1980s, Liz Sanders used ethnography to find the differences between what people say they do and what they actually do (a very powerful technique that we will discuss later). She also used projection to help people express their unconscious needs. Over the last 20 years, the design consultancy IDEO (famous for helping Apple design their first computer mouse) has built a worldwide reputation for using ethnography and design-driven innovation (and the company now employs Fulton Suri).

Today, top companies use ethnography.[13] For example, the systematic analysis of video-recordings of customers interacting with products or receiving services generates deep insights; this technique is described later in this chapter.

Lead Users

The concept that users can contribute to product design is not new. In 1776 Adam Smith recognized that many machines had been invented by 'common workmen'.[14] In the 1920s, farmers modified the Model T Ford to thresh corn and saw wood, and these adaptions were the harbingers of the agricultural machinery industry. In the 1980s, Professor Eric von Hippel at MIT criticized traditional market research for generating few insights. As a solution, he developed the *Lead User Technique*, which taps the expertise of communities of users.[15] For example, mountain bikes were invented by enthusiasts who found normal bicycles ill-suited for rough tracks and used components from motorcycles to build more durable machines. Over the years, the mountain bike community has constantly refined designs and created a vigorous industry.[16]

Impact of the Internet

The internet has strongly influenced market research, as information on user needs can now be gathered online. *Virtual communities* are independent groups of users of particular products and services and studying their online behaviour on websites or mobile applications can generate ideas. Social media can also contain useful information. Similarly, online surveys are easy to organize and large numbers of responses can be gathered (although whether these are representative needs to be carefully considered). For B2C products, online video diaries and the like mean that ethnographic methods can be more widely applied.

Probably the biggest impact that the internet has had on market research is the phenomenon of *big data*. Consumers' internet usage, such as their search and retail behaviour, leaves a digital footprint. Looking for patterns in data (often called *data mining*) can be a useful way to segment customers and sophisticated algorithms are often used. The Japanese airline All Nippon Airways (ANA) is extremely advanced in this area and employs mathematicians to identify new market segments through cluster analysis. Interestingly, ANA finds that it's essential to go out and meet customers from the different segments, to fully understand their motivations. In Chapter 2 we introduced the digital marketing company Red Ventures (Case Study 2-1) and explained how they organize for innovation. Here, Case 3-1 describes how Red Ventures drives innovation based on insights generated from big data.

CASE STUDY 3-1:
RED VENTURES: NOT RED TAPE[17]

Red Ventures is a US-based technology and internet services company with over 3,500 employees distributed across more than 15 locations around the world. Over the last 20 years the company has built a portfolio of influential brands, digital platforms, and strategic partnerships that work together to seamlessly connect millions of people with information and tools to help them discover and decide on key aspects of their life.

Red Ventures owns over a dozen brands that are household names in the US, such as TVGuide, CNET, Lonely Planet, The Points Guy, Bankrate.com and many more. Another example is the widely used website NextAdvisor, which is operated under a partnership with Time Magazine. This offers a one-stop platform to help with all of life's financial decisions (from credit cards to car insurance, from mortgages to tuition fees). MyMove.com provides ways to avoid the otherwise inevitable hassle of moving (from planning the move flawlessly, estimating living costs in a new State, to making a new house into a real home). Lonely Planet, which rightfully has a huge reputation for providing 'local knowledge' content to travellers, is an example of the traditional print to digital transformation that Red Ventures is driving. Concise, timely and inspiring content is an important aspect for all of Red Ventures' brands. For example, NextAdvisor has recently published articles on how to launch a 'side hustle'—how to make extra money parallel to your normal job, through a business idea that matches your passion and personality.

In addition to successfully running its own brands, Red Ventures provides digital marketing expertise to partners, supporting them to manage the digital bridge to their consumers. This includes building and operating platforms that improve every aspect of the consumer's journey either online or offline. So-called 'digital buy flows' are optimized, so that consumers can make informed decisions when buying complex, life-stage products and services such as healthcare. Red Ventures' own brands create a wealth of knowledge on consumer needs, as its websites receive a staggering 500M visits a month! Mapping digital buy flows and the types of questions asked has given Red Ventures a unique capability for designing content which delivers a seamless, personalized experience.

The common denominator in all of Red Ventures' work, whether on its own brands or for clients, is a focus on improving every aspect of the consumer journey and a deep understanding of the data these journeys create. Carlos Angrisano is the manager of Digital Labs, the internal incubator for the Red Ventures organization, where new digital solutions that can serve the entire business are conceived. Digital Labs provides 'big R' (research) for Red Ventures and it uses multiple methods to gain insights. Websites generate big data on consumers' preferences but *"When we need to understand the consumer's lifetime perspective, we also run lots of customer workshops. These enable us to generate different insights compared to the big data. Each insight, regardless of its source, is important but we arrange them into a hierarchy. Only then can we recognize the high-quality insights—ideas about consumers that haven't been spotted before"*, says Carlos. *"Then we use experimentation to check which digital experiences consumers prefer and how we can deliver them based on our proprietary technology."*

The approach taken by Digital Labs is very data-centric, but herein lies a dichotomy. On the one hand, Red Ventures only wants business ideas based on solid data but, on the other hand, it wants novel digital solutions. To deal with this, the teams within Digital Labs are given a lot of autonomy and do not work within strict processes because, as Carlos says, *"They need to be free to apply their raw energy. We like teams to have what we call their 'shared Everests'. We want them to be excited about the problem AND the solution."* Teams in Digital Labs include people with deep experience in all areas of the business, including data science, consumer marketing, digital design and content development.

The key metric for these teams is not to move a current business KPI such as acquisition from A to B but to move a capability, for example machine learning adoption, that can be inserted into their future businesses. Another dichotomy is the pace of learning. To learn faster and increase autonomy Carlos reduced team sprints from four weeks to one week, so everyone is focused on a very specific hypothesis. He also increased his formal reviews from every week to every three weeks to allow teams to reflect, and generate higher quality insights which lead to breakthrough innovations. As Carlos puts it, *"Innovation is an everyday race against red tape... and a race that has to be won."*

DIAGRAM 3-2: DOUBLE DIAMOND MODEL OF DESIGN[19]

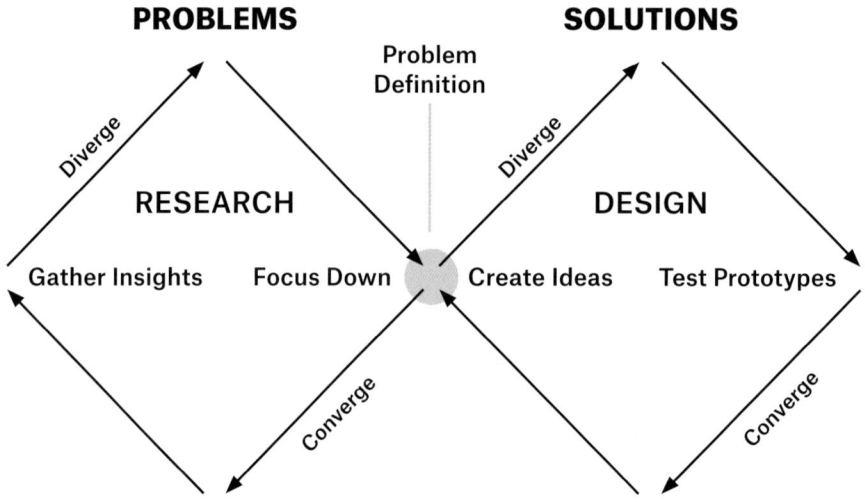

Design-driven Innovation

Design-driven innovation, also known as *design thinking*, is the current buzzword in the innovation field. In recent years it's influenced how companies try to understand their customer needs. Design thinking stems from the creative ways in which industrial designers design products, and it's been popularized by IDEO. The essence of design thinking is to break innovation into two parts: the identification of the customer's problems, and the generation of creative solutions.

The process is best explained based on the *Double Diamond* model developed by the UK Design Council and shown in Diagram 3-2.[18] The first diamond (*research*) includes a divergent and a convergent activity. The first activity is to identify all the challenges the customer faces. Here, design thinking aficionados recommend customer visits and empathizing with customers, to identify the customer's *jobs to be done*. This is the outcome the customer wants to achieve through employing a product or service. Identifying the customer's challenges is a divergent activity, as more and more issues are identified. Note that popular design thinking does not explain advanced techniques for understanding customer needs. Therefore, in this chapter, we will explain in detail how to apply systematic techniques to generate deeper insights.

The next activity is convergent and fixated on defining the most important challenge customers face: *problem definition*. The first diamond stops designers jumping to solutions before they've sufficiently understood the customer's challenges and formulated a precise problem definition. Note that creativity research has demonstrated the importance of developing a clear problem definition before looking for solutions.

The second diamond (*design*) starts with the third (divergent) activity—coming up with creative ways to solve the defined problem. Note that creativity research has demonstrated the importance of developing lots of ideas in problem solving. In the final (convergent) activity, prototypes are tested as the best solution is selected for development.

Overall, the history of market research gives us some important pointers. It shows that deep customer insights are crucial to innovation but that focus groups and direct questioning have limitations. More sophisticated techniques such as ethnography—observing customers in their own environment—are invaluable for surfacing hidden needs (see Case Study 3-2). In recent years, design thinking has led many businesses to place more emphasis on understanding customer needs and testing potential solutions with users.

CASE STUDY 3-2: ALTRO LTD
COVERING AND UNCOVERING[20]

Altro Ltd. is a family-owned UK manufacturer of flooring and wall coverings. It has annual sales of £143 million, employs 800 people, and is a regular top performer in the UK Sunday Times Best Place to Work rankings. Altro operates in the competitive, highly commoditized building materials industry, where customers are conservative and focused on price. The company's products target the education, healthcare, retail, industrial and transport sectors.

Despite the company's success in addressing sectoral needs, it decided to go even further. The company conducted detailed market research in cooperation with Cranfield School of Management. In 2015, Altro created the dedicated role of product insights manager that reports to the company's marketing manager. Altro recruited Antonio Lourenco to drive a more sophisticated approach to identifying customer needs. During his first year, healthcare was Lourenco's priority. He travelled regularly, visiting hospitals, flooring contractors, and specifiers, trying to understand their concerns and hidden needs. The company used ethnographic market research ideas, and Lourenco observed the day-to-day usage of products at customers' facilities. He interviewed facility managers, doctors, nurses, patients and cleaners—everyone that 'used' the products. In total, he visited 21 customer sites and collected more than 15 hours of audio-visual data, the systematic analysis of which led to many actionable insights.

Working with colleagues, Lourenco identified numerous unintended ways in which customers used products, as well as many 'workarounds' where customers had developed their own solutions. For example, in the high-secure environment of psychiatric wards, flooring products were installed on walls to protect the patients in danger of self-harm, and products intended for installation on walls were being installed on ceilings. Lourenco said, *"I thought the gap in the market meant we needed to develop new products. I was surprised to find we already had products that were perfectly suitable to the high-secure environment, when applied correctly. Until now, these products had only been targeted at industrial applications."* The crucial insight uncovered was the need for a product range aimed specifically at high-secure mental health environments, and that offered extreme robustness and safety to both patients and staff. Altro had not realized before that the characteristics of its most robust industrial products were exactly those needed for specialized healthcare applications.

The company's research also showed that healthcare customers had difficulties specifying the products they needed, and many inefficiencies and misunderstandings existed between the different parties involved—from the healthcare administrators to facility managers, architects and contractors. Altro responded in several ways. It now offers a popular Continuous Development Program, which explains interior design principles for professionals involved in flooring and walling decisions (architects, facility managers, etc.). The company created the 'Altro Possibilities Studio' at its factory, which showcases nine different rooms for high-secure and mental health environments. These rooms show different degrees of robustness, ease of use and installation, to match different use scenarios. Between the studio opening in October 2017 and March 2020 (and Covid-19 restrictions), approximately 400 customers visited, ranging from major healthcare trusts to the Ministry of Justice and Mental Health Board. Altro estimates it has won approximately 50 projects as a direct result of the sector expertise demonstrated by the studio. Its focus on high-secure environments has reinforced Altro's brand as a leading healthcare supplier. Lourenco said, *"Our experience in healthcare has demonstrated the importance of identifying hidden customer needs, and now we are applying our techniques in other sectors such as transport."*

PLANNING INSIGHT GENERATION

Insight teams need to conduct a thorough investigation of various innovation strategic options (ISOs) and identify suitable innovation concepts (products, service and business model combinations). Therefore, the senior team needs to provide clear aims for these teams such as:

- Here are the ISO maps with our first-pass ideas for innovations. You need to analyse the markets more deeply and, through this process, come up with better ideas for innovative products, services and business models.
- Make sure you collect clear evidence to support your recommendations.

RESOURCES TO ALLOCATE AND RESEARCH TO CONDUCT

We are often asked how much market research MSBs and SBUs should conduct, because they have limited time and resources. Based on experience, we pragmatically recommend that deep insights into an ISO can be generated from 20 repertory grid interviews and 20 ethnographic visits; possibly a lead user workshop; and good online research. A team of 10 people, working part time but with reserved slots for the insight generation work, will be required to collect and later analyse this data.

It must be stressed that generating deep customer insights involves small samples and achieving a representative sample is not the objective. Instead, you'll base your investigation on an *exploratory sample*—a small number of customers from which to gain market insights.

CHOOSING THE SAMPLE

An important decision is choosing the exploratory sample—deciding who to talk to. The sample should include all members of the *Decision-making Unit* (DMU). A DMU is the group of individuals that make, or influence, the buying decision. In a B2C market like breakfast cereals, products are selected mainly by mothers but children also influence the decision, while fathers usually have little influence. In a B2B market like medical electronics, the DMU consists of doctors and nurses who will use the products, bioengineers who will maintain them, and hospital purchasing managers who will weigh up the investment, running costs, and potential revenues. Working on projects in the medical electronics market, we have typically spread 20 repertory grid interviews across the DMU—interviewing 12 doctors and nurses, 3 bioengineers and 5 finance managers.

GAINING ACCESS

Access can be an issue and there are differences between B2C and B2B markets. In B2C, consumers give up their own time and are paid around €90 per hour for participating. With this motivation, it's relatively easy to recruit people for interviews or ethnographic home visits.

Access is more difficult in B2B markets. For example, purchasing managers at car manufacturers are known to be reluctant to participate in market research. We encounter such issues on all our B2B projects. To resolve this we always look for what will motivate a B2B company to cooperate. Automotive purchasing managers were resistant until we offered them a report on our findings, across the car industry. They were interested in service levels and trends and later they received an aggregate report, which they found very useful. Negotiating access requires creativity, which obviously must lead to legal and ethical approaches. Never, ever, try to collect data without permission.

It's essential to be cognisant of the time pressures customers face. Only collect data (that is, conduct interviews and video-recording) when it's not disruptive. For example, don't attempt to visit greenhouse growers during their harvest season, or a fashion house in the week before the launch of a new collection. Aim to make every visit and every interview effective, time-efficient, and interesting for the interviewee. This means not exceeding the time agreed for the research. A good visit means that the respondent will be willing to cooperate again in the future. (Practical tip: ask for an hour and ensure you finish after 55 minutes!)

Businesses can use their own lists of customers, or use an agency to identify suitable samples. Agencies maintain lists of customers willing to cooperate in market research, but be aware that these people may have already shared their ideas with your competitors. So, when using an agency, it's best to specify that you want to talk to customers who have not recently been involved in market research. On a recent investigation of the well-being food and drinks market we used an agency to recruit 20 different consumers and 5 well-being shop owners, and this worked well.

IDENTIFYING CUSTOMER NEEDS—DATA COLLECTION

To generate deep insights, we recommend three methods: *Repertory Grid Technique*; *Ethnography*; and *Lead User Technique*. This combination was chosen for four reasons: it can be used in both B2C and B2B contexts; it's cost-effective; the techniques are relatively easy to learn and apply; and the techniques provide complementary perspectives. We will also discuss how to use existing data, such as market reports.

REPERTORY GRID DATA COLLECTION

Repertory Grid Technique (RGT)—often referred to as *rep grid*—is a powerful research tool for identifying customer needs. It stems from psychology and helps customers articulate future needs. It's a structured way of interviewing which avoids bias and leads to a matrix of quantitative data—the repertory grid. Rep grid is rarely used well and so your competitors won't have heard of it. (So, think competitive advantage!)

The essence of rep grid is that it requires the interviewee to *compare and contrast* a number of existing things, such as products and services and an imagined 'Ideal Product'. Psychologists know that when people compare and contrast things, it helps them think deeply (uncovering their unconscious mindset). When, for example, products are compared and contrasted, it stimulates customers to articulate their needs. In rep grid, one main question is asked multiple times and the interviewee has to give different answers each time.

To illustrate rep grid, we'll explain how we used it to help a food company investigate the European market for well-being products. This project was conducted with product and R&D managers from the client company. For a month, we immersed ourselves in the well-being market. We read market reports and academic research; trawled the web for secondary data; interviewed customers and shop owners; and visited shops. During an intensive week, we conducted 25 one-to-one rep grid interviews. We will describe here the interview with one consumer, Sarah, conducted in three stages.

Identifying the Elements

The 1st Stage of the rep grid interview is to identify five products that the interviewee knows. Here, it helps to have a pre-prepared list of products, from which the interviewee can choose. Such a list typically includes similar products and products from closely related categories.

Sarah was shown Table 3-2 and asked: *"Which of the following things do you sometimes take to influence your well-being (your physical, mental and emotional health)? Please choose a mix of drinks, foods, supplements and other products you use."* The list included a range of drinks; foods; supplements; and other products. Sarah answered: *"Coffee, yes I drink that every day… And herbal tea; I drink that to help me sleep. At the gym I always have a protein*

TABLE 3-2: LIST OF WELL-BEING PRODUCTS SHOWN TO SARAH (CONSUMER / INTERVIEWEE)

DRINKS	FOODS	SUPPLEMENTS	OTHER
• Coffee • Bullet Coffee • Tea • Herbal tea • Probiotic drinks • Energy drinks • Protein shakes	• Superfoods • Healthy confectionery • Power bars/gels	• Vitamins • Minerals (for example magnesium) • Turmeric (root) • Ginseng • Protein additives	• Aromatherapy • Essential oils • Tinctures • Traditional Chinese medicine • Memory boost products

shake. From the superfoods, I like turmeric. And I like tinctures to build up my bodily resistance."

The name of each product Sarah selected was written on a separate, randomly numbered postcard-sized card, as shown in Diagram 3-3. The random numbering of the cards (5, 1, 4, 3, 2 & 6) meant that the first product selected ["Coffee"] was written on Card 5, the second product selected ["Herbal (sleep) tea"] on Card 1, and so on. Note also that Card 6 was pre-labelled as an 'Ideal Product (imagined)'.

There are two general points to note. What is written on the cards (products) are what are termed the *elements* in RGT terminology. Second, the random numbering of the cards is necessary to mix them up, changing them from the order in which they were selected.

Eliciting and Rating the First Construct

The 2nd Stage of a rep grid interview is to ask the interviewee to compare and contrast three different cards. This identifies how the interviewee perceives products (Stage 2a) and then their ratings (scores) are collected (Stage 2b).

Sarah was shown three cards (a *triad* in RGT terminology). Diagram 3-4 shows that the triad consisted of Cards 1, 2 and 3 (corresponding to "Herbal (sleep) tea"; "Tinctures (resistance)"; and "Turmeric"). These cards were placed on the table in front of Sarah and she was asked: *"How are two of these products similar and different from the third? And why?"* This elicited

DIAGRAM 3-3: STAGE 1—IDENTIFYING THE ELEMENTS (WELL-BEING PRODUCTS)

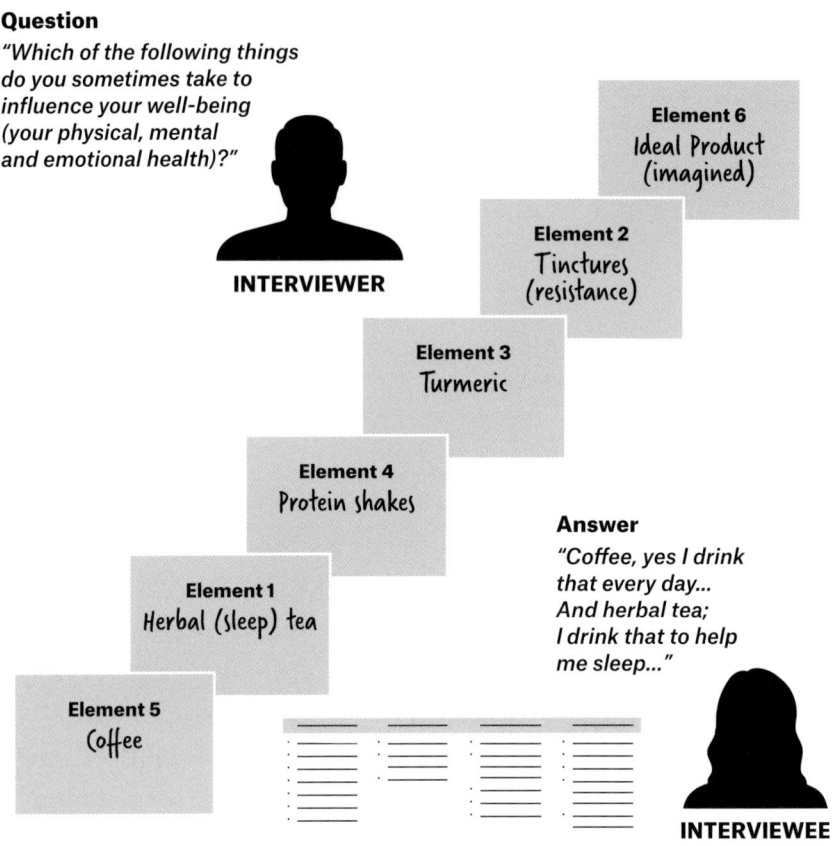

her response, "*I like the taste of turmeric and my tinctures, whereas the sleep tea is too bitter*" (Diagram 3-4).

Interviewees' responses are termed *constructs* in RGT terminology. This term is based on psychology, where individuals are known to 'construct', or 'build', their view of the world (in this case Sarah's view of the world of well-being products). Constructs show us how an interviewee like Sarah differentiates between different products. Sarah's first construct was *taste*, and to gain more explanation of the construct she was asked: "*Can you explain what you mean by 'taste'?*", to which she answered: "*I like silky-smooth tastes, not too sweet and definitely not bitter things.*"

DIAGRAM 3-4: STAGE 2A—ELICITING THE FIRST CONSTRUCT

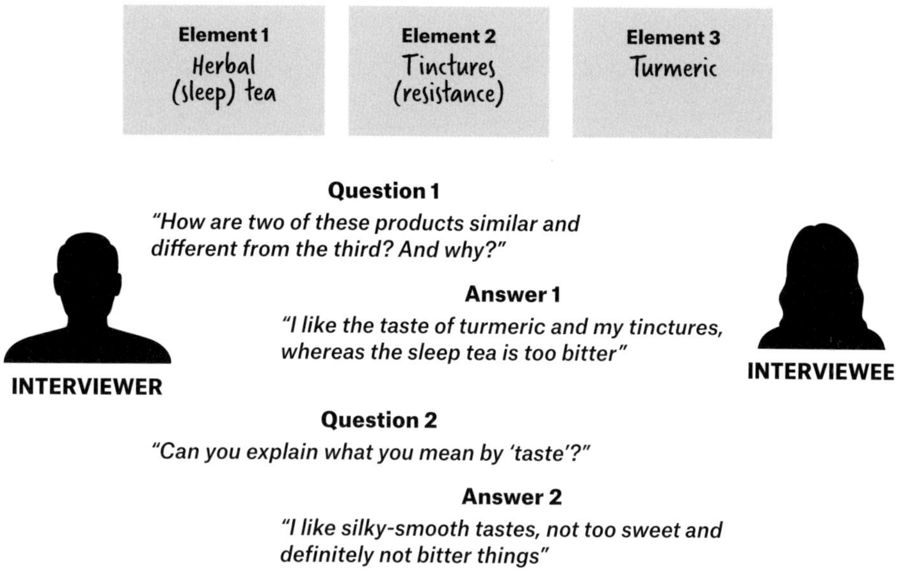

Element 1
Herbal (sleep) tea

Element 2
Tinctures (resistance)

Element 3
Turmeric

INTERVIEWER

INTERVIEWEE

Question 1
"How are two of these products similar and different from the third? And why?"

Answer 1
"I like the taste of turmeric and my tinctures, whereas the sleep tea is too bitter"

Question 2
"Can you explain what you mean by 'taste'?"

Answer 2
"I like silky-smooth tastes, not too sweet and definitely not bitter things"

After the follow-up question clarified the construct, a 5-point scale was made using small Post-it® sticky notes on the table, as shown in Diagram 3-5. Note that the rating scales were anchored using Sarah's own words (for example, the '1' end of the scale was "Bitter"). Sarah was then asked: *"Can you rate all these six products on their taste, on a scale from '1' (Bitter) to '5' (Silky-smooth)?"* After some consideration Sarah explained her ratings as follows: *"I really like the taste of coffee, so I will give coffee a '4'. The Ideal would be a '5'... [thinks] Now the tinctures and turmeric I like but they are not as good as coffee. And protein shakes are a bit metallic and the herbal tea is, well, just bitter."*

Note that rep grid interviews capture the interviewee's own words and prevent bias (such as an interviewer interjecting their own terms or labels). In this sense, RGT really does elicit the spontaneous VOC, and so it's best to record interviews. (Practical tip: ask for permission to make an audio recording.)

Eliciting Further Constructs and Ratings

The 3rd Stage of a rep grid interview is to show the interviewee new triads and ask them the same question multiple times, eliciting new constructs. It

GENERATING DEEP INSIGHTS AND NOVEL SOLUTIONS 149

DIAGRAM 3-5: STAGE 2B—RATING THE ELEMENTS (PRODUCTS) AGAINST THE FIRST CONSTRUCT

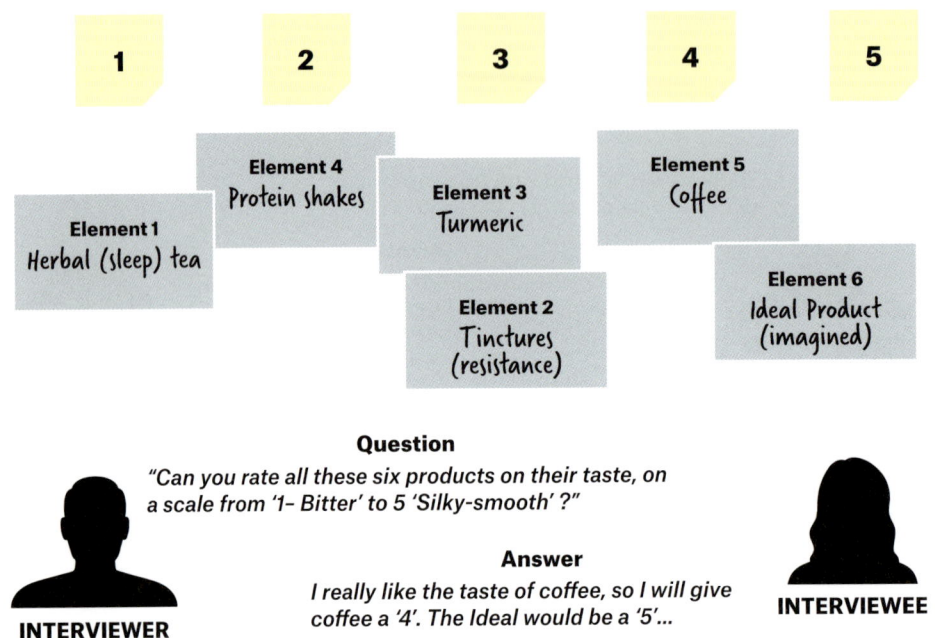

should be noted that the interviewee is not allowed to repeat constructs—each new triad must stimulate a new construct. After each new construct is elicited, the interviewee then rates all six elements (the products on the cards) against the construct.

Diagram 3-6 illustrates how Sarah was shown a new triad consisting of Cards 4, 5 & 6 and asked: "*How are two of these products similar and different from the third? And why?*" This prompted her to say, "*My Ideal would be pure, whereas the protein shakes have a lot of artificial things*". Sarah's answer to the follow-up question provided more clarity: "*I feel artificial things are not good for my body.*" At this point, Sarah was asked to rate all six elements (well-being products) on how pure she perceives them to be, on a scale from '5' ("pure") to '1' ("artificial").

It should now be apparent that rep grid interviews follow defined stages: showing the interviewee three cards (a triad); asking them a standard

DIAGRAM 3-6: STAGE 3A/B—ELICITING AND RATING THE SECOND CONSTRUCT

Element 4	Element 5	Element 6
Protein shakes	Coffee	Ideal Product (imagined)

INTERVIEWER

Question 1
"How are two of these products similar and different from the third? And why?"

Answer 1
"My ideal product and coffee, when I buy organic, are pure... whereas the protein shakes have lots of artificial things."

INTERVIEWEE

Question 2
"Can you explain what you mean?"

Answer 2
"I feel artificial things are not good for my body"

Question 3
"Can you now rate all six products on a scale of 'pure' to artificial"

Answer 3
"Yes, I can rate them... Herbal tea would get a '3'..."

question; eliciting a *personal construct* (that is, an unprompted construct); and then having them rate all six cards against that construct (on a 1 to 5 rating scale). Note that ratings (scores between 1 and 5) are used, and not rankings.

The interview with Sarah identified further constructs. As she was not allowed to repeat constructs, each new triad elicited a new construct and then all six elements (well-being products) were rated; that is, scored against this construct. The full set of constructs and the product (element) ratings formed Sarah's rep grid, which is shown in Diagram 3-7. (A blank grid for interviews is available in the Online Appendix.) At the top of the grid is the standard (compare and contrast) question, which is the same for *every* interview. On

DIAGRAM 3-7: REPERTORY GRID ON WELL-BEING PRODUCTS FROM SARAH

Date: 8/19	Interview: #1		Interviewee: Sarah		Interviewer: KG		
Order of elements: 5; 1; 4; 3; 2; 6. Note: stars indicate the triads.	Herbal tea	Tinctures	Turmeric	Protein Shakes	Coffee	Ideal	
Construct	Element 1	Element 2	Element 3	Element 4	Element 5	Element 6	Construct Pole
1) Good taste	*1	*3	*3	2	4	5	Too bitter
2) Pure	3	4	3	*1	*4	*5	Artificial
3) Easy prep	*4	*4	2	3	*4	5	Hassle
4) Healthier	*4	4	*4	2	*3	5	Less healthy
5) Ongoing	*3	1	1	*3	5	*4	Immediate
6) Not expensive	4	*1	*2	2	*4	3	Expensive
7) Referral	4	4	*5	*1	2	*5	Marketed
8) Smells good	*2	3	4	1	*5	*5	Pungent
9) Brings confidence	1	*4	4	*2	2	*5	No effect
10)							
Would recommend	3	5	5	1	3	5	Would not
2nd Provided construct							

Sarah's grid, note that the names of the six products (elements) have been written in the diagonal boxes across the top of the grid (for example Herbal tea is Element 1). Down the left-hand side of the grid are the nine constructs elicited during the interview (including *Good taste* and *Brings confidence*).

For each construct, the ratings of the elements are entered into the grid (for example Herbal tea received only a '1' for Taste, whereas Coffee scored '4'). The stars before some ratings indicate which cards were in the triad that elicited particular constructs. For example, the first construct was elicited using a triad consisting of Cards 1, 2 and 3 (indicated by the ratings with stars: *1, *3, *3) and the second triad was Cards 4, 5 and 6. The constructs and ratings tell us how an interviewee perceives products from their personal standpoint, and we will explain more on this in the section on data analysis.

Three other points should be noted on Diagram 3-7. First, the column 'Construct Pole' is used to record the opposite end of the construct (for example *Too bitter*). Second, rep grid interviews identify not only product attributes (for example taste and purity) but also interviewees' emotions and feelings (for example *Brings confidence*). Understanding the emotions that interviewees associate with products can be very useful in generating ideas on how to design empathic products or services. Third, at the bottom of the form is what's called a *provided construct*. During most of the interview, the aim is to identify personal (unprompted) constructs, but at the end the interviewer may have specific questions to ask. On Diagram 3-7 it can be seen that the interviewer wanted to know which products the interviewee would recommend. This was asked at the end, when it would not bias the interview. As the construct *Would recommend–Would not* was provided (that is, given to the interviewee), she only needed to give her ratings. Provided constructs allow us to check whether certain product attributes that have not been mentioned as personal constructs are important. Companies often assume that certain product attributes are really valuable to customers, and rep grid allows such assumptions to be tested.

A typical rep grid interview takes just under an hour and will elicit about seven to ten personal constructs (the form has space for up to ten constructs) and the ratings of one or two provided constructs. During rep grid interviews, it's quite common for the interviewee to express some frustration, as they're being pushed to think deeper. Avoid the temptation to end the interview early—encourage the interviewee and give them the opportunity to think up new constructs. The interviewee's emotion indicates that the technique is working!

TABLE 3-3: SIX DIFFERENT REP GRID PROJECTS

	PROJECT	INTERVIEWEES	ELEMENTS CHOSEN	COMMENTS / EXAMPLE INSIGHTS
1	Well-being products	Consumers and shop owners	Different well-being products (see Table 3-2).	Many people mention pureness but, as they only consider organic and pure products, this is a hygiene factor, not a market driver.
2	ECG monitors	Intensive care professionals	Different types of equipment used in intensive care (for example ECG monitor, ventilator, etc.).	Comparing different types of equipment generated many ideas for the ECG manufacturer. It helped the company identify the importance of product attributes such as "easy to train staff" in the medical equipment market.[21]
3	Sterile rubber gloves	Surgeons and nurses	Different types of gloves used for different operations (for example thick protective, thin and tactile, etc.).	Identified a problem that current products did not solve adequately. For example, sterile gloves slipping down the cuffs of sterile gowns, necessitating medical professionals to have to re-sterilize.
4	Farming	Farmers and growers	Different crops and animal husbandry (for example wheat, beef, trees, etc.).	Identified the reasons that many farmers do not use their free land for forestry.
5	Pensions	Women	Different financial services (for example current account, savings, life policy, etc.).	Identified women's financial and emotional barriers to investing in banks ("risky institutions") and how to overcome them.
6	Diabetes	Newly diagnosed patients	Different ways in which patients keep healthy (for example medication, lifestyle, nutrition, etc.).	Identified areas where newly diagnosed patients struggle and where healthcare services are lacking.

It's also possible to conduct rep grid interviews using internet video platforms such as Zoom. The Online Appendix (see www.innovativegrowth.com) includes a checklist for RGT interviews; this will help prevent common mistakes, such as forgetting to have all six cards (elements) rated against each construct. RGT interviews need practice, but people typically become comfortable and efficient after two or three interviews.

Preparing Rep Grid Interviews

The most important thing in preparing rep grid interviews is to decide what the elements should be. For the well-being project, it was a range of well-being products that the interviewees could choose from. Rep grid is a flexible technique and the elements can also be services (in a project for an insurance company, different financial services were used), or even brands (a company might want to know how its brand is perceived in a new market).

To investigate an ISO, the elements of the rep grid interview will be products or services (and, of course, the 'Ideal Product' or 'Ideal Service'). Table 3-3 lists six projects we conducted, with the types of interviewees and the elements chosen. It can be seen, for example, that in an investigation for a manufacturer of electrocardiogram (ECG) monitors, the elements were different machines used in intensive care. This was necessary because the interviewees (intensive care professionals) could not name five ECG machines and so a broader range of equipment was discussed. This worked well and the ECG monitor manufacturer learnt a lot from the discussions on other types of machines. Another example was the work on pensions for women. Different financial service products were compared and contrasted, enabling the interviewees (who were not finance experts) to articulate what they liked and didn't like about financial services and explain their anxieties. Table 3-3 can be used to help identify what type of elements to select for rep grid interviews.

Advantages of Rep Grid Interviews

It's important to note why we're making the effort to conduct 20 rep grid interviews:

- The technique probes deeper than normal questioning and collects the VOC without bias.
- Typically, 7–10 constructs are elicited per interview. These will be a mix of product attributes and sometimes emotions and feelings (for example *"Brings confidence"*).
- After 20 interviews, you'll have elicited lots of constructs. This gives a comprehensive view of how customers perceive products and their attributes.

- Having an *Ideal Product* (imagined product, service or proposition) as an element stimulates the interviewee to consider what attributes an ideal product would have, giving us ideas for novel solutions.

ETHNOGRAPHIC DATA COLLECTION

Ethnography is a powerful technique.[22] Ethnographic data are collected in the customer's home environment (for B2C), or their work environment (for B2B). It entails going 'into the field', something that ethnographers have found to be fundamentally important. For the well-being project, we visited people at home and interviewed them about their use of products including their preferences and where they were stored, etc. .

The main pillar of ethnography is *contextual interviews*, with data collected through video-recording. Two members of the insights team should attend each visit—one to interview and one to video. Mobile phone cameras are good enough for this recording but check that the interviewees' words are clear; a lapel microphone might be necessary in a noisy environment. Obviously, you need to obtain the interviewee's permission to video-record. Videos of contextual interviews are often simply referred to as *ethnos*.

Conducting Contextual Interviews

As their name indicates, contextual interviews are conducted in the customer's own context (home or working environment). The customer is asked to explain what their key activities are during a typical day, or whatever regular cycle determines their main activities. For example, an accountant would be asked about a typical month and a farmer would be asked about a typical year. Contextual interviews take a broader approach than the 'jobs to be done' approach of design-driven innovation. Good ethnographic market research not only identifies all the jobs to be done by the customer but also the key challenges they face and the emotions they experience. Understanding emotions can be important even in B2B markets. For example, contextual interviews with scientists who use electron microscopes showed that they wanted to feel certain they were following the right procedure and would get the best images possible. This led the manufacturer to, for example, improve

TABLE 3-4: OUTLINE OF A ONE-HOUR CONTEXTUAL INTERVIEW

	TOPIC	POINTS TO MAKE / OPEN QUESTIONS TO ASK	TIME
1	Establish rapport (before videoing)	• Thank them for their time; ask demographic questions; stress one-hour maximum and then explain that you will now switch on the camera.	5 min.
2	Key activities	• Can you explain what the main activities are in a typical day / week / year? • What are the most challenging activities and why?	10 min.
3	Purpose of key activities	• When do you / don't you do this? • Why do you use this? • How does it help you? • Who else benefits from it? • How do you feel about it?	10 min.
4	Procedures used	• Can you show me and explain how you conduct this activity? • What makes it easier/harder? • Are there different ways to conduct the activity? • How long does the activity usually take?	10 min.
5	Organization of activities	• Who is responsible for this? • Who else uses this? • What is the relationship between these people?	5 min.
6	Triggers for the activities	• When do you use/do this? • How often? • Who else uses it?	5 min.
7	Spontaneous questions	• Can you explain? What is this? How do you do that?	5 min.
8	'Golden minute' (camera off)	• Tell them you have finished videoing; ask important, sensitive, last questions. Thank them again.	5 min.
		TOTAL	**55 MIN.**

the design by providing regular messages on the display to tell the user that procedures were progressing correctly.

Ethnography is also valuable in the service sector and can be used to observe the delivery of a service. For example, in work with the Deutsche Bahn (German Railways), we had permission to shadow passengers on their travels, to understand their feelings. This helped to identify what are called *pain points*—the moments of a service where the customer's expectations are unmet.

A university ethnographer studying a tribe will have (nearly) all the time in the world but in ethnographic market research our interviewees have limited time, so we must conduct the interviews efficiently. Therefore, Table 3-4 includes rough timings for the stages of a one-hour interview. A good interview is where the customer does 95% of the talking. At the beginning it's important to establish rapport. Asking a few demographic questions over a coffee can help put the interviewee at ease, before the camera is switched on. Then, use open-ended questions for key activities (Topic 2); clarify the purpose of these activities (Topic 3); and observe activities being conducted (Topic 4), etc. In addition to the suggested questions that are selected in advance (from Table 3-4), the two members of the team making the visit must observe actively and ask if there's something that they don't recognize or understand. Ask spontaneous, extra questions such as '*Excuse me, what is this?*' and '*Can you explain?*' Take the opportunity to probe emotions, asking things like '*I notice you're smiling* [or frowning] … *how did that make you feel?*'

During the contextual interview, it's important for the interviewer to be aware of *contradictions*. Ethnographers know that people often say one thing and do another, or make things sound particularly positive, or make bold generalizations. Therefore, if interviewees say things like '*I always…*' '*It is very easy…*' '*I never…*', it's worth asking them to demonstrate the task they've mentioned. For example, one interviewee told us that changing the filter on a device '*Was easy enough…*' and so we asked them to demonstrate it. The interviewee struggled and only then admitted that they always ask their partner to change the filter.

At the end of 50 minutes, tell the interviewee that you're switching off the camera. We call this point of the interview the *golden minute* as, with the camera off, the interviewee will typically answer sensitive questions openly.

A typical question here might be: *"Do you always follow the procedure you demonstrated to us?"* For example, we have had people 'open up' and tell us what corners they would cut if we were not there! Such comments should be written down straight after the visit.

In the Online Appendix we provide a checklist for team members conducting ethnographic market research. This will help prevent common mistakes, such as not having enough memory capacity for the video-recording.

Advantages of Contextual Interviews

It's important to note why we are making the effort to video 20 contextual interviews:

- Ethnography gives you a broad understanding of the challenges and issues your customers face (and the jobs they have to do). This identifies if current products and services address customer needs and where there are gaps—unsolved problems.
- Videoing captures information that would be overlooked on a casual visit and allows a systematic analysis. Video material can also be easily shared with colleagues.
- After 20 contextual interviews, we will have collected comprehensive data on the challenges and issues that your customers face.
- By going 'into the field', you'll discover novel things about your customers that you didn't know and so it's fascinating work for insight generation teams.

LEAD USER TECHNIQUE

Surveys aim for representative samples. Lead user technique takes a very different stance and looks for atypical customers—the outliers. It focuses on specific customers, often big enthusiasts or those who face greater challenges, for example in using equipment in extreme situations. A classic example is that companies have studied the usage of tyres in Formula 1, to develop better tyres for normal road use.

Lead users' requirements are extreme but they become mainstream over time. For example, the outdoor clothing company North Face works closely with some of the world's best mountaineers, to design high-tech, lightweight equipment for extraordinarily difficult alpine mountaineering routes. Working with top mountaineers has led to super-light, stretchable insulating 'puff' jackets that insulate even when wet. The technology uses synthetic rather than down fibres. Puff jackets have now become a winter fashion item that is not only reassuringly warm but also light and comfortable. Similarly, top 'gamers' are often engaged by companies to co-create new online video games.

A word of caution: the extreme needs of some lead users might not be relevant for mainstream customers. For example, the medical implant manufacturer Johnson & Johnson found that some top surgeons' ideas for product design, although interesting, weren't practical for use in regional hospitals. However, when applied correctly, lead user technique looks at the needs of demanding users, collects ideas from users of similar products and services in other markets, and checks the mainstream market for the relevance of the ideas generated.[23]

The selection of a lead user group normally follows two steps. Firstly, identify which of your customers use products or services in the most demanding circumstances. These users will have developed particular expertise in dealing with the challenges they face and may have modified standard products or processes to match the challenges in their working environment.[24] Once extreme users have been identified, the important next step is to identify *analogous users*—users from related fields, who face similar challenges to those in the current market. For example, horticultural growers face challenges in optimizing the climate within a greenhouse and zoo keepers in the reptile house face many similar issues. It can be said that recruiting attendees for lead user workshops requires creative ideas and considerable effort.

A useful way to summarize the discussions in a lead user group is to apply the strategic roadmap covered in Phase 1. This tool can gather lead users' views on market contexts; products and services; and the evolution of technology. Lead users have expert knowledge and so, once the roadmap format has been explained, they're usually very efficient at filling in the details. Their views on market trends and the products needed to address them can be enlightening (and can be compared to the ISO maps generated internally).

Coillte, the Irish forestry and wood products manufacturer, organized a lead user workshop in London. In addition to a few lead users, a highly experienced architect, a construction project manager, a forester, a European building regulations expert, a cabinet maker and a wood products expert attended. The one-day workshop led to a strategic roadmap that was not only pertinent to Coillte but also for all the attendees. As they came from different roles and perspectives, the individuals were motivated to take part by the knowledge that they'd meet other experts.

Advantages of Lead User Workshops
The lead user technique is worthwhile because:

- Lead users have precious knowledge on how products or services perform in demanding situations. Often, lead users will have modified existing products or services to meet these demands.
- The discussions between experts from very different backgrounds throw up unexpected ideas. Note that creativity research indicates that eureka moments emerge when different perspectives interact.
- Important new insights can be extracted from the strategic/ISO roadmaps, which can be easily communicated to others.
- Having engaged lead users means you have a pool of experts who can be brought together again in the future.

COLLECTING SECONDARY DATA

The three data collection methods described all collect empirical data—that is, *primary data*. In addition, the insights team should consider where *secondary data* (pre-existing information) can be used in what's often called *desk research*. Secondary data can be very useful for understanding market size, the expected speed of diffusion, competitors, regulatory aspects and the like. There are five sources of secondary data to consider, which go beyond the common and dangerous myopia of simple Google searches.

First, market reports are available from companies such as Frost and Sullivan and the cost is typically €2,000–5,000 per report. The reports provide a quick overview of a market, with information on market size, key segments, incumbent companies and customer needs. However, they don't include customers' hidden needs and are also available to your competitors. (So, think: No competitive advantage!) Our advice is that the reports give an overview of a market but you still must conduct deeper research. Market reports give you a baseline, but Phase 3 will generate insights that you don't find in published reports.

Second, an often-overlooked source of market data is academic research published in international journals. Academics have the time to study all sorts of things, including markets. For example, on the Irish pensions research mentioned earlier, we found recent, very useful research identifying the barriers to women investing in pensions. The articles were found using a Google Scholar search and each journal article cost about €30—trivial in comparison with what we learnt. Academic papers also include a review of the literature, which often gives an overview of key issues. In addition to Google, the academic databases such as ABI Inform and EBSCO are efficient for finding relevant academic papers.

Third, an important and often unique source of secondary data are your own databases with various customer information. These can provide contact details for fieldwork. In addition, depending on the amount of data you collect, they can give you insights into the buying behaviour of your customers. The obvious example of the power of such data mining is the way Amazon can suggest additional items to customers. Recall also how Red Ventures (Case Study 3-1) combines their big data analysis (over 500M website visits a month), along with customer workshops, to generate deep insights.

Fourth, social media can provide insights and is widely used by B2C market research consultants. It can give you an overview of what's being discussed by your target groups, potentially including comments on products and services. Be aware that what's being discussed doesn't necessary translate into a decision to buy. Similarly, fashion experts stress that social media shows what's popular today but doesn't identify next year's trend.

Fifth, competitors' websites give very valuable information on how they segment their customers; the product advantages that they promote; and the business model(s) they use. Frequently, competitors use the same segmentation and address very similar customer needs. For example, Svensson—the Swedish provider of climate control products and services in the horticultural sector—found that its competitors' websites copied Svensson's segmentation. This led Svensson to a unique segmentation (see Case Study I-1).

Advantages of Secondary Data

The advantages are:
- Some secondary data are relatively cheap and provide useful market information.
- Market reports can build an *initial* understanding of the market, although they are also available to your competitors.
- Secondary data provide a detailed understanding of what is currently known about markets—against which deeper insights can be compared.

IDENTIFYING CUSTOMER NEEDS—DATA ANALYSIS

For the volume of data collected (20 rep grid interviews; 20 contextual interviews; possibly a lead user strategic roadmap; and secondary data), an insight generation team of around 10 people will require three full days for an *Analysis Workshop*. Everyone who has been involved in insight generation should attend and a large dedicated workspace must be found.

Identifying customer needs involves qualitative data, and social scientists emphasize the importance of 'immersing yourself' in such data. By this they mean: taking enough time to get to know and understand the data; comparing and contrasting the results from different techniques; openly discussing and reflecting on the findings; and recognizing patterns in the data. We'll describe practical ways in which the insight generation team can immerse themselves in the data, to ensure deeper insights emerge. Remember, deeper insights mean that your team will be identifying customer needs that your competitors haven't identified. (Think: Competitive advantage!)

The Analysis Workshop should be organized by the innovation manager. However, a facilitator who's experienced in qualitative data analysis can really help drive the analysis to the point where deep insights and novel solutions emerge. During the first two days, the insight teams should concentrate on

TABLE 3-5: ANALYSIS WORKSHOP SCHEDULE AND CHECKLIST

DAY	TOPICS	TASKS	GROUP 1	GROUP 2	TIME
1	Rep grid analysis	☐ Prepare construct cards	✓		2 hours
		☐ Develop construct categories	✓		2 hours
		☐ Analyse construct categories	✓		1 hour
		☐ Analyse element ratings	✓		1 hour
	Ethno coding	☐ Video analysis (coding)		✓	8 hours
		☐ Video analysis (coding)	✓		2 hours
2	Ethno coding Lead user analysis Secondary data	☐ Video analysis (coding)	✓	✓	6 hours
		☐ Compare roadmaps	✓		1 hour
		☐ Identify key findings		✓	1 hour
	Problem definition	☐ Walk the Data Wall – I	✓	✓	½ hour
		☐ Problem(s) definitions	✓	✓	½ hour
3	Final problem definition	☐ Walk the Data Wall – II	✓	✓	1 hour
		☐ Final problem(s) definition	✓	✓	1 hour
	Develop solutions (innovation concepts)	☐ Walk the Data Wall – III Ideation: product, service and business model innovation / Kano Analysis	✓	✓	2 hours
		☐ Prototyping	✓	✓	3 hours
	Team meal with sponsor(s)	☐ Team show the sponsor(s) the Data Wall and celebrate with a team meal.	✓	✓	
		TOTAL WORKSHOP TIME	**24 HOURS**	**24 HOURS**	

customer problems and refrain from jumping to solutions. To ensure this, they should consciously avoid using the words 'product', 'service' and 'solution' for two days! Only when the problem definition is clear, on Day 3 of the workshop, should solutions be generated. The schedule of the *Analysis Workshop* has been carefully mapped out. It incorporates the main advantage of design thinking—the separation of problem definition from solution generation (see Diagram 3-2). It's also based on best practices identified by researchers in the field of creativity.

Table 3-5 shows the typical schedule for a 3-day workshop, based on our experience with many businesses. Analysis is time-consuming and eight *uninterrupted hours* are required each day, so an offsite location is preferable. The 10 or more people involved should be divided into groups of approximately 5, enabling some of the analysis to be conducted in parallel. On Day 1, Group 1 is assigned for six hours to rep grids and then two hours on ethno videos. In parallel, Group 2 is assigned to ethno video analysis for the whole day. As Group 1 will analyse the rep grids, it should include the people that conducted the interviews and it helps if the group includes representatives from different functional areas.

Day 2 continues with both groups working on ethno video analysis for six hours, followed by the analysis of lead user and secondary data. Across Group 1 and 2, over 20 hours are allocated to ethno video analysis; hard work but it enables all the videos to be analysed. In the afternoon of Day 2, the groups will be able to inspect the full findings and *Walk the Data Wall* (explained later in this chapter). Day 2 finishes with the first definition of the customer's main problem(s). Deliberately, this allows the groups to reflect overnight on the customer's main issues (that is, to 'sleep on it'), as creativity research has proven the value of such reflection.

Day 3 starts with walking the wall again and finalizing the problem(s) definition. Once this is clear, the whole insight generation team (consisting of the two groups) will be in a strong position to generate creative solutions to the customer's problems and build simple prototypes. An ideal end to Day 3 is for the senior sponsor to attend and be shown the results.

We now describe how to analyse the data from the three techniques, together with the secondary data.

ANALYSING REP GRID DATA

The analysis of rep grid data requires four steps:

- Preparation of *Construct Cards*.
- Creating *Construct Categories*.
- Analysing construct categories.
- Analysing *Element Ratings*.

Preparing Construct Cards

Across the 20 rep grid interviews, a total of between 140 and 200 different personal constructs will have been elicited. Construct cards are prepared using large postcard-sized cards. For example, the interview with Sarah elicited nine constructs and each of these must be written on a separate card. On each construct card is the construct, its pole and a relevant quote from the interview (a form for this is given in the Online Appendix). It's worthwhile for members of Group 1 of the insight generation team to prepare the construct cards by hand, as this is an opportunity to 'immerse' themselves in the data, requiring them to listen to the recordings and to extract quotes. It also exposes them to many constructs and will get them thinking about categories.

Diagram 3-8 shows the nine construct cards based on Sarah's interview (Interview #1) with the handwriting indicating Constructs #1 to #9. Compare Diagram 3-8 to Sarah's rep grid (Diagram 3-7) and you'll see the same nine constructs. Diagram 3-9 shows the eight construct cards for Interview #2. The card Interview #2 Construct #3 has been placed on the top of the pile for illustrative processes, and comparing this with Diagram 3-8, it can be seen that this construct is about taste and it can be placed in the same category as Sarah's Construct #1.

Creating Construct Categories

Once construct cards have been prepared for all of the interviews, it's time for Group 1 to sort them into categories. A large table, large Post-it® sticky notes and flipchart pens are needed. Each member of the group should take one set of construct cards (that is, one interview). Then, the person with the cards from Interview #1 should read them aloud. Each construct with its

DIAGRAM 3-8: CONSTRUCT CARDS FOR INTERVIEW #1
(WELL-BEING EXAMPLE)

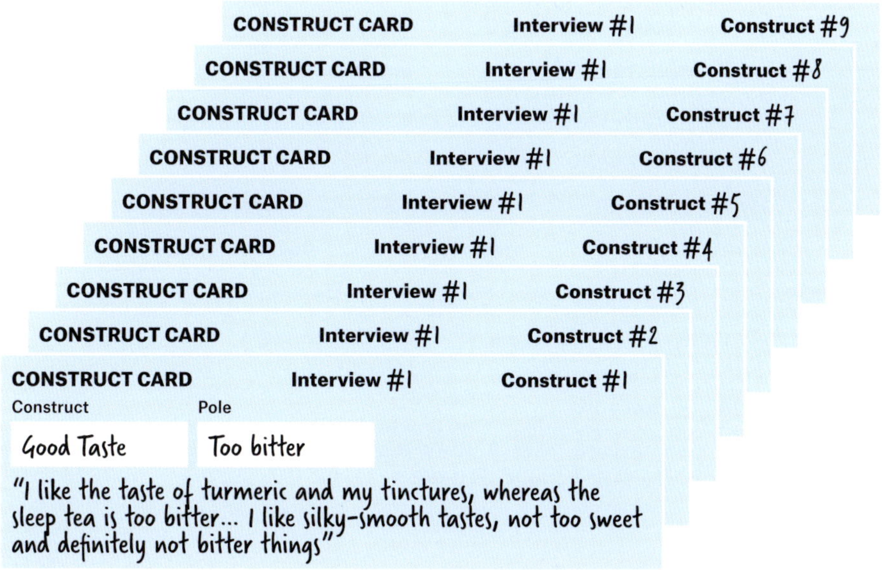

```
            CONSTRUCT CARD      Interview #1      Construct #9
          CONSTRUCT CARD      Interview #1      Construct #8
        CONSTRUCT CARD      Interview #1      Construct #7
      CONSTRUCT CARD      Interview #1      Construct #6
    CONSTRUCT CARD      Interview #1      Construct #5
  CONSTRUCT CARD      Interview #1      Construct #4
CONSTRUCT CARD      Interview #1      Construct #3
CONSTRUCT CARD      Interview #1      Construct #2
CONSTRUCT CARD      Interview #1      Construct #1
Construct       Pole

Good Taste      Too bitter
```

"I like the taste of turmeric and my tinctures, whereas the sleep tea is too bitter... I like silky-smooth tastes, not too sweet and definitely not bitter things"

associated quote should be read out, and then the cards should be placed in a row on the table. Once all of the constructs from Interview #1 have been placed on the table, other members of the group should compare their cards with those on the table. If anyone finds a similar construct, they should explain why they think that particular card should be put into a specific category. It's essential that only one person talks at a time during categorization. Otherwise, chaos ensues.

The process of deciding which construct cards should be grouped together will involve discussion, with the group looking for consensus. Don't forget to consider the quotes, in deciding the categories to which individual construct cards belong. Diagram 3-10 illustrates part of the process, where three categories have been formed. It shows that the first category is labelled *Taste* and it includes Sarah's Construct #1; Interviewee #2 Construct #3; and Interviewee #5 Construct #3. The category has 12 construct cards in total (that is, taste was mentioned by 12 interviewees). Similarly, the second category *Pure* includes construct cards from Sarah (Construct #2) and

DIAGRAM 3-9: CONSTRUCT CARDS FOR INTERVIEW #2
(WELL-BEING EXAMPLE)

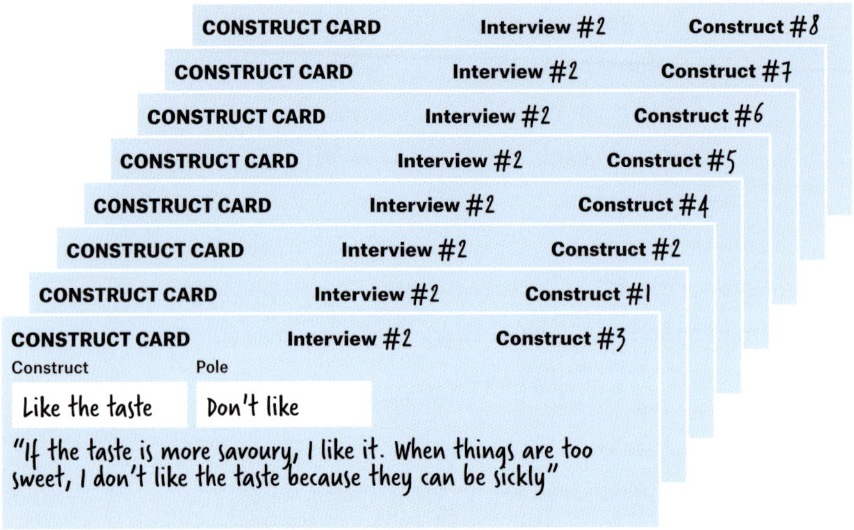

CONSTRUCT CARD	Interview #2	Construct #8
CONSTRUCT CARD	Interview #2	Construct #7
CONSTRUCT CARD	Interview #2	Construct #6
CONSTRUCT CARD	Interview #2	Construct #5
CONSTRUCT CARD	Interview #2	Construct #4
CONSTRUCT CARD	Interview #2	Construct #2
CONSTRUCT CARD	Interview #2	Construct #1
CONSTRUCT CARD	Interview #2	Construct #3

Construct / Pole

Like the taste / Don't like

"If the taste is more savoury, I like it. When things are too sweet, I don't like the taste because they can be sickly"

Interviewee #5, etc. and was mentioned 14 times. The third category was *Healthy* and was mentioned 6 times.

The process of creating construct categories is time-consuming but it gives the group a detailed understanding of customers' constructs, in other words their *mindset*—thoughts, feelings and decision-making about the outcomes they desire. Typically, 15–20 categories emerge, plus a 'Miscellaneous' category, demarcated to have less than 10% of the total number of construct cards. Some categories will contain 10–15 construct cards, others far less.

Analysing Construct Categories

Four questions guide the analysis of construct categories and the findings should be summarized on flipcharts (see Diagram 3-11). The first question is: *What are the most frequently mentioned categories and what does that tell us?* Typically, certain constructs categories will be found in 50% or more of the interviews. As shown on the left-hand flipchart, 22 categories were found and the three mentioned most were *Pure*, *Taste* and *Effective*. Market researchers often assume that anything that is mentioned frequently is important.

DIAGRAM 3-10: CREATING CONSTRUCT CATEGORIES
(WELL-BEING EXAMPLE)

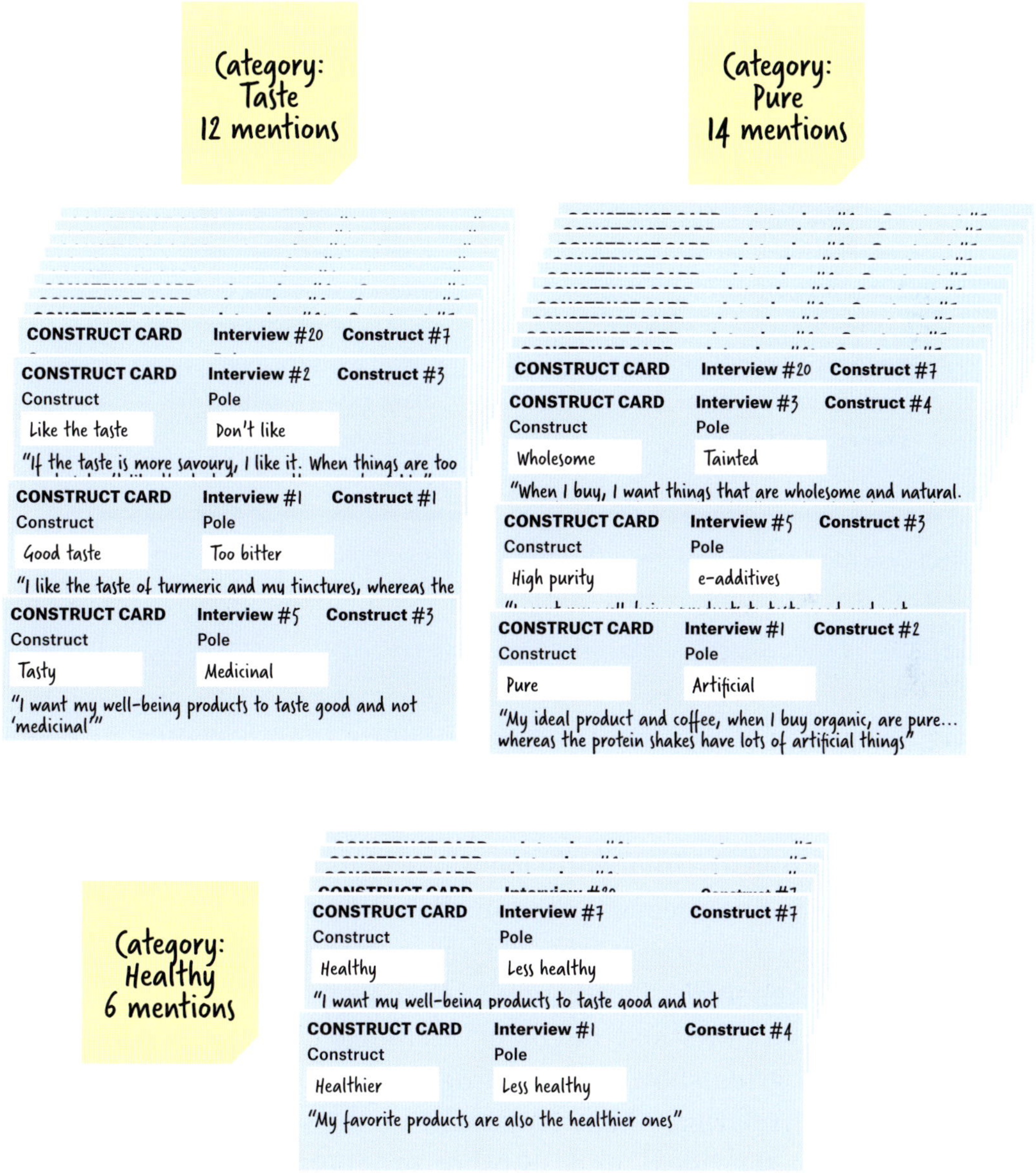

Category: Taste — 12 mentions

CONSTRUCT CARD — Interview #20 — Construct #7

CONSTRUCT CARD — Interview #2 — Construct #3
Construct: Like the taste
Pole: Don't like
"If the taste is more savoury, I like it. When things are too..."

CONSTRUCT CARD — Interview #1 — Construct #1
Construct: Good taste
Pole: Too bitter
"I like the taste of turmeric and my tinctures, whereas the..."

CONSTRUCT CARD — Interview #5 — Construct #3
Construct: Tasty
Pole: Medicinal
"I want my well-being products to taste good and not 'medicinal'"

Category: Pure — 14 mentions

CONSTRUCT CARD — Interview #20 — Construct #7

CONSTRUCT CARD — Interview #3 — Construct #4
Construct: Wholesome
Pole: Tainted
"When I buy, I want things that are wholesome and natural."

CONSTRUCT CARD — Interview #5 — Construct #3
Construct: High purity
Pole: e-additives

CONSTRUCT CARD — Interview #1 — Construct #2
Construct: Pure
Pole: Artificial
"My ideal product and coffee, when I buy organic, are pure... whereas the protein shakes have lots of artificial things"

Category: Healthy — 6 mentions

CONSTRUCT CARD — Interview #20 — Construct #7

CONSTRUCT CARD — Interview #7 — Construct #7
Construct: Healthy
Pole: Less healthy
"I want my well-being products to taste good and not..."

CONSTRUCT CARD — Interview #1 — Construct #4
Construct: Healthier
Pole: Less healthy
"My favorite products are also the healthier ones"

GENERATING DEEP INSIGHTS AND NOVEL SOLUTIONS

DIAGRAM 3-11: SUMMARY OF REP GRID RESULTS
(WELL-BEING EXAMPLE)[26]

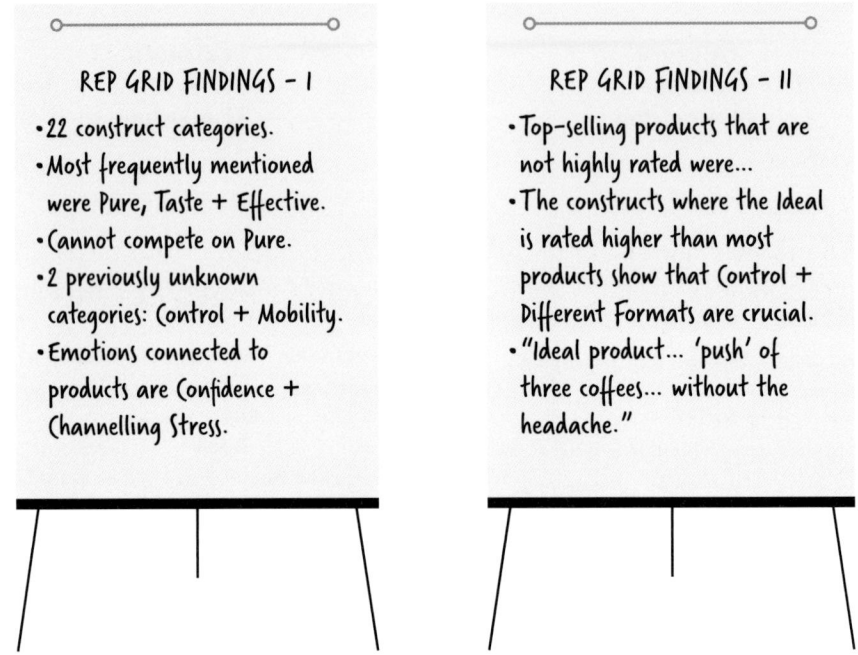

However, frequency of mention is a poor measure of importance, as people often mention things that are obvious but not that important.[25] This is where the time and energy invested in rep grid pays dividends, because RGT helps us identify things that are frequently mentioned but not salient.

This leads to the second question: *What do the ratings of the most frequently mentioned categories tell us?* To answer this, we look at the ratings in the individual rep grids. For example, *Pure* was found to be mentioned in 60% of the interviews and might be assumed to be crucial. However, inspecting the 14 grids showed the ratings given to the 'Ideal' and other products were all relatively high (typically, in the range '3' to '5'). What this means is that the 'Ideal' and all other products were perceived to be relatively pure, as they were all given high ratings. One interviewee even said *"I wouldn't even consider buying something that wasn't pure and so they all get good ratings"*. In other words, although interviewees mentioned pureness frequently, competing on pureness is not an option as customers consider it to be a basic, must-have factor.

The third question is: *What categories are new to us?* This identified two categories of construct not found in existing market research: *Control* and *Mobility*. The former was about how the effect of the well-being product could be managed (for example, in terms of how many hours it lasts, or the level of effect ["*boosting or relaxing*"]). *Mobility* was about how easy it was to carry the well-being with you and to "*have a shot on the move*". Both of these construct categories gave the insight generation team ideas for new solutions on Day 3.

The fourth question to ask is: *What emotions are associated with products?* Rep grid interviews often identify emotions associated with products, and interviewees exhibited high levels of emotion in relation to well-being products. For example, certain products made them "*feel good*" and interviewees said things like, "*I feel good being able to recommend specific products to my friends*".

Analysing Element Ratings

Two questions guide the analysis of the element ratings. The findings should, again, be summarized on flipcharts (see Diagram 3-11). The first question is: *How are top-selling products rated against the constructs?* Looking at the ratings in the individual grids identified several popular well-being products which were not perceived as 'ideal' on every construct. This showed constructs where improvements would be worthwhile.

The second question is: *Are there constructs where the Ideal product is highly rated but all the other products get low ratings?* Individual grids should be inspected, looking for where the Ideal product gets a high rating (that is, '5'), whereas the other products all get lower ratings (typically '3' to '1'). This shows where the Ideal would offer something that current products don't. Such insights can also be recognized from associated quotes. For example, Interviewee #15 said, "*My Ideal Product would have practical packaging so I can carry it with me. These other two products are not easy to take with you.*" Similarly, Interviewee #7 said: "*My Ideal product would give me the 'push' of three coffees when I am stressed at work but without the headache in the afternoon.*"

ANALYSING ETHNOGRAPHIC DATA

Contextual interviews help us understand how customers conduct key activities. Teams will collect approximately 20 hours of videos, and looking for insights in this volume of data is like looking for a 'needle in a haystack'. Therefore, the key to analysing video data is using a *Coding Scheme*.

Ethno Coding

Social scientists use coding to analyse qualitative data systematically. It defines the things to look for in the videos—a list of factors related to customer experience and product usage, in other words their entire customer journey. Table 3-6 gives a generic coding scheme with an explanation of the 12 factors (codes), based on our research.[27] The table includes columns for the times when codes are observed and notes on what was seen.

The first four codes are related to use behaviour. *Uses* prompts the identification of the many ways in which the customer wants to use a product or service. For example, customer videos might show that a vacuum cleaner is used for cleaning floors, carpets, curtains and mattresses. *Misuses* are ways a product is used that the manufacturer did not intend. For example, a user might attempt to vacuum clean a small amount of spilled liquid (although the manufacturer will prohibit this in their operating guide). *Workarounds* are the way in which customers deal with the limitations of current products. For example, women were observed mixing hair conditioner with stain remover, as they found this was less aggressive on delicate clothes. In B2B situations, equipment limitations are often 'solved' using duct tape. *Problems* are the parts of an activity where the customer struggles (and, if encountered regularly, these can lead customers to develop workarounds).

The code *processes* prompts us to determine how customers conduct their key activities, their jobs to be done. "By thoroughly mapping the job a customer is trying to get done, a company can discover opportunities for breakthrough products and services."[28] In a B2C situation such as doing the laundry, customers will have a distinct order in which they do things and so it helps to document their steps. In B2B situations, business processes are often documented (for example using flow diagrams) and it helps to ask for the formal documentation and then observe the process in practice.

The next two codes are *acquisition* and *triggers* for use. Acquisition is concerned with buying behaviour; how the customer acquired the product or service, including the decision-making unit that made the decision. There are normally specific reasons and times when products or services are employed and these are captured under triggers. For a vacuum cleaner the triggers for use could be the weekly clean, an extensive 'spring clean', and a spill. The recognition of the need for a quick way to clean up spills led to Black and Decker's hand-held Dustbuster vacuum cleaner.

Environment is the code that prompts the identification of interesting things in a customer's home environment, or in a B2B work area. This can be where a B2C customer stores their vacuum cleaner and the other cleaning tools they own. In a B2B context, it can be the measurement and test devices used by laboratory scientists in conjunction with an electron microscope. In online contexts, environment refers to the complete user experience (UX) from the device to web or app content and use flow including the specific look and layout (user interface or UI). Coding for environment is easier if the people who recorded the video were inquisitive and asked spontaneous questions whenever they saw something they didn't recognize (see Table 3-4, Item 7).

The last four codes in Table 3-6 are connected with more soft and emotional factors. For example, *emotions* can indicate frustration with current services and products and it can highlight poor user interfaces. *Humour* is a useful emotion to code for separately, as smiles and jokes can reveal customers' honest views on products, services and even themselves. Coding for emotions can even reveal people's underlying motivations. For example, the German domestic appliance company Miele found that parents of a child with a dust allergy felt guilty if they didn't clean their child's bedroom regularly, methodically and slowly. This led to the development of a vacuum cleaner with a dust-level indicator, showing parents when the dust level was low enough, reassuring them they were cleaning effectively and efficiently. Another important emotion (or feeling) is confidence, and scientists using equipment were found to worry whether they had conducted everything precisely, as the equipment gave no indication at certain steps in a complex procedure. This led to significant improvements in the UI; feedback to the

TABLE 3-6: GENERIC CODING SCHEME FOR ETHNOS[32]

	CODE	EXPLANATION	VIDEO #/ TIME	NOTES
1	USES	All of the different ways a product or service is used.		
2	MISUSES	Ways in which a product is used that were not intended by the manufacturer.		
3	WORKAROUNDS	Ways in which the limitations of a product are surmounted by the user through, for example, modifications of the product, or changes to working practices.		
4	PROBLEMS	Typical challenges, issues and problems encountered.		
5	PROCESSES	The process or workflow by which the user completes their task(s) using the product.		
6	ACQUISITION	When, how and why the product was acquired.		
7	TRIGGERS	Reasons for using the product at a particular time.		
8	ENVIRONMENT	The user's environment in which the product is used, including physical or virtual space and other related equipment.		
9	EMOTIONS	Emotions observed in using the product or service, including satisfaction, confidence, enthusiasm, hesitation, frustration, etc.		
10	HUMOUR	Smiles and jokes often give clues that customers are thinking something different from what they are saying.		
11	CONTRADICTIONS	Contradictions are when: customers do something different from what they've said; or where they gloss over problems.		
12	CULTURE	Culture: aspects about the 'culture', the characteristics of groups that use the product. How do customers organize themselves (informally)? What language do they use and what stories do they tell?		

user as each step is successfully completed. Overall, this led to much higher customer satisfaction.

The code *contradictions* is a powerful way to uncover hidden needs, but very few businesses know the approach. There are four types of contradictions to look out for: *disjunctures, gloss, generalizations* and *claims of idiosyncrasy*. Overall, contradictions surface where customers are not being open and honest about their real needs. If undetected, it can appear that customers are fully satisfied, when they are not. Disjunctures are when people say one thing but do something very different. For example, users often claim they follow the manufacturer's procedure, but they can be observed doing very different things. The next type of contradiction is where people gloss over things, to place themselves in a different (usually positive) light. Ethnographers are careful not to believe everything that they're told[29], and so it helps to check people's statements. For example, sport fishermen emphatically denied that the colour of products was important, when asked directly. However, observations showed that the majority of fishermen had chosen their equipment to have matching colours.[30] Similarly, mothers claimed their children always choose healthy options for breakfast, but very different eating habits were observed.[31] If you reflect on how you explain things to others, you'll recognize that you often add a certain amount of 'gloss'!

Generalizations are when people make claims like: *'This is quite easy…'*; or *'It didn't take long to learn…'*; or *'I always…'*; or *'Everyone knows…'*. Whenever people make such statements it's important to check whether what was seen in the video fits with the claim. In many B2B and B2C situations, we've had customers claim that a procedure is easy and when they're asked to demonstrate it, several difficulties can be observed. The final type of contradiction to look for in videos is claims of idiosyncrasy. Here people state that their behaviour is special or unusual, saying: *'I know this is unusual…'*, or *'No one else does it this way…'*; or *'This is really special'*, and so on. For example, in an investigation of logistics centres, individuals in different companies often claimed they had *'Unique needs, you won't see this anywhere else'*, but very similar problems were seen in other logistic centres.

The final code in Table 3-6, *culture*, reveals cultural factors about the way certain activities are conducted. Local styles and traditions often affect customer needs. For example, different countries often have different designs for hand tools; decorators' paintbrushes in Britain will have a rectangular cross-section, whereas in Germany they are circular. In B2C observations of families in London 'doing the washing', the time-honoured British tradition of the 'weekly wash' was found for parents with small children to have been superseded by daily washes. Religious beliefs can also affect the way people do things, such as the process of preparing food.

Several people are needed to code each video, as it's impossible for one person to look out for all 12 codes at the same time. Therefore, the codes should be assigned across the group, with each person responsible for a few codes. During an hour's video, multiple examples of some codes will be found. By identifying and listing every code, teams will understand key activities and discover the details of how customers use products and services. They'll gain insights into customer satisfaction (gains) and customer frustration (pains), which allow teams to generate a comprehensive and accurate understanding of the entire customer journey. As part of coding, team members should identify short excerpts from the videos that illustrate particular findings, in a concise and effective way. These will be crucial when presenting to management and colleagues who were not directly part of the research process. Clarks, a famous footwear brand, even created an intranet platform with video excerpts, so that R&D and marketing could regularly refer back to the data.

Ethnographic Insights

Codes are the means to generate deep insights. Diagram 3-12 shows how codes are noted on the left flipchart with notes (descriptive statistics on the number of times particular codes were seen can also be added). Discussing the codes leads to insights, as shown on the right flipchart. For example, across many well-being videos a workaround was that people had experimented (*"through mixing and matching"*) and put together their own *"Set of products that helps ME!"*, as no company on the market offered a suitable solution, particularly for positive stress management. Discussions also centred on the way that people loved recommending to their friends combinations that they had found helpful. Several video excerpts were found to illustrate these points, as were clips of the way people carried products with them *"on the move"*.

DIAGRAM 3-12: ETHNO FINDINGS AND CONCLUSIONS (WELL-BEING EXAMPLE)[33]

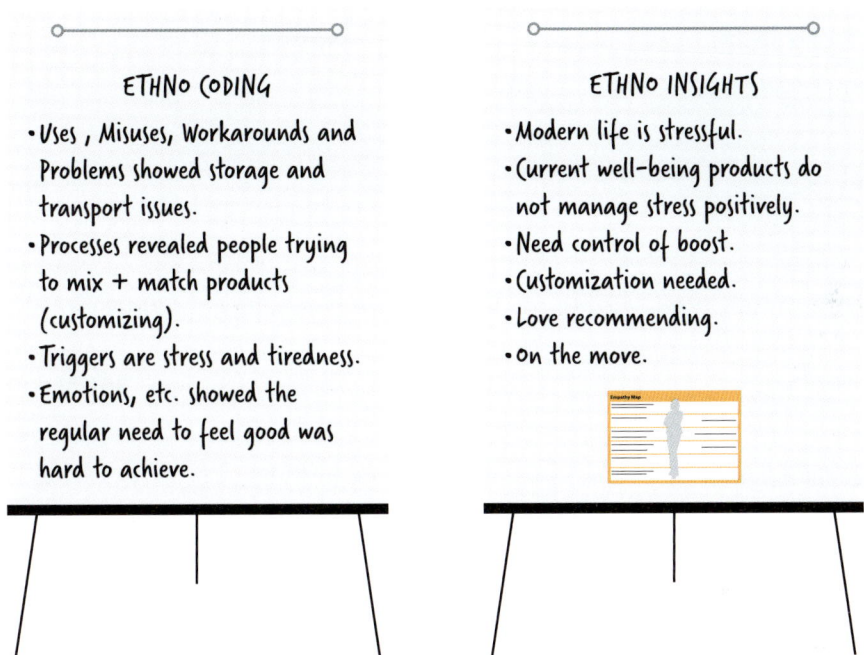

As different videos are coded, it's also useful to print screen shots of the people interviewed and consider the similarities and differences between them and their circumstances. This helps to develop what are called *personas*; fictional customers that typify a particular, needs-based customer segment. To do this, a tool from design thinking is useful. The *Empathy Map* shown in Diagram 3-13 builds directly on coding. It includes space for a typical biography and descriptions of what a customer says and thinks, their pain points, delights (gains), and so on, based on what was observed across similar videos. The value of empathy mapping is in revealing characteristics—especially customers' feelings—that have previously been overlooked and can help identify new customer segments. A word of caution: we often find managers completing empathy maps based only on their own views of what customers say, think, feel and need. Always engage the customer directly and use techniques to eliminate bias.

DIAGRAM 3-13: EMPATHY MAP BASED ON CODING[34]

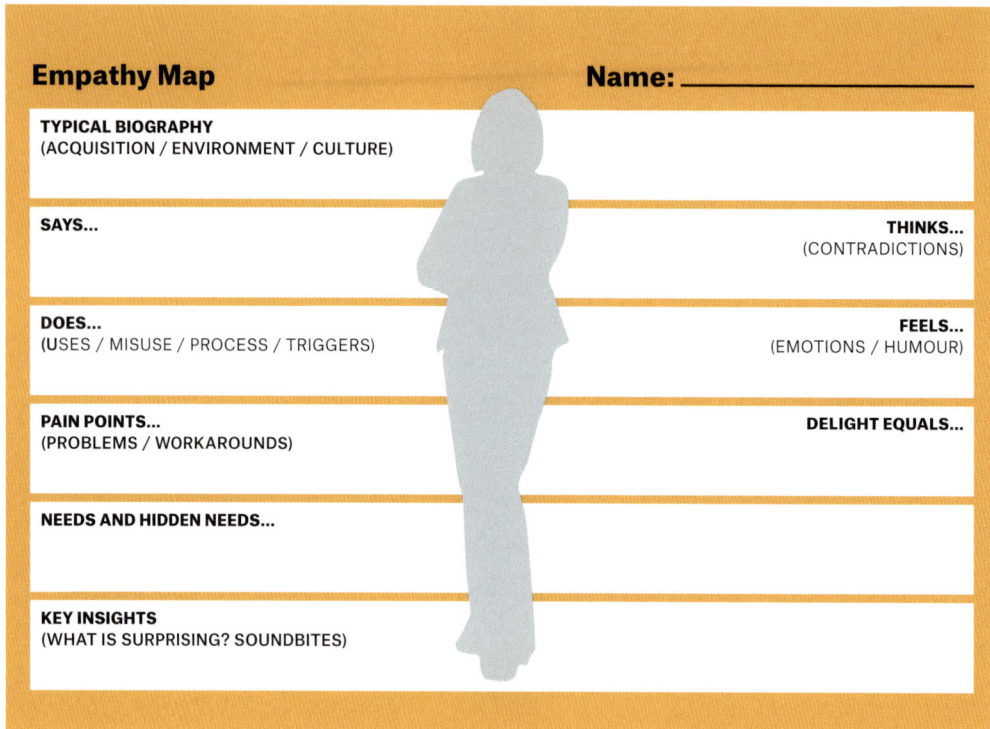

ANALYSING LEAD USER DATA

Lead user data are primarily collected using strategic roadmapping (see Diagram 1-7). As the strategic roadmap collects lead users' perceptions in a very structured way, the analysis is fairly straightforward. The strategic roadmap drawn with lead users should be compared with the one developed by the innovation leads, during innovation strategy development (as described in Phase 1, Shaping innovation strategy). There are four questions to ask to gain the maximum insights from the lead user data. First: *What trends have the lead users identified that were not identified internally?* Answering this question pinpoints issues that the senior team had not recognized, and Diagram 3-14 illustrates how the well-being lead user findings were summarized on flipcharts.

DIAGRAM 3-14: LEAD USER FINDINGS (WELL-BEING EXAMPLE)[35]

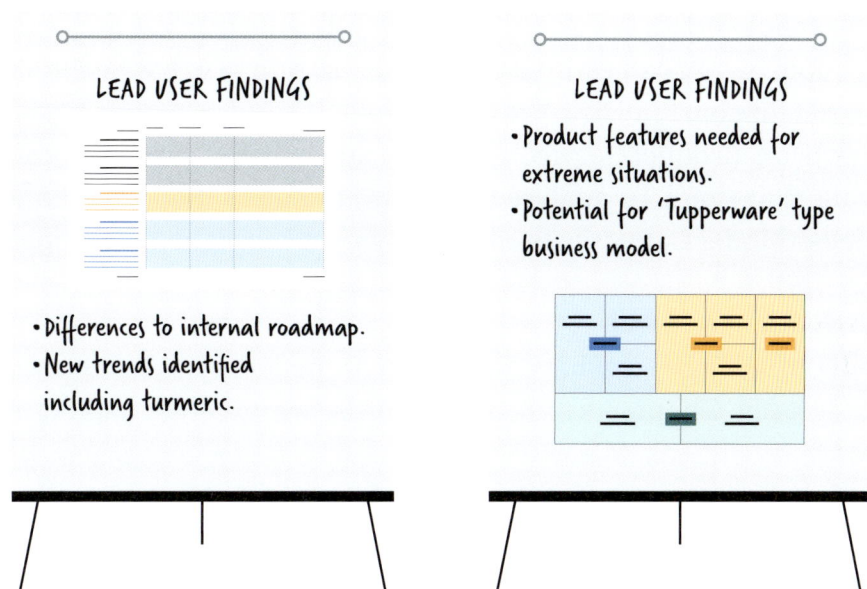

The second question used in analysing lead user data is: *What product, service and business model solutions are perceived as viable by lead users?* Discussions about lead users' ideas for future products and solutions (third swim-lane) can essentially be reserved for Day 3 of the *Analysis Workshop*, when solutions will be discussed. Similarly, lead users' views on the business models that will be important in the future can be very useful, as these are based on external views (that is, without internal bias). These can be collected on a business model canvas (see right-hand flipchart in Diagram 3-14).

The third question is: *How are products used in extreme situations?* Answering this question will generate ideas on which attributes are crucial and how lead users cope with challenging situations.

The fourth question is: *What can we learn from analogous users?* Answering this question can pinpoint ways in which analogous users work. These users come from different markets and situations but they face similar problems. Often, they bring new perspectives and solutions unthought-of in our markets. And creativity research has proven time and again the value of diverse perspectives in problem solving.

ANALYSING SECONDARY DATA

The analysis of secondary data is relatively easy, as it stems from structured reports. Secondary data are useful in determining market size and, comparing different reports, you can estimate the likely margin of error (as indicated on the left-hand flipchart in Diagram 3-15). Next, secondary data can give useful information on product/service features, advertising, pricing, positioning, and buying behaviour. To analyse the typical business models in an industry the Business Model Canvas is used, as shown on the right-hand flipchart.

CREATING A DATA WALL

Recall how, as humans, we have the ability to make new neural connections (see Mindsets in Chapter 2); in other words, we excel at making sense of

DIAGRAM 3-15: SECONDARY DATA FINDINGS

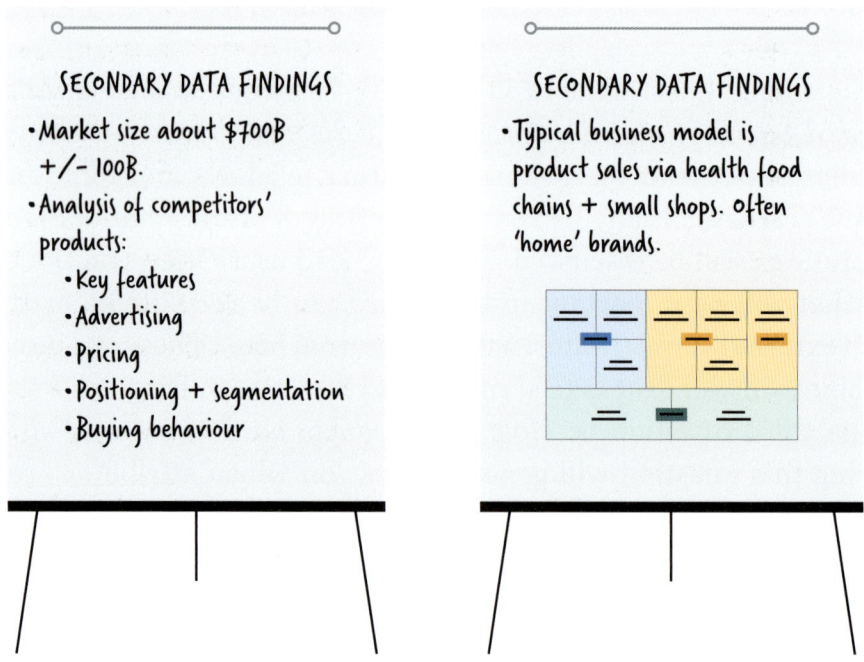

complex data. However, for this to happen the brain requires repeated exposure to the data, and time to reflect. Consequently, an effective way to contend with qualitative data is a *Data Wall* (Diagram 3-16). The results from rep grid, ethnography and lead user technique were all summarized on flipcharts hung on the walls of the conference room. This means that a comprehensive summary of the findings up until now will be visible to the whole insight team. Readers will see that the flipcharts on the data wall are those discussed in the previous sections on the analysis of individual techniques (see Diagram 3-16).

A data wall is the equivalent of the *incident board* that is used by detectives in murder investigations. Incident boards typically have photographs of the scene of crime; pictures of suspects; forensic reports; mobile phone reports; other evidence, etc. In TV shows we often see teams of detectives discussing 'the case', looking for links between clues on their incident board. Through repeated inspection of the board and discussion, detectives spot associations between the events connected with the crime, including things they previously overlooked. An incident board enables detectives to 'immerse' themselves in the evidence, which is analogous to our use of a data wall.

Walk the Data Wall

Once the data wall is created, team members can *Walk the Data Wall*, inspecting the results, asking specific questions, thinking about the answers, and discussing them. Diagram 3-16 illustrates how this complex, iterative process works; it shows that the conclusions from discussions are summarized on two flipcharts, shown at the front. The process of discussion within the team is supported by asking five questions:

- *How can the customers' main problem(s) be defined?*
- *What does triangulation tell us?*
- *What do we see that our competitors have not recognized?*
- *What hidden needs can be identified?*
- *Which new segments can we identify?*

DIAGRAM 3-16: WALK THE DATA WALL FOR PROBLEM DEFINITION (WELL-BEING EXAMPLE)

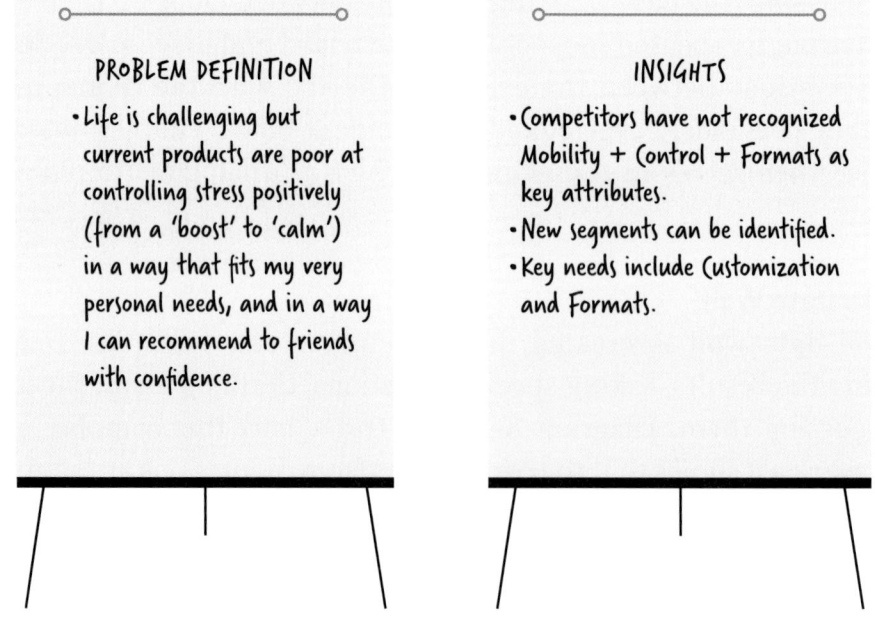

Answering the above questions forces the findings from the different techniques to be compared, and the secondary data to be considered. The *Walk the Data Wall* approach is a challenging but intriguing way for to the team to further 'immerse' themselves in the data and generate deep insights. As indicated in the *Analysis Workshop* schedule (Table 3-5), *Walk the Data*

Wall is conducted three times to ensure that that sufficient 'immersion' is achieved.

In the well-being project, the *Walk the Data Wall* approach was very effective in defining the problem (see left hand, front flipchart in Diagram 3-16). The findings from the rep grids showed the importance of factors such as *Mobility and Control* and showed existing products had significant limitations. The emotions identified showed that dealing with stress and relaxing were perceived as essential but difficult to achieve with today's products. It's important to compare the findings from the different techniques—this is called *triangulation* (the name comes from the way surveyors measure the height of a mountain from different directions). Comparing the results from the techniques allowed the team to confirm in the videos many of the things found in the rep grid data. For instance, in the videos people often showed their personal 'set' of well-being products, explaining how long they had taken to find which products went well together, in controlling stress positively. They also mentioned that they enjoyed swapping ideas with friends. So, lots of the points from the rep grid could be confirmed in the ethno findings. Similar confirmation was found in the results of lead user technique. In the comparison of ethno personas and current market segmentation, significant differences were found. (Later, this enabled a unique marketing strategy.)

CASE STUDY 3-3: BASF
WALKING THE VIRTUAL DATA WALL[36]

The *Walk the Data Wall* approach has been used to help more than 20 companies gain the deepest insights from their customer data. In all but one case, the data analysis process was conducted in conference rooms with the insight teams physically present. In 2021, Yannick Griveau, Head of Cereal Crop Systems at BASF, launched a project to collect data from visits to farms across Europe. Jennifer Rech, Crop Management, led the project and comprehensive data were collected in six countries.

DIAGRAM 3-17: WALKING THE VIRTUAL WALL AT BASF, WITH EMPATHY MAPS AND SUMMARY FLIPCHARTS

When the time came for data analysis, travel was restricted due to Covid-19 and so Jennifer could not arrange a physical meeting for several months. As an alternative and to avoid further delays, she came up with a very creative approach. This was to have teams from the six countries analyse their data in a 3D virtual environment called BASF Spaces. This allowed team members to adopt avatars, to move virtually between their designated meeting rooms, share data, and discuss findings with colleagues. This included more than 30 people walking a virtual data wall (see Diagram 3-17) and generating deep insights on agricultural markets. As Jennifer explains, *"We wanted to analyse our customer data in a systematic and creative way. This required the cross-functional teams from different countries to analyse their own data and then consolidate this into a European picture. Using BASF Spaces, we were able to build a virtual environment which not only made this process possible but also made it engaging and fun for our teams. The participants were just amazed at how much we could achieve virtually."*

The ground-breaking work of BASF shows that virtual conferencing systems will revolutionize data analysis in the future.

From a management perspective, Yannick was focused on the outputs of the process and how these could support business growth. He says, *"This project was an extremely valuable experience for everyone involved as it refreshed our view of customer needs. We confirmed some things we already knew but started to see things in a different light. For example, people often talk about the unique challenges farmers face in different countries. Through this work, we identified a core set of challenges that transcend national boundaries. Based on these, we're generating unique business ideas that will drive growth."*

CREATING NOVEL SOLUTIONS—IDEATION

We developed the *Walk the Data Wall* to create an effective way to analyse data within time and resource constraints. The approach develops a clear problem(s) definition(s), which gives a solid platform from which the insight generation team can develop novel innovative solutions. With a clear problem definition, it's surprising how quickly a team can come up with multiple, novel solutions. As Einstein said, "If I had an hour to solve a problem, I'd spend 55 minutes thinking about the problem and five minutes thinking about solutions." This indicates how the investment in time and effort to understand the customers' problems pays dividends.

To support the team's creativity, we recommend brainwriting so that many diverse ideas are generated. And, at this point in the *Analysis Workshop*, the team are again allowed to use the words 'product', 'service' and 'solution' and their creativity in linking problems to solutions is crucial. Certain individuals in the team will have technical expertise that can enable them to be creative in the solutions they generate. Case Study 3-4 gives an example where recognizing customer needs combined with creative use of technical expertise paid dividends.

CASE STUDY 3-4: SKINOURISHMENT CLIMB ON AND ON AND ON![37]

Who on earth came up with the idea? A skin-care product specifically for people with 'challenged skin' brought on by harsh environments? Who on earth would want the product? And would the market even be big enough to be interesting?

The name of Tommy Caldwell has been known in climbing circles for years but it was his free ascent of The Dawn Wall on Yosemite's El Capitan that has made him a household name in the US. Even Barack Obama played tribute to his climb, which included rock climbing at a grade of 5.14c. (For non-climbers, a grading of 5.14c signifies climbing that is RIDICULOUSLY HARD.) At the end of his climb, Tommy gave an interesting product testimonial: *"Out of the hundreds of pounds of gear it took to climb The Dawn Wall, the most crucial was my 1oz. tin of climbOn."* The *SKINourishment* company's product climbOn contains esoteric-sounding ingredients mixed into a paste that helped Tommy protect his hands from the extreme wear and tear of 19 days' rock climbing, on the vertical granite of Yosemite.

The climbOn product is the brainchild of American Polly Glasse. Her approach to innovation demonstrates the importance of a specific aspect of creative thinking. Psychology researchers have found that creative breakthroughs ('aha' or 'eureka' moments) do not happen spontaneously but occur when an expert with a deep knowledge of their field learns a new fact, or gains a new insight. Polly grew up on an organic farm and her deep expertise of natural ingredients comes from a lifelong interest in nature, eastern medicine, aromatherapy, herbal ingredients and their therapeutic value. However, she is not just an expert. She supplements her expertise with an unusual flair for identifying customer needs and potential markets that others would miss.

Polly had a successful career and ran her own medical transcription company. However, after an accident where the family home burnt to the ground, Polly decided the time was right to make her hobby into a new career. She focused first on all purpose skin-care: *"I was inspired by our skin. It is our largest organ and some people use up to 12 products daily, containing around 168 different ingredients, including numerous synthetic ones."* Talking to people, Polly knew that many had concerns about synthetic ingredients in products used daily. So, she took to her (new) kitchen to blend ingredients into unique, ultra-natural products. The brand *Ivy's Herbal Delights* was launched in 1995 and word-of-mouth quickly led its first product—a face creme—to be in high demand and soon Polly was supplying local hotels and retailers. The 'it is pure and natural (and absolutely nothing synthetic)' skin creme quickly established a loyal following. (Tellingly, the company website also tells you the ingredients that their products will never include.) And on from this?

From skin cremes came other products such as body care, and hands and feet. Describing how she invents products Polly says: *"In everything I formulate I am thinking about the emotional-mental-aspect as well as the physical aspect of customers. For example, in choosing essential oils, I might look for anti-bacterial properties but I will also be looking for ingredients with calming properties. Choosing the right ingredients is a complex process, based on the many things I have studied over the years. But...* [she pauses], *at the same time, the process is very simple—ingredients need to be synergistic and the right combinations just seem to fall into place."* And on from this?

From all-purpose skin-care came products for rock-climbers. Again, these came from Polly's discerning of customer needs. Meeting climbers who complained about trashed hands led to climbOn paste. Another problem that rock-climbers complain about is muscle strain. The product for this is RIDICULOUS! Paste, which has a reassuring aroma and a warming, soothing effect. The list of ingredients reads like a Latin dictionary, including: Shorea stenoptera butter, Butryospermum parkii, Nippohae rahnoides and Zingiberaceae. The *climbOn!* range of products, with their Dawn Wall graphics and sustainable packaging, have attracted a cult following among climbers, and created a completely new market (with significant sales). And on from this?

With her new brand *Polyn* ('skin care for body + mind + soul'), Polly has added further target markets to the business. This includes baby care products, skin nourishing and more, all based on organic ingredients made in Texas. As Polly says: *"Most of our top-selling products were derived for a person who had a need not met by traditional products. Our customers inspire me and it inspires me when I can match their needs to the right ingredients."* And on from this? Polly is sure to go on inventing new products and creating new markets. And On and ON!

Brainwriting

At this point in ideation, the insight generation team members should individually *Walk the Data Wall* for a third time, focusing on three questions (see Diagram 3-19), to generate ideas that solve the defined customer problem(s). Each idea should be written on single post-its using brainwriting techniques (see Phase 1). Ideas can then be discussed, with the best ones enhanced and potentially combined. In addition, the market viability of ideas should be checked, using the *Kano Model.*

Kano Analysis

The Japanese quality movement had a big influence in putting the voice of the customer at the centre of innovation. A VOC tool was developed by Noriaki Kano (Diagram 3-18).[38] The horizontal axis is the *Degree of Implementation* of a feature (the time and effort that's been invested in making the features effective). The vertical axis is *customer satisfaction*. Kano identified three categories of product (or service) features and the influence they have on customer satisfaction:[39]

1. *Performance Features.* These are the easiest Kano category to understand; the features that increase customer satisfaction as their degree of implementation is increased. These are the features that customers talk about most. For example, megapixels, the resolution of a camera, is widely discussed and mobile phone companies have improved this feature dramatically in recent years. The performance

features curve shows that every improvement in implementation leads to an increase in customer satisfaction.
2. *Basic Features.* These are features that a product or service 'must have'; without them the offering will be unacceptable to customers (in marketing, these are called *hygiene features*.) For the well-being product, pureness was recognized as a 'must-have' feature. Viewing the basic features curve shows that a certain level of implementation is essential, otherwise customers will not buy. However, the curve reaches a plateau, indicating that further increases in the degree of feature implementation do not lead to increased customer satisfaction.
3. *Excitement Features.* These features are new to the market and immediately lead to customer satisfaction. They bring unexpected value but customers are unlikely to ask for them, as they are related to hidden needs. A recent example of an excitement feature is the iPhone Portrait function that the background of photographs can be blurred, mimicking the 'depth of focus' advantage of professional cameras.

DIAGRAM 3-18: KANO MODEL OF PRODUCT (OR SERVICE) FEATURES

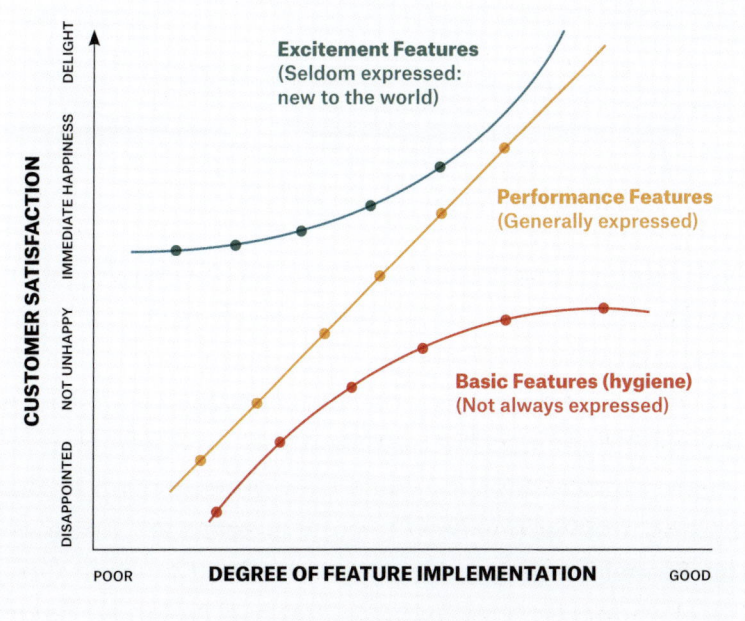

DIAGRAM 3-19: WALK THE DATA WALL FOR SOLUTION GENERATION (WELL-BEING EXAMPLE)

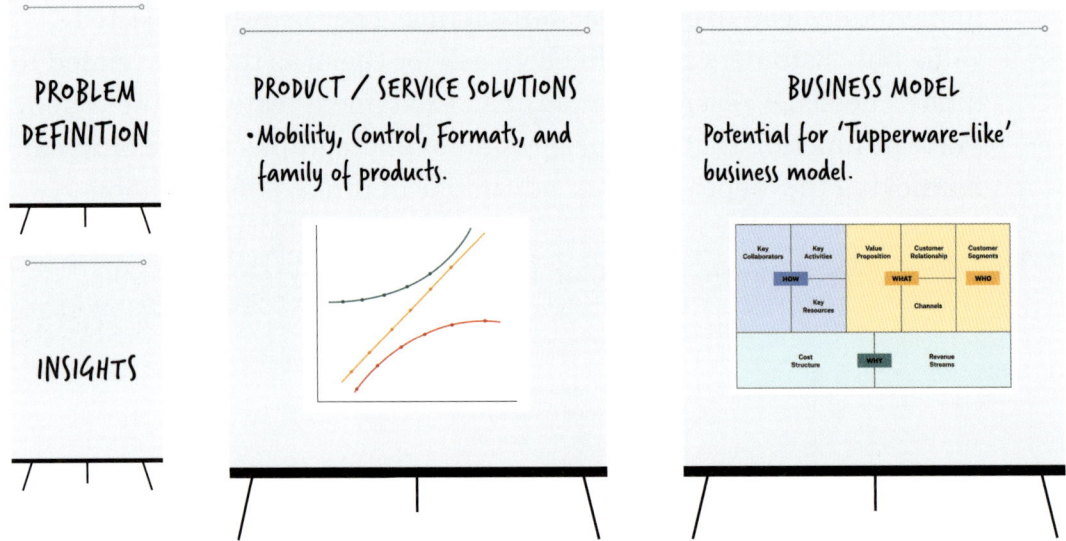

The Kano Model is excellent for comparing the insight generation team's ideas against competitors' existing products/services. A good rule of thumb is that a proposed innovation should provide one or two excitement features; it should exceed the performance of competitors on all the performance features; and it should include the basic features. In dynamic markets, excitement features are quickly copied and so they quickly drop to the next curve. Therefore, making innovations hard to copy is essential. Readers should note that the Kano Model covers much of the thinking of Blue Ocean Strategy, which identifies product/service features that can no longer be differentiated, or can be accentuated (made into excitement), as part of an innovative value At this point, teams should also consider the business model; for example, a Tupperware-like business model was perceived as relevant to well-being.

OUTPUT OF ANALYSIS WORKSHOP

Diagram 3-19 shows how on Day 3 of the *Analysis Workshop*, the insight generation team's ideas will have summarized the overall findings on four flipcharts: *Problem Definition*; and related *Insights*; *Product/Service Solutions*; and *Business Model* ideas. These flipcharts provide the majority of the information necessary to define innovation projects and can be used for the presentations to senior management in Phase 4, Selecting projects for implementation..

As the *Analysis Workshop* draws to a close, your team will have developed a deep market understanding and will have generated initial novel solutions. After all their hard work, a fitting finish is for the senior sponsor to be taken through the results and the findings, followed by a team meal. The sponsor's presence will motivate the insight generation team and can also give them an indication of the way members of the senior management team will react to their findings. The five outputs of the *Analysis Workshop* are:

1. A deep understanding of customer needs.
2. Creative product, service and business model solutions.
3. An appreciation of expected buying behaviour.
4. An estimate of market size.
5. A clear grasp of competitors.

MINDSET MATTERS

The people involved in Phase 3 are the insight generation teams, the innovation manager, senior sponsors, and, potentially, specialists (for example experts in hidden needs techniques). It's important to understand how these groups think, feel and behave during this challenging phase. Generating deep customer insights is an essential part of your innovation journey but it will, by its nature, arouse feelings of uncertainty and ambiguity. However, with the right mindset, training and management support, Phase 3 can also be one of the most exciting parts of the innovation journey. For example, many of the employees involved in Mölnlycke Health Care's scouting teams (which we call insight generation teams) spontaneously enthused that it was the most gratifying experience in their professional careers to date (see Case Study 5-1). Employees at Bank of Ireland (Case Study 2-3) had similar views.

At the beginning of Phase 3, the insight generation teams will feel apprehensive as they're tasked with developing previously unknown insights and novel solutions. Plus, they have lots new techniques to learn and apply for the first time (and this can make your brain hurt!). However, these are all normal feelings and a bit of adrenaline boosts individual performance! Later, when team members have made several customer visits, it becomes easier but never routine.

For Phase 3 to work, the innovation manager has a lot to organize. They must ensure the insight generation team is competent in the techniques; that enough time is allowed so that the data collection is finished on time; and they must arrange the *Analysis Workshop*.

Each insight generation team will have a senior sponsor, who must be directly involved. When senior managers participate in customer data collection, it not only reinforces the importance of this work to the team but also helps senior managers to interact with their customers on a whole new level. In *Walk the Wall* sessions, senior managers always tell us they've seen things for the first time or, where they had hunches in the past, things have now become much clearer.

Finally, the senior team should be aware that Phase 3 is an important opportunity to mould the culture of the business. Customer-centricity is an espoused value in most companies (see both Case Study 2-3 on Bank of Ireland and Innovation Values Map Diagram 2-4). This is not surprising as truly understanding customer needs and meeting them is the essence of a great business. Learning and applying the tools and techniques provided in Phase 3 will go a long way to make customer-centricity a truly lived organizational value. As the insight generation team members are drawn from the different functions of the business, their enthusiasm and knowledge of customer needs will spread and further embed business-wide innovation in your organization.

SUMMARY

- The history of market research shows that sophisticated techniques are essential to generate deep customer insights as the basis for novel solutions.
- Three systematic techniques, in combination, are effective at identifying customers' hidden needs. These are rep grid technique, ethnography, and lead user workshops. These techniques can be used by the insight generation team to collect valuable field (customer) data.
- Secondary data are also a useful source of market insights.
- A three-day *Analysis Workshop* is needed to analyse the data collected. This uses ideas from design thinking and creativity research to ensure that deep insights are generated.
- The workshop will generate: a deep understanding of customer needs; novel product, service propositions and business model solutions; an appreciation of expected buying behaviour; a good estimation of market size; and a clear grasp of competitors.
- Now, the insight generation teams are ready to present their ideas in Phase 4 portfolio management meetings.

Phase 4
Selecting projects for implementation

Selecting projects for implementation

INTRODUCTION

At this point on your innovation journey, the insight generation teams will have conducted a deep analysis of several *Innovation Strategic Options* (ISOs). These market investigations will have generated customer insights and, based on these, the insight teams will have prepared proposals for *innovation projects*. Their proposals must now be assessed by senior management. The number of proposals will need to be reduced, in order to achieve a good match with the resources available. In essence, Phase 4 involves the insight teams presenting their ideas and management making carefully weighed decisions on which projects to back. It's therefore the bridge between insight generation and getting innovation projects to market (Diagram 4-1).

DIAGRAM 4-1: PHASE 4 IN THE INNOVATION JOURNEY

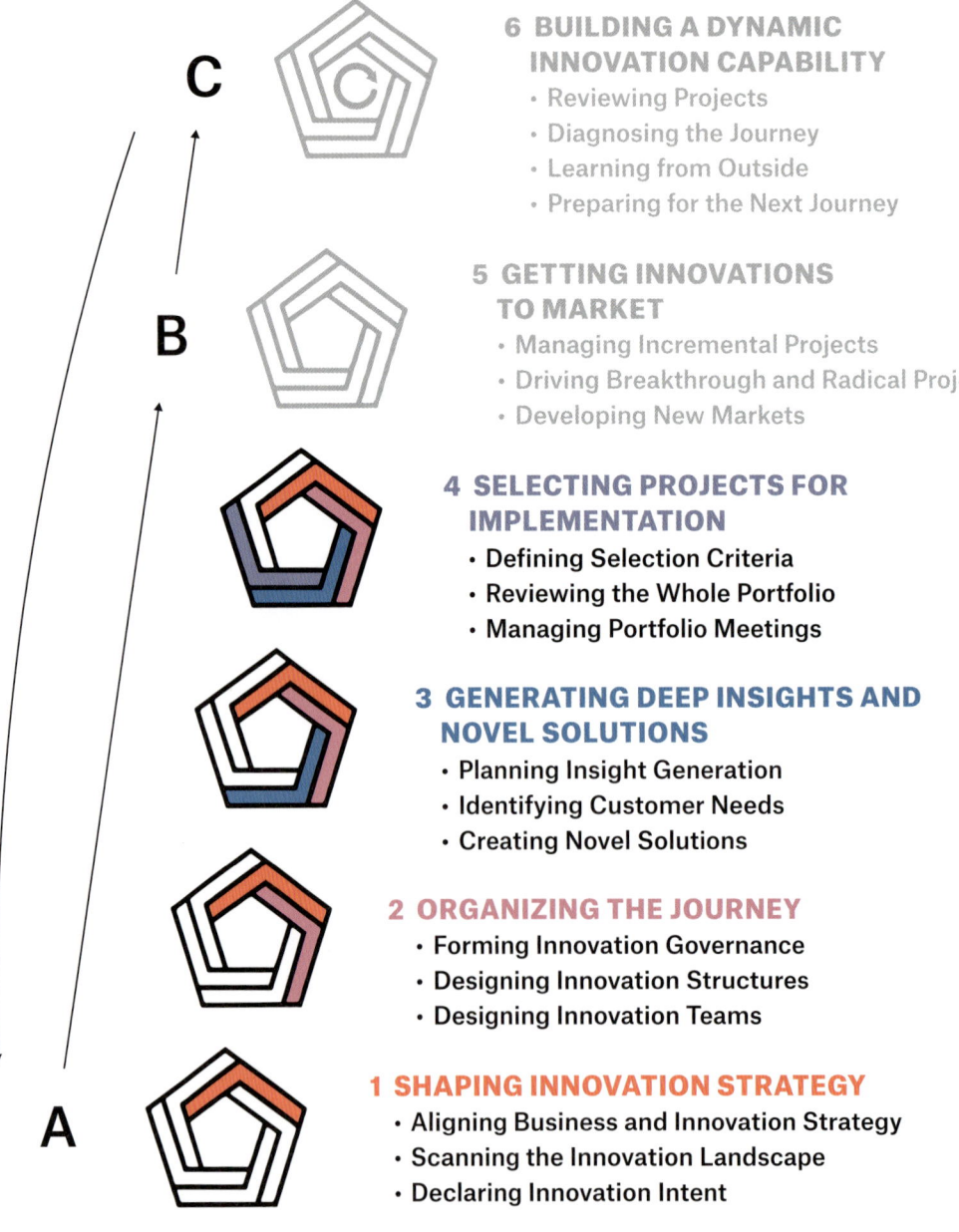

Selecting the projects to implement and deciding which ones to drop is called *Innovation Portfolio Management*. The decisions taken determine whether or not your innovation strategy will be successful. Some of the projects being considered will be incremental and some will be more radical innovations, and you have to achieve an appropriate balance between these categories of innovation. It's crucial that you use a systematic approach to select projects, otherwise the process will be prone to negative bias.

Table 4-1 summarizes the key themes covered in this chapter (Phase 4). It can be seen that there are three actions (or steps) to take: define selection criteria; review the whole portfolio; and manage portfolio meetings including decision-making and communications. Businesses that already have a portfolio management process should take the opportunity to compare their current approach against the methods discussed here.

In many businesses, project selection is based solely on financial calculations. However, these calculations are only appropriate for incremental projects and projects in their later stages. Therefore, we present not only financial selection methods but also *Strategic scoring* (based on management's perceptions of potential projects).

The main people involved in Phase 4 are the insight generation teams, who present their proposals, the senior management team who make the decisions, and the manager designated to chair portfolio management meetings and record the decisions. The chair's role is a challenging one and it strongly influences innovation strategy. Therefore, the senior team should assign their innovation manager or another of their best people to the task. A finance manager with experience of marketing can, for example, be an excellent choice. Once assigned, this manager must take responsibility for all of the issues raised in this chapter.

Portfolio management is laden with mindset matters. Certain managers may have a bias towards particular projects, which they think are important for favourite customers. Managers may also hope to identify 'big winners', forgetting that business successes such as Nespresso didn't emerge overnight. Another mindset matter is that the senior team might stick within its comfort zone and 'kill' all radical ideas. At its worst in large corporates, portfolio management is riddled with organizational politics and decisions based on gut

TABLE 4-1: PHASE 4—KEY THEMES AND CHECKLIST

THEMES	DETAILS
Actions to take	☐ Define selection process ☐ Review the whole portfolio ☐ Manage portfolio meetings— decide and communicate
Tools and concepts	☐ Financial tools for selecting projects ☐ Strategic scoring
People responsible	☐ Insight generation teams ☐ Senior management team ☐ Portfolio management meeting chair ☐ Innovation manager
Mindset matters	☐ Biased decision-making due to blinkered information ☐ The senior team being too conservative ☐ Political gaming and a reliance on intuition ('gut feelings') ☐ Portfolio management becomes a 'dry', numbers process
Outputs	☐ An effective process for evaluating innovation projects ☐ A balanced set of innovation projects has been selected ☐ Appropriate resources are allocated to the chosen projects

feelings. Research has found that "an over-reliance on subjective opinion and the absence of mechanisms to generate more evidence-based inputs… [leads] to inappropriate portfolio decisions".[1] Hopefully, mid-sized businesses (MSBs) and strategic business units (SBUs) will not suffer the same level of politics, but defining a set of objective criteria is still essential.

When insight generation teams' ideas are rejected, it needs to be done in a way that doesn't demotivate them. Here, clear criteria make decisions more transparent. The final mindset issue is that portfolio management meetings can be very 'dry', based only on financials and abstract discussions of projects. Here the designated chair needs to create an appropriate atmosphere in the meetings. A feeling of diligence is essential (as these are strategic decisions), combined with a degree of edginess (as wrong portfolio decisions can be costly).

Portfolio management meetings should be invigorating (to understand how, see Case Study 4-1 on Richardson Sheffield).

There are three essential outputs of this phase: an effective portfolio management process has been applied (and which can be used repeatedly); a balanced set of innovation projects has been selected; and sufficient time and resources have been allocated to these projects.

CASE STUDY 4-1: RICHARDSON SHEFFIELD CUTTING-EDGE PORTFOLIO MANAGEMENT[2]

Based in Sheffield in the UK, Richardson's Knives design and manufacture high-quality kitchen knives. The company is part of the Dutch Amefa Group and is famous for its luxury products that carry a 30-year guarantee. Early on, the company learnt the importance of not only making portfolio decisions transparent but also making portfolio management meetings motivational for all concerned.

Initially the company had a typical approach to portfolio management. Small teams of marketing and engineering people were tasked to develop new product ideas, based on market needs. Every six months the different teams were required to write a 10-page business case, describing their ideas. The senior management team would read the business cases (or, frequently, only the executive summaries) and, in a 'behind closed doors' meeting, choose the 1–2 ideas they considered most promising. Teams received minimum feedback on why certain ideas were selected, whereas others were rejected. Richardson's R&D Manager, David Williams, realized that this didn't motivate anyone involved (and even the teams whose projects were selected lamented that they didn't really know why their ideas were chosen). Consequently, he got the senior team's backing for him to re-design the process. In the new process, teams were again tasked with developing market-oriented ideas. However, instead of full business cases, each team writes a 1–2-page executive summary and prepares a 'exhibition stand' with a prototype of their idea and graphics on the market opportunity, market size, etc. A large conference room is reserved for the different teams to set up their displays, creating the atmosphere of an industrial fair. Then, having read the executive summaries, management spends a couple of hours walking round the different teams' displays, talking to the teams, making notes and getting a clear understanding of each proposal. Next, the senior team holds a meeting to make its selection decisions and, on the same day, announces and explains them to the teams.

The company is convinced that since changing its innovation portfolio management from closed meetings to a transparent process, with interaction between the teams and management, it's making more effective portfolio decisions. Even the teams whose ideas are rejected now understand why, and so take it as a challenge to develop even better ideas next time. In addition, David Williams's senior colleagues have said that the new process has made them recognize the importance of having skilled and motivated teams to take the best ideas to market.

ESSENTIAL BACKGROUND

Portfolio management should be objective and transparent. Before we describe the key steps towards this, it is important to understand the aims of innovation portfolio management; why weak portfolio management stifles business performance; and how biases harm decision-making.

AIMS OF PORTFOLIO MANAGEMENT

There are four aims of portfolio management,[3] which should become a mantra during all portfolio discussions:

1. To ensure that each and every innovation project selected will achieve a good return for your business. Whenever two similar projects are considered, the one that offers the best opportunities should be chosen.
2. To ensure that the range of projects chosen matches your innovation intent (commercial, category and capability goals). It's surprising how

many organizations fail to choose the right set of projects to match their strategic goals.
3. To achieve category balance—meaning a suitable mix of incremental (black-space), breakthrough (grey-space) and radical (white-space) projects. A balance between short-term and long-term projects is also recommended.
4. To build capability, through transparency and learning mechanisms within the portfolio management process.

IMPACT OF INEFFECTIVE PORTFOLIO MANAGEMENT

A business without an effective portfolio management process will suffer from slow decision-making; poor projects not being terminated ('killed'); too many projects in the pipeline; and a glut of incremental projects.[4] Without transparent criteria and checks on decision-making, decisions such as whether to terminate a project will tend to be postponed. This wastes resources (and capabilities), and this will frustrate innovation teams, who know that a management 'sword' is hanging over their project. Some managers think that introducing more projects into the pipeline increases the pressure on teams and thus increases project output. This thinking is flawed; having too many projects causes substantial delays at the bottlenecks. Cramming more projects into the development funnel doesn't increase output. Remember, 'less is more' in portfolio management.

BIAS IN PORTFOLIO MANAGEMENT

Choosing projects in an objective fashion is difficult because humans in general, and specifically managers, are susceptible to biased mindsets. We are just not as rational as we like to think![5] This recognition has led to the field of *Behavioural Economics*.[6] Bias affects both the way we gather the information on which we base our decisions and also the way we make those decisions.[7]

Biases in gathering information
Portfolio management decisions need to be based on comprehensive, unbiased information.[8] However, in collecting information we're subject to: *confirmation bias, salient information bias* and *information avoidance bias*.

People tend to focus on information that supports their view, and this is called confirmation bias. The danger in portfolio management is that the arguments in favour of a particular project might be built on confirmatory evidence with no consideration of—or even a blindness to—*contradictory evidence*.

Salient information bias takes place when vivid information presented by engaging or charismatic presenters tends to be weighed more heavily than, for example, statistical information. In portfolio management, this can mean that managers are swayed by emotions stirred by a good 'marketing story' when they should be looking for a convincing argument backed by substantial, objective evidence.

Information avoidance is avoiding talking about new and complex issues because such learning is painful. In portfolio management, this could mean that an insight generation team avoids engaging with new technologies required to succeed in new markets. Or it could mean that a team that's struggling, glosses over technical feasibility issues by stressing 'massive' market potential.

Bias during decision-making

Bias also influences the way decisions are made. Here, there are six main biases: *conservatism, the law of small numbers, anchoring, procrastination, sunk costs fallacy* and *inconsistency*.

Conservatism is people's inbuilt bias towards their existing views and beliefs when they receive new information. Managers feel more confident making decisions in their comfort zone (and typically, therefore, concerning incremental innovations). In innovation projects, conservatism can lead managers to avoid new information (the outside view) that contradicts their current view of the market (the inside view).

Another problem is that people tend to consider small samples to be representative of the populations from which they are drawn—this is the law of small numbers. In portfolio management, this could mean that a small number of qualitative interviews are claimed to be representative of the whole consumer market. (Note, in Chapter 3 it was pointed out that insight generation teams should gain deep insights from small groups but then check them with larger samples, as necessary.)

Anchoring bias is the inclination to be influenced by numbers that are not appropriate. One example is when a manager, having been presented with information such as a market size figure, uses that number as the starting point for all subsequent discussions. In portfolio management, this can mean that next year's sales forecast is based too strongly on this year's results (and, for example, does not take account of competitors' moves, which will reduce your market share). So, you need to watch out for anchoring bias.

Procrastination is the tendency to delay decisions, particularly difficult ones. In portfolio management, the classic mistake is to keep postponing the termination of a poorly performing project, hoping that things will improve (as the expression says: 'throwing good money after bad'). Related to procrastination is the *sunk costs fallacy,* where people continue investing in something that isn't working, as they've already invested a lot in a project. Investments should be assessed looking forward rather than backwards.

Portfolio decisions can be subject to inconsistency, where different judgements are made in very similar situations. Inconsistency will arise when the chair of portfolio management meetings makes no record of *how* decisions were reached. Without such records, the senior team won't be able to learn from past decisions. Research shows learning is essential to good portfolio management.

With *nine* types of bias identified, it should be absolutely clear that ad hoc decisions based on managers' intuition will be poor portfolio decisions—and consequently poor strategic decisions. However, if you understand bias, you can take actions to avoid its negative influence in portfolio management meetings. Later, when we discuss how to run portfolio management meetings, we'll provide a set of 'bias-busting' questions to apply.

DEFINING SELECTION CRITERIA

The first step in designing a reliable portfolio management process is understanding the right selection criteria for different categories of innovation. Large corporations often develop complex sets of criteria and even run portfolio simulations. Such approaches are less relevant in MSBs and SBUs and so, throughout the following discussion, the emphasis will be on practicality and simplicity.

TYPES OF CRITERIA

Most businesses rely solely on their accountant's analysis in making portfolio decisions. Accountants focus on calculations such as *Net Present Value* (NPV) and *Return on Investment* (ROI). NPV looks at the duration of a project and considers costs and returns over coming years. An investment that will be needed in the future is 'discounted' down as it isn't as 'costly' as an investment needed today. Similarly, NPV considers income this year as more valuable than returns in the future. At its most basic, NPV is a calculation that considers 'a bird in the hand is worth two in the bush' (to use the English expression). The calculation ROI is the ratio of net profits to costs.

The limitations of NPV and ROI calculations are that they are based on estimations. Estimates of future sales can be reasonably accurate for existing markets but are far less accurate in emerging markets. Consequently, if all portfolio management discussions are based on financial calculations, decisions will be skewed towards known markets and incremental innovation (black-space) and, thus, away from breakthrough and radical (grey- and white-space). This is compounded by managers feeling more comfortable making decisions about markets which they are familiar with. When the senior team remains within its comfort zone (conservatism bias), companies get caught in the incremental innovation trap. Overall, businesses need to avoid killing grey- and white-space projects by applying too much financial and left-brain logic.[9]

All management discussions about market size, sales potential and the like should include an estimate of the accuracy of the estimates. Thus, rather than talking about a market size of 10,000 units a year, it's better to talk about a market size of 10,000 ± 2,000 units. Why? It makes the senior team and project teams more cautious when making decisions based on unreliable figures. (This is similar to the way that a physicist never makes a measurement without also assessing the error on that measurement.)

Often in grey- and white-space markets it is very difficult to make accurate estimates of an innovation's potential. Here, *Strategic scoring* methods are as important as financial calculations, but many accountants are less familiar with them. When there's no direct way to measure project risk or the size of a new market, managers' perceptions can be used as a *proxy* measure. A proxy is an indirect measure, when an exact one is either unavailable or takes too much time and effort to derive. Rather than acquiescing to gut feelings, scoring systemizes managers' perceptions by collecting them on appropriate scales with *anchors*. Anchoring is the use of descriptions of different points on a scale. For example, if managers were considering the potential market size of a new market, they might do this on a scale from 'low' (score '1') to 'medium' (score '3') to 'large' (score '5'). Where possible, it's better to quantify anchors, for example specifying the size of a market as €5M rather than simply as 'large'. To avoid anchoring bias, discussed earlier, it's necessary to choose appropriate anchors.

Every project needs to be evaluated in terms of *opportunity*—the benefit it will bring to your business—and the *feasibility*—both the technical and commercial viability of the project.[10] However, there are three important differences in how breakthrough and radical projects should be treated compared to incremental projects. The first difference is that financial calculations shouldn't be used for early-stage breakthrough and radical projects. The second difference is that as they are riskier, breakthrough and radical projects may require additional risk assessment. The third difference is that breakthrough and radical projects need to be assessed regularly and you should not make an early decision to fund them all the way to market. Here, we can learn from venture capitalists, who don't try to spot 'big winners' straight away. Rather, venture capitalists break the funding decision into stages and only allocate funding in tranches, with follow-up funding only approved if demanding targets are met. Note that simple opportunity and feasibility ratings were the criteria we used to assess innovation strategic options in Phase 1.

ASSESSING BREAKTHROUGH AND RADICAL PROJECTS

Table 4-2 is a template for managers to assess breakthrough and radical innovations. It indicates that five criteria should be selected for opportunity and five for feasibility, together with suitable anchors. The right-hand column of Table 4-2 leaves space for actual scores to be given.

TABLE 4-2: ASSESSMENT CRITERIA FOR EARLY-STAGE RADICAL AND BREAKTHROUGH PROJECTS

BREAKTHROUGH AND RADICAL PROJECTS		ANCHORS	PROJECT'S VALUES
Five Opportunity criteria [select from Table 4-3]	1		max value=5
	2		max value=5
	3		max value=5
	4		max value=5
	5		max value=5
Five Feasibility criteria [select from Table 4-4]	1		max value=5
	2		max value=5
	3		max value=5
	4		max value=5
	5		max value=5

CHOOSING CRITERIA, ANCHORS AND WEIGHTINGS

Portfolio decisions involve uncertainty and so it helps if managers give scores on several criteria, the results of which can be averaged. This avoids the risk that scoring on one criterion is so uncertain as to be meaningless. A good rule of thumb is to use five criteria to evaluate the opportunity and five criteria for feasibility, from the lists in Tables 4-3 and 4-4.[11]

Table 4-3 gives a selection of 10 opportunity-related criteria which have been collected from our research. An MSB or SBU can and should choose the five that fit best with its business. For a business designing its first portfolio management process, we recommend the first five criteria. Businesses with an existing process should compare their criteria against Tables 4-3 and 4-4. Having the senior team decide which criteria they consider most appropriate ensures management buy-in and prevents later argument about whether the right criteria are being used.

As shown in Table 4-3, for consistency all scorings are made on a scale of '1' (low) to '5' (high). Anchoring statements can and should be made as specific as possible. For example, in Table 4-3 the market size can be directly

TABLE 4-3: CRITERIA FOR EVALUATING OPPORTUNITY (WITH EXAMPLE ANCHORS)

	CRITERIA	EXPLANATION	EXAMPLE ANCHORS		
			LOW SCORE (1)	MEDIUM SCORE (3)	HIGH SCORE (5)
RECOMMENDED OPPORTUNITY CRITERIA					
1	Market size	What is the size of potential market?	Small ~€0.5M p.a.	Medium ~€1M p.a.	Large ~€2M p.a.
2	Existing demand	How big is the existing market demand?	Low	Medium	High x units / year
3	Customer value	Does the innovation give customers new value?	None	Some	Significant
4	Competitive advantage	Does the innovation bring a lead over competitors?	Insubstantially	Reasonably	Significantly
5	Learning potential	Will the project generate valuable knowledge for the business?	No	Somewhat	Very much so
ALTERNATIVE OPPORTUNITY CRITERIA					
6	Gross margin per unit	What margin will the innovation generate?	Low for example 2%	Medium for example 10%	High for example 25%
7	Brand image	Does the innovation add to the business's brand image?	Insubstantially	Reasonably	Significantly
8	Market growth	What is the expected market growth?	Low for example ~1%	Medium for example ~5%	High for example ≥10%
9	Cost savings	What level of cost savings to the business will it bring?	Low	Medium	High for example €xx savings
10	Customer relations	Project strengthens relationships with customers?	Unchanged	Stronger	Much stronger

linked (anchored) to a business's typical markets, with a 'large' market shown as €2M. Identifying specific, numeric anchors helps managers make consistent scorings.

Managers in some businesses have asked us about the value of different weightings for the criteria. Our advice: keep it simple! Portfolio decisions are based on uncertain data and so, if these are then weighted, extra ambiguity ensues. Therefore, we do <u>not</u> recommend different weightings for each of the opportunity and feasibility criteria. It is better that the whole portfolio management process remains simple and transparent. It also avoids unproductive discussions about which criteria should be given higher weightings.

Table 4-4 gives a selection of 10 feasibility criteria. Again, for simplicity, we indicate the five that we would recommend, including Criterion #1 (whether the innovation fits with business strategy).[12] Criterion #3 is whether there is a suitable team and project leader available. We highly recommend this often-overlooked criterion. Venture capitalists stress that breakthrough and radical projects require teams that have the ability to pivot—change their business model significantly—when the original business idea doesn't work (see Case Study I-2 on Shotgun). Innovation teams require both flexible and agile mindsets (as discussed in Chapter 2). Without such a team, even an exceptionally attractive project might be better shelved until a team with the right composition of skillsets and mindsets is available (see Innovation Team Design Matrix, Table 2-5).

DEALING WITH RISK

Breakthrough and radical projects are by their nature far riskier than incremental ones. Research shows that only 29% of radical projects are on time, whereas 58% of incremental ones are.[13] This doesn't mean that such projects shouldn't be selected, as they can bring very significant returns. Rather, for such projects it makes sense to supplement the opportunity-feasibility assessment with a risk analysis.

Table 4-5 is a tool for assessing risk. Remember that risk is defined as the *probability of an event* multiplied by the *severity of the consequences*. So, it helps to identify the main things that could go wrong—both technical and commercial adverse scenarios. For each scenario, the probability is assessed

TABLE 4-4: CRITERIA FOR EVALUATING FEASIBILITY
(WITH EXAMPLE ANCHORS)

	CRITERIA	EXPLANATION	EXAMPLE ANCHORS		
			LOW SCORE (1)	MEDIUM SCORE (3)	HIGH SCORE (5)
RECOMMENDED FEASIBILITY CRITERIA					
1	Strategic fit	Does the innovation fit with strategy?	Not at all	Partially	Fully
2	Financial resources	Is appropriate finance available?	No	Partially	Fully
3	Innovation team	Is a suitable team and leader available for the project?	Not at all	Partially	Fully
4	Technical capability	Can the necessary technical capability be deployed?	Not available / difficult to develop	Partially	Fully available, or can be built
5	Marketing capability	Can the necessary sales and marketing capability be deployed / developed?	Not available / difficult to develop	Partially	Fully available, or can be developed
ALTERNATIVE FEASIBILITY CRITERIA					
6	Manufacturing capability	Can the necessary manufacturing capability be developed / deployed?	Not available / difficult to develop	Partially	Fully available, or can be developed
7	Market knowledge	What degree of market knowledge do we have?	Low: no reliable, current data	Partial: market investigations quite good	High: market investigations are accurate and current
8	Product differentiation	Can the innovation be fully differentiated?	No, the innovation is similar to the competition	Partly; the innovation includes features that are better than the competition	Yes, the innovation includes unique features
9	Sustainable competitive advantage	Is the competitive advantage from the innovation sustainable?	No, the innovation is easy to copy	Partly, as the innovation is challenging to copy	Yes, the innovation is very hard to copy
10	Organizational backing	Does the project have the full backing of the whole organization?	No active support from stakeholders	Partial support	Strong support from all relevant stakeholders

on a scale of '1' to '0'; with '1' (extremely likely) to '0.5' (likely [a 50% chance of this happening]) to '0' (no likelihood). The consequences are assessed on a scale of '1' (low negative impact) to '5' (very high negative impact).

Table 4-5 shows an example risk assessment from the medical sector. The project has been disguised to avoid any commercial drawbacks for the company in question. The project involved a clever, innovative drug delivery system, invented by a respected company scientist. The aim was to sell the product to several pharmaceutical companies, enabling patients to inhale a range of different drugs more effectively. In terms of risk, the R&D manager perceived challenges with producing a fine 'mist' necessary for inhalation unless an expert could be re-allocated to the project; and the air flow through the delivery system could lead to undesirable eddies (leading to some of the drug not being inhaled). The marketing and commercial directors perceived three risks: regulatory approval might be specific to the molecule (drug) being delivered and so limit the use of the device to specific drugs; pharmaceutical companies were rumoured to be developing their own drug delivery systems; and current market projections had not considered that pharmaceutical companies might insist on sole rights to the delivery system, thus reducing net sales.

TABLE 4-5: TECHNICAL AND COMMERCIAL RISK ASSESSMENT TOOL (WITH EXAMPLE DATA)

RISKS	SCENARIOS	PROBABILITY [SCALE 0-1]	CONSEQUENCES [SCALE 1-5]	RISK SCORE
Technical	1. Producing fine mist	1	5	5
	2. Air flow	0.5	2	1
	—	—	—	—
Commercial	1. FDA approval specific to drug	0.25	3	0.75
	2. Pharma's own solutions	0.1	1	0.1
	3. Sole rights	0.75	3	2.25
			Average Value =	1.8

The management team then assigned scores for probability and consequences. In the ensuing discussion, it was recognized that the cleverness of the device and the excellent presentations the inventing scientist had made had led the senior team to overlook the risks (an example of salient information bias in action). Using the results of the risk analysis, however, led the company to assign a physicist to solve the fine mist issues and the commercial director proactively discussed sole rights with pharmaceutical companies.

The utility of a risk analysis for breakthrough and radical projects is threefold. Firstly, having identified risk scenarios, project teams can take steps to mitigate them before the next tranche of funding is allocated to the project. Secondly, by considering potential technical and commercial risks, managers are less likely to be influenced by salient information bias, where a superficially attractive project is not assessed critically enough. Thirdly, risk can be considered when the whole portfolio is reviewed (as we discuss later in this chapter).

ASSESSING INCREMENTAL AND LATER-STAGE PROJECTS

Since incremental projects address known markets (black-space), financial calculations *are* appropriate for assessing opportunity. Thus, NPV or ROI can be used, as shown in Table 4-6. By their nature, incremental projects are

TABLE 4-6: ASSESSMENT CRITERIA FOR INCREMENTAL AND LATER-STAGE PROJECTS

BREAKTHROUGH AND RADICAL PROJECTS		ANCHORS	PROJECT'S VALUES
Opportunity financial criteria	NPV or ROI calculations based on reasonable estimates, as these are known markets. However, include an estimate of errors.		€xx +/- xx M
Five *Feasibility* criteria [select from Table 4-4]			max value=5
			max value=5
			max value=5
			max value=5
			max value=5

more certain, but feasibility should still be considered. For this, it makes sense to take the same criteria as adopted for breakthrough and radical projects (in grey- and white-space). Therefore, it can be seen that the big difference in assessing incremental and later stage projects is that opportunity scores can be replaced by opportunity financial criteria (calculations).

REVIEWING THE WHOLE PORTFOLIO

Portfolio management aims to: select the projects which will bring good returns; enable the implementation of innovation intent; achieve category balance; and build a transparent selection process. To support portfolio management discussions and decisions, three diagrams are presented (Diagrams 4-2, 4-3 and 4-4). In the explanation, we present real data from a business which we call TechProdLine, that offers production line equipment and services. This business employs 2,000 people and currently markets its specialist devices to medical, automotive and food manufacturers. Several innovation projects were under consideration. At the time of a major portfolio review, a project budget of €1.8M was available and 10 projects were under consideration, which are disguised as Projects A to J.

BUBBLE DIAGRAMS

The *Bubble Diagram* (Diagram 4-2) displays the whole portfolio with *opportunity* on the vertical axis and *feasibility* on the horizontal axis. Note that for breakthrough and radical projects the opportunity is a scoring (as indicated by the left axis labelling), whereas for an incremental project the opportunity is a quantitative NPV or ROI (as indicated by the right axis labelling). Of course, having a mix of scores and calculations on one diagram is a compromise, but one worth accepting so that all the data can be displayed together.

Diagram 4-2 shows TechProdLine's 10 projects, and the size of the project 'bubbles' is proportional to the investment. The projects are colour-coded to match TechProdLine's four business areas (medical, automotive, food and new opportunities). It can be seen that Projects B, E, F, D and H represent both high opportunity and high feasibility, although Project E requires a large

DIAGRAM 4-2: BUBBLE DIAGRAM FOR TECHPRODLINE

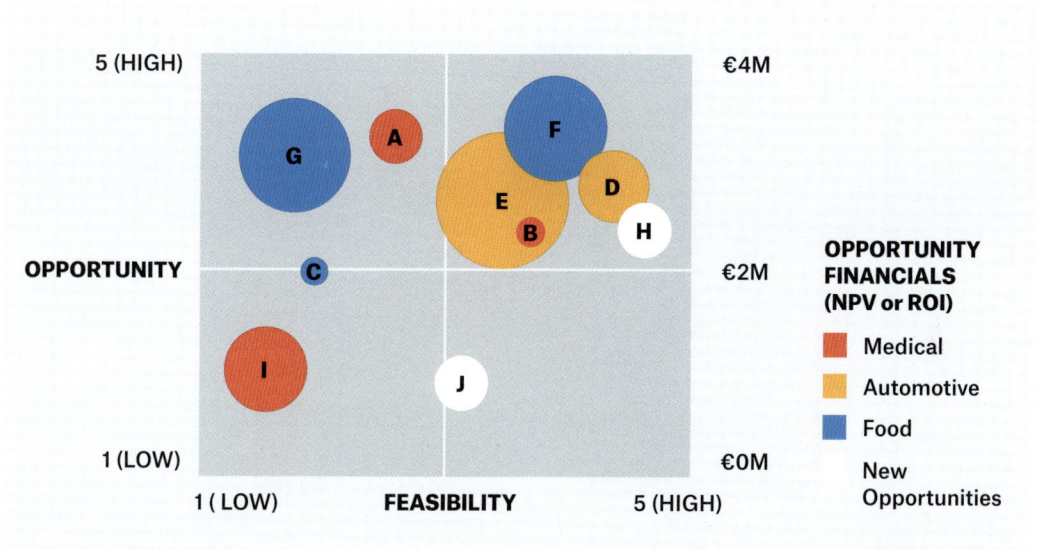

investment. Project G presents good opportunities but has low feasibility and represents a comparatively high annual investment. Projects I and J are both scored low on opportunity. Note that Diagrams 4-3 and 4-4 are also colour-coded to indicate which business area the projects address.

Bubble diagrams are most useful for checking that individual projects represent a good opportunity and that there is balance in the portfolio between risk (feasibility) and return (opportunity). In their portfolio meeting, TechProdLine's senior team noted from the bubble diagram that Projects I and J weren't very attractive and the relatively large investment in Project I was for the medical business, which wasn't currently a strategic priority.

OPPORTUNITY-INVESTMENT DIAGRAMS

The second diagram that can display the whole portfolio and thus support discussions is the *Opportunity-Investment Diagram*.[14] On this diagram, the horizontal axis should be taken as the *constrained resource* (i.e. the most scarce or precious resource)—typically the innovation budget or people's time (measured in full time equivalents (FTEs)).

DIAGRAM 4-3: OPPORTUNITY-INVESTMENT DIAGRAM FOR TECHPRODLINE

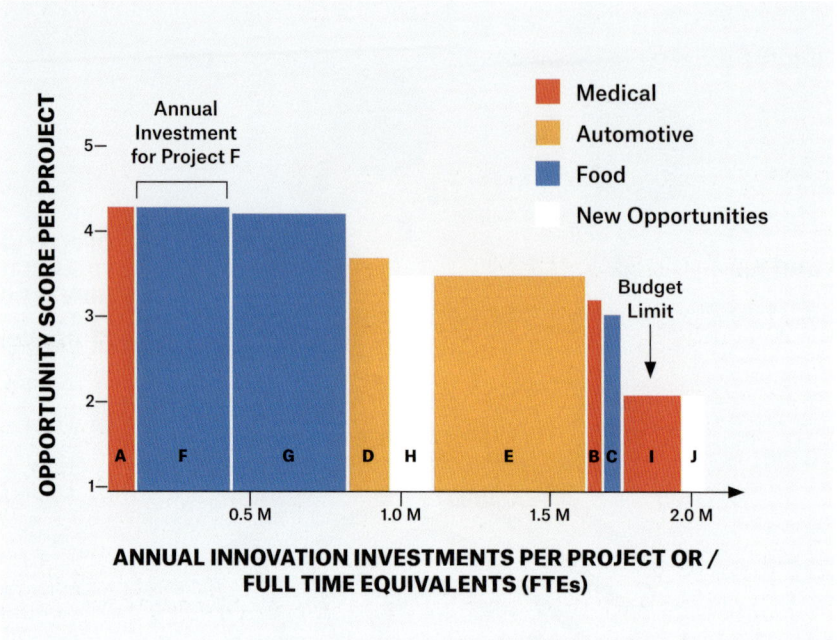

For TechProdLine, where innovation projects often require significant investments in technology, budget is the constraining factor rather than FTEs, so the horizontal axis shows project budgets. The vertical axis of the bar chart is the opportunity score, and each project is represented as a bar, the width of which is the annual investment or FTEs required and the height the opportunity score. Marked on the horizontal axis is the available annual budget (which for TechProdLine was €1.8M).

The diagram helps with decisions when projects need to be dropped (or shelved) to meet budget constraints. For TechProdLine's senior team, Project J was seen as important as it was an innovation strategic option targeting a new market. Therefore, the provisional decision was made to shelve Project I (although the manager for the medical business area was against this). Project J was perceived as a relatively low investment but also a low feasibility. Therefore, it was subjected to a risk analysis (using Table 4-5) and then steps to mitigate the risks were taken.

The discussions based around Diagram 4-3 helped TechProdLine consider new opportunities. These can open up new market prospects and develop new capabilities. The importance of selecting projects that develop strategic capabilities is shown by Case 4-2.

CASE STUDY 4-2: SOFTBANK ROBOTICS BECOMING EMOTIONAL[15]

SoftBank Robotics designs and manufactures interactive and friendly humanoid robots, to support humans in their day-to-day activities. The company was founded in France in 2005, acquired by a Japanese group in 2012 and currently has 500 employees. It is a world leader, with expertise in hardware, software, artificial intelligence and psychology. SoftBank Robotics has chosen to target six industries: retail, finance, government, healthcare, tourism and education, and already has an installed base of over 25,000 robots.

SoftBank has developed the hardware and software for two main platform products: 'Pepper', and 'Nao^6'. The Pepper robot is 120cm tall, has 20 degrees of freedom in its movement, and is not only able to recognize human emotions but also to express them. It can communicate in 20 languages and it also makes use of facial expressions and body language. With an array of sensors and cameras, it can navigate autonomously and is an open, fully programmable platform. As an example, in order to make sense of the hidden meanings in conversation, IBM's Watson computing technology has been successfully implemented on Pepper's platform. Pepper is often used in retail as a sales associate, providing product consultation and personalized recommendations. In hospitality, Pepper is already being used to greet hotel guests and offer advice.

The Nao^6 is the 6th version of the Nao platform, a 58cm programmable robot aimed primarily at education and research. It has seven touch sensors located on its head, hands and feet, plus ultrasonic sensors and cameras to monitor its environment and movement (for example, recognizing shapes, objects and even people). Nao can be programmed to inform and educate students in an interactive way. As Nao can recognize human reactions, it is able to ascertain when students have understood what has been explained to them. Currently, it can interact in 20 different languages.

"*Most people think of robots as performing simple, physical and computational tasks in a logical, detached way*", says Charles Broussaudier VP, Chief Information & Software Officer. "*Our vision at SoftBank is that robots are more adaptable when they can recognize, interpret and respond to human emotions. Robots should not be thought of as gadgets, as they have huge potential for deep interaction.*" An example is that Pepper is being used to interview abused children. It has been found that a robot that can quickly establish trust and empathy through conversation, and is more effective than adult professionals at encouraging children to talk about their trauma.

Softbank Robotics has transitioned quickly from the *start-up* to the *scale* stage of the business cycle (see Introductory Chapter on business life cycles). The watershed came in 2012, when SoftBank ordered Pepper robots for each of their Japan shops. Charles says, "*That forced us quickly to 'industrialize' our product, production process and logistics. We changed quickly from a laboratory making prototypes to an organization that can design, manufacture and support robust, reliable robots.*" Industrialization and formal business processes brought with them the danger that innovation would be stifled. "*We didn't want to lose our inventive, start-up atmosphere*", says Edouard Lagrue,[16] Strategic Innovation Director and head of SoftBank's Protolab. He stresses, "*Despite the fast growth and our strict quality procedures, we are proud that we have been able to maintain a culture of innovation. We are still passionate about designing unique robots that will make a positive impact in the world.*"

With so many areas where robots can be used, there are many directions in which the company could develop. "*Pepper and Nao reflect a strategy of designing platforms products, which third parties program for use in specific applications and environments*", says Edouard. "*However, our business model is not just that of a B2B platform provider. We also have the capability to be a B2B solutions provider, active in selected, specific applications.*"

Edouard is currently working on portfolio management issues. *"Innovation is about ensuring the whole company innovates strategically. This means our portfolio management process must select the right projects to enable our platform strategy. However, it is also about ensuring that the portfolio includes projects that build our capability to offer services and it is about experimenting with business models. Most companies think of their portfolio just in terms of products but, for us, portfolio management is wider. When we assess projects, we are considering the amount of product, platform, service and business model innovation they can deliver. So, it is about assigning our resources to projects that build not only markets but also our capabilities."*

PORTFOLIO DASHBOARD

Four simple pie charts—a *Portfolio Dashboard*—can help ensure that the aims of portfolio management are met (Diagram 4-4). Due to their simplicity, the charts can be easily and regularly updated and they enable the senior team to check that the portfolio is balanced.

Diagram 4-4 includes data from TechProdLine and the top-left chart shows the 10 projects by their time to market. TechProdLine's managers considered this as showing a reasonable spread, with about 60% of projects to be launched in the next two years and two projects needing four years (long development times for TechProdLine). Checking different project timeframes also helps senior managers recognize what consultants McKinsey call the *three horizons*[17] mentioned in Phase 1, Chapter 1. This approach emphasizes that investments in current businesses will bring cash flow within the next 1–2 years (termed *Horizon 1*); investments in current businesses will bring growth and then cash flow over the next 2–3 years (termed *Horizon 2*); whereas new businesses may take 4+ years to come to fruition (termed *Horizon 3*). Time horizons help management to be realistic and patient—developing breakthrough and radical innovations takes time, as does building market demand.

DIAGRAM 4-4: PORTFOLIO DASHBOARD FOR TECHPRODLINE

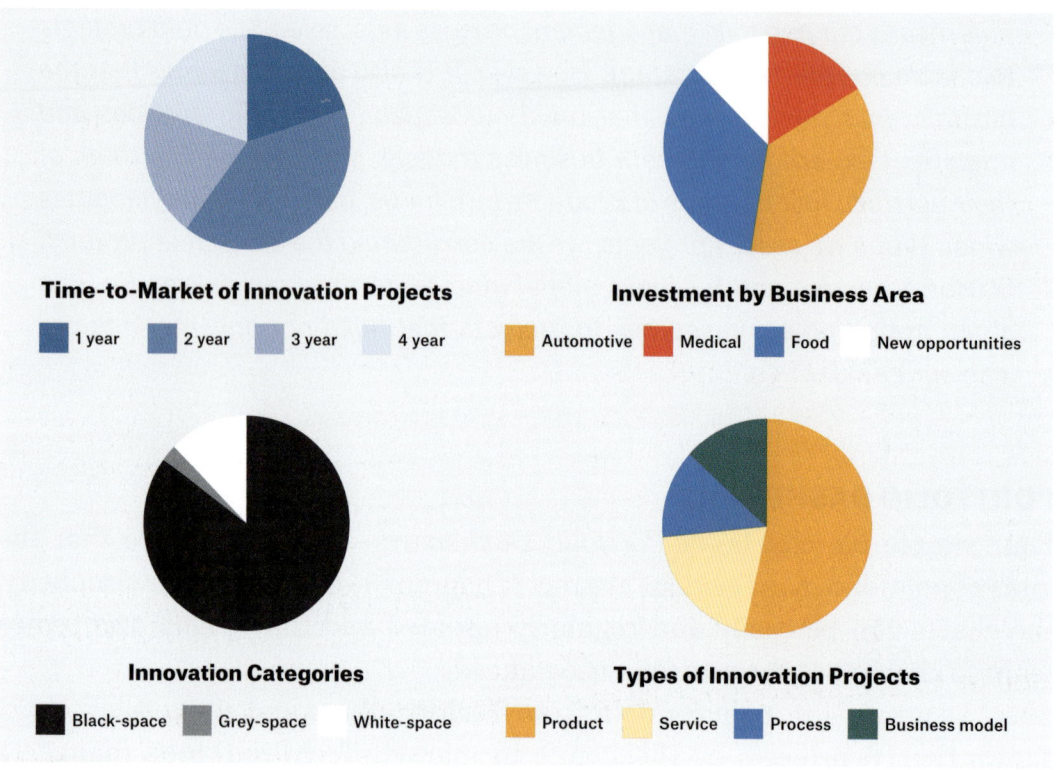

The top-right chart indicates the balance of projects across business areas. Here, TechProdLine's management team perceived that the high investment in food and automotive reflected current business successes and that the investment in new opportunities needed protection. At the time medical investment was being reduced, so this led to Project I being shelved, with the manager of the medical business area agreeing, albeit reluctantly.

The bottom-left chart is the category balance between black-, grey- and white-space projects. This reminds managers of the importance of ambidextrous innovation. Here, the senior team was concerned that the investment was skewed towards incremental projects and there were very few breakthrough ones. The decision was made to identify two new (grey-/white-space) opportunities.

Finally, the bottom-right chart checks that managers are investing in business-wide innovation. We recognize that many projects will include several dimensions of innovation. However, they can be grouped by their primary dimension (i.e. product, service, process and business model innovation). Remember, process innovations such as manufacturing and service-delivery methods can be hard to copy and, thus, they can be a source of long-term competitive advantage. Business model innovation is often overlooked during new product development and this was the case at TechProdLine, until the dashboard exposed the issue.

MAKING PROJECT COMPARISONS

Comparing incremental projects with breakthrough and radical ones is like comparing apples with pears. Because of this, we have mixed opportunity scoring for breakthrough and radical projects with financial calculations for incremental ones. This is a compromise, but portfolio management is more of an art than a science, and it should be remembered that "numerical input informs but doesn't dictate decisions".[18]

There are many other diagrams that can be used for portfolio management but, from experience, we've found that bubble diagrams, opportunity-investment and a dashboard suffice. Note that a number of companies offer innovation management software packages, and these include multiple portfolio management displays. We've found that it's more cost-effective for a business to develop its own simple dashboard, based on an Excel spreadsheet with automated diagrams.

In explaining portfolio management, we've discussed TechProdLine's portfolio and some of the decisions that the business made. This leads us to consider how meetings should be prepared and run.

MANAGING PORTFOLIO MEETINGS

PREPARATION FOR MEETINGS

Once the senior team has agreed criteria, a portfolio management meeting can be held. This will be an important meeting as a mix of existing projects will be compared to the proposals from the insight generation teams. These teams should be informed of the selection criteria and encouraged to share their evidence on which their proposals are based. Evidence helps managers make better assessments of each project. A spreadsheet to capture and aggregate individual managers' scorings, and which automatically generates diagrams, will need to be prepared.

The designated chair of portfolio meetings should consider how to make the portfolio management process engaging (see Case Study 4.1: Richardson Sheffield). The finance manager must prepare for the meeting by confirming the funding available for innovation projects. This is essential, because if budgets are unclear then portfolio management decisions can't be made effectively. It's also extremely frustrating for all involved when an insight team comes with a great proposal to which the answer is *'Yes: It looks good but we don't have the funding'*.

RUNNING MEETINGS

Portfolio meetings are a key governance mechanism. They must be held on a regular basis, as was decided by the senior team in Phase 2. An annual meeting is simply not enough because of the importance of portfolio management to innovation strategy, and because it is essential to ensure that sufficient resources are allocated to projects. If your business serves fast-moving consumer goods markets or fashion, then more reviews will be needed (we know of a fashion company that reviews its collections in monthly portfolio meetings). A trigger for a portfolio review meeting can also be that insight generation teams have just finished a set of further ISO investigations. So, depending on the characteristics of the business, the designated chair of portfolio management meetings must arrange both regular meetings and occasional special meetings.

Table 4-7 gives a suggested agenda for a portfolio meeting. First, the designated chair needs to introduce the meeting, stating what its aims are. These are typically the four generic aims of portfolio management (discussed earlier), plus the aim to identify which insight generation team proposals will receive funding. Second, a short historical review allows previous decisions to be considered (and learning to take place).

TABLE 4-7: SUGGESTED PORTFOLIO MEETING AGENDA

	AGENDA POINT	EXPLANATION	TIME	TOOLS TO APPLY
1	Introduction	• Meeting chair explains the aims of the meeting and the agenda.	5 min.	
2	Historical review	• Short discussion on previous portfolio decisions and their impacts.	15 min.	Bubble diagrams from previous meetings.
3	Project-by-project presentation	• Insight generation teams explain their project proposals (20 min. each).	Depends on number of proposals	
4	Senior management team scores each project's opportunity and feasibility	• Opportunity and feasibility scoring by individual managers. • Potentially supplemented by a risk analysis.	30 min.	Copies of Table 4-2 for each project for each member of the senior team. Table 4-6 for incremental projects.
5	Break	• Entry of individuals' scoring data into a spreadsheet. • Calculation of average opportunity and feasibility scores by project, with standard deviations.	30 min.	A spreadsheet to average the senior team's scoring results.
6	Discussion of project scores	• Discussion of implications where scores have large standard deviations.	20 min.	
7	Project funding decisions	• Display in bubble and opportunity-investment diagrams. • Comparison of potential projects against resources. • Consideration of portfolio maximization; balance; and link to strategy.	45 min.	Bubble diagrams; opportunity-investment diagrams (Diagrams 4-2 and 4-3), plus Portfolio Dashboard [Diagram 4-4].
8	Capturing how each decision was made	• Checking decisions. • Project-by-project short notes on decision made and key discussion points.	20 min.	Table 4-8 is a checklist that should be used for each decision.
9	Announcements	• Senior management team decides when and how to make the announcements.	15 min.	
		TOTAL	**4 HOURS**	

The third agenda item is where the insight generation teams present their proposals (either as a formal presentation or in an industrial show format). Next, individual members of the senior team are asked to score the projects using the agreed criteria for opportunity and feasibility. Data entry takes place ideally during a break, after which the scores where there are large standard deviations can be discussed. Large deviations between individual managers' scores often uncover important aspects of a project that need discussion. For example, in one meeting we ran the innovation manager had important information about project risk that others were not aware of. This led to a consensus within the senior team that the feasibility score should be lowered, based on the innovation manager's input. Note that several tools should be used in supporting the decision process, as indicated by the right-hand column in Table 4-7. For example, Table 4-2 should be used as a project scoring sheet.

TABLE 4-8: PORTFOLIO DECISION CHECKLIST

	QUESTIONS TO ASK	SUB-QUESTIONS TO AVOID BIAS	
1	Was the decision based on good evidence (data collection)?	Was contradictory evidence considered?	☐ Yes
		Was the information about very attractive (salient) projects considered critically?	☐ Yes
		Was any information avoided?	☐ No
2	Was the decision soundly made?	Was the decision too conservative?	☐ No
		Was the decision made on 'small numbers' only?	☐ No
		Was the decision influenced by irrelevant numbers?	☐ No
		Was procrastination avoided?	☐ Yes
		Was the decision consistent with other similar ones?	☐ Yes
3	Does the decision support the aims of portfolio management?	Does the project help maximize returns?	☐ Yes
		Does the project help balance?	☐ Yes
		Does the project support strategy?	☐ Yes

Next, it's important to display the data in the key three diagrams discussed earlier. (This should be built into the pre-prepared spreadsheet.) The diagrams form the basis for the discussion and decisions on which projects remain in the portfolio. It's important to avoid bias and so Table 4-8 is a prudent checklist. Managers should bear in mind that the scorings and diagrams support the discussion, but the decisions are made by the senior team.

The final part of the portfolio meeting should be spent deciding when and how to announce the decisions. As stressed throughout, transparency has a direct effect on motivation and so we recommend that the decisions are quickly and clearly communicated. Case Study 4-3 shows how important clear and fact-based communications are in announcing portfolio management decisions.

CASE STUDY 4-3: VMT VISION POWER PROJECT DETERMINATION[19]

VMT Vision Machine Technology Bildverarbeitungssysteme GmbH is a supplier of image-processing and robot-guidance systems used in the automotive, medical technology and pharmaceutical, and logistics sectors. The company employs 130 people worldwide and has an annual revenue of around €20–25M and is based near Mannheim in Germany. VMT is part of the Pepperl + Fuchs Group, a world leader in sensor products, with 6,300 employees and annual revenues of €715M.

VMT is a true solutions provider: supplying hardware and software, products and services, and it has an installed base of over 1,000 image-processing systems at customers' manufacturing sites around the world. The hardware that VMT has developed consists of laser and imaging components, which generate detailed images for the monitoring and control of complex manufacturing equipment. The company's image-processing software enables ultra-high-speed measurements checks on output quality, with AI technology used to predict and prevent 'outliers' (production output that is outside specifications). VMT can also provide robots with 'intelligent vision', in order to pick and place components with precision.

Operating in a technology-driven market means that VMT is constantly considering which technologies it needs to adopt and customers themselves often ask for a solution based on a particular technology. The Managing Director of VMT is Dr.-Ing. Michael Kleinkes, an engineer by training, who has recently completed an MBA. As customers have very specific production requirements, Michael says: *"Our strategic challenge is to be able to offer customer-specific solutions that are based on standard building blocks. To address this challenge, for example, we have a standard software platform that is used in all our systems. This software allows us to switch on certain functionality whereas other functions are switched off. This means we can customize our solutions and even change the appearance of the user interface, to meet specific customer needs."*

Michael stresses that VMT is managed as a project and service company. Customers come to VMT with their production problems and VMT's engineers work in close cooperation with clients: to specify the issues; to develop hardware and software; to install and test the equipment; and then to transfer the technological know-how (so that customers can gain maximum value from their systems). This compels VMT's engineers to build close working relationship with their clients. *"To support this, we conduct on-the-job training for our engineers, so that they can not only manage the technical issues but also become adept at listening to customer needs"*, says Michael. *"This means that our engineers bring back precious insights giving us ways to improve our systems."*

Michael has three recommendations on portfolio management, based on his experience both as an R&D manager and now as MD. His first point is about moving to new technologies: *"Have a good evaluation process when you are considering implementing a new technology. Set a number of milestones rather than making a single 'go' decision; you need to conduct multiple trials before making the final decision."*

His second point is about 'killing' projects: *"Engineers enjoy solving problems and so they are determined to take on even the most difficult projects. However, there is a commercial imperative to problem-solving; the investment must make financial sense. And sometimes, it makes sense to kill technically feasible projects."* Michael knows that this can be difficult for an R&D team to accept: *"Project termination is not just 'a decision'; it is also about communicating why the decision was made, so that it is not a 'slap in the face' for R&D."*

His third point is: *"As humans we seem to be very poor at 'letting go'. Although we all know about sunk costs, people still argue: 'Let's go on'; or 'It's a crucial project'; or 'We can rescue it'; or 'We can solve the problem'. There are always a thousand arguments for continuing a project. So, make sure that you have the determination to kill projects, otherwise you will end up with a set of 'walking zombie' projects, eating into your R&D budget!"*

MINDSET MATTERS

The people involved in Phase 4 are the senior team, the meeting chair, the innovation manager, and insight generation teams. The senior team should understand the importance of scoring methods and feel the gravity of portfolio decisions, as these determine your actual strategy. The decisions they made should have taken them beyond their comfort zone, otherwise the portfolio discussed is all about black-space. Senior managers should also feel that they've selected a balanced mix of projects, some of which address new areas of market opportunity, and not just their personal favourites. The senior team should check that they've taken the opportunity to give probing but positive feedback to the different insight generation teams that have made project proposals. Remember, senior managers carry the responsibility for making their decisions transparent and understood.

Before the first portfolio meeting, the designated chair will understandably be somewhat apprehensive about whether the criteria chosen will stimulate valuable discussions and lead to appropriate decisions. However, when portfolio decisions are based on evidence and bias is avoided, the four aims of portfolio management will be met. Later meetings will be easier as the senior team become familiar with the format. Sometimes, to avoid this familiarity leading to superficial discussions, the chair will need to challenge the status quo.

Insight generation teams should feel that their proposals have been viewed objectively and should remain motivated, irrespective of the decision made. For teams whose proposal was chosen, they should know exactly why management viewed it positively against the selected criteria and the team should be excited that their proposal was selected. For teams where their proposal was turned down, they should know exactly why rejecting (or shelving) the project was perceived by senior managers as the right decision. If this is the case, then when projects are turned down the respective teams can view them as good business decisions (that they can learn from) and not as 'rejection'.

It is worth noting that most managers from SBUs are subject to a rigorous corporate innovation approach, including portfolio management. Consequently, senior managers from SBUs may feel that building their own specific innovation portfolio mechanisms is futile. In our extensive work with SBUs, we find that specific innovation portfolio mechanisms overcome two issues that hinder SBU innovative growth. First, corporate innovation programmes tend to focus narrowly on the traditional industry dimensions (for example in the food industry the thrust is for new products and formats). This means that business-wide innovation growth opportunities are lost. Second, it is rare for corporations to fully appreciate the innovation potential of an SBU until it's brought to their attention (for example process innovation capabilities). Senior teams that proactively share opportunities for innovative growth with their corporate parent will cause their SBU to become recognized as a powerhouse of growth and will increase their autonomy.

Once your business has run a portfolio management meeting to consider insight generation teams' proposals, you've reached a momentous point in your innovation journey. Now, innovation projects are becoming real and must be managed in a way to maximize their chance of market success! Consequently, there should be palpable new energy in your organization as it moves to Phase 5, Getting innovations to market.

SUMMARY

- Portfolio management decisions are strategic and so it makes sense to develop a practical but systematic process for assessing projects and managing the whole portfolio.
- Financial calculations are only useful for incremental projects. Therefore, scoring mechanisms are crucial for balanced portfolio management.
- Every project needs to be considered in terms of *opportunity* and *feasibility*. A set of criteria needs to be agreed for each of these.
- Portfolio management is laden with mindset matters, such as conservatism and favouritism. Failing to address these demotivates everyone involved and reduces organizational learning.
- Regular portfolio management meetings should ensure that your business maximizes its return; achieves a balance in terms of risk and return and across business areas; and reflects your chosen strategy. Therefore, regular governance meetings are one of the senior management team's most strategic responsibilities!
- Portfolio meetings choose the projects that will move to Phase 5, Getting innovations to market.

Phase 5
Getting innovations to market

Getting innovations to market

INTRODUCTION

Now that you've selected your portfolio of innovation projects, your business is ready to bring the best ones to market. Phase 5 is about action. It's a stimulating but risky part of your innovation journey. It requires dedicated, highly skilled and motivated innovation project teams with the full backing of senior management. In this phase, it's essential to start developing markets from the outset. Your business must acquire market knowledge, such as how to explain 'value' to customers effectively, before an innovation is launched. Too many businesses forget this and then lose their nerve when sales are slow to develop. Therefore, Phase 5 is the culmination of the journey from 'A' to 'B'. It's about managing incremental (black-space) projects and driving breakthrough (grey-) and radical (white-space) ones; it also includes developing new markets (Diagram 5-1).

DIAGRAM 5-1: PHASE 5 IN THE INNOVATION JOURNEY

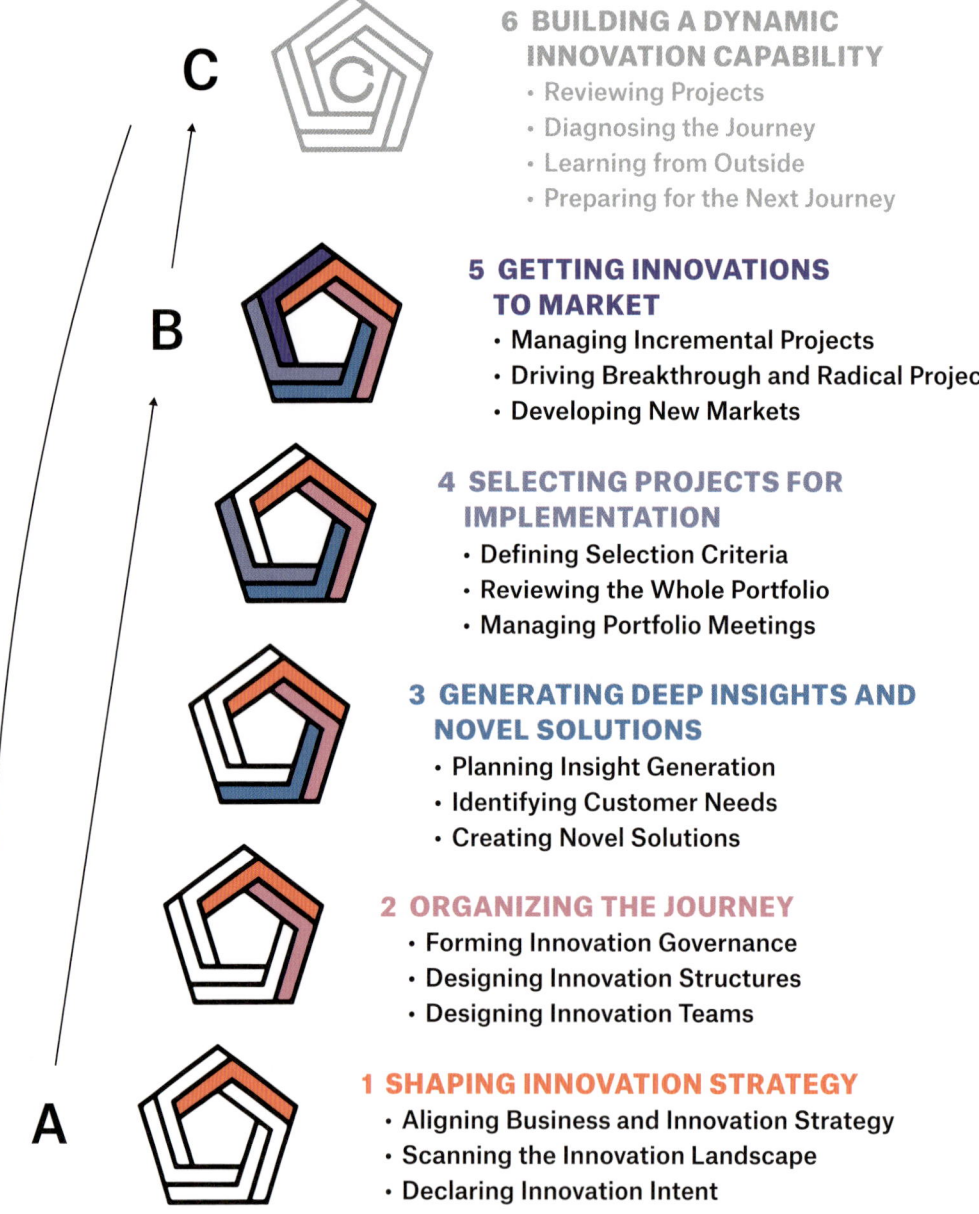

6 **BUILDING A DYNAMIC INNOVATION CAPABILITY**
- Reviewing Projects
- Diagnosing the Journey
- Learning from Outside
- Preparing for the Next Journey

5 **GETTING INNOVATIONS TO MARKET**
- Managing Incremental Projects
- Driving Breakthrough and Radical Projects
- Developing New Markets

4 **SELECTING PROJECTS FOR IMPLEMENTATION**
- Defining Selection Criteria
- Reviewing the Whole Portfolio
- Managing Portfolio Meetings

3 **GENERATING DEEP INSIGHTS AND NOVEL SOLUTIONS**
- Planning Insight Generation
- Identifying Customer Needs
- Creating Novel Solutions

2 **ORGANIZING THE JOURNEY**
- Forming Innovation Governance
- Designing Innovation Structures
- Designing Innovation Teams

1 **SHAPING INNOVATION STRATEGY**
- Aligning Business and Innovation Strategy
- Scanning the Innovation Landscape
- Declaring Innovation Intent

A word on terminology: innovation and product development are often treated as if they are synonymous. However, the term new product development (NPD) is relatively narrow and product-centred. As we've said several times, innovation is a business-wide capability leading to not only new products but also services, processes and business models. We focus on appropriate *Innovation Development Processes* (IDP) and not just NPD.

In our experience, most service businesses have neither an 'R&D department' nor a distinct service innovation development process. This often causes these businesses to struggle with innovation and sometimes stagnate. Therefore, service businesses will have more work to do in Phase 5 as they must define suitable innovation development processes and assign teams to this work for the first time.

Every manufacturing business with an R&D department will have some form of new product development process, probably a variation of the ubiquitous *Stage-Gate*™ approach that's been around for the last 30 years. Such processes are very suitable for incremental innovation but they're less appropriate for breakthrough and radical projects. Therefore, Phase 5 starts by pinpointing the weaknesses of the current NPD process and rectifying them; and, crucially, developing more *agile* innovation development processes for managing breakthrough and radical projects. However, Phase 5 is much more than defining management processes; it's about successfully launching a portfolio of projects, from black- to white-space, onto the market.

As seen in Table 5-1, there are three actions to take: review your current innovation process(es); develop effective innovation development processes for breakthrough and radical projects; and drive selected projects through the development process to successful market introductions. At a high level, Phase 5 decides *how to maximize the chance of success of each project*. Also keep in mind that every project must be periodically screened (evaluated) and some should be killed (or shelved) because tolerating a poorly performing project drains precious resources from potentially better projects!

Phase 5 covers concepts like *Stage-Gate*™, *Spiral Development* and the screening tool *RWW* (real-win-worth analysis). A classic tool, based on *Diffusion of Innovation* theory, will be presented. We also discuss *Value-based*

TABLE 5-1: PHASE 5—KEY THEMES AND CHECKLIST

THEMES	DETAILS
Actions to take	☐ Review your current innovation process(es) ☐ Tailor your innovation development process for breakthrough and radical projects ☐ Drive innovation projects to market
Tools and concepts	☐ Stage-Gate™ ☐ Spiral development ☐ RWW Analysis ☐ Diffusion of innovation ☐ Value-based pricing ☐ Hard-to-copy innovation
People responsible	☐ Innovation manager ☐ Senior management project sponsors ☐ Innovation project teams with their project leaders
Mindset matters	☐ Functional silos ☐ Senior team members should adopt a venture capital mindset ☐ Everyone involved in innovation needs to test assumptions and mitigate risks
Outputs	☐ Effective processes for bringing black-, grey- and white-space innovations to market ☐ A number of innovations introduced to the market ☐ Some projects shelved or killed but in a positive way

pricing. This is simply because, having dealt with the risks and challenges of bringing an innovation to market, businesses need to set the pricing appropriately. Solutions that meet customers' deeper needs can and should achieve higher margins.

The main people involved in Phase 5 are the innovation manager—who oversees everything—innovation project teams, and senior sponsors. Getting innovations to market is prone to mindset matters, as it involves multiple business functions. Professionals working in particular roles, such as R&D and marketing, will have different, often opposing goals. For example, R&D would like to fix the specifications (so-called *spec freeze*) as early as possible, whereas marketing would like to be able to respond to market trends during the project. Another mindset matter is that different functions such as finance and IT have strong professional cultures, which can exacerbate cross-functional tensions.

During Phase 5 the senior team must act like venture capitalists—treating innovation as a series of 'small bets' rather than looking for the one 'big winner'. The senior team also need patience and steady nerves because the markets for breakthrough and radical products take time to develop. Finally, in developing innovations it's imperative that everyone surfaces and tests assumptions. This is because important decisions may be based on implicit, incorrect assumptions. An example of this took place some years ago when GlaxoSmithKline assumed that a new drug would have 'blockbuster sales' and so decided to build a number of factories to meet the demand. Post-introduction, the demand was much lower than assumed and several factories had to be quickly closed. The fact that even a respected multi-national can make a mistake like this shows the importance of dealing with the uncertainty of innovation projects.

There are three crucial outputs of Phase 5. Firstly, your business will have defined effective innovation development processes for black-, grey- and white-space projects. Secondly, a wave of new products, services, processes and business models will have been developed and launched. This will mean that new markets and segments have been created and sales are ramping up. Finally, along the way some projects will have been shelved or killed in a transparent and positive manner.

ESSENTIAL BACKGROUND

Some managers and innovation project team members will be familiar with concepts such as cross-functional (or multidisciplinary) teams and product development. However, to ensure that everyone involved in Phase 5 has the same level of understanding, we give a short overview here.

INNOVATION—SUCCESS AND FAILURE

Product development has been defined as "The creation of products with new or different characteristics that offer new or additional benefits to the customer",[1] and for years the focus in both research and practice has been on 'product'. Product-centric mindsets cause businesses to miss growth opportunities, as service offerings can generate significant revenues. Similarly, product-centric businesses are vulnerable to disruptive business models.

Product, service and business model innovation are risky, and radical projects are particularly hard. The harsh reality is that products, services and business models can and do fail. The rate of new product failure is widely quoted in the popular press to be 80–90%.[2] At this point, readers will be wondering why we're recommending that businesses should develop new products, when they have such a low chance of success! Fortunately, recent research shows that the 80–90% failure rate is simply wrong. The urban legend of this high failure rate grew out of the confusion between raw ideas and commercialized products. *Product failure rate* refers to the percentage of new products that are launched on the market and fail and the true figure is 30–40%, in most markets. Research provides even better news—businesses with a deep understanding of customer needs have fewer product failures. The whole of Phase 3 was about generating deep insights and novel solutions. Although this is hard work, it pays dividends at the innovation development stage.

Table 5-2 is based on data from a survey of over 450 manufacturers and shows that breakthrough and radical projects are more difficult to manage. Although 58% of incremental innovations are 'on-time', only 44% of breakthrough and 29% of radical projects meet their schedules. Similarly, 68% of incremental innovations met their market objectives, whereas only 59% of breakthrough and 46% of radical projects meet market objectives. However, we reiterate that successful breakthrough and radical innovations typically achieve greater returns. Businesses should also view the figures in Table 5-2 as typical performance at other companies and do all they can to ensure that each and every one of their own projects bucks the trend.

It's important to note that projects tend to meet their technical objectives more often than their market objectives. As shown in Table 5-2, 53% of radical projects met technical objectives but only 46% met their market objectives. This shows the importance of managing not only technical feasibility but also market (commercial) viability, when opportunities are being developed.

TABLE 5-2: CHARACTERISTICS OF INCREMENTAL, BREAKTHROUGH AND RADICAL PROJECTS[3]

PROJECT CATEGORY	ON-TIME	ON-BUDGET	MET TECHNICAL OBJECTIVES	MET MARKET OBJECTIVES
Incremental	58%	62%	73%	68%
Breakthrough	44%	49%	66%	59%
Radical	29%	32%	53%	46%

HISTORY OF PRODUCT INNOVATION

Humans have innovated since the beginning of time. A short historical discussion illuminates the challenges in managing innovation.

Artefacts and Artisans

The very earliest human artefacts—stone-age tools—were made around 3 million years ago. Early in history, the production of artefacts became a specialized task. The ubiquitous wheel was developed in Mesopotamia around 3500 BC, and by this date skilled crafts had already emerged. Extraordinary levels of craftsmanship developed in, for example, pottery. Mass production also took place in ancient times, with Egyptian artisans cutting 2.3 million blocks of stone for the Great Pyramid, with millimetre accuracy. However, the limited availability of skilled artisans constrained the spread of many artefacts.

The First Industrial Revolution

The dictionary definition of a product is 'something that is made to be sold, usually something that is produced by an industrial process'.[4] The first industrial revolution, which enabled products to be made in vast quantities on mechanized 'production lines', started in Britain in about 1760 and lasted until about 1860. Concurrently, societal change led to consumer demand and the emergence of marketing. The story of Josiah Wedgwood (1730–1795) illustrates this.

Wedgewood was a potter who kept meticulous notes on how he produced particular finishes. This technical knowledge became crucial to his business and he defined procedures for moulding and transferring patterns onto items in his factory. Wedgwood's designs were often inspired by Etruscan pottery but he also responded to market needs. He recognized the aspirations of 'middling England', selling masses of tea sets, and when vases became fashionable, he developed 100 different models. Wedgwood typically priced his products higher than competitors, as he believed that a cheap price implied low quality. His marketing stratagem was to gift products to the nobility (the influencers of the day!) and then leverage their patronage. For example, he sent 1,000 parcels of pottery to German nobles, which cost £20,000 (a staggering €4.5M today). Germany became a major market and helped establish Wedgwood as one of the first international brands. Wedgwood's story is an early example of technical knowledge combined with commercial skills.

Second Industrial Revolution
Sophisticated production lines emerged in the second industrial revolution (1870–1915), enabling the supply of products at lower cost, as epitomized by the approach of Henry Ford (1863–1947). His famous quote that "You can have any colour you like, as long as it is black" indicates his emphasis on production priorities rather than customer preferences. (At the time, black paint dried much faster than any other colour and this enabled faster, lower cost production.) Ford was aware that with lower prices, he could address a larger market. The Model 'T' sold for $850 in 1908 but the price was lowered to only $290 in 1924. Pricing for the masses was a spectacular success and over 15 million cars sold from 1908 to 1927.

Mass production focused interest on the production process, rather than how products were conceived and designed. Typically, entrepreneurs took personal responsibility for product design.[5] For example, Ford personally influenced the design of the Model 'A', all the way to the blockbuster 'T'. Similarly, Henry Royce (1863–1933), co-founder of Rolls-Royce and a brilliant engineer, shaped every one of Rolls-Royce's products, from cars to aero engines.

As new technologies emerged, the demand for products increased and greater design capacity was needed. This led to *Research and Development* (R&D) departments in companies such as GE, Kodak and AT&T[6] in the early 1900s and the product development process emerged. Initially NPD was a strictly sequential process: with market ideas passed to R&D, where development was conducted and a prototype built, which was then passed to manufacturing to plan production.

The economic impact of innovation became clearer in the 1930s through the work of Austrian economist Joseph Schumpeter (1883–1950). He identified different aspects of innovation[7], including new products, new methods of production, and the opening of new markets. Schumpeter is particularly remembered for pinpointing that innovation can disrupt industries in what he called *creative destruction*.

Third Industrial Revolution

The third industrial revolution, also called the information age, began with the introduction of semiconductors and integrated circuits (1950s), then mainframe computers (1960–70s), personal computers (1980s) and the internet (1990s). Parallel to these technological advances, economies and many industries shifted from product-based to information and service ones.[8] However, despite the long history of innovation, the study of how it is managed is only recent. Innovation management has only been taught in business schools since the late 1980s, and the main academic journals in the field were founded in 1970s and 1980s.[9] And most innovation research has been heavily biased towards products.

A barometer of the interest in new product development and innovation is the set of articles published in the *Harvard Business Review*. Harvard has published over 400 articles on innovation in total, with the number of articles published each year increasing over time. In the 1970s, the main topics included ideas on how to test-market new products and explore new markets.

In the 1980s, Harvard published pieces on the limitations of sequential product development, the need for cross-functional teams, and getting products to market faster. In sequential product development the work is focused in R&D, and manufacturing is only involved at a late stage. R&D engineers were not concerned about manufacturing issues and would simply pass the responsibility for production 'over-the-wall' to manufacturing, leading to problems and high manufacturing costs. Also, in the 1980s, the importance of understanding customer needs became recognized (although this was intuitively obvious to entrepreneurs such as Wedgwood and Ford). The Mitsubishi shipyards in

Japan put customer needs centre stage and coined the phrase 'listening to the *Voice of the Customer* (VOC)'.[10] The seminal work of Canadian professor Bob Cooper on the Stage-Gate™ process, starting in the 1980s, cannot be ignored. Cooper studied companies that were proficient at NPD and found that non-sequential approaches were emerging. From these, he developed the Stage-Gate™ process, which coordinates cross-functional teamwork.

The 1990s continued with further articles on NPD processes, cross-functional teams and faster product development. The focus was on *time to market* involving all departments from the beginning—*concurrent engineering*. This helped prevent problems in manufacturing.

Since 2000, a lot of Harvard articles have focused on the front end of innovation. The themes covered in these articles have included recognizing the importance of exploring new markets and new methods for understanding deep customer needs. The role of senior managers in driving the success of NPD has also been discussed. Finally, the biggest wave of interest was in how technology has enabled new business models which transform markets, so-called *Disruptive Innovation*.

From 2010, *Harvard Business Review* has published articles on *corporate entrepreneurship*, *open innovation*, and *business model innovation*. Most recently, *design-driven innovation* has become 'fashionable'. We use the '*f*-word' quite deliberately as, in the whole innovation management field, there's an undertone that only the latest techniques are useful (because many people think that everything about innovation management must be the 'latest'). Here, caution is necessary as the latest innovation management tool applied in isolation won't boost your business's innovation performance, and so throughout this book we have selected a mix of established and emerging techniques.

In the years from 2020, the main drivers of innovation are digital, environmental and social, including the Covid-19 pandemic. The technologies we have mentioned earlier include artificial intelligence, the internet of things and what is known as the fourth industrial revolution (Industry 4.0). Many organizations will employ digitization to enhance the production and delivery of their products, services and business models, which we cover in Phase 6. Remember, innovation is about learning, and digitization is certain to support faster learning in novel ways in the coming years.

CASE STUDY 5-1:
MÖLNLYCKE HEALTH CARE: LESS OF A PAIN[11]

Mölnlycke is a leading provider of single-use wound care and surgical products based in Gothenburg, Sweden. It has manufactured gauze and wound care products since the 1920s and surgical drapes since the 1960s. The company has over 7,900 employees and generated revenues of €1,793M in 2020. Mölnlycke's SafeTac technology is famous for being the first gel-based wound dressing. The use of gel means that the surface of the wound is protected when dressings are changed, promoting faster healing and, at the same time, significantly reducing the pain for patients. The inventor of SafeTac, Thomas Fabo, worked in Mölnlycke's R&D but spent much of his time visiting hospitals to understand wound care. He recognized something that others had overlooked—changing the dressing is often very painful for the patient. As he says, *"The hospital staff didn't see the problem they simply had the attitude that 'wound care hurts'"*.

In 2015, as Mölnlycke developed ambitious growth plans, it built its 'scouting' capability—cross-functional teams using sophisticated

DIAGRAM 5-2: MÖLNLYCKE'S DUAL PATH INNOVATION DEVELOPMENT PROCESS (IDP)

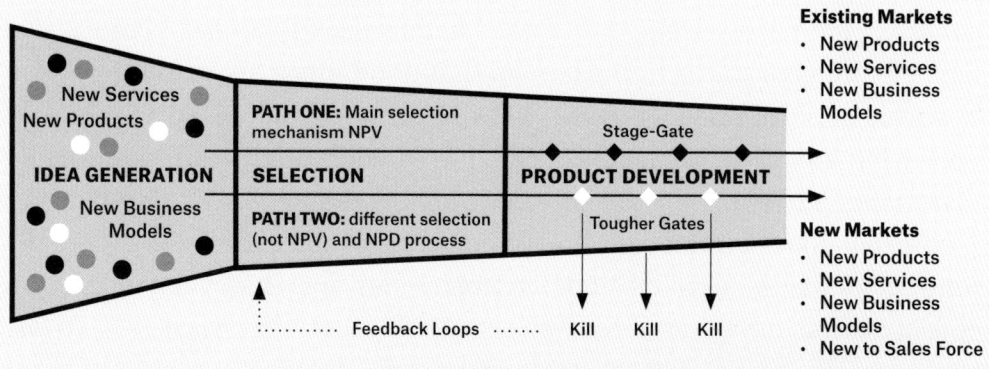

approaches to generate the deep customer insights. The teams used ethnography, repertory grid technique, and lead user technique to uncover ideas. Mölnlycke's finance director found that using systematic methods for gaining insights was *"very positive in moving us from decisions based on 'feelings' about what customers want, to decisions based on verified insights"*. The ideas proposed by the scouting teams were so convincing that management approved and funded five different projects. These ranged from incremental (but important) ideas to radical ones. Barry McBride, R&D Manager says, *"Bringing out new revolutionary solutions takes a long time. For us, it is equally important… to develop and improve the products already existing in our range."*

BUILDING AN INNOVATION DEVELOPMENT PROCESS

Mölnlycke's next challenge was to commercialize its ideas and it was decided that a different financing and management was needed for the radical projects. Two parallel processes were developed for the commercialization of its innovations, as shown in Diagram 5-2. Path 1 is for incremental innovations and project selection is based mainly on net present value (NPV) and projects follow a traditional Stage-Gate™ process. Radical projects require a different climate if they are to survive and prosper. For this reason, Path 2 includes different selection criteria at the early stages and funding is allocated in tranches. Development along Path 2 focuses as much on developing the market and the sales channel as on the product itself. As the global marketing manager conceded, *"You cannot build a new category and have huge sales in months."* Path 2 also includes tougher gates to make sure that good ideas are also interesting business opportunities, to make sure resources are allocated to the most promising areas. As Mölnlycke's Finance Director said: *"You have to dare to do some big things but you shouldn't spread resources too thinly."*

Since it started managing breakthrough and radical projects differently from incremental projects, the company has increased its innovation output. And scouting remains central to Mölnlycke: *"We always have to talk to customers and watch them doing their work"* stresses Barry McBride.

MANAGING INCREMENTAL PROJECTS

Incremental innovation (black-space) is crucial to maintain market share and sustain margins in a business's core markets. It shouldn't be perceived as the poor relative of breakthrough (grey-space) and radical innovation (white-space). Incremental innovation can be implemented relatively quickly, and it brings faster financial returns than breakthrough and radical projects, depending on market development. Teams working on incremental projects should not feel their work is less innovative. Moreover deep insights nearly always identify how to grow black-space and new ways to segment black-space markets. For example, Svensson, the Swedish company producing climate control products for greenhouse growers, found that a new segmentation boosted sales in existing markets (see Case Study I-1).

The tried-and-tested Stage-Gate™ process works well for both incremental products and services and it forms one of two innovation development paths at Mölnlycke Health Care (see Case Study 5-1). We explain below how Stage-Gate™ can be applied during incremental projects, and how potential enhancements can be applied to the process.

STAGE-GATE™ PROCESS

Diagram 5-3 shows the typical process with five stages from *scoping* to *launch*. At each stage, all functional areas are involved and responsible for specific tasks. At the gates, the senior team evaluates the work of the functional areas, reviewing the deliverables and, thus, whether the project should be allowed to progress to the next stage. The advantages of the Stage-Gate™ process are that it prevents key tasks being overlooked and coordinates the work across functional areas.

During the *scoping* stage the concept is defined, and this should be based on the insights work. The Kano Model (explained in Chapter 3) is an effective way of summarizing innovations. The Stage-Gate™ process includes checklists for the deliverables at each stage. The diagram shows, for example, the *Stage 1 Deliverables* for six different functions, from marketing

DIAGRAM 5-3: THE STAGE-GATE™ APPROACH TO PRODUCT DEVELOPMENT[12]

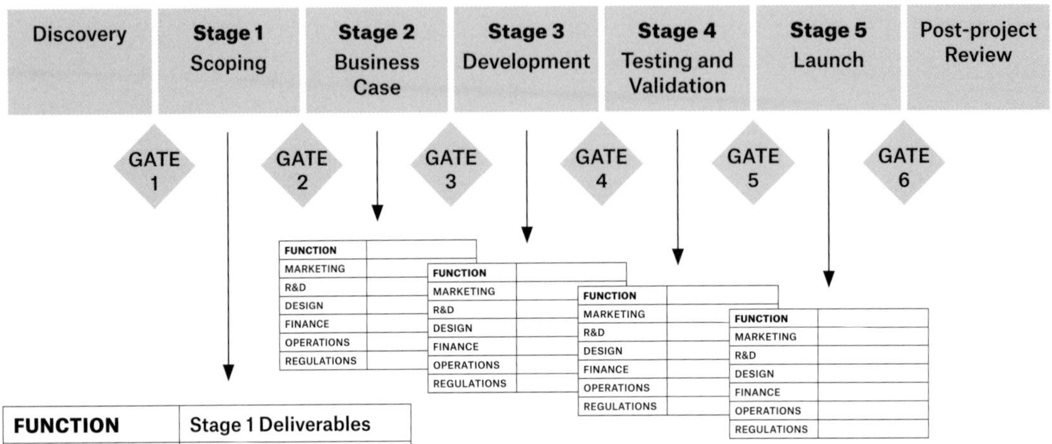

Discovery	Stage 1 Scoping	Stage 2 Business Case	Stage 3 Development	Stage 4 Testing and Validation	Stage 5 Launch	Post-project Review

Gates between stages: GATE 1, GATE 2, GATE 3, GATE 4, GATE 5, GATE 6.

At each gate, the following functions are assessed:
FUNCTION — MARKETING, R&D, DESIGN, FINANCE, OPERATIONS, REGULATIONS

FUNCTION	Stage 1 Deliverables
MARKETING	Identify market needs and size
R&D	Identify the potential architecture
DESIGN	Initial ideas on the UX and CX
FINANCE	Project cost estimation
OPERATIONS	Initial idea on manufacturing or service delivery mechanisms
REGULATIONS	Identify relevant rules

to regulations. Typically, marketing is responsible for identifying customer needs and estimating the potential market size. Similarly, finance is responsible for making an estimate of the project costs and return on investment in Stage 1 (and, of course, ROI calculations are possible for incremental projects—see Phase 4, Chapter 4). The deliverables per stage are specific to a company, although the Stage-Gate™ processes of different companies in the same sector will be similar (with, for example, a strong emphasis on regulatory requirements in the medical sector). For simplicity, Diagram 5-3 does not show every deliverable at each stage but these will, of course, be a crucial part of a fully defined Stage-Gate™ process. Top-level deliverables per stage are shown in Table 5-3.

The senior team has three options at each gate: to approve the project; to defer approval until certain deliverables are met; or to kill or shelve the project. Research shows that many companies don't apply the gates in a robust way. In other words, projects often pass through gates easily, without sufficient scrutiny. Here, managers must ensure that they don't fall into the information avoidance and sunk-costs fallacy traps (explained in Phase 4), and that they terminate projects where appropriate.

Enhancing Stage-Gate™ Processes

Even businesses that have used a Stage-Gate™ process for years can and should make improvements. Three enhancements are recommended, as shown in Table 5-3: industrial design enhancements; business model enhancements; and sustainability enhancements.

Design is about improving the appearance of a product, its usability (termed *UX*), and the overall customer experience (termed *CX*). Furthermore, design can help products have a deeper meaning for customers (that is, customers identify themselves closely with a product, service and /or brand). Of course, the success of Apple's products and its digital services has been based heavily on industrial design. For example, at the height of its success, the iPod achieved cult status in youth culture. Industrial designers are visually oriented people and businesses can gain value from their drawing skills and distinct creative mindset, either as development team members or as external consultants. Table 5-3 suggests *Industrial design enhancements*, where designers can add value to the Stage-Gate™ process.[13] For example, designers can make sketches that bring customer needs to life at the scoping stage, help develop prototypes, and provide good ideas on how to present the product at the launch.

An aspect that nearly all companies' Stage-Gate™ processes overlook is business model innovation. Every innovation project should review the main business models in a market and consider whether a new or enhanced business model can be developed to support the new product or service (here, the business model canvas discussed in Chapter 1 is the appropriate tool). Business model innovation can bring sustainable competitive advantage but business models should also be tested before they are launched.

TABLE 5-3: ENHANCEMENTS TO THE STAGE-GATE™ PROCESS[14]

ENHANCEMENTS	STAGE 1: SCOPING	STAGE 2: BUSINESS CASE
Typical deliverables per stage	• Preliminary market assessment (size; potential and acceptance). • Preliminary technical, manufacturing and regulatory assessment. • Cursory business analysis (time and costs).	• User needs and wants analysis. • Competitor and market analysis. • Concept tests. • Detailed technical assessment. • Business and financial analysis.
Industrial design enhancements	• Producing illustrations of customers' needs. • Narrowing down ideas while maintaining creativity. • Rating and selecting concepts.	• Discussing research and generating ideas. • Check plausibility of designs. • Justify product idea and costing.
Business model enhancements	• Assess current business models using BM Canvas.	• Assess financial impact of potential business models.
Sustainability enhancements	• Ensuring sustainability is considered in detail at this early stage, when innovation teams are busy with other issues. • Identifying production methods that have lower negative impacts. • Conducting life cycle cost (LCC) calculations.	• Demonstrating how sustainability can have a positive impact on profit. • Top management sponsor sustainability at the project level. • Determining how manufacturing, distribution, use, re-use and end-of-life impact sustainability.

STAGE 3: DEVELOPMENT	STAGE 4: TESTING AND VALIDATION	STAGE 5: LAUNCH
• Product / service development. • Iterations with customers (acting on their feedback). • Develop test marketing and production plans.	• Full customer tests. • Market test. • Trial production.	• Implement production and marketing plans for the market launch.
• Developing UX concepts and working on aesthetics. • Creating a prototype of the final concept. • Working to resolve production issues.	• Present to customers to see if it meets their needs. • Creating test plans and analysing feedback. • Refining the design.	• Help getting the branding right. • Ideas on how to present the product/service. • Communicating the design effectively through visuals.
• Develop different models using the BM Canvas.	• Conduct market tests of business models.	• Make new or enhanced business models clear to customers during the innovation launch.
• Establishing the ecological, social and economic implications of various solutions. • Source sustainable materials. • Organizing production, distribution and recycling to minimize environmental impacts.	• Having different prototypes that can be used to gauge the sustainability of the product. • Reserving enough time and resources to evaluate different prototypes in terms of their sustainability. • Minimizing packaging.	• Meeting challenging 'green manufacturing' targets as manufacturing is scaled up. • Attaining sustainability performance that is superior to competitors. • Tracking and continuous improvement of sustainability.

The third way that Stage-Gate™ can be enhanced is to integrate sustainability thinking into the business-wide innovation process, as indicated in Table 5-3—*Sustainability enhancements*.[15] Although the scientific evidence for global warming is clear and unambiguous, many businesses are not yet fully considering sustainability. Sustainability must be considered throughout innovation and, in coming years, products, services and business models that demonstrate that they are truly sustainable will command a market premium (as we will discuss further in Chapter 6).

MSBs and SBUs can be faster to act on sustainability than corporate juggernauts, such as some car companies. A stark example of a company behind the sustainability curve is BMW. The CEO said in December 2019 that he rejected any criticism of his company's dependence on sales of large, energy-inefficient SUVs, saying these vehicles *"are driven by perfectly normal people"*. Of course, his argument completely misses the point—products used by the mass of normal people are the ones where any progress on sustainability will make the biggest impact. Just consider the 'Fridays for Future' movement and it's obvious that sustainability is going to have a huge influence on the buying behaviour of the next generation. Industries such as fashion now realize they must change the way they design and manufacture products plus the way they market them (advising consumers about the negative impacts of fast fashion); and explore circular business models.

Service Products

Service products are different to products; they cannot be stored and their delivery—the customer experience (physical and digital)—is a key part of their value proposition. The Stage-Gate™ process is ubiquitous in manufacturing businesses, whereas most service businesses have neither an R&D department nor a new service development process. If this is the case in your business, you'll need to define your own process, with required deliverables for each stage by functional area to be defined, and gate criteria selected to fit your business. This can be achieved in a 1-day workshop, where representatives of all functional areas meet to define a process (based on Diagram 5-3 and Table 5-3).

From our experience with service businesses, we have two tips. Firstly, a service Stage-Gate™ process does not have to be complicated but it should clarify the roles of different departments, and coordinate their work. In particular, in businesses without an R&D department it should clarify where the main responsibilities for innovation lie. Secondly, in many service businesses the constrained resource is IT, and this will often slow new service development. For example, in regional banking, the capacity for changing IT systems is limited and this determines the speed at which innovations can be implemented.

DRIVING BREAKTHROUGH AND RADICAL PROJECTS

In keeping with the prior phases, breakthrough and radical projects should be managed using different, tailored innovation development processes (Case Study 5-1, Mölnlycke calls them Path 2). Exciting and risky, these grey- and white-space projects can bring significant growth but need considerable attention and strong nerves. Managing a breakthrough or radical project requires an experimental mindset; dealing with trial and error, together with the thrill of getting new things to market.

CHALLENGES IN BREAKTHROUGH AND RADICAL PROJECTS

The more breakthrough or radical a project is, the riskier it is. For example, developing a *new* product, with a *new* technology, for a *new* market is particularly risky. Expressing this in a mathematical way, it can be said that: New+New+New=(Risk)^3. Consequently, breakthrough and radical innovations require teams with wider skills. These projects must be evaluated differently, as discussed in Phase 4, and also require a different development process.

Table 5-4 summarizes the main challenges with breakthrough and radical projects. It can be seen that the technical challenges are the same for both types of projects and depend on whether a new technology is being used. New technologies always bring with them unexpected problems and so the teams require spare capacity to deal with them.

TABLE 5-4: TYPICAL RISKS OF INNOVATION PROJECTS[16]

TYPE OF PROJECT	TECHNICAL CHALLENGES	MARKETING CHALLENGES	PROJECT MANAGEMENT CHALLENGES
Breakthrough Projects	• Similar for breakthrough and radical projects. • Depends on whether the product/service is based on new technology. • Unknown problems are inevitable with new technologies.	• The innovation must be clearly differentiated from other products/services in existing markets. • Company expertise in next space markets must be built. • The pricing of the breakthrough product needs to be set carefully.	• Planning can be based on previous similar projects. • Some spare capacity needed.
Radical Projects	• As above	• Completely new markets must be created. • Sales can take longer than expected to rise. • A new business model might be appropriate. • Value-based pricing must be used.	• Radical projects' schedules are hard to plan and manage. • Spare capacity is essential. • Innovation project teams have much to learn about technology and markets.

The main marketing challenge for breakthrough projects is to clearly differentiate the new product/service from existing ones and to explain the value of feature(s) and benefit(s) to prospective customers. Here, marketeers must develop communications that hammer home the value to customers, otherwise there is a danger that the new product will be perceived as similar to other products/services on the market.[17] The pricing must also be set appropriately, avoiding the danger of under-pricing of unique features. If the breakthrough innovation is being launched in a new market, then marketeers must quickly build their knowledge of this market. For radical projects, new markets and business models need to be created, and pricing is a crucial issue as there are no benchmarks. Sales are often slower than expected in grey- and white-space markets.

Managing projects successfully requires planning, but planning breakthrough and radical projects is not always easy. Breakthrough projects can be scheduled based on similar previous projects, but unexpected problems must be anticipated. For radical projects there is nothing on which to base estimates,[18] and the inevitable technical problems that arise in radical projects mean that spare capacity is essential. Without this slack, every problem that arises will throw the schedule back and cause high levels of frustration in the team. Teams that have enough capacity can take pride in quickly and efficiently solving each problem that arises. The value of understanding technical feasibility and commercial viability is shown by the experience of EuroCaps (Case Study 5-2).

CASE STUDY 5-2: EUROCAPS
NOT JUST NPD, BUT BUSINESS-WIDE INNOVATION![19]

EuroCaps is based in Tredegar, South Wales in the UK and is a world-class manufacturer of soft gelatin capsules, supplying the nutritional supplement and over-the-counter (OTC) industries. It belongs to DCC, a multi-billion pound FTSE 100 listed company. EuroCaps employs 270 people, has annual revenues of £45M and the company is very proud of the complex products it can manufacture, such as Vegesoft®, a vegetarian, non-gelatin capsule. However, employees are equally proud of the journey the company has made. In just over ten years, the company has been transformed: from being a manufacturer of highly commoditized products (such as cod liver oil capsules), to being a highly respected player in the industry (creating complex capsules for its clients). This change has come with the full support of DCC, an organization that challenges its individual businesses to grow but gives them a high degree of autonomy backed by investment and advice, as needed.

Contract softgel manufacturing is an industry producing straightforward products, earning low margins, and experiencing strong competition.

With numerous competitors in regions with much lower labour costs than the UK, management at EuroCaps realized that a change in strategic direction was imperative. Two options were considered: competing on cost (through lean management and continuous improvement); and competing on innovation (through an ability to design and manufacture complex products). Managing Director Brett Tomlin says, *"It was important to pick one strategy and go with it. We knew that you can't succeed at being both ultra-lean and innovative. When we chose to innovate, we appreciated that it would be a challenge moving from 'easy things anyone can do' to becoming a specialist supplier."* At the start of EuroCaps' innovation journey, the company ran extensive workshops to gain employees' support and to collect their ideas on how to reinvent the business model. These workshops were instrumental in setting the direction for the company's new culture, which today is focused on a problem-solving mindset, where *'No, we can't do that…'* is not an acceptable answer and conversations quickly move on to *'Let's find a way…'*.

Gelatin-based capsules are ubiquitous—most of us know them from the various nutritional supplements people take. Yet, most of us have no idea of the science and engineering that go into their design and production. It is in the high-tech world of capsule science and engineering that EuroCaps excels; it offers a differentiated service for developing specific capsules to meet clients' new product development (NPD) schedules.

Clients working on NPD will typically come to EuroCaps with an idea that needs to be developed into a product. Capsules must remain stable, be easy to swallow, and should dissolve at an appropriate speed. For example, EuroCaps can supply softgels that dissolve either in the stomach or in the intestine. After initial discussions between a technical sales specialist and the client, EuroCaps will assign people from their cross-functional teams to work with the client on NPD including the choice of softgel and the capsule design. With expertise ranging from biology to chemistry, to food science and engineering, cross-functional teams advise the client on a capsule that will meet demanding regulatory standards, and which can be quickly launched onto the market. Furthermore, EuroCaps often provides its clients with unique solutions that give them a tangible competitive advantage in their markets. Supporting clients this way is a key factor in winning EuroCaps significant additional business (and meeting the DCC Group's challenging growth expectations).

The majority of contract manufacturers focus solely on delivering what the client requests. However, in addition to its development teams, EuroCaps has an Innovation Team responsible for identifying market trends and emerging technologies; for example, spotting ideas from one market that can help clients in other markets. The core Innovation Team can draw additional expertise from across the company to form Wider Innovation Teams to proactively develop new solutions that can be offered to clients. Innovation Team members pride themselves on, as Brett Tomlin says, *"finding tricky problems to solve that will put EuroCaps in a position to offer our clients a unique range of products"*. Innovation Teams constantly scout for technological advances that can address the demanding requirements of the nutritional supplement industry. This has led EuroCaps to develop first-to-market organic, vegetarian softgels, which have been launched by a major European brand. EuroCaps will also start to manufacture 'nutritional gummies', which offer a novel, alternative way to take nutritional supplements (they are similar to the gummy bear confectionery from Haribo in Germany) and will open an entirely new market for EuroCaps (and, again, help to meet the DCC Group's growth expectations).

Unusually for a company with a science and engineering mindset, EuroCaps has succeeded in creating a culture that is equally driven by service innovation. *"Our Development and Innovation Teams are constantly refining the ways in which we interact with clients so that both they and us can remain at the cutting edge"*, explains Brett. He continues, *"It can be difficult to see where the nutritional market will go next but part of our service to customers is providing answers to that very question. We always have to be proactive, developing the ideas that will drive NPD in the nutritional sector in the future."*

SPIRAL DEVELOPMENT

In addition to being product-centric, Stage-Gate™ has been criticized for still being sequential and somewhat inflexible. For example, the specifications are fixed at an early stage (so-called *spec freeze*). This can cause problems in fast-moving markets, where competitive moves and market needs can necessitate specification changes mid-way through a project. A more appropriate approach for breakthrough and particularly radical projects is *Spiral Development*. The spiral approach was initially developed for software projects but it works well for any breakthrough or radical project. As can be seen from Diagram 5-4, the total development time is divided into three, corresponding to three rounds of the spiral, each of which passes through four quadrants.

The *Requirements Quadrant* is where the innovation project team generates an initial understanding of customer requirements and how they can be addressed. Here, the work of the insight generation team will be extremely useful. Once an initial idea has been conceptualized, the next quadrant is *Design and Refine Quadrant*. Some innovation project teams start off with the easier requirements on the initial cycle, whereas others 'jump into the deep end' and attempt the more challenging functionality. Either way, the design of an innovation will neither be fixed nor finished on the first round of the spiral. The third quadrant is *Prototyping*, where a prototype is built that can be demonstrated to customers and discussed with them.

The fourth quadrant, *Testing Quadrant*, is particularly important, as detailed customer feedback is obtained on reactions to the prototype. This feedback can be used to improve the innovation but it is also the opportunity to assimilate market knowledge. This market knowledge should encompass customer perceptions and emotions related to the innovation, potential market size, and the price the customer is willing to pay. If Gate 1 at the end of round 1 leads to the project being approved, then the second round begins with the updated requirements being defined, based on customer feedback, and so on.

At the beginning of the spiral process, it isn't possible to create a realistic, detailed project schedule for radical projects (as also indicated by Table 5-2). This is because, on the first round of the spiral, teams will be working on things that they haven't developed before. For example, it may involve new technology or functionality, where teams are at the limits of their experience. This is the reason that the interior of the first round is not shaded, indicating that the team will be on a steep learning curve. The team will become more efficient in the second and third rounds. At the end of the first round (Gate 1), the team will have enough information to create a realistic project plan, detailing the functionality they'll be able to achieve on the second and third rounds of the spiral.

Spiral Process Gates

The gates in spiral development should be robust. If a project doesn't make sense, it's better to cancel or shelve it early, rather than waiting for the launch and subsequent failure. It's important to use appropriate criteria and, from experience,[20] we recommend using the *RWW* tool to investigate whether the market is promising. Supplementing these criteria, the *Diffusion of Innovation* theory allows us to evaluate the chance of an innovation succeeding. Both of these tools are discussed later in this chapter and the Gate 1 decision should be based on the analysis they provide.

Although the spiral approach helps manage breakthrough and radical innovation, it can't prevent problems emerging. Problems are part and parcel of breakthrough and radical innovation! So, there is one certainty—teams will encounter problems that were unknown at the start of projects. Teams require spare capacity to deal with these problems. This is very different from incremental projects, where the type of problems that emerge are familiar and easier to plan for. It also explains why more radical projects are often late and miss technical and commercial objectives (see Table 5-2). Put another way, incremental projects can be managed to be lean (to maximize efficiency) but radical ones require spare capacity (often called slack).[21]

Project Team Kick-off Meetings

It is helpful to run a kick-off meeting with the whole innovation project team at the start of a breakthrough or radical project (as mentioned in Phase 2). In the 1990s it was common for important projects to have off-site kick-off

DIAGRAM 5-4: SPIRAL DEVELOPMENT PROCESS FOR BREAKTHROUGH AND RADICAL PROJECTS

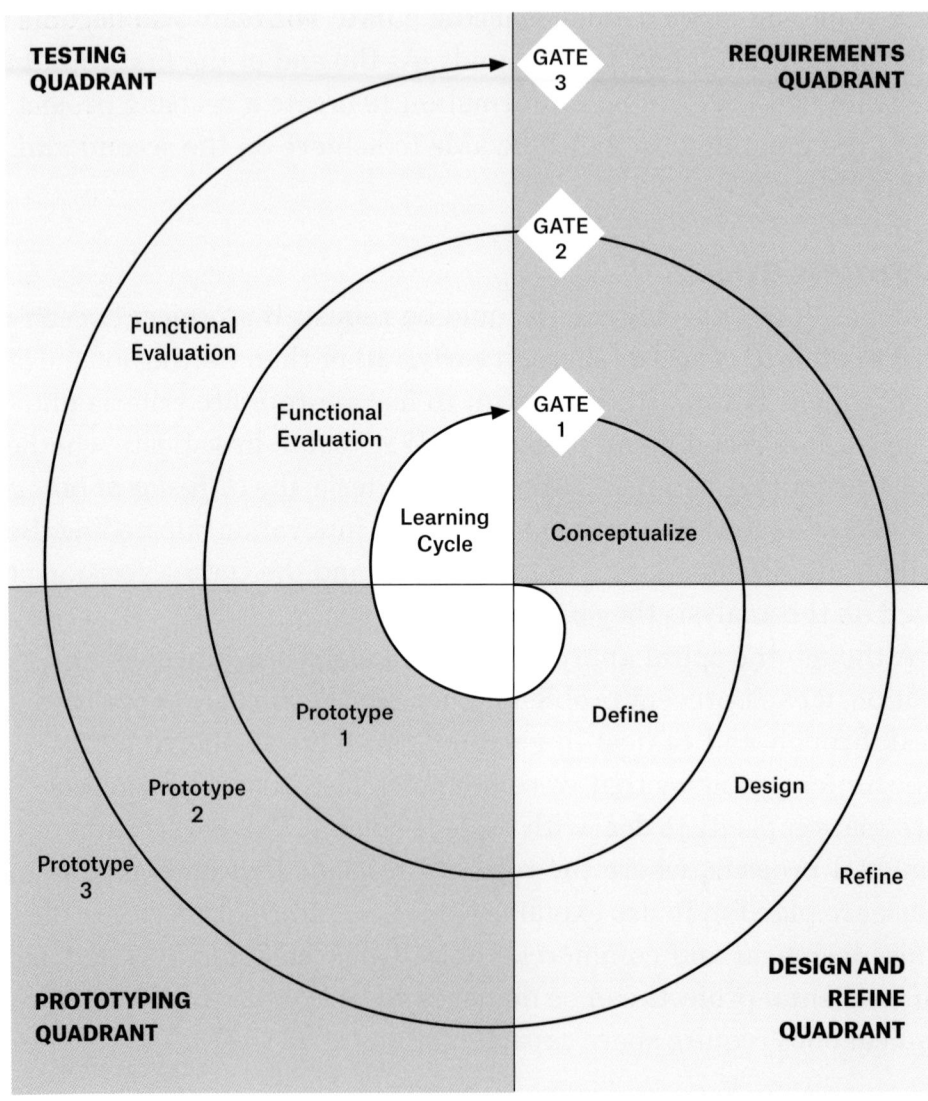

meetings, but this is no longer typical. However, if your management team expects big things from the project team, then developing great team dynamics is well worth the investment. The presence of the senior sponsor is essential at the kick-off and, for example, sharing a meal with the team signals management's support. If your senior sponsor isn't willing to invest their time in supporting the project team, then something is wrong! At kick-off meetings the focus is on developing a team charter, based on the four characteristics of high-performing innovation teams (clear goals; composite mindsets and skillsets; suitable processes; and team dynamics).

We reiterate that the senior sponsor must be actively involved not only in the kick-off meeting but also on a regular basis. It's surprising how many senior managers want innovative growth but then try to delegate all of the work to the teams. Senior managers should not underestimate how strong a message their active involvement sends, not only to the project team but also to the rest of the business. Regular interaction with the senior sponsor also acts as a catalyst to keep projects on schedule. Nuesoft Technologies (Case Study 5-3) illustrates how the CEO actively managed the successful transition from an existing (client-server) business to a new Software as a Service (SaaS) business.

CASE STUDY 5-3: NUESOFT SIMULTANEOUS OLD AND NEW BUSINESS MODELS[22]

In 1993 Massoud Alibakhsh, a computer engineer, founded Nuesoft Technologies within Georgia Institute of Technology's Advanced Technology Development Center. His intent was to help medical practices simplify their complex administration processes. At the height of the dot.com bubble in 2000, Nuesoft had a board of investors, 30 employees, three million dollars in revenues and were being wooed by WebMD. They offered a customizable client-server technology called Medicat. The profit model consisted of a software licence of $25,000 per desktop, including on-site servers, and an annual support fee of 15% per licence. A small sales team on 15% commission targeted larger medical practices with 10 to 40 healthcare professionals and completed about six sales a year with an average price of $350,000. Scaling this business model was linear, dependent on adding sales and operations people.

In 2000, Massoud was also designing a new business model, which a few people started calling 'Software as a Service' (SaaS), to provide an affordable offering to the considerable 'small medical practice' market. However, he was hit with two big problems. First, the dot.com bubble burst and his investors wanted to extract their investments. Second, to develop a first-to-market SaaS business model, he had to protect his core client-server business (maintaining it and keeping his investors happy) and, at the same time, develop the new SaaS business. Massoud says *"SaaS is so well known today and many of our ideas seem trivial in hindsight, but at the time they were firsts. We never knew how the market would respond, so there was a lot of trial and error with the technology, proposition, marketing and pricing. Post dot.com bubble our investors were reluctant to go on this innovative journey, which was considered risky and would take time; however, I knew it was the future."*

With a good sense of the needs of smaller medical practices and a rough idea that the new SaaS business model would not require customers to buy expensive hardware and would require some kind of subscription, Massoud set about organizing the team to develop and scale. As shown in Diagram 5-5, Massoud remained the sponsor. He hired Dr Shahram Famorzadeh, who had expertise in distributed computing on public networks (the internet), as both team leader and CTO. Other essential members included an experienced marketing lead, a junior 'internet' marketer, and a hardware and a software engineer. Extended members, who contributed at various phases, included a former consultant who helped design digital business models (and also served as COO for the core business); and a handful of highly active current customers who took part in pilot testing. Shahram says *"We valued talking things through as a team; this appeared to others as arguing, but we were really*

DIAGRAM 5-5: BUSINESS MODEL INNOVATION TEAM

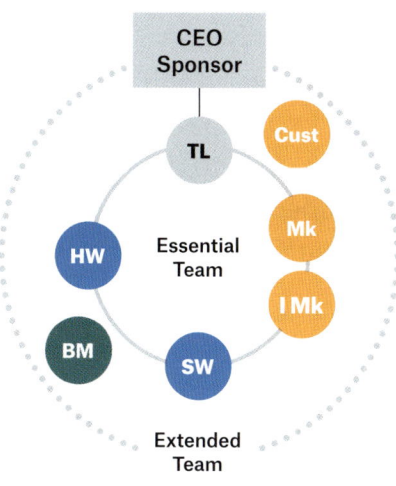

- **CEO** : Sponsor
- **TL** :Team Leader (also CTO)
- **Mk** : Marketing Leader
- **I Mk** : Internet Marketer
- **HW** : Hardware Specialist
- **SW** : Software Specialist
- **BM** : Digital Business Models (also COO)
- **CUST** : High Active Customers

testing each other's thinking before testing ideas with customers to see what worked".

The SaaS value proposition was branded NueMD and the business model was refined, setting the standard for SaaS pricing with a monthly subscription per doctor which they estimated had three support staff who would use the software. This profit model was very different from Nuesoft's original one as the average sale was a lot less at $5,000 including 20% sales commission, but after one year recurring profits were a lot higher. In 2004 the team solved its two big problems. Nuesoft sold the legacy Medicat business and in doing so paid off investors. Now with full control of NueMD and initial sales funding growth, they accelerated scaling—adding an electronic health records product and a billing product. Over the next decade they increased revenue fivefold, doubled margins and grew to 200 employees.

Reflecting on the journey, Massoud's advice to other businesses who have to manage one core business and develop the next is: *"The team's skills, mindset and motivation are everything. Daily, the innovation team had to flip between today's business and creating tomorrow's. Most people could not do this, especially sales and support, so we kept them separate. The innovation team was purposely small, tight and constantly communicating. We reminded ourselves of the overall vision, clarified customer problems like pricing and interface ones like how to navigate like a browser, and explored how to keep the technology secure and figure out what is now known as search engine optimization. If I had to do it all again, I would focus on how to communicate and learn together better."*

In 2018 Nuesoft merged with the other main player in the market, AdvancedMD, to form the leading medical practice provider with revenues of approximately $145M and 600 employees.

MANAGING SPIRAL-CRITICAL PATHS

On the first round of the spiral, the team will be learning. It's important to identify the *critical path* of the project during this learning period. The critical path is where the bottleneck will occur, slowing a project's progress. In projects where there is complex software, often the coding and testing can take longer than expected. In service companies, the bottleneck might be getting the IT function to make links to legacy databases, whereas for B2B products it could be verifying the long-term durability of components.

In incremental projects, the team has a wealth of prior experience and so can predict bottlenecks. For breakthrough and radical projects, this is not the case. Nevertheless, the project team will have had experiences with other projects that can give them an idea where bottlenecks will occur. A useful tip is that team members responsible for the task that emerges as the bottleneck will be the ones that become stressed. So, monitor team stress to spot problems as early as possible. If bottlenecks aren't spotted early enough, they become harder to solve. For example, if a struggling software team is allocated extra people, these new engineers will need to be trained by the current team, which will mean further schedule delays.

PROTOTYPE TESTING

The popular management book *The Lean Startup* explains how to develop digital products quickly.[23] The most relevant concept is to treat innovation development as a set of experiments, or hypotheses (views, beliefs) to be tested. Part of this thinking is to produce what is termed a *minimal viable product* (MVP)—a prototype with the minimum set of features necessary for a meaningful demonstration to customers. Unfortunately, the minimal viable product concept has been widely misunderstood. It's often interpreted as launching products with minimal functionality. This is wrong; minimal viable products are used to gather customer feedback and this is used to design the final product. The aim is not to launch stripped-down functionality but to launch functionality that meets the highest priorities.

During the first round of the spiral, when the *Testing Quadrant* is reached, the first prototype can be shown to customers. The lean startup approach recommends asking customers four questions, to ascertain the value the product can bring and the market opportunities available.[24] However, product and market viability are too complex to cover with just four questions (remember, at many points in this book we recommend putting more effort into your analysis than your competitors). Therefore, we recommend taking the time to conduct a thorough *Real-Win-Worth* (RWW) analysis (Table 5-5).

The 17 questions in Table 5-5 should be answered carefully. What do we mean by this? For example, teams can simply answer 'yes' to Q1; there is a need or desire for the product. However, Table 5-5 includes a column where the evidence should be noted, so that management can weigh it up as they make their gate decisions. The innovation project team leader should summarize the evidence, for example detailing where they've spoken to customers and conducted prototype tests. Where possible, these tests should be filmed because a lot can be learnt from such videos. For example, the Irish forestry company Coillte tested prototypes of a recreational service. Permission was

TABLE 5-5: THE RWW SCREENING QUESTIONS

	TOP-LEVEL QUESTIONS	2ND-LEVEL QUESTIONS	3RD-LEVEL QUESTIONS	ANSWERS AND EVIDENCE
1	Is it real [R]?	• Is the market real?	1. Is there a need or desire for the product (or service)? 2. Can the customer buy it? 3. Is the size of the potential market adequate? 4. Will the customer buy it?	
		• Is the product (or service) real?	5. Is there a clear concept? 6. Can the product be made (or the service delivered)? 7. Will the final product (or service) satisfy the market?	
2	Can we win [W]?	• Can the product (or service) be competitive?	8. Does it have a competitive advantage? 9. Can the advantage be sustained? 10. How will competitors respond?	
		• Can our organization be competitive?	11. Do we have superior resources? 12. Do we have appropriate management? 13. Can we understand and respond to the market?	
3	Is it worth doing [W]?	• Will the product (or service) be profitable at an acceptable risk?	14. Are forecasted returns greater than the costs? 15. Are the risks acceptable?	
		• Does launching the product (or service) make strategic sense?	16. Does the product (or service) fit our overall growth strategy? 17. Will top management support it?	

obtained to video children and their parents participating in various recreational activities in the forest. The analysis of these videos allowed important, previously unrecognized customer needs to be identified. For example, it showed that parents really valued personalized feedback on their child's progress in outdoor activities.

DEVELOPING NEW MARKETS

During breakthrough and radical projects, there should be equal emphasis on both the development of the innovation and the development of the market. As prototypes are tested in the fourth quadrant of the spiral process, the RWW questions will illuminate market issues. However, to understand more deeply how innovations will be received by the market, several key concepts can be applied. Some of these are based on the research of American professor Everett Rogers[25] and, in addition, pricing will be considered. When market understanding and pricing are integrated into Spiral Development, it maximizes the chance of market success.

DIFFUSION OF INNOVATION

Some customers are more open to innovation than others. Diagram 5-6 shows the *Adoption Life Cycle*. The horizontal axis represents the time at which individual customers adopt an innovation and the vertical axis the percentage of customers (adopters) buying at a particular time. It can be seen that the number of customers buying at a particular time follows a normal, Gaussian distribution—the blue curve. The cumulative number of customers as the innovation *diffuses* into the market is also shown—the red curve.

The first customers that adopt or buy an innovation are termed the *innovators*. They are always interested in the 'latest thing' and scan the market for new products, technologies, and services. They'll be the consumers with the latest mobile devices, and the businesses that like to be associated with the latest technology. Innovators know that not every innovation will be that effective but this won't dilute their interest in the latest technology, or

DIAGRAM 5-6: ADOPTION LIFE CYCLE

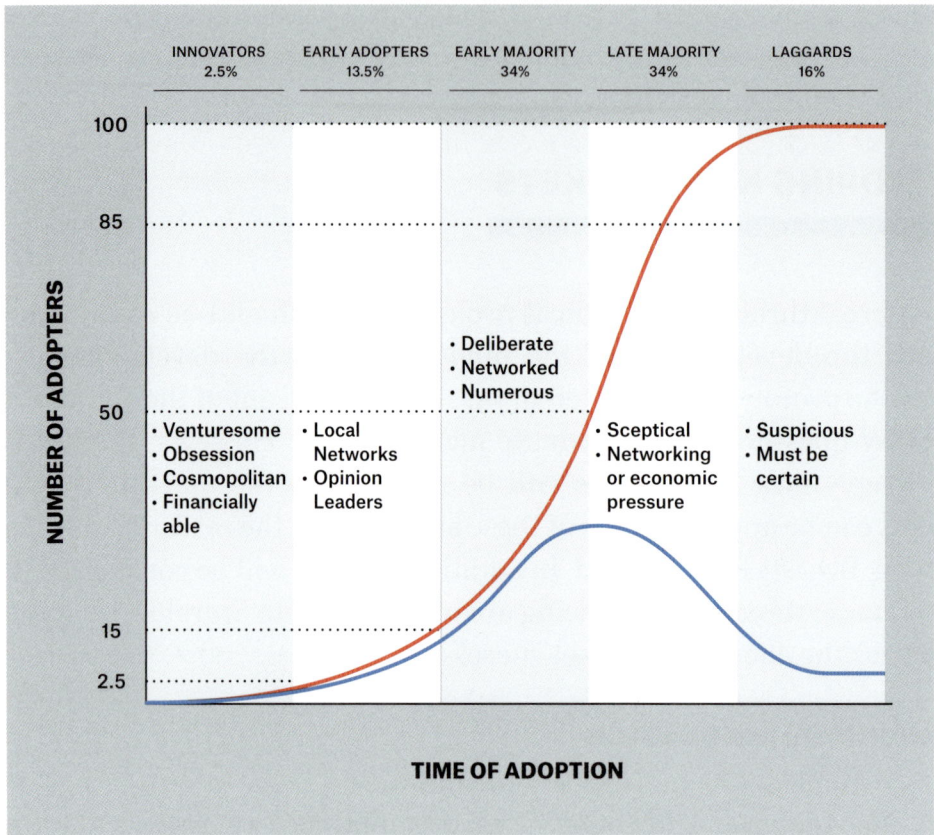

discourage them from trying things out. (Very often, innovators are where you will find the lead users discussed in Phase 3, Chapter 3.)

The *early adopters* come next; they are more critical in that they want to obtain specific benefits from the innovation and they are often opinion leaders. Both innovators and early adopters have the time and money to invest in the latest innovations, are typically in contact with people with similar views, and are influenced by how they are perceived within these peer groups.

The *early majority* are numerous and, when they start buying, it means that the mainstream market has been reached. However, these customers are deliberate and have to be convinced that the innovation not only functions but also brings measurable benefits. In contrast to innovators and early adopters, who look out for interesting innovations, the early majority require unambiguous proof of the benefits.

The fourth group, the *late majority* are more cautious and have less experience with new things. Therefore, the value of the innovation needs to be obvious to them, as they are not willing to experiment like the innovators and early adopters. Consequently, the late majority need clear pre-sales advice and often look for the security of buying from an established company or well-known brand.

The final, fifth group of buyers are the *laggards*, who will adopt only reluctantly and when forced to do so. In some B2C markets, the five types of buyer can be, at least partially, predicted by age. However, it's an over-simplification to say that older people are always laggards and, in many markets, there can be innovators who are older.

Crossing the Chasm

Diagram 5-6 shows the adoption curve as a normal distribution, with specific percentages given for each customer group (for example, early adopters are shown as 13.5%). A word of caution here; it is an idealized view and an actual curve won't necessarily follow a Gaussian distribution. The biggest risk is that an innovation is adopted by the innovators and early adopters but never by the early majority. Transitioning sales from early adopters to the early majority can be difficult and is called *Crossing the Chasm*.[26] The 'chasm' metaphor makes us aware that our marketing plan for a breakthrough or radical innovation should include specific actions to not only capture the interest of innovators and early adopters but also bridge (the chasm) to the early majority. The early majority need hard evidence that an innovation will deliver extra value and they can adopt it easily. The early majority's scepticism means that, frequently, innovations don't become widely adopted.

Factors Impacting Diffusion

There is a danger that project teams convince themselves that an innovation will be positively perceived by customers.[27] Internal views are often biased (remember confirmation bias in Phase 4) and so prototype testing is

TABLE 5-6: FACTORS THAT IMPACT DIFFUSION (ADOPTION) OF INNOVATIONS

	FACTOR	IMPACT	RELATIONSHIP	ASSESSMENT QUESTIONS WITH CUSTOMERS	ANSWERS AND EVIDENCE
1	Relative advantage	+	The greater the perceived advantage (compared to alternatives), the more likely the innovation will be adopted.	• What are the benefits of the innovation in your perception? In terms of the time saved, reduced costs and confidence in the innovation? • Does the innovation have any limitations compared to existing products or services in your opinion?	
2	Observability	+	The more easily the advantages of the innovation can be observed, the more likely it will be adopted.	• Could you observe the advantages of the innovation easily? • How could the innovation be designed so that the unique benefit(s) are more evident?	
3	Trialability	+	The easier it is for users to try out the innovation, then the more likely it will be adopted.	• Is it easy for the customer to trial the innovation and perceive its benefit(s) first hand? • Can small-scale trials be conducted?	
4	Compatibility	+	The more compatible the innovation is to the existing product, process or service, the more likely it will be adopted.	• Do you perceive the innovation to fit with your normal way of working? Why? • How can the innovation fit better with your current way of working?	
5	Complexity	−	The more complex an innovation is perceived to be, the less likely it will be adopted.	• Do you perceive the innovation as complex? Why? • How could the innovation be made simpler?	
6	Perceived risk	−	The riskier an innovation is perceived to be, the less likely it will be adopted.	• Do you perceive any risks associated with the innovation? What are they? • How can each of these risks be minimized?	

essential. Another practical finding from the research of Everett Rogers is that there are six factors which characterize a customer's perception of an innovation and therefore its adoption (Table 5-6).

Four factors positively impact diffusion (indicated by a '+' in the IMPACT column). The first factor is the *relative advantage*, compared to similar existing innovations (also called the benefit-cost ratio). Not surprisingly, the greater the advantage of an innovative product (or service) relative to existing products (or services), the more likely people are to adopt it. Some businesses make the tacit assumption that the advantage of a product / service will automatically lead to adoption. But, of course, there are other factors. Three other factors can positively tip the balance in favour of adoption (diffusion). These are: the *observability* (that is, the advantage is easy to observe); the *trialability* (Is it easy for the customer to try out the innovation?); and *compatibility* (Is the innovation compatible with the way the customer works and their existing mindset?).

The two factors that negatively impact diffusion are the *perceived risk* and *complexity* (indicated by a '-' in the table). If changing to a new product (or service) is perceived as risky, then customers won't adopt, even though it would bring a relative advantage. Similarly, if an innovation appears complex, customers are reluctant to take the time to understand it.

Scrutinizing the six factors allow us to understand how customers perceive an innovation. Some of the diffusion of innovation questions overlap with RWW but this is not a problem, as the two approaches are complementary. The assessment questions in Table 5-6 can be used to guide discussions with customers assessing a prototype.

SEGMENTATION AND VALUE-BASED PRICING

Two important parts of market development are identifying customer segments and knowing how much customers are willing to pay. There are several ways in which pricing is set incorrectly.[28] For example, if an innovation is crammed with features to address all customers, it might be too expensive for some segments. Similarly, a lack of understanding of the value the innovation can create for customers leads to under-pricing. Remember that your business has invested significant time and effort in preparing its innovations for market and so it's essential to gain a healthy return on investment. Remember, also, that your breakthrough and radical innovation projects solve customers' hidden needs. Such needs are unknown by competitors, so your innovation will be unique and it should be priced accordingly.

Pricing can lead to big mistakes. Working recently with a building materials company, we learnt of a blundering example. The company in question, which must remain anonymous, produces fire-resistant materials. Founded by a European inventor 100 years ago, it has always sold products by weight. Recently, it developed a new product which offered significantly greater fire resistance and which was, by chance, 20% lighter. Marketing cooperated with finance to set the price based on internal calculations of production costs and an expected margin. When a company bases its price on its costs with an added margin, this is called *cost-plus pricing*. The company had always used this approach, and no one questioned (or even recognized) the assumptions on which it was based. When the product was launched, the sales for use in high-rise constructions were unexpectedly high and the company consulted an architect with expert knowledge. The company was shocked to learn that their new product was, in the architect's opinion, under-priced. Why? The new, significantly lighter material enabled huge savings in the foundations of high-rise buildings. Although the improved fire resistance was important, the lower weight solved many other issues as well. *'Most customers would have paid twice as much for this product'* was the architect's summary. The moral of the story is to have a deep understanding of the problems you are solving for customers, and to know how much they are willing to pay—this is the essence of *value-based pricing*.

Insight generation teams should have summarized the key problems that customers need to solve (the jobs to be done). During spiral development you will be gathering customers' feedback on prototypes that demonstrate how customer issues will be addressed. Concentrate on identifying the time and effort an innovation saves; different customer segments; and the innovation features that fit certain segments. This can allow options to be designed to fit different segments.

Development is the right time to also conduct willingness to pay conversations with customers. It is best to ask four questions (Table 5-7), applied in Quadrant 4 of the Spiral. The first three can be asked on the first round of the Spiral and the 4th question can be added on the second round (based on the

TABLE 5-7: WILLINGNESS TO PAY QUESTIONS[29]

	QUESTIONS	ANSWERS AND CONCLUSIONS
1	What do you think would be an acceptable price? Why?	
2	What do you think would be a high price? Why?	
3	What do you think would be a low price? Why?	
4	Would you buy this product for €xxx? Why?	

results of the first-round conversations). Note that the 'why' questions are often particularly revealing on customers' purchasing thoughts.

MARKET PLANNING AND LAUNCH

From the preceding discussions on market development, it will be clear that innovators and early adopters have different perceptions compared to the early majority. Therefore, marketing plans are needed to address these different groups and cross the chasm. A simple tool, shown in Table 5-8, can be used for market development. The table firstly includes space for notes on how the three different groups have varying perceptions of the innovation (based on answers to the diffusion of innovation questions in Table 5-6). Secondly, it includes space for specific promotional actions to be planned.

We will explain an example from our own experience: planning the launch of an intelligent electrocardiogram (ECG) monitor.[30] To accelerate planning, 24 customer visits were organized in one week. A team of three marketing experts visited different medical facilities, from university clinics to local cardiologists. All of the potential customers were given a demonstration of an advanced prototype and asked questions about their perception of the machine (based on the diffusion of innovation questions in Table 5-6). From this the characteristics of the different types of customers were generated and actions to promote the product to them identified. From Table 5-8 it can be seen that the innovators and early adopters were found to be university

TABLE 5-8: MARKET PLANNING TOOL WITH EXAMPLE FINDINGS FOR AN INTELLIGENT ECG MACHINE

ADOPTERS / STAGE	ADOPTERS' CHARACTERISTICS AND THEIR PERCEPTIONS OF THE INNOVATION	ACTIONS TO PROMOTE ADOPTION
Innovators	University hospitals are very open to innovation. The ECG machine was perceived as a potential time-saver, quickly identifying patients where cardiologists should focus their time. The perceived risk was that abnormal ECGs would be missed.	Professors of cardiology were asked to objectively evaluate the machine; write an article on how it could be used; and give presentations on their findings. In return, their departments were given significant discounts on equipment and free maintenance.
Early Adopters	Larger regional hospitals were interested but sceptical that their staff had the time to learn how to use the new machine effectively. Some ECG technicians were worried that their role was threatened.	Early adopters were invited to the professors' presentations and offered trial machines for two weeks. Free training for their staff was provided for every machine purchased.
Crossing the Chasm		Links between larger regional and more local hospitals were found to be strong, in terms of staff contacts and cooperation. Building on these links, seminars and workshops were organized to explain and offer trials of the new equipment.
Early Majority	Local hospitals and larger physician practices.	Based on the strong links between hospitals in a region, multiple hospitals were invited to free staff training sessions in the larger hospitals.

hospitals and regional cardiology centres, with large workloads on analysing ECGs. In particular, crossing of the chasm was accelerated by seminars and workshops on the new machines.

During spiral development, there are three opportunities where the project team can show versions of the product to customers (initially the minimally viable product, then an advanced prototype and finally the finished product). At each of these times, the project team will have an opportunity to build their market knowledge. This will inform marketing's launch plan.

A crucial part of the launch plan is to consider the sales channel and how different members of the decision-making unit can be convinced of the advantages of the innovation. For breakthrough and radical innovations, salespeople will require training on the new features and benefits.

At the innovation launch, unique features must be promoted effectively. Here, it's important to clearly communicate the problems that the innovation addresses. Try to be as specific as possible; saying things like 'this device will save 10 minutes' preparation time'. An example is Swedish manufacturer Mölnlycke's new surgical gloves. A particular advantage of these was that their cuffs were designed so that they would not slip down the arms of a surgical gown. Typical other products would slip occasionally, forcing medical professionals to leave the operating room to re-sterilize. The problem was so accepted that medical staff perceived it as annoying but normal and Mölnlycke had to develop clear communications and ways to demonstrate the advantage, to get customers to perceive that Mölnlycke's gloves were better.

MINDSET MATTERS

The people involved in Phase 5 are innovation project teams and their team leaders, the innovation manager, senior sponsors and the rest of the senior team. If you're a member of an innovation project team, you're at the leading edge of innovation. As innovation is risky, you should be aware that conducting such projects isn't purely a technical challenge. Emotions can and should run high during Phase 5 and cross-functional tensions can be productive, if handled appropriately. Different functions such as R&D, finance and marketing will have different, sometimes opposing objectives. These trade-offs should be aired openly and the team should find ways to make the best decision for the project and not for one function.

Teams working on incremental (black-space) innovation might feel that this isn't as exciting or as important as breakthrough (grey-space) and radical (white-space) projects. However, the business life cycle showed that incremental innovations protect the core business. These teams must take pride in conducting their projects quickly and efficiently, and delivering tangible returns. For breakthrough and radical project teams, the experience will be stimulating and taxing. Such projects explore the limits of markets and sometimes technologies, and so team members must come to work expecting the unexpected and having the energy and resilience to solve whatever problems the project 'throws at them'.

Remember, innovation project team leaders must have the right mindset and tools for the incremental, breakthrough, or radical project they are assigned to. Kärcher, the German producer of high-pressure cleaning devices for home, garden and professional use, regards innovation as a learning process, where project leaders must solve emerging, unexpected problems. Kärcher's top innovation team leaders are trained to learn from previous projects and to develop a 'sixth sense' for anticipating what the next problem to arise will be (and that they will need to solve). Project team leaders should remain calm when problems arise as, if they become stressed, this can become contagious. Therefore, 'calm under pressure' and 'perseverance' are essential traits for team leaders.

Innovation managers must be versatile in Phase 5; they must constantly switch from one project to another, switching mindsets from black- to grey- to white-space. They'll have to remind colleagues, senior sponsors and especially the senior team that implementing a portfolio of different projects is challenging, but it is building ambidextrous capabilities that will sustain long-term innovative growth.

Senior sponsors should interact regularly with their innovation project teams, challenging them in a positive way about their work—both the speed of progress and the commercial viability of the idea. This sort of proactive interaction helps innovation project teams far more than if they only meet their senior sponsor at gate meetings, or worse, only when the project is struggling. As a sponsor, you can hone your interactions with teams by regularly asking the same questions: *What hypotheses have you proved and disproved?* And: *What assumptions are you making going forward and how do you propose to test them?*

Throughout Phase 5 managers from the senior team will be acting like venture capitalists, monitoring the progress of the portfolio of innovations. The aim is to get the whole portfolio of innovations to market successfully, but if a project doesn't make technical or commercial sense it should be culled. Once innovations hit the market, steady management nerves are needed because the markets for breakthrough and radical products take time to develop.

SUMMARY

- The traditional Stage-Gate™ process works well for managing incremental innovation projects. Such projects are imperative as they defend and extend existing market share and margins.
- Breakthrough and radical innovation projects need to be managed using an agile, spiral process. Unknown problems are bound to emerge and so project teams need the capacity to deal with them.
- In parallel to the development of breakthrough and radical products (or services), project teams must develop new markets.
- At the end of Phase 5, you will have accomplished one of the most exciting and risky parts of your innovation journey, and will have launched a range of innovations onto the market.
- Phase 6 will be about learning from the whole of your innovation journey and building further innovation capabilities to sustain future growth.

Phase 6
Building a dynamic innovation capability

Building a dynamic innovation capability

INTRODUCTION

By now, your business has completed its first *Innovation Journey*, having navigated from 'A' to 'B'. Several innovations will have been implemented and it's now time to review what worked well and what can be improved to drive future growth, as your business context inevitably changes. Some businesses, emboldened by initial success, rush to exploit the results and don't reflect on how they reached this point. Other businesses, chastened by a less than successful project, may skip reviews altogether. Whether you had a resounding success or

DIAGRAM 6-1: PHASE 6 OF THE INNOVATION JOURNEY

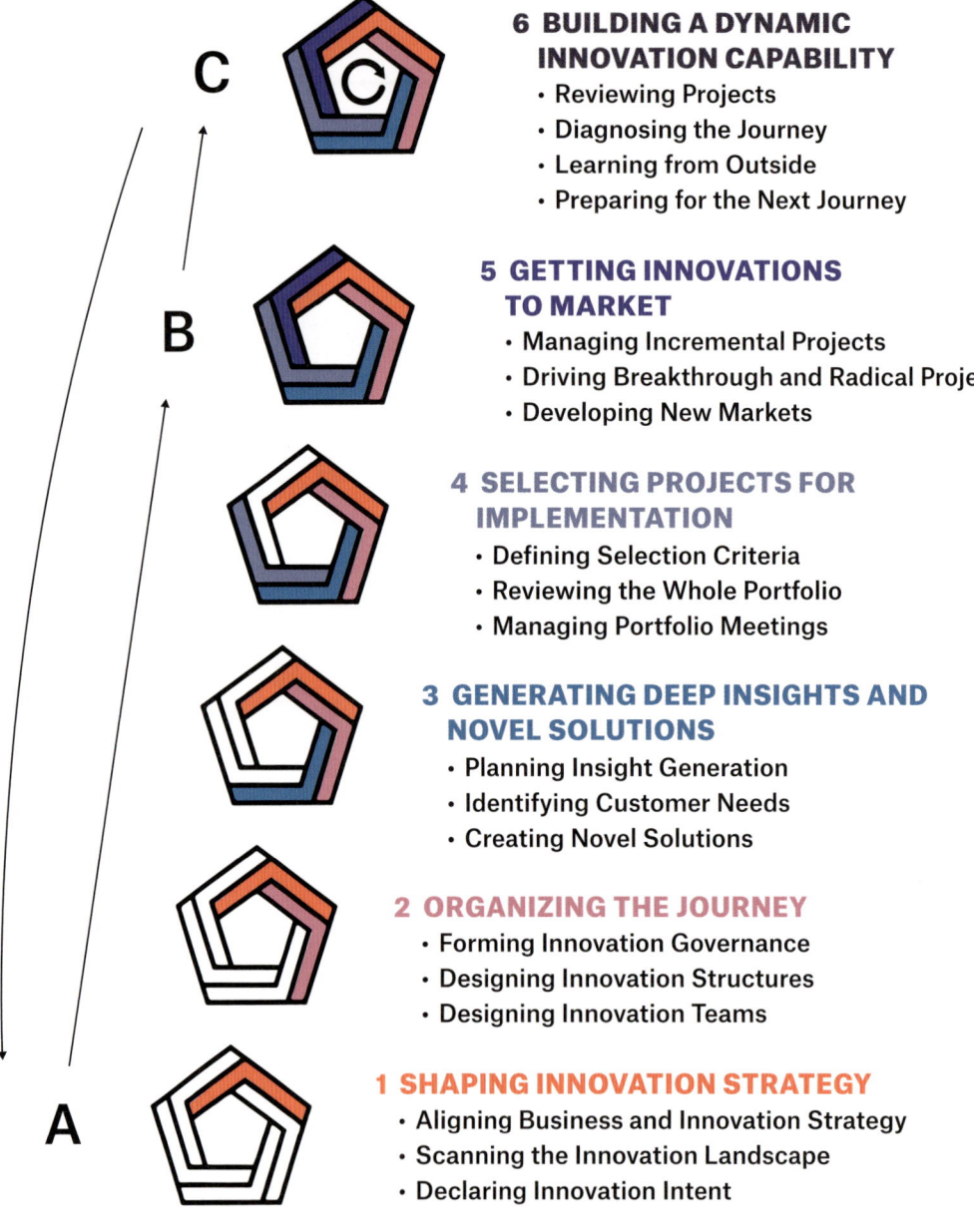

more mixed results, it's vital that you learn from the journey. Only then can you build a dynamic innovation capability ('C'), which will ensure your business can be successful in changing contexts.

Diagram 6-1 indicates that Phase 6 consists of reflecting on the whole journey. In engineering terms, Phase 6 provides a positive feedback loop to enhance your innovation capabilities. In psychology terms, it helps to develop the right mindset for your next *Innovation Journey*. And reflecting on what you achieved versus your intended goals will help you decide which innovation capabilities to concentrate on building for the next journey.

Reflecting on the *Innovation Journey* is best done using what's termed an *Action Learning Cycle*. This ensures that conscious learning takes place, with the four steps shown at the top of Diagram 6-1 (they are usually shown as an iterative cycle).[1] Step 1 reviews each innovation project. In Step 2, the senior team conducts a diagnosis of the journey. The first two steps are inward-looking, whereas Step 3 looks externally, aiming to learn from other businesses. Step 4 brings it all together in a senior team workshop that facilitates collective reflections (deciding which capabilities to discard, improve and renew) and prepares for the next journey.

TABLE 6-1: PHASE 6—KEY THEMES AND CHECKLIST

THEMES	DETAILS
Actions to take	☐ Review completed innovation projects ☐ Diagnose the journey ☐ Learn from the outside ☐ Prepare the next journey
Tools and concepts	☐ Project review workshops ☐ Journey diagnostic
People responsible	☐ Project teams ☐ Innovation manager ☐ Senior team
Mindset matters	☐ Learning through conscious reflection ☐ Dynamic leadership
Outputs	☐ Journey diagnosis ☐ Next journey initial goals

Table 6-1 summarizes the key themes covered in this chapter. There are the above four actions (or steps) to take in building a dynamic innovation capability. The main tools are *Project Reviews* and a *Journey Diagnostic Tool*, which assess the extent to which innovation capabilities ('C') have been built.

The people responsible are the project teams, innovation manager and the senior team. A strategic, learning-oriented mindset is required to reflect on the innovation management capabilities you've built to date and how they can be further enhanced to make your business dynamic. The key outputs are a comprehensive journey diagnosis and goals for the next journey.

ESSENTIAL BACKGROUND

Saying that today's businesses need to be able to handle extreme levels of change has become a cliché. Nevertheless, top businesses *do* possess particular innovation capabilities that enable them to dynamically cope with change. To build such a capability, it helps to understand the nature of change and the essentials of organizational learning.

RELENTLESS CHANGE

How change will actually play out in your business context is unclear and emergent. What is clear, however, is that just reacting to change inevitably leads to decline. Over the past 50 years the average lifespan of a successful corporate has dropped from 50 to 20 years and the lifespan of a successful business model has dropped from 15 to 5 years in many markets.[2] Of the numerous drivers of business contexts, two very different ones stand out for mid-sized businesses (MSBs) and strategic business units (SBUs). First, digital technology enables new entrants to build highly competitive business models. Second, 'purpose' is a meaningful, genuine way to engage customers, employees, wider communities and investors alike, and will guide successful businesses in the future.

Digitally Enabled Business Models

From the first industrial revolution (1760–1860) to the third (1950–2000), technologies such as power, computers and automation radically changed some industries and created new ones. Today, the fourth industrial revolution (Industry 4.0)[3] is based on the rapid convergence of computational power; increased bandwidth and storage capacity; burgeoning digital data; network effects; and digital product mobility for sales and supply. This is enabling both start-ups and technology giants to create digital business models that can decimate small businesses and squeeze traditional MSBs (including retailers, distributors and manufacturers).[4]

There are more digital start-ups with innovative business models vying for customers than ever before. Since the 2008 global recession, venture capital investment in start-ups has grown by 17% a year.[5] In 2013 the term *unicorn* was coined to describe 39 privately owned Silicon Valley technology start-ups valued at over $1 billion.[6] As of 2021, 892 unicorns in 45 countries have achieved a total valuation of $3 trillion[7], funded by a range of sources—crowdfunding, angels, accelerators, traditional and corporate venture capital.[8]

In most industries, groups of digital start-ups are driving disruption, such as 'FinTech' in finance and 'EdTech' in education. They attack established players, such as retail banks, with cheaper and simpler (digital) propositions, initially for a niche market, before adding services and increasing margins. For example, London-based Revolut is a neobank; a financial services technology firm that streamlines mobile and online banking through clever apps, software and other technologies. It was established in 2015, originally offering only debit cards and e-wallets. Revolut now offers stock and cryptocurrency trading, business accounts and payments insurance, and even credit.[9] This enabled Revolut to gain 4.5 million new customers in 2020 alone, taking their total to 14.5 million. Digital business models require far fewer physical assets, so they can be scaled quickly. In addition, this means that private funders are willing to cover losses for several years before market dominance and profit is achieved.[10]

Disruptive innovation is by no means the exclusive realm of start-ups. At the established end of the business life cycle, large 'tech' companies can also shake things up. In 2000, the top five valued companies—General Electric, ExxonMobil, Pfizer, Citigroup and CISCO—had business models that controlled physical resources within well-defined value chains. In 2021 the top five—Apple, Alphabet, Microsoft, Amazon and Facebook[11]—had digital platform business models that orchestrate global value ecosystems, spanning traditional industry boundaries. Amazon has disrupted retail, entertainment and cloud computing and is using its cash and vast collection of customer and supplier data to attack the pharmacy, business lending, logistics, groceries, smart homes and insurance markets.[12] You might not fear that Amazon or Apple will enter your industry directly, but you should worry that their business models will inspire others to disrupt your markets. Don't wait for this to happen—be the first mover!

Purpose-led Businesses
Today's successful business models create and capture 'value' for multiple stakeholders. Value should be considered in terms of the functional, social, emotional and economic worth that different stakeholders stand to gain. Meeting the expectations of a range of stakeholders is a question of *purpose*— why a business exists. Purpose, also called Mission, guides the selection of long-term goals (vision) and how they will be achieved (organizational values).

Purpose is a topic that has been extensively studied for over 80 years (often referred to as the *Theory of a Firm*) but is even more pertinent today. Not only millennials[13], but also the wider public wants to buy from, work for, invest in, and associate themselves with the 'right' sorts of businesses—that means businesses that say they are environmentally and socially responsible and demonstrate this year-on-year. Just as business strategy needs to be transformed as the macro and market context changes, so too does purpose.

In his 1954 seminal book *The Practice of Management*,[14] Peter Drucker regarded the purpose of a business as to serve the customer, and customer-centricity is the stated primary purpose of the above-named, top five valued companies. In 1970, the economist Milton Friedman claimed that the only responsibility of a business is to deliver value to shareholders[15] and the role of managers is solely to maximize profits.[16] Today, leading management thinkers contend that stakeholder-centricity is essential for success. Influential books such as *Conscious Capitalism* (2013)[17] and *Stakeholder Capitalism* (2021)[18] encourage businesses to think in this way. Firstly, by broadening their view of stakeholders to include employees, contractors, suppliers, and the communities and environment in which the business operates. Secondly, by ensuring their purpose addresses pressing environmental and societal issues. Climate change-related disasters and the Covid-19 pandemic have intensified the urgency of such issues. For example, the World Economic Forum has highlighted five main risks[19]: climate change; infectious diseases; loss of biodiversity; shortage of natural resources; and environmental damage. Similarly, the United Nations has flagged social inequality as an increasing problem impacting much of the global population, and new technologies such as artificial intelligence and robotics are likely to exacerbate the problem.[20]

The adoption of *Corporate Social Responsibility* (CSR) practices by large, medium and small businesses peaked ten years ago. CSR should help businesses self-regulate, so that they have a positive impact, through environmentally friendly products, philanthropy and volunteering. However, the way some companies have approached environmental issues has been seen as 'greenwashing'. For example, fashion companies are under scrutiny for labelling products as 'environmentally friendly' but doing far too little to moderate consumption, pollution and waste. A crass example is that up until recently, Burberry purposely burnt unsold stock every year! Such moves have led the term CSR to acquire negative connotations.

The newer term *Environmental, Social and Governance* (ESG) designates businesses which monitor their Environmental impacts quantifiably (for example carbon emissions, water use and waste), analyse their Social impacts (for example customer, supplier, consumer and community aspects); and monitor their Governance (for example monitoring board diversity, limiting lobbying, and preventing corruption). Investors are increasingly interested in ESG and today over 90% of the world's biggest companies report their ESG performance.[21] Disappointingly, and similarly to CSR, research shows there is still a big *purpose gap* between what businesses say they do and their actions.[22] However, the positive news is that companies that genuinely strive for ESG, such as the outdoor clothing company Patagonia, engender hyper-loyal customers, attract the best employees and achieve the highest performance[23] (see Case Study 6-1). Thus, purpose presents MSBs and SBUs with a way to differentiate what they do, why they do it, and who and how they serve.

CASE STUDY 6-1: PATAGONIA
TRUE PURPOSE[24]

Patagonia Inc. was born almost 50 years ago in a tin shed in Ventura, California. The founder, Yvon Chouinard, a renowned mountaineer and self-taught blacksmith, originally made climbing hardware from material salvaged from junkyards. Despite, or perhaps because of its humble beginnings, Patagonia has evolved into an international outdoor clothing brand, with over 2,300 employees and $1B revenues. Patagonia is highly respected within its industry and beyond.

Patagonia aspires to design great products that stand out from the competition, and minimize environmental impact. Many of the company's employees share their customers' passion for outdoor sports and caring for the environment. The company proudly measures its product development cycles in years (not weeks, like many in the industry) because it is striving for unique and robust products that last longer... and longer (as Patagonia offers inexpensive—often free—and convenient repair services). Product development is not rushed as it is all about getting things right. Getting things right includes using advanced techniques such as *biomimicry*, which imitates the way nature solves problems. For example, ideas from nature have helped create high-performing, enduring wetsuits made from FSC Certified Yulex natural rubber, rather than harmful, non-renewable neoprene. The company also strives to uncover deep customer insights and act on them. For example, it found that clothing co-branded for corporate clients has a shorter lifespan, as people are less likely to wear it if they move companies. Accordingly, Patagonia has downscaled corporate sales. Similarly, not only does it sell new clothes based on a classic retail business model, but through the company's longstanding Worn Wear initiative it also encourages resale of used products, featured alongside new ones (currently US only). The company is totally transparent about its supply chain and has the goal to be carbon neutral by 2025 and is proactively encouraging partners and others to follow suit. For example, Patagonia's exceptionally high score in the demanding B-Corporation accreditation has inspired apparel companies to try to emulate its performance. Patagonia also allocates 1% of company revenues to grassroots environmental groups, and invests in environmentally and socially responsible start-ups, via the US-based venture arm Tin Shed Ventures.

Although Patagonia is the very definition of an innovative business, it refrains from describing itself using the 'i-word'. Communication and language matter to the company, which believes that 'innovation' is becoming synonymous with companies still striving for growth without proper consideration for the environment, and with those individuals extolling how technology can make other planets habitable rather than finding ways to protect our home one. The Patagonia organization has clearly identified that its most vital resource is not just its innovation but its purpose.

Evelyn Doyle is Head of People for the Europe, Middle East and Africa (EMEA) region. Before Patagonia, she worked in HR for various NGOs and corporations, and says of the last five years: *"Patagonia's two 'faces' never cease to amaze me. The warm-hearted, outdoor sports-loving, free-spirited people that you meet every day. But these same people become relentless and tireless in the pursuit of our mission."* Evelyn and colleagues believe there are several aspects of the organizational culture at Patagonia that drives its purpose.

The organization understands that running a business always involves dealing with contradictions. Patagonia is a commercially successful clothing business that openly accepts that it causes some environmental harm. This led Chouinard, who turned 80 in 2018, to change the mission from *"Build the best product, cause no unnecessary harm, use business to inspire and implement solutions to the environmental crisis"* to simply *"Patagonia is in business to save our home planet"*. Evelyn recounts that Chouinard's direction was *"You are smart people, go figure out what this means and how to truly live it"*, which sparked a period of organizational reflection.

Evelyn's then boss Ryan Gellert (who was then general manager for EMEA and is now the global CEO) and senior team colleagues engaged Patagonia's entire EMEA organization. Off-site workshops, held over several months, were used to reflect on the new mission and define exactly what it meant for stakeholders. What others might consider to be seeking unnecessary consensus and pedantic wordsmithing was a process to co-create a more dynamic organization, even more focused on environmental and societal impact. External facilitators 'held up a mirror' and taught Patagonia's people how to authentically empathize with different stakeholders and collaborate. *"This made us feel very uncomfortable at times, as we realized we did not have the answers to many big issues. However, it was these moments of humility that opened up so many new insights and possibilities"*, says Evelyn. These collective learning moments are something that has defined Patagonia's work over the past half century. For example, the organization has acknowledged that it is not as socially inclusive as it could be and this has led to the re-evaluation of every aspect of the business, from recruitment to marketing and the sports ambassadors the company partners with. A radically different learning programme, 'Patagonia Earth University', brings together cross-functional cohorts in a nature setting around a campfire to discuss topics such as 'Growth'—clarifying what 'good growth' entails—and 'Revolutions'—how to connect your individual voice and role to Patagonia's purpose.

While the organizational renewal continues to be driven by employees, Patagonia management still actively leads. For example, despite the loss in revenue, management has taken tough decisions about the sales partners it works with, prioritizing those who share the brand's values and moving away from companies who are not as invested in taking an active role in this work, or conduct business in ways that breach Patagonia's values. Looking forward, Patagonia's senior managers are exploring how to develop more and faster business breakthroughs at the same time as maintaining consensus and setting the right priorities. Purpose drives every one of Patagonia's management decisions.

Summarizing, Evelyn muses *"Patagonia is an unusual organization. Usually, after five years in a position I have found that the level of challenge declines. Here, it is the opposite, as we have so many capabilities to build, if we are to help save our home planet. Here, I can put my mind, heart and soul into my job, and so I know no better place to work than Patagonia."*

DYNAMIC INNOVATION CAPABILITY

What differentiates top businesses is less about digital disruption or a powerful purpose per se and more about a business's capability to change itself in synch with its changing external context. In Chapter 2 we explained that many businesses persevere with a set strategy and the same organization, even though their macro and market contexts change significantly. Achieving growth in changing contexts requires *Dynamic Innovation Capabilities*. These capabilities *sense* and *seize* opportunities and *reconfigure* an organization, responding with little or no delay.[25] Such capabilities might sound complicated, but the good news is that on the *Innovation Journey* you applied tools that already started to build these capabilities.

Sensing opportunities is connected with the capability to develop strategic roadmaps (Phase 1), generate deep insights, and to come up with novel solutions to customer problems (Phase 3). Seizing is intricately linked to your innovation development processes, where the novel solutions were tested with target customers, and innovations were taken to market (Phase 5).

So, the journey from 'A' to 'B' already started to build sense and seize capabilities. In Phases 2 some reconfiguration took place, with mapping and embedding of innovation values (Diagram 2-4), and by designing your business-wide innovation organizational structure (Diagram 2-5). Now, your organization's ability to learn from the whole journey will determine how good it will be at reconfiguring itself.

ORGANIZATIONAL LEARNING

In Chapter 2, we explained how innovation is dependent on learning curves. In short, the faster your business can learn (climbing steep learning curves), the better it is at innovation. Organizations 'learn' at the individual, team, organizational and inter-organization levels, using two modes of learning.[26] *Adaptive learning* occurs when the achievement of goals is jeopardized, but a quick review remedies the situation. An example would be if an innovation project slips behind schedule and the team works all hours to find ways to catch up and launch on time. Adaptive learning is reactive, drawing mostly on fixed mindsets and existing organizational capabilities developed through operating in and defending black-space.

Generative learning is triggered by reflection, when we question our intended goals and the mechanisms being used to achieve them. So, for example, if product launches are consistently late, we question if the schedules were achievable, if processes were suitable, and even if the overall innovation intent was realistic. Generative learning is proactive and requires the right mindset to think in abstract terms, transitioning from specific examples to broad, meaningful conclusions. It relies on a reflective and curious mindset to conceive novel ways to achieve growth in black-, grey- and white-space.

It's important to note that individuals and teams that are successful at adaptive learning often struggle when generative learning is required. Since generative learning is proactive, it requires a climate of *psychological safety*—where people don't fear being criticized; they accept constructive conflict; they value being asked 'naive' questions; and they admit errors.[27] Therefore, senior managers must fully engage in the organizational learning process, encouraging everyone involved to reflect, using the four action learning steps.

STEP 1—REVIEWING INNOVATION PROJECTS

Each individual project should be reviewed within 6–10 weeks of completion.[28] A *Post-project Review* will encourage learning, helping to enhance capabilities and recognize a team's achievements.[29] Such reviews are a practical way to mould an innovative culture that values evidence-based learning. We recommend a facilitator from outside the team, who is skilled at probing both tacit and sensitive issues.[30] The facilitator, often the innovation manager, should foster a no-blame, generative learning climate in every review.

Team performance should be checked against the team charter (introduced in Chapter 2, and also in the Online Appendix). To reiterate, the charter is based on the four characteristics of high-performing innovation teams. These are: clear and challenging goals; appropriate skillsets and mindsets; tailored processes; and positive team dynamics. Table 6-2 is a post-project review template which covers each characteristic and captures a team's answers to three questions: *What Worked Well? What Did Not Work Well?* and *How Can We Improve?* Make sure to use the brainwriting technique (explained in Chapter 1) so that everyone's viewpoint is captured. In addition, we recommend two techniques for stimulating open discussion about the more implicit team dynamics. The first is called the *I Like – I Wish Technique.* Each team member is asked to write two things they liked about the actions of all other team members and to express one wish.[31] For example, a team member might reflect on a colleague, saying *'I liked that your inputs were always succinct and I liked that you warned the team when you needed extra time to complete a task'*, and *'I wish you had shared more of your experience with less experienced colleagues'*. Remind everyone that this isn't a blame game. Then, one by one, get each project team member to share their feedback. Team members receiving feedback should only respond with points of clarification and thanking colleagues for their views. The technique gives team members insights on how their mindsets and actions impact others. Another technique is to task teams with creating a 5-minute video answering the question *What did the team learn from this project?* Videos can be tagged with key words and shared with other teams.

Throughout the post-project review, the facilitator should stimulate discussion and capture learning using the template. After a post-project review, the innovation manager or facilitator is responsible for feeding the post-project review conclusions (Table 6-2) into the overall Phase 6 action learning cycle. Table 6-2 summarizes the post-project review conducted by an innovation team at the Irish forestry company Coillte. The team was tasked

TABLE 6-2: INNOVATION POST-PROJECT REVIEW TEMPLATE

CHARACTERISTICS OF HIGH-PERFORMING INNOVATION TEAMS	WHAT WORKED WELL? (KEEP/EMBED)	WHAT DID NOT WORK WELL? (DISCARD/IMPROVE)	HOW CAN WE IMPROVE? (WITHIN TEAM/ORGANIZATION)
CLEAR AND CHALLENGING GOALS Goal and priority assumptions clear and mutually agreed between the team and senior team?	• We had a clear and ambitious challenge: 1) Who visits the forest? 2) What are their met/unmet needs? 3) How can we better serve them? 4) How can we make a profit?	• Managing the expectations of the senior team. They wanted a definitive 'answer' early on that fit their comfort zone of land development ideas, such as hotels, parks developed by partners.	• Give the Senior team a full understanding of the innovation journey and prime them to consider broad insights and ideas before definitive answers are available. More frequent meetings.
APPROPRIATE SKILLSETS AND MINDSETS Required knowledge and mindsets were well identified and accessible?	• The skillsets and mindsets identified for the team were intuitively correct. • Team leader brought a fresh perspective to recreation and was passionate about creating something new.	• Too many of the team were part-time, which meant their engagement was too low, despite their genuine enthusiasm. • Key experts within Coillte were hard to access and relevant reports and presentations were either unavailable or held little value without a discussion with the author(s).	• Team members need sufficient time and the full support of their line managers. • Experts' knowledge needs to be captured and made available within Coillte.
TAILORED INNOVATION DEVELOPMENT PROCESSES Suitable tools and techniques were identified for key activities and phases and team was skilled/supported to use them?	• The 'light' project management and KPIs worked well. • The inventory of tools and introductory training (for example design thinking) helped the team get going. • The Phase 3 hidden needs techniques led to several breakthrough insights.	• It would have saved time if the hidden needs training was given earlier. • Some of the training (for example value chain analysis) was superficial and expert hands-on support would have been better.	• Recognize the team's skill gaps earlier and provide tailored, hands-on training and support.

CHARACTERISTICS OF HIGH-PERFORMING INNOVATION TEAMS	WHAT WORKED WELL? (KEEP/ EMBED)	WHAT DID NOT WORK WELL? (DISCARD/ IMPROVE)	HOW CAN WE IMPROVE? (WITHIN TEAM/ ORGANIZATION)
POSITIVE TEAM DYNAMICS Team had agreed ways of working and lived them?	• The team was passionate about doing something different for recreation. • Team lead updated people formally every week and also informally. • The dedicated workspace was indispensable.	• The decision-making processes within the team and with senior manager were opaque and frustrating for some people. • Part-time team members were not present during many team sessions.	• Spend more time on team 'on-boarding' and 'orientation'. • Clarify how decisions will be made. • Ensure all team members have sufficient time together.

with creating a recreational service, which would build a new business making at least €1M profit per annum within 36 months. The post-project review meeting included everyone involved in the project. It can be seen that the team thought that they had clear goals but, when they proposed ideas, many senior team members had a strong conservative bias and lacked an open mindset. Similarly, in considering team dynamics, the Coillte innovation team thought that more time should be made available to 'on-board' and 'orientate' team members in future projects.

A substantive aspect of the post-project review is to recognize and celebrate a team's accomplishments. Senior sponsors' participation signals to the team that learning is highly valued, irrespective of whether their project was fully successful or not. For example, at the German company Kärcher (which manufactures high-pressure cleaning equipment) the Chief Technology Officer attends every post-project review, to hear teams' learning points first-hand and then to host a celebratory meal.

STEP 2—DIAGNOSING THE JOURNEY

In Step 2, the senior team should assess which innovation capabilities were effective during the first journey, using the *Journey Diagnostic* tool, which covers Phases 1-5. Diagram 6-2 shows the section of the tool covering

DIAGRAM 6-2: JOURNEY DIAGNOSTIC— PHASE 1: SHAPING INNOVATION STRATEGY

1. SHAPING INNOVATION STRATEGY	LOW (1)	MEDIUM (3)	HIGH (5)	RATING
1.1 ALIGNING BUSINESS AND INNOVATION STRATEGY	The business and innovation strategies were not aligned. Financial growth goals were unrealistic and made only vague reference to 'innovation'. The senior team was not engaged.	The business and innovation strategy were tied to financial growth goals. A dedicated manager facilitated the innovation strategy and partly engaged the senior team.	The business and innovation strategy addressed ambitious financial growth goals. The process was led by an innovation manager who fully engaged the senior team. Innovation-related growth was clear.	— 5
1.2 SCANNING INNOVATION LANDSCAPE	Only existing opportunities were considered and the wider innovation landscape was ignored. These opportunities. were superficially investigated based on intuition.	A limited innovation landscape with some new opportunities was considered. Ad-hoc teams investigated growth opportunities but without proper roadmapping.	The full innovation landscape was scanned to find opportunities. Suitable teams were designated to investigate innovation strategic options (ISOs) with comprehensive roadmaps.	— 5
1.3 DECLARING INNOVATION INTENT	Conservative and /or grandiose commercial goals were articulated. These relied solely on incremental innovation (black-space) and / or hype. Innovation capabilities were overlooked.	Ambitious yet unrealistic commercial goals were set with a poor balance of growth in black-, grey- and white-space. Innovation capability gaps were only partially discussed.	Clear, ambitious yet realistic commercial goals were set. These led to a balanced growth in black-, grey- and white-space. Innovation capability gaps and well-defined means to close them were identified.	— 5
1.4 STRATEGIC MINDSET	The senior team remained in its comfort zone, acted in a myopic conservative way and relied on gut-feelings.	The senior team moved arbitrarily beyond its comfort zone, with some long-term thinking and some broader innovative opportunities.	The senior team fully stepped out of its comfort zone, systematically moving between short- and long-term thinking and exploring the breadth of innovative growth.	— 5
			PHASE 1 SCORE	— 20

Phase 1, Shaping innovation strategy. The other four sections of the tool are given in the Online Appendix (www.innovativegrowth.com).

The far left-hand column of Diagram 6-2 provides short descriptions of the four specific innovation capabilities needed in developing innovation strategy, starting with *Aligning Business and Innovation Strategy* (1.1), through to *Strategic Mindset*—how the senior team thinks, feels and behaves in relation to business growth (1.1). For each capability, a rating on a scale of '1' (low) to '5' (high) should be given; anchoring statements are provided to assist managers. Managers should assign ratings in the column on the right, based on their perceptions of the capabilities. (The online appendix version allows for specific comments to be made about each rating). Managers should sum up their overall assessment, giving a score out of 20 points. The tool follows exactly the same format for Phases 2-5. This enables senior managers to rate the effectiveness of their company's innovation capabilities over the entire Innovation Journey, leading to a total score out of 100 points.

The *Journey Diagnostic* tool should be completed separately by each member of the senior team and submitted to the innovation manager, who can then calculate the average ratings, standard deviations (which shows the variation in ratings across the senior team), and the overall score. These are summarized using Diagram 6-3, which has space where the senior team can annotate their perceptions on the strengths and weaknesses of their organization's innovation capabilities. The ratings and any specific comments should then be discussed by the senior team. Common themes, contradictions and cases where there are large standard deviations—that is, where different managers have assigned very different scores—will lead to potent insights. Discussions enable the senior team to identify which capabilities to enhance and how (add ideas for capability improvement on the right part of Diagram 6-3).

Note that the journey diagnostic uses self-assessments and is perception-based. Therefore, don't treat the scores as 'absolutes', but rather as a means to identify which capabilities require attention and how to make pragmatic improvements.

DIAGRAM 6-3: JOURNEY DIAGNOSTIC TOOL—SUMMARY

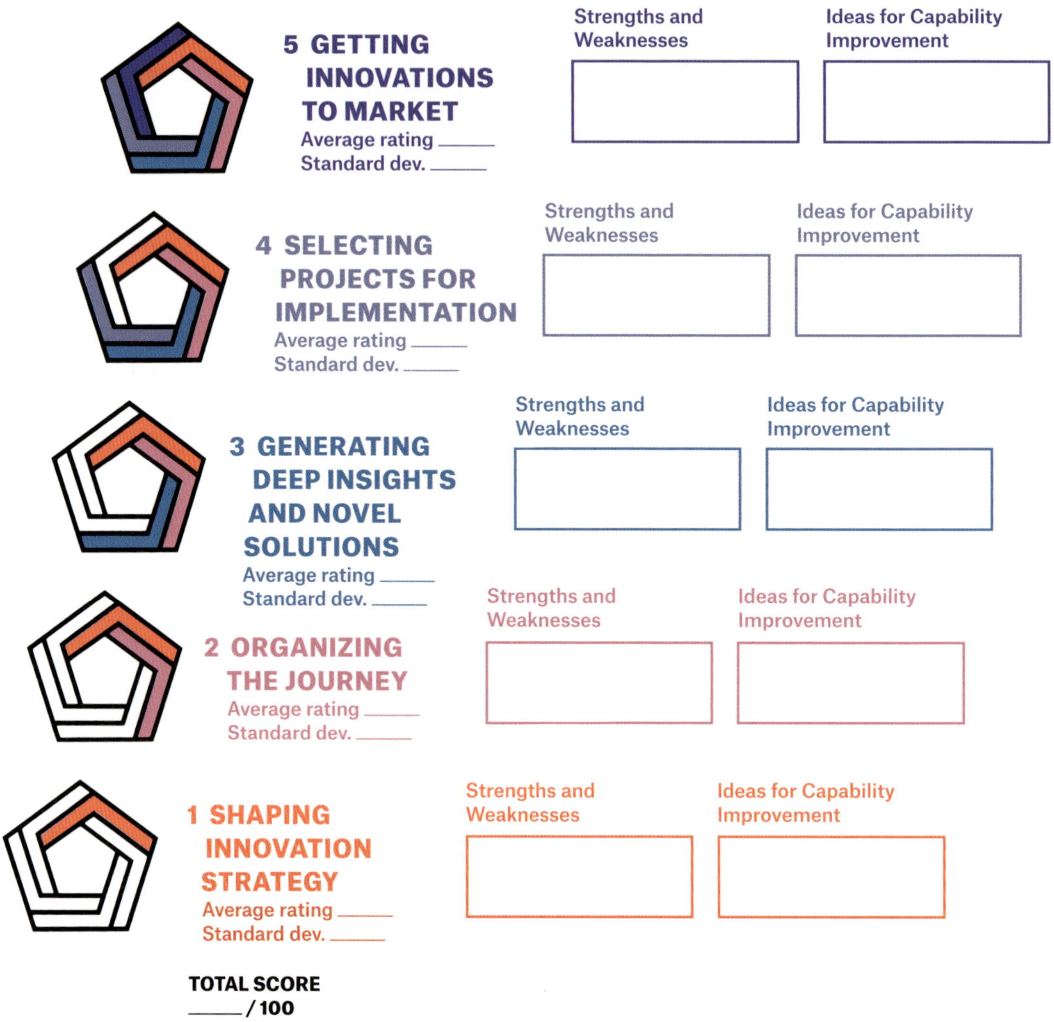

5 GETTING INNOVATIONS TO MARKET
Average rating _____
Standard dev. _____

Strengths and Weaknesses

Ideas for Capability Improvement

4 SELECTING PROJECTS FOR IMPLEMENTATION
Average rating _____
Standard dev. _____

Strengths and Weaknesses

Ideas for Capability Improvement

3 GENERATING DEEP INSIGHTS AND NOVEL SOLUTIONS
Average rating _____
Standard dev. _____

Strengths and Weaknesses

Ideas for Capability Improvement

2 ORGANIZING THE JOURNEY
Average rating _____
Standard dev. _____

Strengths and Weaknesses

Ideas for Capability Improvement

1 SHAPING INNOVATION STRATEGY
Average rating _____
Standard dev. _____

Strengths and Weaknesses

Ideas for Capability Improvement

TOTAL SCORE
_____ / 100

STEP 3—LEARNING FROM OUTSIDE

Steps 1 and 2 of the action learning cycle took the inside view, looking at innovation projects and capabilities. Managers should also take an outside view, as much can be learnt by considering the innovation capabilities of other companies[32] (the importance of an outside view to counter myopic mindsets was explained in Chapter 2). Learning should be based on selected company case studies, and three contemporary topics, digital business models; purpose-led businesses; and the future of work.

LEARNING FROM EXTERNAL CASES

Throughout this book we have shared case studies exemplifying different innovation capabilities. Now, the aim is to reflect on which case studies are most relevant to your business and to think about which other businesses you can also learn from.

It helps to specify your learning objectives. Asking: *Which businesses are good at innovation?* is too broad; and, for example: *Which businesses are good at providing a superior digital customer experience that could be applied in our markets?* is a better question to ask. If the objective is to imitate other businesses, then look at organizations with similar characteristics (size, industry, customers) to your own.[33] If the objective is to learn about something not yet seen in your market, then case studies in analogous markets are more relevant. For example, a business unit of a major bank was looking at customers' 'financial wellbeing'. As part of this investigation, the business unit looked at what healthcare organizations are doing to improve physical and mental wellbeing and generated many ideas based on this.

To identify and approach external companies, be sure to leverage your organization's networks to open doors. Positive engagement will be founded on trust and mutual benefit. Convey your intentions and address confidentiality concerns up-front. Clarify the value for the other company; for example, mutual learning from exchanging ideas on very different markets. Agree reciprocal visits and prepare by checking your partner company's markets and by crafting open questions. When on site and if permitted, take photographs or videos as these will reinforce the learning when you write a summary of the visit. Share the summary with the external organization as it will be useful for them to see how their innovation capabilities are perceived. Such nascent inter-organizational connections often evolve into fruitful collaborative relationships. For example, we know of two MSBs from the agricultural and automotive fields that run joint workshops on identifying customer needs. Employees find that these workshops have enabled them to understand a very different market, which has stimulated novel ideas for their own markets.

LEARNING FROM DIGITAL BUSINESS MODELS

Digitalization will disrupt most businesses at some time. Even when it doesn't disrupt, digitization will impact the way customers are served and can help optimize existing business models. Therefore, it's prudent for the senior team to understand the role of *digital business models*—how different participants (for example consumers, suppliers) are digitally integrated to collectively create and capture value.

A well-known example of a digital business model is the accommodation platform Airbnb. The success of this 'platform' business model is based on four factors.[34] First, the platform creates value for the consumer (including greater choice, cheaper accommodation, and cooking facilities) *and* suppliers (for example hosts generating income from previously underutilized space). Second, Airbnb's platform is professional, easy to use, and efficient for the consumer (a good customer experience), and has helpful tools for hosts joining the platform. It has become what is known as a *destination*—a 'go-to' platform (in this case for people seeking accommodation). Third, the platform generates positive *network effects* as more consumers adopt, rate their experiences, and attract more consumers (this is termed *same-side network effects*), which then attracts more hosts (*cross-side network effects*). Fourth, Airbnb's ownership of the platform allows them to collect substantial amounts of data, which enables the company to learn how to improve the current offering and create new propositions. Airbnb has grown an evolving value ecosystem that is hard to copy and now comprises a range of participants, including rental managers, cleaners, and photographers who portray properties. Adding new participants is quick and inexpensive and Airbnb capture 3% of revenues from their seven million hosts and 10–15% from their 150 million guests.[35]

Digital Business Model Framework

Airbnb's digital business model is easy to describe but harder to emulate in different markets, such as B2B. To better understand your current digital business model and potential alternatives, the *Digital Business Model Framework* (Diagram 6-4)[36] is useful. Based on extensive research at MIT, this framework identifies two dimensions to concentrate on. The first is to build a business model that moves a business from a *partial* knowledge of its end-customers, to a *complete* one. A 'complete' view of end-customers means knowing who they are, constantly following their purchasing and other interactions with you and other network participants and, crucially, finding out their deeper, unmet needs. The second dimension to concentrate on is designing a business model that isn't just based on a linear, upstream-downstream *value chain* (where boundaries and decisions on pricing, IP and branding are clear-cut) but rather on a *value ecosystem* (where boundaries are blurred and participants' roles are interdependent).

Diagram 6-4 shows how the two dimensions delineate the patterns inherent in digital business models. In the *Supplier* business model, a company produces products or services but sells them to end-customers through intermediaries. This means the supplier business slots into another business's value chain, has little or no contact with end-customers, and so has only partial knowledge of end-customers' needs. As the supplier business model is based on incremental innovation and low margins, it often leads to suppliers losing power, and consequently isn't an attractive long-term position. A classic example of this is automotive suppliers that have no contact with end-users and sell components to powerful manufacturers following cost-plus, open book accounting practices. Even suppliers with strong technical expertise have lost power in recent years, despite talk of 'partnerships with suppliers' within the industry. Some car manufacturers are discouraging suppliers from patenting inventions, to avoid single-sourcing and the higher costs that entails. Of course, this traps suppliers into incremental innovation and working within the manufacturer's value chain. Consequently, they have nothing unique to offer and they can only build a digital platform for order fulfilment but without unique content. Put simply, the supplier digital business model is dependent on the product or service being offered, and often just its pricing. Therefore, it's subject to commoditization.[37]

With an *Omnichannel* business model, a company has direct contact with end-customers and interacts with them via multiple channels, ensuring a positive customer experience. It's key to 'own' and maintain customer relationships. Strong interaction with customers enables a B2C company to understand the 'life events' that drive consumer needs. Recall Bank of Ireland (Case Study 2-3), where the organization bolstered its B2C customer-centricity and digital capabilities. The bank investigated its customers' life events—from student life to running a business, to seniors' wealth management. Based on these insights, the bank now tailors its services to enable customers to manage their personal finances at any stage of life. It has started to create a go-to platform, with different digital tools to help customers' financial planning. Services are delivered via a carefully designed mix of digital and physical services. In B2B markets, a deep understanding of customers' business processes and business challenges is the equivalent of understanding B2C life events. A B2B example of this is where manufacturers that have previously sold only via

DIAGRAM 6-4: DIGITAL BUSINESS MODEL FRAMEWORK

	Value Chain	Value Ecosystem
Complete (Knowledge of your end customer)	**Omnichannel** • 'Own' the customer relationship • Create multiproduct customer experience to address life events • Customer chooses channels • Integrated value chain	**Ecosystem Driver** • Become the destination in your space • Add complementary and possibly competitor products • Ensure great customer experience • Match customer needs with providers • Extract 'rents'
Partial	**Supplier** • Sells through other enterprises • Potential for loss of power • Core skills: low-cost producer, incremental innovation	**Modular** • Plug-and-play product/service • Able to adapt to any ecosystem • Constant innovation of product/service

Knowledge of your end customer: Know the identity, purchase history with your company and other firms, and customer goals

Business design
Who controls key decisions like brand, contracts, price, quality, participants, IP and data ownership, regulation

retailers have now added a *Direct-to-Consumer* (D2C) platform, where customers can buy products and services directly. Put simply, the omnichannel business model primarily depends on the (digital and traditional) customer experience offered.

The *Modular Producer* business model is based on designing products or services that can easily adapt to many value ecosystems, such as PayPal does in digital payments. Since markets are hypercompetitive, this business model is dependent on constant innovation and remaining price-competitive. The financial service company Fexco was established in 1981 by Brian McCarthy, as a one-man foreign exchange business. Today it has over 2,500 employees. Its leading currency conversion service is 'plug and play', and it provides instant and transparent currency exchange for customers in stores, ATMs or online points of sale. Put simply, the modular producer business model requires you to be the preferred supplier and is contingent on the strength of the platform it plugs into.

The *Ecosystem Driver* business model is based on a digital platform that becomes *the* destination not only for customers but also for other participants, as illustrated earlier with Airbnb. The platform ensures a deep knowledge of end-customers and orchestrates a value ecosystem, rather than a linear value chain. It typically requires a fraction of the traditional high levels of resource ownership (for example, Airbnb does not own property). Put simply, the ecosystem driver business model is dependent on the attractiveness of the product or service being offered, the usefulness of the information provided by the platform ('content'); a great customer experience; and a virtuous network that outshines all others.

Recall how Red Ventures (Case Study 3-1) initially operated call centres for telecoms and financial companies, as a B2B service supplier. It now owns and operates 100 'destination platforms' in areas such as financial services (Bankrate), healthcare (Healthline), travel (Lonely Planet) and technology (C-Net). The Red Ventures digital insights lab focuses on customer and partner insights and building 'must-visit' websites that are easy to use and offer content that draws in users. Underpinning its success has been a culture that persistently focuses on customer needs, innovation, straight-talking and learning (Case Study 2-1).

Optimizing Your Digital Business Model

Use Diagram 6-4 to identify your current business model and your digital aspiration. The ecosystem driver model is attractive as it's highly profitable and generates significant growth, although it's very hard to attain and maintain. Gaining a competitive advantage through digitization depends on your capability to move up and to the right.

Capabilities to move up include using deep insights about customers to identify the novel products or services needed; which components of the offer can be delivered digitally; and what content is useful to the customer and will draw them to the platform. Insights will also indicate how an integrated, multi-product, multi-channel customer experience can be configured. For a B2B manufacturer, this could consist of a digital platform that allows customers to place custom orders based on their exact technical requirements, a 3-D digital showroom, the ability to order samples via the digital interface, digitally enabled after-sales service, and a host of application information about how products can be used with components from other manufacturers in end-products. Such content starts to make a digital platform more valuable to customers, especially when it supports them in improving their own business processes in unique ways. Through network effects, this will draw in more customers.

Capabilities to move right include the ability to create a digital platform that enables your business to be placed at the centre of a value ecosystem of participants. Visualizing how your business can achieve this will be demanding as it requires generative learning. So, take the time with your management team to draw a possible ecosystem where your business is at the centre, and where the ecosystem satisfies the customer's need for not only your products and services but also related ones. The aim is to transform your business into the preferred digital destination for your customers. Note that your IT function will need to think differently; moving from systems support to understanding how to create a digital platform that creates value for customers and other ecosystem participants.

Case 6-2 describes how the racing bike manufacturer Pinarello has moved its business model 'up and to the right'. The business is fiercely committed to understanding the needs of their key customers—top riders and racing teams—and so it's increased not only its sponsorship but also the level of interaction with leading teams. It's also added its own shops to its retail channels. In moving to the right, Pinarello has replaced its linear, local supply chain with a digitally enabled global ecosystem. This gives the company access to not only the components it needs for manufacturing but also the latest technology and know-how for developing the best bikes possible.

CASE STUDY 6-2: CICLI PINARELLO LEADER OF THE (PELOTON) PACK[38]

Founded in Treviso, northern Italy, in 1952 by Giovanni Pinarello, Cicli Pinarello is a top brand in the global racing bike industry. Over the years, Pinarello has established itself as the benchmark for innovation in the highly competitive professional sector, and today it is the official provider for Team Sky.

Pinarello generated a turnover of €50 million in 2018 and employs 45 people at its headquarters in Treviso. Most of Pinarello's employees are engineers and technicians who work on pre-production (R&D and product development) and post-production functions (painting and finishing) activities, as the bulk of Pinarello's production is outsourced to Asian original equipment manufacturers (OEMs). Pinarello's obsession for innovation comes from the family's enduring passion for racing bikes and professional competitions—for example, Fausto Pinarello, son of Giovanni and the company's current President, has been involved in professional cycling all of his life.

Pinarello's business has changed significantly since the application of carbon fibre components for racing bikes in the early 1990s. In common with other leading companies such as Cannondale, Bianchi and Wilier Triestina, the use of carbon fibre forced Pinarello to reorganize and internationalize its production and supply chain. Pinarello had to reconsider its purchasing strategy and turned to global suppliers located in low-cost economies, as the production of carbon fibre bike frames is a labour-intensive process.

The company switched from small and specialized local suppliers to large, international and cost-effective vendors. Working intensely with foreign suppliers triggered the redesign of Pinarello's product development cycle and this was carefully done in a way that also enhanced the company's innovation capabilities. The new product development cycle, which now begins and ends in Treviso but takes shape thanks to the production skills of Asian suppliers, has been enabled by the use of 3-D printing technology. 3-D printing is used by Pinarello engineers to obtain a real sample of the new frames designed in Italy but refined and completed overseas. This facilitates the interaction between the different parties involved in the product development cycle, while at the same time allowing Pinarello to keep control of such a high-order activity.

When challenged about the company's decision to manufacture entirely offshore and dissipate the production know-how accumulated over decades, Fausto, calmly responded: *"Our design skills and ability to read the market's trends come from other activities."*

So, what are Pinarello's enviable innovation capabilities based on? As in all complex business contexts, the answer lies in a mix of factors. First, Pinarello's unwavering support and commitment to professional cycling competitions and riders provide an ongoing, unmatched source of innovation ideas for the company. Working with some of the most famous professional cyclists in the world—lead users, if you will (for example Miguel Indurain, Mario Cipollini, Jan Ullrich and Egan Bernal)—constantly drives Pinarello to apply advanced technologies to develop higher performing bicycles. The product innovation cycle always starts at Pinarello's Treviso headquarters, where engineers and technicians work on the development of new product ideas and produce sketches of the new bicycles. Pinarello's new products have unique designs, which blend together the tradition of Pinarello with the best of Italian contemporary design.

Once they have been manufactured overseas, bike frames are finished in Treviso. It's in this final phase that the distinguishing design of Pinarello is crafted by experienced professionals. When asked about the threats posed by new global competitors, Fausto responded: *"Try to make a bike like ours if you can. Try to make it as sexy as ours. It won't happen any time soon."

In 2015 Pinarello was acquired by L Catterton, a US private equity firm which owns many luxury brands, such as fitness training equipment provided by Peloton, and CorePower Yoga. Through Catterton's influence, Pinarello is expanding its channels to market, including opening retail stores in London, Manchester and Mallorca. The passion for products at Pinarello is sure to keep them ahead of the (Peloton) pack.

LEARNING FROM PURPOSE-LED BUSINESSES

Many businesses place stakeholders in a pecking order: shareholders, customers and employees. More progressive businesses value all their stakeholders and don't place them in a strict hierarchy. This helps close the purpose gap discussed earlier, where a company's claims about its perspective on the environment, society and governance (ESG) lack authenticity.

Transforming a traditional business into a distinctive, purpose-led one such as Patagonia (Case Study 6-1) is complicated. There's no blueprint, as every business is unique, including yours. So, start by looking at each of your stakeholders' needs in comparison with your current ESG goals and decide what must be changed. Resolving the complex, strategic trade-offs between profits, carbon emissions and providing a modern workplace for employees will stretch the mindset and skills of your senior team, as it takes you onto new ground.

To help you with this move, you can apply some familiar tools again. First, the business model canvas is a useful lens to consider the range of environmental issues and their impact on different stakeholders across the business. Diagram 6-5 shows some probing questions you can ask to raise awareness of environmental issues, when discussing your business model(s). Second, you can apply the techniques for identifying customer insights provided in Chapter 3 to understand the needs of different stakeholders. Third, use the innovation values map (Phase 2, Diagram 2-4) to ensure that your organization will be authentic about being purpose-led. Similarly, these three tools can also be used to innovate on social issues, for example how you engage the people to both operate and grow your business into the future.

DIAGRAM 6-5: BUSINESS MODEL CANVAS THROUGH AN ENVIRONMENTAL LENS

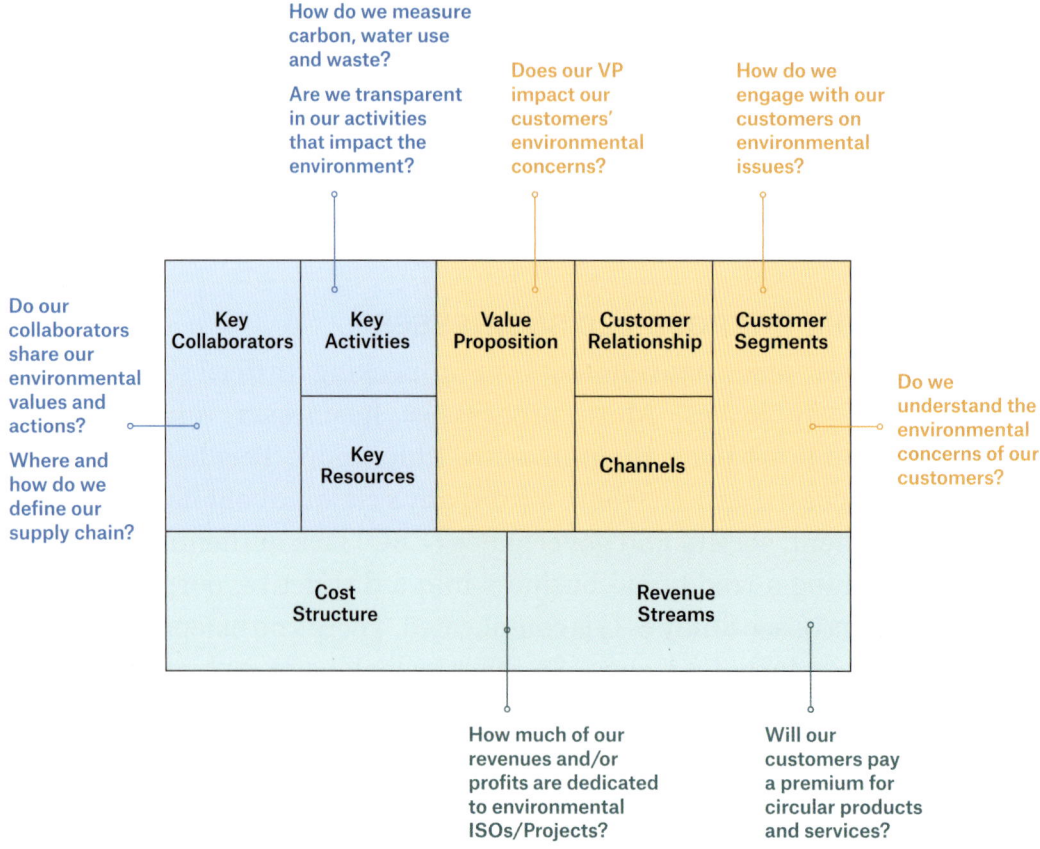

THE FUTURE OF WORK

It's accepted that satisfied employees are more productive and lead to competitive advantage. This has led companies to compete for 'talent' and to try to be the 'best' place to work. Modern MSBs and SBUs must offer an attractive, innovative workplace for their employees—be they full or part-time, contracted or sub-contracted.

The *future of work* is a term that refers to the many management innovations emerging today.[39] In particular, it recognizes the impact on employees of three things: digitization (AI, robotics and virtual work tools), the gig economy and globalization. Covid-19 accelerated the adoption of many workplace innovations, especially remote home-working. Tech companies and start-ups were quick to leverage modern ways of working to attract talent. Some medium-sized and family-owned businesses have been more conservative and have returned to 100% 'in the office' rather than a hybrid approach. Your senior team must have a strategy in place for the future of work.

The fast, Covid-driven adoption of home-working has highlighted many advantages but also some limitations. Numerous surveys have shown that employees perceive increased productivity, less commuting, and greater access to experts positively. The disadvantages are blurred work–life boundaries, stress and the reinforcement of functional silos—all of which stifle innovation. The big assumption is that hybrid working will easily create an effective mix of home- and at-the-office working. Your HR team should investigate how to create and maintain a culture of innovation in a hybrid working environment, and this includes understanding the thoughts and feelings of your employees on this. For example, the insurer Laya Healthcare used the lockdown situation to study its employees' work and life needs. This enabled them to draw a 'future of work roadmap', including different working models. Being proactive enabled Laya to experiment with the way employees conduct their work and to strengthen its culture of innovation.

A positive aspect of the future of work is that most employees want to know how they can contribute to business-wide innovation. Participation in innovation is highly motivating for many people. On your first *Innovation Journey*, the number of people involved in insight generation teams and innovation project teams will have been limited. Involving more people will create momentum for your next journey and help to embed a culture of innovation in your organization.

It's worth involving participants from other organizations. The popular concept of *open innovation* advocates sourcing knowledge and ideas from outside, as you can't expect to build all of the required expertise internally.[40] You should consider links to universities and research institutes. Many MSBs and SBUs don't know how keen most business and engineering schools are for companies to propose and host projects. Hosting projects offers businesses the opportunity to investigate markets and technologies in a cost-effective way. In addition, collaborating with start-ups can help to source unique business ideas. In the past, the model was large corporates acquiring start-ups' ideas. Today, the model is centred on temporary accelerator programmes, where businesses of all sizes co-develop insights, solutions and markets.[41]

Governments are also increasingly funding MSBs and SBUs to interact with start-ups and behave more entrepreneurially.[42] So, some of the market and technological investigation work for your *Next Innovation Journey* may be conducted in close cooperation with other organizations, which might also be the first step in building a value ecosystem.[43] Look for local communities of innovators and entrepreneurs to leverage an accelerator programme to fast-track ideas.[44] Open innovation is also about sourcing knowledge externally, in ways that can position your business at the heart of an emerging ecosystem or as a part contributor to another (for example licensing-out IP).[45]

In driving incremental innovation, the power of process improvement should not be forgotten. This book hasn't focused on operational improvements, but such process innovations can: reduce costs significantly; improve margins; involve more people; and create momentum. See Case Study 6-3 for how one factory is looking for every small innovation that can count.

CASE STUDY 6-3: CRANFIELD FOUNDRY
EVERY INNOVATION COUNTS[46]

Foundries are usually found in historical locations, with easy access to power, resources and markets. In contrast, the Cranfield Foundry occupies a green field site in North Macedonia and it began its first test operations in November 2019. Investors wanted to build a modern, environmentally friendly foundry that could supply customers in Europe and the Middle East with competitively priced quality castings, on time and without hassle. By the end of 2021, the business had grown to 150 people, supplying products to diverse range of customers.

The foundry's high-quality castings are made using metals that meet demanding EU standards, including 'grey iron' (Standard EN-GJL 150-350) and 'ductile iron' (EN-GJS 350-800). The company strategy is to be a highly reliable 'job shop', producing limited runs of castings that match the specific needs of customers. The Foundry currently makes complex fittings and valves; drainage covers; elements for railway infrastructure; automotive and agricultural components; and decorative, custom-made designer products. To facilitate the fast production of products for very different markets, production is equipped with the latest kit from the best suppliers. This helps makes the Cranfield Foundry a safe and environmentally friendly environment. For example, the furnace is 100% electric powered; non-contaminating, 'clean' scrap metal is used to reduce emissions; the casting process is designed to maximize sand and water recycling; and safety is the number one priority for all team members.

The CEO is Dariusz Dziuba, a Polish manager with an engineering background and the ability to combine an eye for detail with a clear understanding of the 'bigger picture'. He has 20 years' international experience in various industries; across the disciplines of manufacturing, R&D, and consulting. Dariusz studied for his MBA at Cranfield School of Management in the UK and this not only inspired the choice of the Foundry's name but also informed his approach to managing operations and managing people in distinct ways.

First, in terms of creating an organizational culture: *"We agreed our strategic direction and then decided what culture we would need to support it. Then, we set about creating it... from day one! We hired accordingly, looking for energetic and open-minded people who understood that results, in large part, are the outcome of processes and systems"* says Dariusz. Candidates' skills were considered but a strong emphasis was put on attitude —employees must be team players, creative problem solvers, and eager to drive process improvements. Management regards manufacturing operators as real experts, and *"Consequently, we don't hire if we can't find the ideal candidate. It's as simple as that"*, says Dariusz.

Second, in terms of learning, *"Starting from 'zero' has its benefits but it also has drawbacks. In our case we had funds to turn a green field into a modern foundry but no parent company to learn from. This means that we have to be good at moving up the learning curve, time and time again."* says Dariusz. In a dynamic and unpredictable business context, working at Cranfield Foundry often felt *"Like a start-up on steroids. We didn't pivot our business model but we certainly had to pivot our project scope and operating model constantly"* says Dariusz, with a smile.

Third, in terms of incremental innovation. As the facilities were being constructed, new hires were tasked with creating a culture of continuous improvement. This led to collecting 'micro ideas' from staff; looking for every minute change that could contribute to significant improvements in process efficiency. In cooperation with external IT professionals, an IT system, called 'DaMIS' (Daily Micro Improvement System) was developed for tracking every small change and its contribution to working practices and the business (and a commercial version of the software was also produced. See www.leanshaman.com). With the attitude that no change is too small, the Cranfield Foundry incremental innovation system focuses on employees' ideas that will bring improvements rather than looking for quantitative assessments. *"Our employees are the process experts and if they think an improvement is worthwhile and does not generate excessive risk, even when its financial impact can't be measured, then we GO FOR IT!"* says Dariusz. In the last three years, on average each employee generated eight ideas per year, which is well above market average. *"There is something amazing about how small, often trivial improvements can go unnoticed. But their combined benefits are significant, plus implementing them creates a snowball effect, motivating the submission of further ideas. Overall, everyone wins: the customer, shareholders, employees, suppliers and even the environment we operate in"* says Dariusz, *"No improvement idea should be considered too small, every innovation counts."*

STEP 4—PREPARING FOR THE NEXT JOURNEY

In the fourth and final Step of the action learning cycle, the innovation manager should run a workshop with the senior team, to prepare the *Next Innovation Journey*. The workshop will use the learning gathered in Steps 1–3, in deciding which innovation capabilities to *discard*, to *improve* (codify and embed) and which to *renew* (adopt, create and apply next). To enable the senior team prepare for the workshop, the innovation manager must circulate a comprehensive, easy-to-read summary document of the evidence collected on the first journey. It should include the actual *Innovation Journey* performance measures (see Table 2-3) and the original commercial, category and capability goals and a synthesis of the outputs from the action learning cycle Steps 1, 2 and 3.

We suggest a one-day meeting off-site, divided into three morning and three afternoon sessions (see Table 6-3). The morning sessions cover Steps 1, 2 and 3. The workshop itself requires constructive, open dialogue to foster generative learning and stretch the senior team. The facilitator's role is paramount and they must challenge the senior team's thinking, create shared insights and align decisions. For example, when reviewing Step 1, the facilitator might have to shift a senior sponsor from 'explaining away' a failed project, to pinpointing root causes to avoid. Or, for Step 3, the facilitator will have to delineate the insights from external cases and how they can be applied in your business.

The afternoon sessions all relate to Step 4 and promote generative learning. The first session begins by considering actual performance compared to the original innovation intent and what the new innovation intent should be. For each commercial, category, and capability goal, each team member should write down potential goals for the next journey ('B 2.0'). The facilitator should map these out, leading the discussion and alignment of views. For the second afternoon session, we recommend that the senior team step back and consider how to come up with a much more ambitious innovation intent. Stretching goals can be a powerful way to achieve impossible things.[47] The team should set an exponential goal and conduct several rounds of brainwriting to shape radical solutions. Exponential goals make most managers anxious but this

TABLE 6-3: STEP 4 SENIOR TEAM WORKSHOP

WORKSHOP AIM	To prepare the next Innovation Journey by identifying which innovation capabilities to discard, improve and renew.	
SESSIONS	**TOOLS TO DISCUSS AND QUESTIONS TO ANSWER**	**INNOVATION CAPABILITIES: ACTION ITEMS**
Review innovation projects (Step 1)	• Table 6-2—innovation post-project review forms. • *What can we learn about our innovation capabilities from previous projects?*	
Journey diagnosis (Step 2)	• Table 2-3 (journey measures). • Diagrams 6-2 and 6-3—journey diagnosis. • *What can we learn about our innovation capabilities from the Journey Diagnosis?*	
Learning from outside (Step 3)	• External cases and contemporary topics. • *What can we learn about innovation capabilities from other companies?*	
Innovation performance (Step 4)	• *What can we learn from our performance compared to our original innovation intent ('B')?* • *What should be the new innovation intent ('B 2.0')?*	
Innovation intent (Step 4)	• *How could we achieve a much more ambitious innovation intent ('B 2.0+')?*	
Final reflections (Step 4)	• *Has everybody had the chance to raise all their ideas, concerns and learning?*	

turns to excitement when they start to identify creative ways to achieve the goal. The third afternoon session re-grounds the senior team, with the facilitator checking that everyone's views have been adequately heard. Then the facilitator summarizes the action items related to innovation capabilities and the next *Innovation Journey* using the template (Table 6-3).

Make sure that action items are as specific as possible. We reiterate, don't expect your people who operate the day-to-day business to intuitively be successful innovators, across your business. Individuals will need specific training to be good at innovation—something businesses frequently fail to invest in.[48] When considering training, innovation simulations are an ideal way to quickly help employees understand the intricacies of cross-functional innovation and inspire them to take on more ambitious goals.[49] In Phase 6, your senior team has consciously assessed your innovation capabilities 'C' and prepared the way for the next journey. Case Study 6-4 shows how the animal nutrition company Alltech has made successive innovation journeys and built a dynamic innovation management capability that sustains growth.

CASE STUDY 6-4: ALLTECH INNOVATION: THE NEXT GENERATION[50]

Dr Pearse Lyons, an Irish biochemist with an expertise in yeast fermentation, began his career at Guinness but emigrated to the US. In 1980, he founded Alltech with $10,000 savings and a vision to 'sustain our planet and all things living on it'. Over the years, the family-owned company has grown to over $3B revenues, it now employs over 5,000 people, and it sells products in three business areas—animal nutrition and feed, crop science and beverages. The theme behind Alltech's success is an unerring commitment to purpose-led, innovative growth.

In its early years, Alltech worked alongside farmers and distillers to support the production of ethanol. When the demand for this fuel substitute dropped, the company pivoted into animal health. Pearse's expertise led to the breakthrough product Yea-Sacc, which uses live yeast to improve livestock digestion and increase milk yields. The founder also developed a distinctive approach to innovation. First, this was based on extensive interaction with farmers, feed companies and animal nutritionists, to gain insights into farmers' problems. Second, farmers' problems were solved according to the *ACE Principle*—requiring all the company's endeavours to contribute to the safety and wellbeing of Animals, Consumers and the Environment. With a strong community of scientists and an expert sales force, Alltech built a high-margin animal nutrition business generating $500M revenues in 2010.

In 2011, as the market context changed, the executive team reconsidered the company's strategy. Faced with intensive price competition; consumer demand for organic foods; and environmental concerns about livestock greenhouse gas emissions, Alltech needed to adapt. A three-track strategy emerged, with a stretch goal to grow revenues to $3B by 2018. The first track extended the core business by acquiring feed companies and marketing directly to farmers. The second was to grow geographically and into new areas. Alltech built a significant presence in China, the world's largest animal nutrition market; it developed an aquaculture business line through Alltech Coppens; and it expanded into the booming craft beer market. The third track augmented products with digital services, for example 'InTouch', which combines data collected from feeder wagons with herd management software and insights from centralized nutritionists to provide farmers with real-time advice to increase feeding efficiency and animal performance.

In March 2018, sadly Dr Pearse Lyons passed away and son Dr Mark Lyons embarked on a new innovation journey for Alltech. Mark recalls *"We had so many strengths and so many possibilities to explore. However, my father Pearse had always been the locus of innovation. In his absence, we knew we had to codify his approaches and build a more systematic approach to innovation across the company."* Mark engaged managers throughout the company to co-create a new vision for Alltech—Working Together for a Planet of Plenty™. This viewed agriculture as having potentially the greatest

DIAGRAM 6-6: ALLTECH'S INNOVATION FRAMEWORK – THE 'WHEEL'

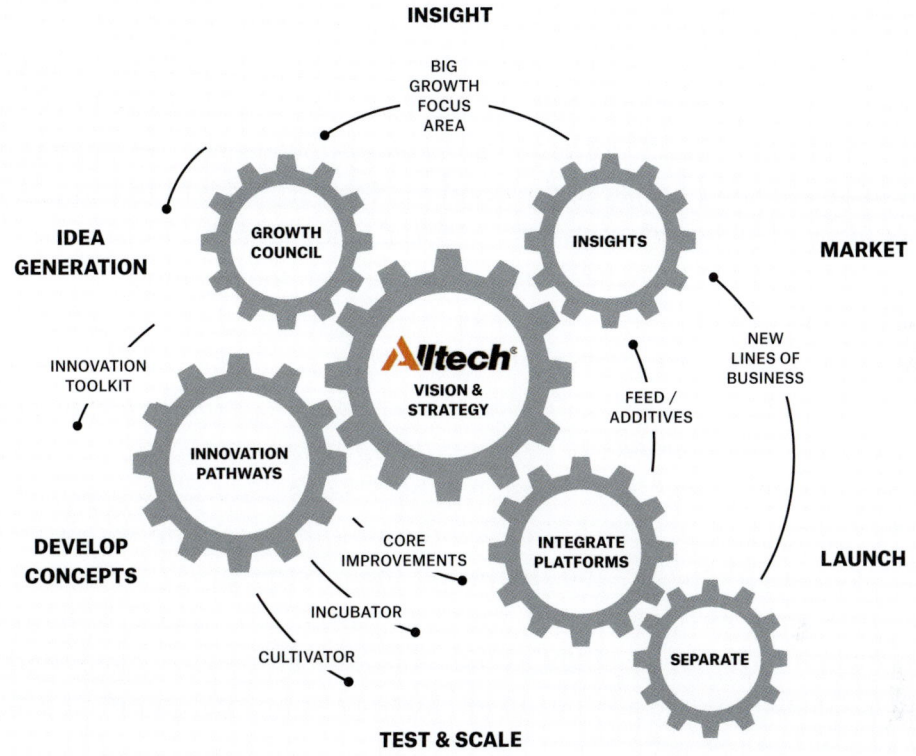

impact on the planet and envisioned Alltech solving food production problems in completely novel and sustainable ways. To support company-wide ingenuity, the management team set about codifying their entrepreneurial origins by creating a new Innovation Framework (depicted by the all-embracing 'wheel' with sub-components in Diagram 6-6).

At the centre of the 'wheel' is the innovation vision and strategy that defines the 'big growth' focus areas and guides all innovation activity. Market insights are gathered from multiple sources to spark ideas within these focus areas. Ciaran Black, who helped design and implement this Innovation Framework, notes *"At Alltech, there is no shortage of ideas, therefore it is essential to specify and shortlist the big growth areas, otherwise the* wheels spin but we don't move very far forward. Critically the 'Growth Council' decides on priorities and resource allocation. We then guide innovations initiatives along three main pathways."* Core improvements progress within the existing business; more radical initiatives where most of the capability resides in-house take the 'Incubator' pathway; and the 'Cultivator' pathway works with start-ups and intrapreneurial teams to develop new markets. All innovations undergo rapid testing and are then scaled into the core business, or by creating new separate entities. Once launched in the market, new learnings keep the wheel turning and refresh the strategy.

The Innovation Framework has been enhanced in recent years. As Ciaran notes: *"We continually review our approach and have made some changes that create deeper internal and external collaborations and give us the capability to explore more fundamental business model innovations of scale."* For example, the Pearse Lyons Cultivator first worked like a typical accelerator, a three-month bootcamp where start-ups focused on refining and delivering their 'pitch' at the Alltech ONE Conference. In all, close to 25 start-ups raised over $40M in funding and several have successfully exited. Now, the emphasis has shifted to deeper collaboration from the outset. Internal 'sponsors' co-develop joint value propositions with start-ups and quickly progress to commercial pilot projects, which provide a route to market for start-ups and an opportunity for Alltech customers and partners to de-risk and accelerate the deployment of new technologies within their business. Another learning relates to the 'InTouch' service for farmers. Originally, this was a closed system focused on productivity but with the 'Planet of Plenty™' vision, the service has evolved to address the sustainability challenges which have now become so crucial to farmers. To do this, Alltech offers an 'E-CO$_2$' service—accredited environmental analyses that capture farm emissions data and create clear recommendations. InTouch is now also a digital platform, where other technology suppliers can add 'plug & play' software services.

Reflecting on Alltech's latest innovation journey Dr Mark Lyons shared the following insights: *"As innovation was in our DNA, we automatically assumed that we were good at it. However, winning with products—the basis of our early success—is not the same as knowing how to win with service solutions. This requires a significant shift in our business model. So, we've made sure that our Innovation Framework continues to develop the new skills and mindsets that can bring about fundamental change. This takes time and, while it is important to be patient, it is also critical to move quickly to establish the right innovation capabilities that will create the 'product plus service' solutions that our 'Planet of Plenty™' vison requires. My father was always emphasizing curiosity as well as speed, and these remain two of our core values today."*

MINDSET MATTERS (IN CONCLUSION)

Processes and technology make innovation possible, but people make it happen. Other than fleeting references to the passion and playfulness needed to generate ideas, books and articles on managing innovation have largely overlooked how feelings can make or break innovation. Throughout this book we've highlighted and clarified the impact of mindsets. For example, it's people's mindsets that determine whether they see opportunities, or just complain about unwelcome turbulence. Mindsets also determine if thoughts and feelings will lead to plans and actions.

As you plan for your *Next Innovation Journey*, you must reflect on the mindsets of your key stakeholders. Innovation across black-, grey- and white-space means habitual mindsets and engrained organizational cultures have to change and become dynamic. Your first journey will have made some changes to your culture and, building on this, we have three pieces of advice to create the dynamic innovation capabilities that will drive your *Next Innovation Journey*.

Stay the innovation course: If, for example, you've launched breakthrough innovations that are selling well, your people will be eager to innovate further. If the results are less positive, people may feel deflated but remember, innovative growth happens outside most people's comfort zone so the journey to success is rarely straightforward. Moreover, remember your business has already made enhancements to its innovation capabilities. For example, it now has a shared language of 'business-wide innovation' and it's learnt and applied sophisticated tools and techniques. Therefore, you're now far better equipped to move adeptly through unknown terrain.

Energize your innovation community: The senior team and every innovation team should talk openly and frequently about capabilities and progress. Use constructive dialogue, aided by our tools, to surface the intellectual, emotional and behavioural challenges your organization faces, so they can be dealt with. Leaders should promote candid discussions, and this will foster focused learning and solidarity that is invaluable when dealing with the inevitable cul-de-sacs and wrong turns of innovative growth. Moreover, nothing energizes individuals more than a feeling of true environmental and social purpose. Remind people *why* they are innovating.

Expand your community of innovators: Raising your ambitions will require you to enlarge the innovation community in your business. Aim to create a 'pull' where more people understand *where* and *what* they can contribute. Encourage your current innovators to share their experiences with potential innovators. You'll be pleasantly surprised by how many people, both internal and external, ask to join the innovation cause.

We've had the great fortune to work with, learn from and be inspired by managers driving responsible, innovative growth in many businesses around the world. Together with managers, we have developed and applied the tools and techniques discussed in this book. Innovation management is much more about practice than theory. It's only when businesses try new things that knowledge can progress and value is created.

We are grateful to the many businesses involved in this work and look forward to further enlarging this community of innovators. As you make your first or successive innovation journeys, we encourage you to connect (see: www.innovativegrowth.com) and share your experiences of achieving innovative growth!

SUMMARY

- It's imperative to step back and reflect after your initial innovation journey. This will enable you to identify the innovation capabilities you'll need to drive the next journey and stage of business growth.
- The conscious reflection on your journey should include four steps: review each innovation project; conduct a top-down diagnosis of the overall journey; learn from other businesses; and critically consider your digital business model, your purpose, and the future of work in your business. These all proactively prepare for the next, more ambitious journey ('B 2.0' and beyond).
- It's essential for management to have a generative mindset, resolving problems in the current business and generating solutions to generate new growth.
- Through reflection, you can continue to enhance your dynamic innovation capabilities across the five phases, so that your business can sustain innovative growth.

REFERENCES AND NOTES

INTRODUCTION

1. Anonymous (2015) The mighty middle: Medium-sized firms are the unsung heroes of America's economy. *The Economist.* Available from: https://www.economist.com/news/business/21564893-medium-sized-firms-are-unsung-heroes-america's-economy [Accessed 31st August 2020].
2. HSBC (2017) *Hidden impact: Unlocking the growth potential of mid market enterprises 2017.* Available from: https://slidelegend.com/queue/hidden-impact-hsbc-commercial-banking_5a9698701723dd1eae00a6e3.html [Accessed 31st August 2020].
3. North, D., Baldock, R. & Vickers, I. (2011) *Research into mid-size business growth.* BIS (Department for Business Innovation & Skills, UK). Available from: https://assets.publishing.service.gov.uk/government/uploads/system/uploads/attachment_data/file/16422/11-1409-research-mid-size-business-growth.pdf [Accessed 31st August 2020].
4. Hurley, J. (2017) *Britain's mid-sized machine.* Available from: https://aibgb.co.uk/steps-to-growth-strategy/britains-mid-sized-machine [Accessed 13th August 2020].
5. See:
   - gov.uk (2011) Official Statistics: Mid-sized businesses: international comparisons. Available from: https://www.gov.uk/government/statistics/mid-sized-businesses-international-comparisons [Accessed 1st September 2020].
   - Mazers (2017) Optimizing mid-sized businesses: A performance analysis of Europe's mid-sized companies. Available from: https://www.mazars.ie/Home/Privately-Owned-Business/New-POB-page/Privately-Owned-Business/Insights/Optimizing-Mid-Sized-Businesses-Mazars-Research [Accessed 13th August 2020].
6. Bowen, A. (2018) Mid-market enterprises – the neglected middle child. *Business & Finance.* Available from: https://businessandfinance.com/mid-market-enterprises-the-neglected-middle-child/ [Accessed 31st August 2020].
7. Leonard, R. (2016) According to Ricoh Europe's mid-sized businesses could be missing out on €433bn annually. *Irish Tech News,* September 12th. Available from: https://irishtechnews.ie/according-to-ricoh-europes-mid-sized-businesses-could-be-missing-out-on-e433bn-annually/ [Accessed 13th August 2020].
8. Table based on information from: Cebulla, A. (2011) Summary notes for the Department of Business, Innovation and Skills (BIS), *National Institute of Economics and Social Research*, UK. Available from: https://www.gov.uk/government/statistics/mid-sized-businesses-international-comparisons [Accessed 1st September 2020].
9. Irish figure based on: CSO (2012) (Central Statistics Office, Ireland). Available from: https://www.cso.ie/en/releasesandpublications/ep/p-bii/businessinirelandabridged2012/smallandmediumenterprises/ [Accessed 1st November 2020].
10. Malshe, A., Roper, S., Eeekhoff, J., Gubitta, P., Parigi, B. & Campagnolo, D. (2012) *The mighty middle: why Europe's future rests on its middle market companies.* Available from: https://www.middlemarketcenter.org/research-reports/european-economy-rests-on-mid-market-companies [Accessed 15th July 2021].

11 Malshe, A., Roper, S., Eeekhoff, J., Gubitta, P., Parigi, B. & Campagnolo, D. (2012) *The mighty middle: why Europe's future rests on its middle market companies*. Available from: https://www.middlemarketcenter.org/research-reports/european-economy-rests-on-mid-market-companies [Accessed 15th July 2021]. [Quote on p. 9].

12 By 'business' we infer a distinct business model, clear markets, and a senior management team that has the autonomy to develop and execute their own strategy.

13 The book explains the idea that companies must escape the 'red ocean', where all companies are competing (and the attacks of 'sharks' are turning the sea red). By redefining products, the idea is that a unique set of attributes can enable a company to find the 'blue ocean', where there is no competition.

14 Osterwalder, A. & Pigneur, Y. (2010) *Business model generation: A handbook for visionaries, game changers, and challengers*. Hoboken, NJ, Wiley.

15 See, for example:
   - Weigel, T. & Goffin, K. (2015) Creating innovation capabilities: Mölnlycke Health Care's 'Journey', *Research Technology Management*, 58 (4), 28–35.
   - Kierans, I. (2015) *Developing a business model innovation capability within an established company*. PhD Thesis, Cranfield School of Management, UK.

16 Wikipedia, Innovation management: https://en.wikipedia.org/wiki/Innovation_management [Accessed: 17th December, 2021].

17 See:
   - O'Reilly III, C. A. & Tushman, M. L. (2004) The ambidextrous organization. *Harvard Business Review*, 82 (4), 74–81.
   - O'Reilly III, C. A. & Tushman, M. L. (2016) *Lead and disrupt: How to solve the innovator's dilemma*. Stanford, CA, Stanford University Press.

18 Case based on:
   - Visits to Svensson between 2018 and 2020.
   - An interview with CEO Anders Ludvigson on 3rd December 2019.
   - The company website: http://www.ludvigsvensson.com/climatescreens/about-us [Accessed 8th September 2020].

19 Theodore Levitt developed the concept of the product life cycle (see: Levitt, T. (1965). Exploit the product life cycle. *Harvard Business Review*, 43 (6), pp. 81–94). Later, this thinking evolved into looking at the entire organizational or business life cycle and also industry life cycle.

20 Business life cycles have been researched for over 50 years; for a good summary see:
   - Lester, D. L., Parnell, J. A. & Carraher, S. (2003) Organizational life cycle: A five-stage empirical scale. *International Journal of Organizational Analysis*, 11 (4), 339–354.

21 For more information on white- and black-space, see:
   - Hamel, G. & Prahalad, C. K. (1994) *Competing for the future*. Cambridge, USA, Harvard Business School Press.
   - Maletz, M. C. & Nohria, N. (2001) Managing in the whitespace. *Harvard Business Review*, 79 (2), 102–111.
   - Johnson, M. W. (2010) *Seizing the white space: business model innovation for growth and renewal*. Boston, USA, Harvard Business School Publishing.

22 March, J. G. (1991) Exploration and exploitation in organizational learning. *Organization Science*, 2, 71–87.

23 O'Reilly III, C. A. & Tushman, M. L. (2016) *Lead and disrupt: How to solve the innovator's dilemma*. Stanford, USA, Stanford University Press.

24 Authors' own table, based on a wide range of the literature.

25 Case based on:
   - Interviews with Tristan Le Corre in February 2020, July 2021 and December 2021.
   - Le Corre, T. (2020) *The birth of distancing*. Tristan's Newsletter. Available from: https://tristanlecorre.substack.com/p/the-birth-of-disdancing?r=33bwb&utm_campaign=post&utm_medium=web&utm_source=copy [Accessed 8th September 2020].

26 The original research on the Pentathlon Framework led to a textbook used on many MBA and MSc programmes. See:
   - Goffin, K. & Pfeiffer, R. (1999) *Innovation management in UK and German manufacturing companies*. London: Anglo-German Foundation, Report Series.
   - Goffin, K. & Mitchell, R. (2017) *Innovation management: Effective strategy and implementation*. 3rd ed. Basingstoke, UK, Palgrave Macmillan Academic Publishers.

27 Case based on:
   - Extensive work with the Heitkamp & Thumann Group over several years.

- Goffin, K., Beznosov, A. & Seiler, M. (2021) Countering commoditization through innovation: Challenges for European B2B companies. *Research Technology Management*, 64 (4), 20–28.

28 This is a direct quote from a very experienced innovation manager working in an organization with different SBUs. One of the challenges the innovation manager is facing is that corporate headquarters has fully embraced lean management thinking and is reluctant to invest in innovation projects that do not have as clear returns as process re-engineering projects.

CHAPTER 1

1 Several longitudinal studies based on senior manager input show that innovative companies outperform their peers on measures of revenue, profits, growth, and market capitalization. For example, see:
   - Jarkuzelski, B., Chwalik, R. & Goehle, B. (2018) What the top innovators get right. *Strategy + Business*, 93 (Winter).
   - The world's most innovative companies, Forbes.com Available from: https://www.forbes.com/special-features/innovative-companies-list.html [Accessed 15th October 2020]
2 Pisano, G. P. (2015) You need an innovation strategy. *Harvard Business Review*, 93 (6), 44–54.
3 Giles, L. (2013) *Sun Tzu on the art of war*. Abingdon, UK, Routledge.
4 Drucker, P. F. (1954) *The practice of management*. New York, USA, Harper & Row.
5 Levitt, T. (1960) Marketing myopia, *Harvard Business Review*, 82 (7–8), 138–149.
6 March, J. G. & Simon, H. A. (1958) *Organizations*. New York, USA, Wiley.
7 The SWOT framework was first described as part of the Stanford Research Institute and intended to help make complex strategic assumptions, based on imperfect knowledge, more explicit. Learned, E. P., Christiansen, C. R., Andrews, K. & Guth, W. D. (1969) in *Business policy, text and cases*. Irwin, Illinois, Homewood.
8 Francis Aguilar, created 'ETPS Analysis' in Aguilar, F. J. (1967) *Scanning the business environment*. New York, USA, Macmillan. This evolved into the PESTEL acronym, including Environmental (for example impact on nature and society) and Legal (for example regulation) factors.
9 Ansoff, H. I. (1965) *Corporate strategy: an analytic approach to business policy for growth and expansion*. New York, USA, McGraw-Hill.
10 McKinsey & Co. (2008) Enduring Ideas: The GE–McKinsey nine-box matrix. McKinsey Quarterly. Available from https://www.mckinsey.com/business-functions/strategy-and-corporate-finance/our-insights/enduring-ideas-the-ge-and-mckinsey-nine-box-matrix [Accessed 10th December 2021].
11 Michael Porter's influential work on strategy considers where to play and how to win. See:
   - Porter, M. E. (1980) *Competitive strategy*. New York, USA, Free Press.
   - Porter, M. E. (1985) *Competitive advantage: creating and sustaining superior performance*. New York, USA, Free Press.
   - Lafley, A. G. & Martin, R. L. (2013) *Playing to win: how strategy really works*. Boston, USA, Harvard Business School Publishing.
12 Grant, R. M. (2019) *Contemporary strategy analysis: text and cases*. 10th ed. Chichester, UK, John Wiley & Sons.
13 See:
   - Barney, J. B. (1991) Firm resources and sustained competitive advantage. *Journal of Management*, 19, 99–120.
   - Barney, J. B. & Hesterly, W. S. (2010) *Strategic management and competitive advantage*. New Jersey, USA, Pearson.
14 Hamel, G. & Prahalad, C. K. (1996) *Competing for the future*. Boston, USA, Harvard Business School Press.
15 Teece, D. J., Pisano, G. & Shuen, A. (1997) Dynamic capabilities and strategic management, *Strategic Management Journal*, 18(7), 509–533. More recent work which focuses on innovation is Teece, D. J. (2009) *Dynamic capabilities and strategic management: Organizing for innovation and growth*. Oxford, UK, Oxford University Press.
16 Mintzberg, H. (1994). The fall and rise of strategic planning. *Harvard Business Review*, 72 (1), 107–114. For a review of the 10 schools of strategy process, see Mintzberg, H., Ahlstrand, B. & Lampel, J. (1998) *Strategy safari: a guided tour through the wilds of strategic management*. New York, USA, Free Press.
17 Christensen, C. M. (1997) *The innovator's dilemma: when new technologies cause great firms to fail*. Boston, USA, Harvard Business School Press.

18 We will mainly use the term *value ecosystems*. See:
   - Christensen, C. M. & Raynor, M. E. (2003) *The innovator's solution: Creating and sustaining successful growth*. Boston, USA, Harvard Business School Press.
   - Parolini, C. 1999. *The value net: A tool for competitive strategy*. Chichester, England, John Wiley & Sons Ltd.

19 For example see:
   - Tushman, M. L. & O'Reilly III, C. A. (1996) Ambidextrous organizations: Managing evolutionary and revolutionary change. *California Management Review*, 38 (4), 8–30.
   - O'Reilly III, C. A. and Tushman, M. L. (2008) Ambidexterity as a dynamic capability: Resolving the innovator's dilemma. *Research in Organizational Behaviour*, 28, 185–206.

20 Baghai, M., Coley, S. & White, D. (2000) *The alchemy of growth: practical insights for building the enduring enterprise*. USA, Basic Books; and Reeves, M., Love, C. & Mathur, N. (2012) *The most adaptive companies 2012: winning in an age of turbulence*. Available from: https://silo.tips/download/report-the-most-adaptive-companies-winning-in-an-age-of-turbulence [Accessed 10th December 2021].

21 Pisano, G. P. (2017) Toward a prescriptive theory of dynamic capabilities: connecting strategic choice, learning, and competition. *Industrial & Corporate Change*, 26 (5), 747–762.

22 Reeves, M., Love, C. & Tillmanns, P. (2012) Your strategy needs a strategy. *Harvard Business Review*, 90 (9), 76–83.

23 Osterwalder, A. & Pigneur, Y. (2010) *Business model generation*. Hoboken, USA, Wiley & Sons, Inc. [We changed 'partners' to 'collaborators' for consistency with our history and added the overarching questions].

24 Christensen, C. M., Hall, T., Dillon, K. & Duncan, D. S. (2016) Know your customers 'Jobs to be done'. *Harvard Business Review*, 94 (9), 54–62.

25 Gassmann, O., Frankenberger, K., Choudury, M. & Csik, M. (2020) *The business model navigator*. 2nd ed. Harlow, UK, Pearson Education.

26 Symon, F. (2015) Ryanair seeks to become 'Amazon for travel' in Europe. *Financial Times*. Available from: https://www.ft.com/content/489bb90c-707a-4438-ae6b-29dc15d1df55 [Accessed 15th October 2020] and Kennedy, J. (2017) Ryanair's Colin O'Brien: We will be a tech company with an airline attached. *Silicon Republic*. Available from: https://www.siliconrepublic.com/enterprise/ryanair-colin-obrien-digital-ecommerce-apis [Accessed 15th October 2020].

27 Case based on:
   - Extensive contact with Company X over a three-year period.
   - Participation in innovation strategy workshops; market research; and portfolio management meetings.
   - Conducting customer visits with the CEO and marketing manager.

28 Anthony, S. D., Johnson, M. W., Sinfield, J. V. & Altman, E. J. (2008) *The innovator's guide to growth: putting disruptive innovation to work*. Boston, USA, Harvard Business Press.

29 Case based on:
   - Work conducted by the authors and Advanced Organisation with Coillte's Senior Team and Innovation Director from 2008–15. This included: business strategy, innovation strategy and organizational change.

30 Case based on:
   - An Internet interview with Maxim Nelemans on 19th August 2020.
   - https://www.fashionpower.eu/ [Accessed 12th April 2020].
   - https://www.youtube.com/watch?v=jryJyCjxh-Vs [Accessed 12th April 2020].

31 Phaal, R., Farrukh, C. J. P. & Probert, D. R. (2007) Strategic roadmapping: A workshop-based approach for identifying and exploring innovation issues and opportunities. *Engineering Management Journal*, 19 (1), 16–24.

32 Amara, R. (2006) The Age. In Ratcliffe, S. (Ed.) (2006) *Oxford essential quotations*. Oxford, UK, Oxford University Press. Available from: https://www.oxfordreference.com/view/10.1093/acref/9780191826719.001.0001/q-oro-ed4-00018679 [Accessed 29th September 2020].

33 Teece, D. J., Raspin, P. G. & Cox, D. R. (2020) Plotting strategy in a dynamic world. *MIT Sloan Management Review*, 62 (1), 28–33.

34 This strategic roadmap is based on a market analysis conducted for Company X by Colin Goffin in August 2021. Used with permission.

35 Case based on:
   - Work conducted by the authors and Dr Ed Molloy with European Beer Supply senior management team in 2012.
   - The Guinness Storehouse is Ireland's #1 tourist attraction, with ca. 1.7M visitors per year.
   - The 'Kilmainham Gaol Strategy' name was

based on the location of the workshops in a hotel next to the famous Kilmainham Gaol (Jail) in Dublin. The name was used as a metaphor for breaking out of a current COGS mindset (jail) into new growth.

36 Heim, U. (2017) Building a reliable innovation engine. Available from: https://www.mckinsey.com/business-functions/operations/our-insights/building-a-reliable-innovation-engine [Accessed 13th August 2020].

37 Nagji, B. & Tuff, G. (2012) Managing your innovation portfolio. *Harvard Business Review*, 90 (5), 66–74.

CHAPTER 2

1 See:
   - Kates, A. & Galbraith, J. R. (2007) *Designing your organization: Using the Star Model to solve 5 critical design challenges*. San Francisco, CA, Jossey-Bass.
   - Tushman, M. L. & O'Reilly III, C. A. (1996) Ambidextrous organizations: Managing evolutionary and revolutionary change. *California Management Review*, 38 (4), 8–30.
   - Tushman, M. L. & Nadler, D. (1986) Organizing for innovation. *California Management Review*, 28(3), 74–92.

2 Morgan, G. (1997) *Images of organization*. Thousand Oaks, USA, Sage Publications.

3 Weber, M., Parsons, T. & Tawney, R. H. (1930) *The Protestant ethic and the spirit of capitalism*. London, UK, George Allen & Unwin Ltd.

4 Taylor, F. W. (1911) *The principles of scientific management*. London, UK, Harper and Brothers.

5 Mayo, E. (1933) *The human problems of an industrial civilization*. New York, USA, Macmillan & Co.

6 For an overview of sociotechnical systems theory see: Cummings, T. & Worley, C. (2015) *Organization development and change*. 10th ed. Mason, USA, Thomson/South-Western.

7 See:
   - Burns, T. & Stalker, G. M. (1961) *The management of innovation*. London, UK, Tavistock Publications.
   - Morand, D. A. (1995) The role of behavioral formality and informality in the enactment of bureaucratic versus organic organizations. *Academy of Management Review*, 20 (4), 831–872.
   - Sine, W. D., Mitsuhashi, H. & Kirsch, D. A. (2006) Revisiting Burns and Stalker: Formal structure and new venture performance in emerging economic sectors. *Academy of Management Journal*, 49 (1), 121–132.

8 Tushman, M. L., & O'Reilly III, C. A. (1996) Ambidextrous organizations: Managing evolutionary and revolutionary change. *California Management Review*, 38 (4), 8–30.

9 Most modern schools of psychology recognize the interplay of thoughts (conscious and unconscious), feelings and behaviours leading to action (a behaviour with intent). These three operations have brain centres: thinking (neocortical) brain; the emotional (limbic) brain and body functioning (reptilian) brain.

10 The estimated percentage of our thoughts that are conscious range from 5% to .05% depending on the definition and perspective taken. Unconscious thoughts and feelings greatly control our actions. See:
    - Carruthers, P. (2017) The illusion of conscious thought. *Journal of Consciousness Studies*, 24 (9–10), 228–252.
    - Dijksterhuis, A. & Nordgren, L. F. (2006) A theory of unconscious thought. *Perspectives on Psychological Science*, 1(2), 95–109.
    - Horowitz, M., Clecio Falcao Araujo, V. & Hoffmann Sampaio, C. (2017) Unconscious thought theory and marketing: A novel perspective for new insights. *Consumer Behavior Review*, 1 (1), 11–23.

11 Brown, P., Kingsley, J. & Paterson, S. (2015) *The fear-free organization: Vital insight from neuroscience to transform your business culture*. London, UK, Kogan Page.

12 Schein, E. H. (1999) *The corporate culture survival guide: sense and nonsense about culture change*. San Francisco, USA, Jossey-Bass.

13 Dweck, C. S. (2006) *Mindset: The new psychology of success*. New York, USA, Random House.

14 *Confirmation bias*—where we selectively search for inputs that confirm our prior beliefs or values, which in turn creates dopamine-induced harmony. See:
    - Nickerson, R. S. (1998) Confirmation bias: A ubiquitous phenomenon in many guises. *Review of General Psychology*, 2 (2), 175–220.

15 Kahneman, D. (2011) *Thinking, fast and slow*. New York, Farrar, Straus and Giroux.

16 An attack on our self-image and self-esteem can trigger the amygdala, which controls fight or flight responses. Daniel Goleman refers to *amygdala*

hijacking as an immediate and intense reaction that is out of proportion for the situation. See:
- Goleman, D. (1995) *Emotional intelligence: Why it can matter more than IQ.* New York, USA, Bantam Books.

17 Hill, L. A., Brandeau, G., Truelove, E. & Lineback, K. (2014) *Collective genius: The art and practice of leading innovation.* Boston, USA, Harvard Business Review Press.

18 Edmondson, A. C. (2019) *The fearless organization: Creating psychological safety in the workplace for learning, innovation and growth.* Hoboken, USA, John Wiley & Sons.

19 Leading strategists recognize the role that shared mindsets and culture play in causing *strategic inertia*—the inability to see, shape or implement new growth strategies. See:
- March, J. G. (1991) Exploration and exploitation in organizational learning. *Organization Science*, 2(1), 71–87.
- Sydow, J., Schreyögg, G. & Koch, J. (2009) Organizational Path Dependence: Opening the Black Box. *Academy of Management Review*, 34 (4), 689–709.
- Christensen, C. M., Raynor, M. & McDonald, R. (2015) What Is Disruptive Innovation? *Harvard Business Review*, 93 (12), 44–53.

20 Chesky, B. (2014) Don't Fuck Up the Culture. Blog to team. Available from: https://medium.com/@bchesky/dont-fuck-up-the-culture-597cde9ee9d4 [Accessed 9th February 2021].

21 See:
- McCord, P. (2017) *Powerful: building a culture of freedom and responsibility.* CA, Silicon Guild.
- McCord, P. (2014) How Netflix Reinvented HR. *Harvard Business Review*, 92 (1/2), 70–76.
- The Netflix slide deck is available from: https://igormroz.com/documents/netflix_culture.pdf [Accessed 9th February 2021].

22 Schein, E. H. (2004) *Organizational Culture and Leadership.* 3rd ed. San Francisco, USA, Jossey-Bass.

23 Truss, C., Shantz, A., Soane, E., Alfes, K. & Delbridge R. (2013) Employee engagement, organisational performance and individual well-being: exploring the evidence, developing the theory. *International Journal of Human Resource Management*, 24 (14), 2657–2669.

24 Kuhn, J. S. & Marsick, V. J. (2005) Action learning for strategic innovation in mature organizations: key cognitive, design and contextual considerations. *Action Learning: Research and Practice*, 2 (1), 27–48.

25 Case based on:
- https://www.redventures.com/about/who-we-are [Accessed 14th February 2021].
- An interview with Hallie Cornetta on 15th December 2020.
- An interview with Eoghan Nolan on 13th November 2020.
- Smith, B. (2021) You've never heard of the biggest digital media company in America. *New York Times*. Available from: https://www.nytimes.com/2021/08/15/business/media/red-ventures-digital-media.html [Accessed 20th April 2021].

26 Kotter, J. P. (1995) Leading change: Why transformation efforts fail. *Harvard Business Review*, 73 (2), 59–67.

27 See:
- Argenti, P. A., Howell, R. A. & Beck, K. A. (2005) The strategic communication imperative. *MIT Sloan Management Review*, 46 (3), 83–89.
- Garvin, D. A. & Roberto, M. A. (2005) Change through persuasion. *Harvard Business Review* 83 (2), 104–112.

28 Beckhard, R. & Harris, R. T. (1987) *Organizational transitions: Managing complex change.* Reading, USA, Addison-Wesley Publishing.

29 Case based on:
- https://www.dcc.ie/ [Accessed 10th November 2020].
- An interview with Rob Flanagan on 13th November 2020.
- Annual Report Year ending 31st March 2020 https://www.dcc.ie/~/media/Files/D/DCC-v2/documents/agm-pdfs/pdfs/2020/dcc-annual-report-2020.pdf [Accessed 16th March 2021].
- Investor presentation November 2020 https://www.dcc.ie/~/media/Files/D/DCC-v2/documents/results-and-presentations/2020/company-overview-presentation-nov-2020.pdf [Accessed 16th March 2021].
- French LPG https://www.butagaz.fr/actualites/actu-click-collect-butagaz [Accessed 16th March 2021].

30 See:
- McGregor, L. & Doshi, N. (2015) How company culture shapes employee motivation. *Harvard Business Review Digital Articles*, 2–9. Available from: https://hbr.org/2015/11/how-

company-culture-shapes-employee-motivation [Accessed 16th May 2021].
- Bailey, C., Madden, A., Alfes, K., Shantz, A. & Soane E. (2017) The mismanaged soul: Existential labor and the erosion of meaningful work. *Human Resource Management Review*, 27 (3), 416–430.

31 Sullivan, J. (2017) Ouch, 50% Of New Hires Fail! 6 Ugly Numbers Revealing Recruiting's Dirty Little Secret. Available from: https://www.ere.net/ouch-50-of-new-hires-fail-6-ugly-numbers-revealing-recruitings-dirty-little-secret/ [Accessed 24th December 2020].

32 See:
- Amabile, T. M. (1996) *Creativity and innovation in organizations.* Harvard Business School Background Note 396-239.
- Amabile, T. M. & Pratt, M. G. (2016) The dynamic componential model of creativity and innovation in organizations: Making progress, making meaning. *Research in Organizational Behavior*, 36, 157–183.

33 The concept of T-Shaped skills originated with the recognition that R&D scientists and engineers have to work with experts in different scientific disciplines to create a solution. To work in such multidisciplinary teams requires a basic understanding of the different disciplines and the teamwork and project management skills to work effectively together. This concept has been adopted by consultants such as IDEO, McKinsey and IBM. See:
- Johnston, D. L. (1978) Scientists become managers – The 'T'-shaped man. *IEEE Engineering Management Review*, 6 (3), 67–68.
- Iansiti, M. (1993) Real-world R&D: Jumping the product generation gap. *Harvard Business Review*, 71 (3), 138–147.
- Bartlett, C. A. (1996) *McKinsey & Co.: Managing knowledge and learning.* Harvard Business School Case 396–357.
- IfM and IBM. (2008) *Succeeding through Service Innovation: A Service Perspective for Education, Research, Business and Government.* Cambridge, UK: University of Cambridge Institute for Manufacturing. Available from: http://www.ifm.eng.cam.ac.uk/ssme/ [Accessed 19th December 2020].
- Hansen, M. T. (1991) IDEO CEO Tim Brown: T-shaped stars: The backbone of IDEO's collaborative culture. *Chief Executive.net* Available from: https://chiefexecutive.net/ideo-ceo-tim-brown-t-shaped-stars-the-backbone-of-ideoaes-collaborative-culture__trashed [Accessed 18th December 2020].

34 There are several people-related innovation assessments: See:
- Burch, G. S., Pavelis, C. & Port, R. L. (2008) Selecting for creativity and innovation: The relationship between the innovation potential indicator and the team selection inventory. *International Journal of Selection and Assessment*, 16 (2), 177–181.
- Kirton, M. J. (2003). *Adaption–innovation in the context of diversity and change.* New York, USA, Routledge.
- Kirton, M. J. (1984) Adaptors and innovators: why new initiatives get blocked. *Long Range Planning*, 17 (2), 137–143.
- O'Reilly, C. A. III, Chatman, J. & Caldwell, D. F. (1991) People and organizational culture: A profile comparison approach to assessing person-organization fit. *Academy of Management Journal*, 34 (3), 487–516.

35 McGrath, R. G. & Macmillan, I. C. (2009) *Discovery-driven growth opportunity: a breakthrough process to reduce risk and seize opportunity.* Boston, USA, Harvard Business Press.

36 Andrew, J. P., Sirkin, H. L. & Butman, J. (2006) *Payback: reaping the rewards of innovation.* Boston, USA, Harvard Business School Press.

37 Govindarajan, V. & Trimble, C. (2010) *The other side of innovation: solving the execution challenge.* Boston, USA, Harvard Business School Publishing.

38 See:
- Amabile, T. M. & Pratt, M. G. (2016) The dynamic componential model of creativity and innovation in organizations: Making progress, making meaning. *Research in Organizational Behavior*, 36, 157–183.
- Beckhard, R. (1972) Optimizing team building effort. *Journal of Contemporary Business*, 1 (3), 23–32.
- Fischer, B. & Boynton, A. (2005) Virtuoso teams. *Harvard Business Review*, 83 (7/8), 116–123.
- Pritchett, P., Tichy, N. M. & Cohen, E. (1998) *The leadership engine: Building leaders at every level.* Atlanta, USA, Pritchett & Hull Associates.
- Edmondson, A. C. (2012) *Teaming: How organizations learn, innovate, and compete in the knowledge economy.* San Francisco, USA, Jossey-Bass.

- Goffin, K. & Mitchell, R. (2017) *Innovation management: Effective strategy and implementation.* 3rd ed. Basingstoke, UK, Palgrave Macmillan Academic Publishers.
39 Kierans, I. (2015) *Developing a business model innovation capability within an established company.* PhD Thesis, Cranfield School of Management, UK.
40 Super, J. F. (2020) Building innovative teams: Leadership strategies across the various stages of team development. *Business Horizons*, 63 (4), 553–563.
41 Pentland, A. S. (2012) The new science of building great teams. *Harvard Business Review*, 90 (4), 61–69.
42 See:
   - Blank, S. (2019) Why companies do "Innovation Theatre" instead of actual innovation. *Harvard Business Review Digital Articles*, 2–5 Available from: https://hbr.org/2019/10/why-companies-do-innovation-theater-instead-of-actual-innovation [Accessed 18th December 2020].
   - Mollick, E. (2019). What the Lean Startup Method gets right and wrong. *Harvard Business Review Digital Articles*, 2–4. Available from: https://hbr.org/2019/10/what-the-lean-startup-method-gets-right-and-wrong [Accessed 18th December 2020].
43 Pisano, G. P. (2015) You need an innovation strategy. *Harvard Business Review*, 93 (6), 44–54.
44 Case based on:
   - Work conducted by the authors with BOI and New Ireland from 2015 to 2019 that included developing internal capability to generate deep customer insights and solutions, review and make recommendations for sprint cycles, and the development of innovation options and project plans.
   - Interview with Seán Ó Murchú on 11th September 2020.
   - Interview with John Nugent on 14th December 2020.
   - The Governor and Company of the Bank of Ireland Annual Report (2020). Available from: https://investorrelations.bankofireland.com/app/uploads/BOI-Annual-Report-2020.pdf [Accessed 19th April 2021].
   - *Net interest income* is the difference between revenue generated from the interest earned on assets such as loans, mortgages and securities over the interest paid out on the institution's deposits.
   - Presentation from CEO Francesca McDonagh on Cultural Transformation https://iob.ie/news/culture-leadership-francesca-mcdonagh [Accessed 24th February 2021].
   - https://www.bankofireland.com/about-bank-of-ireland/press-releases/2020/ifac-collaborates-with-bank-of-ireland-to-launch-next-generation-farm-financial-management-and-planning-tool/ [Accessed 24th February 2021].

CHAPTER 3

1 Goffin, K., Beznosov, A. & Seiler, M. (2021) Countering commoditization through Innovation: Challenges for European B2B companies. *Research Technology Management*, 64 (4), 20–28.
2 Booth, C. (ed.) (1902–3) *Life and labour of the people in London* (17 volumes). London, UK, Macmillan.
3 Catterall, M. & Ibbotson, P. (2000) Using projective techniques in education research. *British Education Research Journal*, 26 (2), 245–256.
4 Fram, E.H. & Cibotti, E. (1991) The shopping list studies and projective techniques: A 40 year view. *Marketing Research*, 3 (4), 14–22.
5 Haire, M. (1950) Projective techniques in marketing research. *Journal of Marketing*, 14 (5), 15–33.
6 Robert K. Merton, is the father of well-known terms like 'self-fulfilling prophecy' and 'role models'. Both terms have filtered from his academic work into everyday language.
7 Denzin, N. & Lincoln, Y. (eds.) (1994) *Handbook of qualitative research.* Thousand Oaks, USA, Sage.
8 Reese, W. (20020) Behavioral scientists enter design. In Squires, S. and Byrne, B. (eds.) (2002). *Creating breakthrough ideas: The collaboration of anthropologists and designers in the product development industry.* Westport, USA, Bergin and Garvey.
9 Deszca, G., Munro, H. & Noori, H. (1999) Developing breakthrough products: Challenges and options for market assessment. *Journal of Operations Management*, 17 (6), 613–630.
10 Elliot, R. & Jankel-Elliot, N. (2003) Using ethnography in strategic consumer research. *Qualitative Market Research*, 6 (4), 215–223.

11. Malinowski, B. (1984) *The argonauts of the Western Pacific*. Long Grove, USA, Waveland Press.
12. Evans-Prichard, E. E. (1940) *The Nuer: A description of the modes of livelihood and political institutions of a Nilotic people*. Oxford, UK, Oxford University Press.
13. Markham, S. K. & Lee, H. (2013) Product Development and Management Association's 2012 comparative performance assessment study. *Journal of Product Innovation Management*, 30 (3), 408–429.
14. NESTA (2008). *The new inventors, how users are changing the rules of innovation*. National Endowment for Science, Technology and the Arts (NESTA) Research Report. Available from: new_inventors_report.pdf (nesta.org.uk) [Accessed 20th December 2022].
15. Von Hippel, E. (1986) Lead users: A source of novel product concepts. *Management Science*, 32 (7), 791–805.
16. Lüthje, C., Herstatt, C. & von Hippel, E. (2002) The dominant role of 'Local' information in the user information. The case of mountain biking. *MIT Sloan Working Paper*, No. 4377-02.
17. Case based on:
    - https://www.redventures.com/about/what-we-do [Accessed 4th February 2021).
    - An interview with Carlos Angrisano on 14th December 2020.
    - https://time.com/nextadvisor/in-the-news/starting-a-side-hustle/ [Accessed 4th February 2021).
18. Drew, C. (2019) The double diamond 15 years on… Available from: https://medium.com/design-council/the-double-diamond-15-years-on-8c7bc594610e [Accessed 16th September 2020].
19. Design Council (2019) Framework for Innovation: Design Council's evolved Double Diamond. Available from: https://www.designcouncil.org.uk/our-work/skills-learning/tools-frameworks/framework-for-innovation-design-councils-evolved-double-diamond [Accessed 23rd July 2021].
20. Case based on:
    - Goffin, K., Beznosov, A. & Seiler, M. (2021). Countering commoditization through innovation: Challenges for European B2B companies. *Research Technology Management*, 64 (4), 20–28.
21. Goffin, K. (1994) Understanding customers' views: A practical example of the use of repertory grid technique. *Management Research News*, 17 (7/8), 17–28.
22. Leonard-Barton, D. (1995) *Wellsprings of knowledge: Building and sustaining the sources of innovation*. Boston, USA, Harvard Business School Press.
23. Herstatt, C. (2001) Search fields for radical innovations involving market research. Technical University of Hamburg-Harburg, Germany, Working Paper No. 10.
24. Herstatt, C. & von Hippel E. (1992) Developing new product concepts via the lead user method: A case study in a 'low-tech' field. *Journal of Product Innovation Management*, 9 (3), 213–221.
25. Griffin, A. & Hauser, J. R. (1993) The voice of the customer. *Marketing Science*, 12 (1), 1–27.
26. We conducted a comprehensive study of the well-being market for a food manufacturer in 2019. However, the illustrative findings given here are based on the results of exercises conducted with several classes of Mannheim MBA students.
27. Goffin, K., Vaernes, C., Koners, U. & van der Hoven, C. (2012) Beyond the voice-of-the-customer: Ethnographic market research. *Research Technology Management*, 55 (4), 45–53.
28. Bettencourt, L. A. & Ulwick, A. W. (2008) The customer-centred innovation map. *Harvard Business Review*, 86 (5), 109–114. Quote from p109.
29. Arnould, E. J. & Wallendorf, M. (1994) Market-oriented ethnography: Interpretation building and marketing strategy formulation. *Journal of Marketing Research*, XXXI, 484–504.
30. Rosenthal, S. R. & Capper, M. (2006) Ethnographies in the front end: Designing for enhanced customer experiences. *Journal of Product Innovation Management*, 23 (3), 215–237.
31. Fellman, M. W. (1999) Breaking tradition. *Marketing Research*, 11 (3), 20–24.
32. Modified from: Goffin, K., Vaernes, C., Koners, U. & van der Hoven, C. (2012) Beyond the voice-of-the-customer: Ethnographic market research. *Research Technology Management*, 55(4), 45–53.
33. Illustrative findings based on well-being product investigations with Mannheim MBA students.
34. There are many simple versions of the empathy map such as: Gray, D., Brown, S., & Macanufo, J. (2010) *Gamestorming: A playbook for innovators, rulebreakers, and changemakers*. Sebastopol, USA, O'Reilly Media Inc. Our version was designed to generate deep insights by integrating the results of video coding.
35. Illustrative findings again based on well-being product exercises with Mannheim MBA students.

36 Case based on:
    - A project with BASF conducted in 2020–21.
    - Extensive discussions with Yannick Griveau and Jennifer Rech from BASF on the capabilities of virtual meeting technology, 2021–22.
37 Case based on:
    - Discussions with Polly Glasse at the ISPO industrial show in Munich February 2019 and a telephone interview with her in April 2019.
    - https://www.polyn.co/ [Accessed 1st September 2020].
38 Kano, N., Saraku, N., Takahashi, F. & Tsuji, S. (1996) Attractive quality and must-be quality. *Journal of the Japanese Society for Quality Control*, 41, 39–48.
39 Matzler, K. & Hinterhuber, H. (1998) How to make product development projects more successful by integrating Kano's model of customer satisfaction into quality function deployment. *Technovation*, 18 (2), 25–38.

CHAPTER 4

1 Kester, L., Griffin, A., Hultink, E. J. & Lauche, K. (2011) Exploring portfolio decision-making processes. *Journal of Product Innovation Management*, 28 (5), 641–61. (Quote from p. 659.)
2 Case based on an MBA project and interviews with David Williams.
3 Cooper, R. G. (1998) *Product leadership*. Reading, USA, Perseus Books. Three goals were identified by Cooper but, based on our experience supporting MSBs with portfolio management, we see it as essential to add learning as a separate point. Otherwise, there is a danger that portfolio decisions will be inconsistent.
4 Tjaturpriono, H. A. (2017) *Unravelling the routines in new product development portfolio management*. PhD Thesis. Cranfield School of Management, UK.
5 Reitz, M. (2011) Is your company choosing the best innovation ideas? *MIT Sloan Management Review*, 52 (4), 47–52.
6 Kahneman, D. (2012) *Thinking, fast and slow*. London, UK, Penguin.
7 Gino, F. & Pisano, G. (2008) Toward a theory of behavioural operations. *Manufacturing & Service Operations Management*, 10 (4), 676–691.
8 Reitz, M. (2011) Is your company choosing the best innovation ideas? *MIT Sloan Management Review*, 52 (4), 47–52.
9 Rigby, D. K., Gruver, K. & Allen, J. (2009) Innovation in turbulent times. *Harvard Business Review*, 87 (6), 79–86.
10 Goffin, K. & Mitchell, R. (2017) *Innovation management: Effective strategy and implementation*. 3rd ed. Basingstoke, Palgrave Macmillan.
11 Mitchell, R., Hunt, F. & Probert, D. (2010) Valuing and comparing small portfolios. *Research Technology Management*, 53 (2), 43–54.
12 Tjaturpriono, H. A. (2017) *Unravelling the routines in new product development portfolio management*. PhD Thesis. Cranfield School of Management, UK.
13 Markham, S. K. & Lee, H. (2013) Product Development and Management Association's 2012 comparative performance assessment study. *Journal of Product Innovation Management*, 30 (3), 408–429.
14 Kandybin, A. (2009) Which innovation efforts will pay? *MIT Sloan Management Review*, 51 (1), 53–60. Kandybin proposed a similar diagram but this used ROI to compare projects, which is inappropriate when the mix includes breakthrough and radical projects. For breakthrough and radical projects, the estimation of profit over coming years is likely to be inaccurate.
15 Case based on:
    - Telephone interviews with Charles Broussaudier and Edouard Lagrue on 18th December 2019.
    - The company website https://www.softbankrobotics.com/corp/profile/ [Accessed 20th February 2020].
    - A company visit on 17th February 2020.
16 Edouard Lagrue of SoftBank Robotics also read an early draft of this chapter and contributed very useful ideas on portfolio management.
17 Heim, U. (2017) Building a reliable innovation engine. McKinsey. Available at: https://www.mckinsey.com/business-functions/operations/our-insights/building-a-reliable-innovation-engine [Accessed 13th August 2020].
18 Brown, B. & Anthony, S. D. (2011) How P&G tripled its innovation success rate. *Harvard Business Review*, 89 (6), 64–72. (Quote from p. 71.)
19 Case based on:
    - An interview with Dr.-Ing. Michael Kleinkes on 9th November 2020.
    - Langenscheidt, F. & Venohr, B. (Eds.) (2015).

Lexikon der Deutschen weltmarktführer. Cologne, Germany, Deutsche Standards.
- VMT Pepperl + Fuchs (2015). 'Bildverarbeitung und Lasermesstechnik' Brochure No. 262862. Available at: https://vmt-vision-technology.com/83/company/growth-locations [Accessed 1st November

CHAPTER 5

1. See: http://www.businessdictionary.com/definition/product-development.html [Accessed 1st January 2019].
2. Castellion, G. & Markham, S. K. (2013) Perspective: New product failure rates: Influence of argumentum ad populum and self-interest. *Journal of Product Innovation Management*, 30 (5), 976–979.
3. Markham, S. K. & Lee, H. (2013) Product Development and Management Association's 2012 Comparative performance assessment study. *Journal of Product Innovation Management*, 30 (3), 408–429. [Note percentages have been rounded for clarity.]
4. Cambridge Dictionary online; https://dictionary.cambridge.org/dictionary/english/product
5. Anthony, S. D. (2012) The new corporate garage. *Harvard Business Review*, 90 (9), 45–53.
6. Usselman, S. W. (2013) Research and development in the United States since 1900: An interpretive history. Economic History Workshop, Yale University, 11th November. Available from: usselman_paper.pdf (yale.edu) [Accessed 20th December 2022].
7. Schumpeter, J. A. (1934) *The theory of economic development*. Boston, USA, Harvard University Press.
8. See:
   - Eden, L. (2018) The fourth industrial revolution: Seven lessons from the past. In van Tulder, R., Verbeke, A. & Piscitello, L. (eds.), *International business in the information and digital age* (Progress in international business research Vol. 13), Bingley, UK, Emerald.
   - World Trade Organization (2019) The future of services trade Available from World Trade Report 2019: The future of services trade (wto.org) [Accessed 16th April 2020].
9. For example, *Research Policy* was founded in 1971 and the *Journal of Product Innovation Management* was founded in 1984.
10. Hauser, J. R. & Clausing, D. (1988) The House of Quality. *Harvard Business Review*, 66 (3), 66–73.
11. Case study based on:
    - Extensive contacts with Mölnlycke over several years.
    - Weigel, T. & Goffin, K. (2016) Creating innovation capabilities: Mölnlycke Healthcare's 'Journey'. *Research Technology Management*, 58 (4), 28–35.
    - Sjöden, K. (2019) Efter soperplåstret: Så ska sårvården förbättras. *Göteborgs-Posten*, Sunday 10th March (newspaper article in Swedish).
12. Based on Cooper, R. G. (2001) *Winning at new products*. Cambridge, USA, Perseus Publishing.
13. Goffin, K. & Micheli, P. (2010) Maximizing the value of industrial design in new product development. *Research Technology Management*, 53 (5), 29–37.
14. Table prepared by the authors based on a number of sources including: Cooper, R. G. (2001) *Winning at new products*. Cambridge, USA, Perseus Publishing; Goffin, K. and Micheli, P. (2010) Maximizing the value of industrial design in new product development. *Research Technology Management*, 53 (5), 29–37; and discussions with BASF (a company which has integrated BMI into their NPD process).
15. Goffin, K. (2112) Sustainable new product development. In: Bradshaw, D. & Grayson, D. (eds.) *Cranfield on sustainability*. Austin, USA, Greenleaf Publishing, 105–118.
16. Authors' own table, based on ideas collected working with various companies.
17. Goffin, K., Beznosov, A. & Seiler, M. (2021) Countering commoditization through innovation: Challenges for European B2B companies. *Research Technology Management*, 64 (4), 20–28.
18. McGrath, R. G. & MacMillan, I. C. (1995) Discovery-driven planning. *Harvard Business Review*, 74 (3), 44–54.
19. Case based on:
    - An interview with Brett Tomlin on 7th January 2021.
    - https://www.eurocaps.co.uk/ [Accessed 22nd January 2021].
20. Here we particularly acknowledge the advice of Dr Matthias Seiler, who has tested various criteria in the companies where he has worked.
21. Richtnér, A., Åhlstrom, P. & Goffin, K. (2014) 'Squeezing R&D': A study of organizational slack and knowledge creation in NPD, using

the SECI model. *Journal of Product Innovation Management*, 31 (6), 1268–1290.
22. Case based on:
    - One author's engagement with Nuesoft Senior Team over the period 2000–2019.
    - Interviews with Massoud Alibakhsh 10th July 2019 and 3rd March 2021.
    - An interview with Shahram Famorzadeh 8th April 2021.
23. Ries, E. (2011) *The lean startup*. London, UK, Penguin.
24. The four questions recommended in *The lean startup* are (p64):
    1) Do consumers recognize that they have the problems you are trying to solve?
    2) If there was a solution, would they buy it?
    3) Would they buy it from us?
    4) Can we build a solution for that problem?
25. Rogers, E. M. (2003) *The diffusion of innovations*. 5th ed. New York, USA, The Free Press.
26. Moore, G. A (1991) *Crossing the chasm*. New York, Harper Business.
27. McGrath, R. G. & MacMillan, I. C. (1995) Discovery-driven planning. *Harvard Business Review*, 74 (3), 44–54.
28. Ramanujan, M. & Tacke, G. (2016) *Monetizing innovation*. New Jersey, USA, Wiley.
29. Based on: Ramanujan, M. & Tacke, G. (2016) *Monetizing innovation*. New Jersey, USA, Wiley. Enhanced based on the authors' experience.
30. Example based on Keith Goffin's experiences in launching medical products at Hewlett-Packard.

CHAPTER 6

1. See:
    - Coughlan, P. & Coghlan, D. (2011) *Collaborative strategic improvement through network action learning: The path to sustainability*. Cheltenham, UK, Edward Elgar.
    - Kierans, I. (2015) *Developing a business model innovation capability within an established company*. PhD Thesis, Cranfield School of Management, UK.
    - Oliver, J. (2008) Action learning enabled strategy making. *Action Learning: Research and Practice*, 5 (2), 149–158.
2. See:
    - Reeves, M. & Püschel, L. (2015) Die another day: What leaders can do about the shrinking life expectancy of corporations. *BCG Perspectives*. Available from: https://www.bcg.com/publications/2015/strategy-die-another-day-what-leaders-can-do-about-the-shrinking-life-expectancy-of-corporations [Accessed 10th April 2021].
    - Boston Consulting Group (BCG) Business model innovation delivers competitive advantage. Available from: https://www.bcg.com/capabilities/innovation-strategy-delivery/business-model-innovation [Accessed 10th April 2021].
    - Govindarajan, V. & Srivastava, A (2016) Strategy when creative destruction accelerates. Tuck School of Business Working Paper No. 2836135.
3. See:
    - Schwab, K. (2016) The Fourth Industrial Revolution. Geneva, CH, World Economic Forum. Available from: https://www.weforum.org/agenda/2016/01/the-fourth-industrial-revolution-what-it-means-and-how-to-respond/ [Accessed 14th January 2021].
    - Eden, L. (2018) The Fourth Industrial Revolution: Seven lessons from the past. In van Tulder, R., Verbeke, A. & Piscitello, L. (eds.) *International Business in the Information and Digital Age* (Progress in International Business Research, Vol. 13). Bingley, UK, Emerald Publishing Limited, 15–35.
4. See:
    - Taylor, K. (2021) In 2020, big businesses got bigger and small businesses died. The vicious cycle won't stop until we take action. *Insider*. Available from: https://www.businessinsider.com/in-2020-big-businesses-got-bigger-small-businesses-died-2020-12?r=US&IR=T [Accessed 15th August 2021].
    - Govindarajan, V., Srivastava, A. & Enache, L. (2021) The U.S. Economy is leaving Midsize Companies behind. Available from: https://hbr.org/2021/02/the-u-s-economy-is-leaving-midsize-companies-behind [Accessed 15th August 2021].
    - Dennis, S. (2021) Retail reality: It's death in the middle. Available from: https://www.forbes.com/sites/stevendennis/2017/12/04/retail-reality-its-

death-in-the-middle/?sh=5a3e3a036341 [Accessed 15th August 2021].
- Carey, A. (2018) From the 'squeezed middle' to the 'magnificent middle market'. Small Business Charter. Available from: https://smallbusinesscharter.org/business-advice/squeezed-middle-magnificent-middle-market/ [Accessed 15th August 2021].
- Carr, J. & Jones, G. (2017). Optimizing mid-sized businesses. Available from: https://www.mazars.com/content/download/933260/48592872/version//file/Optimize%20White%20Paper_FINAL_UK_single.pdf [Accessed 15th August 2021].

5. Graham, A. (2020) State of the Venture Capital Industry 2019. Toptal. Available from: https://cdn2.hubspot.net/hubfs/2799924/Finance%20Decks/Whitepapers/Finance/State_of_the_Venture_Capital_Industry_in_2019_-_02.pdf [Accessed 10th April 2021].

6. Lee, A. (2013) Welcome to the Unicorn Club. TechCrunch Available from: https://techcrunch.com/2013/11/02/welcome-to-the-unicorn-club/?guccounter=1 [Accessed 10th April 2021].

7. See:
   - Startup Genome (2020) The new normal for the global startup economy and the impact of Covid. Available at: https://startupgenome.com/report/gser2020 [Accessed 12th April 2021].
   - CBI Insights (2021) The complete list of Unicorns. *CBI Insights*. Available from: https://www.cbinsights.com/research-unicorn-companies [Accessed 12th April 2021].

8. Kenney, M. & Zysman, J. (2019) Unicorns, Cheshire cats, and the new dilemmas of entrepreneurial finance. *Venture Capital*, 21 (1), 35–50.

9. Anon. (2021) Europe's biggest neobank wants to take over the world. *The Economist*. Available from: https://www.economist.com/finance-and-economics/2021/06/24/europes-biggest-neobank-wants-to-take-over-the-world [Accessed 24th July 2021].

10. Hoffman, R. & Yeh, C. (2018) *Blitzscaling: The lightning-fast path to building massively valuable businesses*. New York, USA, Crown Publishing.

11. Dogs of the Dow (2021) Largest companies by market cap today (top 50 list) Available from: https://www.dogsofthedow.com/largest-companies-by-market-cap.htm [Accessed 24th July 2021].

12. CBI Insights (2020) The 9 industries Amazon could disrupt next. Available from: https://www.cbinsights.com/research/report/amazon-disruption-industries/ [Accessed 24th July 2021].

13. Truss, C., Shantz, A., Soane, E., Kerstin, A. & Delbridge, D. (2013) Employee engagement, organisational performance and individual well-being: exploring the evidence, developing the theory. *The International Journal of Human Resource Management*, 24, 14.

14. Drucker, P. F. (1954) *The practice of management*. New York, USA, Harper & Row.

15. Friedman, M. (1970) A Friedman doctrine—The social responsibility of business is to increase its profits. *New York Times*, 13th September. Available from: https://www.nytimes.com/1970/09/13/archives/a-friedman-doctrine-the-social-responsibility-of-business-is-to.html [Accessed 21st August 2021].

16. Jensen, M. C. & Meckling, W. H. (1976)—Theory of the firm: Managerial behavior, agency costs and ownership structure, *Journal of Financial Economics*, 3 (4), 305–360.

17. Mackey, J. & Sisodia, R. (2013) *Conscious capitalism: liberating the heroic spirit of business*. Boston, USA, Harvard Business Review Press.

18. Schwab, K. & Vanham, P. (2021) *Stakeholder capitalism: A global economy that works for progress, people and planet*. Hoboken, USA, John Wiley & Sons.

19. World Economic Forum (2020) The global Risks Report. Available from: https://www.weforum.org/reports/the-global-risks-report-2020 [Accessed 15th August 2021].

20. Inequality in a rapidly changing world. Available from: https://www.un.org/development/desa/dspd/wp-content/uploads/sites/22/2020/01/World-Social-Report-2020-FullReport.pdf [Accessed 15th August 2021].

21. Sustainability Reporting is Growing, with GRI the global common Language. Available from: https://www.globalreporting.org/about-gri/news-center/2020-12-01-sustainability-reporting-is-growing-with-gri-the-global-common-language/ [Accessed 15th August 2021].

22. See:
   - Gast, A., Illanes, P., Probst, N., Schaninger, B. & Simpson, B. (2020) Purpose Shifting from Why to How. (2021) *McKinsey Quarterly*. Available at: https://www.mckinsey.com/business-functions/organization/our-insights/purpose-shifting-from-why-to-how [Accessed 15th August 2021].

- Rosenberg W. (2020) The purpose gap. Corporate Reporting, PwC. Available from: https://pwc.blogs.com/corporatereporting/2020/10/the-purpose-gap-october-2020.html [Accessed 22nd December, 2021].

23 See:
- Research by CONE. Available from: https://www.conecomm.com/research-blog/2016-millennial-employee-engagement-study [Accessed 10th June 2021].
- The business case for purpose. Harvard Business Review Analytic Services. Available from: https://hbr.org/resources/pdfs/comm/ey/19392HBRReportEY.pdf [Accessed 10th June 2021].

24 Case based on:
- An interview with Evelyn Doyle, Patagonia Head of People Europe, Middle East and Africa, on 14th June 2021.
- The Harris Poll (2021) Corporate reputation rankings. *Axios*. Available from: https://theharrispoll.com/axios-harrispoll-100/ [Accessed 15th June 2021].
- Chouinard, Y. (2016) *Let my people go surfing: The education of a reluctant businessman.* New York, USA, Penguin Books.
- Stanley, V. How to become a mission driven company like Patagonia. *You Tube*. Available from: https://www.youtube.com/watch?v=VPt-0InbY6RA [Accessed 15th June 2021].
- O'Rourke, D. & Strand, R. W. (2016). Patagonia: driving sustainable innovation by embracing tensions, *California Management Review*, 60, 102–125.
- Beer. J. (2019) Exclusive: Patagonia founder Yvon Chouinard talks about the sustainability myth, the problem with Amazon—and why it's not too late to save the planet. *Fast Company*. Available from: https://www.fastcompany.com/90411397/exclusive-patagonia-founder-yvon-chouinard-talks-about-the-sustainability-myth-the-problem-with-amazon-and-why-its-not-too-late-to-save-the-planet [Accessed 25th October, 2021].

25 Teece, D. J. (2009) *Dynamic capabilities and strategic management: Organizing for innovation and growth*. Oxford, UK, Oxford University Press.

26 See:
- Argyris, C. (1999) *On organizational learning*. Oxford, UK, Blackwell Business.
- Senge, P. M. (1994) *The fifth discipline*. New York, USA, DoubleDay.
- Regner, P. (2005) Adaptive and creative strategy logics in strategy processes. *Strategy Process*, 22, 189–210.

27 Garvin, D. A., Edmondson, A. C. & Gino, F. (2019) Is yours a learning organization? *Harvard Business Review*, 86–93.

28 Hill, L. A., Brandeau, G., Truelove, E. & Lineback, K. (2014) *Collective genius: The art and practice of leading innovation*. Boston, USA, Harvard Business Review Press.

29 Koners, U. & Goffin, K. (2007) Learning from post-project reviews: A cross-case analysis. *Journal of Product Innovation Management,* 24 (3). 242–258.

30 Goffin, K. & Koners, U. (2011) Tacit knowledge, lessons learned and new product development *Journal of Product Innovation Management*, 28 (3), 300–318.

31 Ian Kierans learnt this technique at a Stanford d.School workshop (design thinking) in 2013.

32 Cohen, W. M. & Levinthal, D. A. (1990) Absorptive capacity: A new perspective on learning and innovation, *Administrative Science Quarterly*, 35, 128–152.

33 Cassol, A., Marietto, M., Toniel, G. & Werlang, N. B. (2021) Interorganizational learning and absorptive capacity: Empirical research in small and medium enterprises, *Revista de Administração Mackenzie*, 22 (1), 1–28.

34 See:
- Van Alstyne, M. W., Parker, G. G. & Choudary, S. P. (2016). Pipelines, platforms, and the new rules of strategy, *Harvard Business Review*, 94 (4), 54–61.
- Zhu, F. & Iansiti, M. (2019) Why some platforms thrive and others don't, *Harvard Business Review*, 97 (1), 118–125.

35 Nath, T. I. (2021). How AirBNB makes money. Available from: https://www.investopedia.com/articles/investing/112414/how-airbnb-makes-money.asp [Accessed 15th August 2021].

36 Weill, P. & Woerner, S. (2018) *What's your digital business model? Six Questions to Help You Build the Next-Generation Enterprise*. Harvard Business Review Press, Boston, MA, USA.

37 Goffin, K., Beznosov, A. & Seiler, M. (2021) Countering commoditization through innovation: Challenges for European B2B companies. *Research Technology Management,* 64 (4), 20–28.

38 This case was written by Dr Giulio Buciuni and is based on his engagements and research with Pinarello and other product companies that

innovate across their value chains in different locations. See also:
- Buciuni, G. & Finotto, V. (2016) Innovation in global value chains: Co-location of production and development in Italian low-tech industries. *Regional Studies*, 50 (12), 2010–2023.
- Buciuni, G. & Pisano, G. (2021) Variety of innovation in global value chains. *Journal of World Business*, 56 (2), 1-13.
- BRAIN Staff, Greenwich, Conn. (2016) Pinarello sold to private equity firm involving LVMH. *Bicycle Retailer and Industry News*. Available from: https://www.bicycleretailer.com/international/2016/12/06/pinarello-sold-private-equity-firm-involving-lvmh#.YP2Wr45KiUk [Accessed 25th July 2021].

39   See:
- OECD (2021) The future of work. Available from: https://www.oecd.org/future-of-work [Accessed 15th August 2021].
- Kropp, B. (2021) 9 trends that will shape work in 2021 and beyond. *Harvard Business Review Digital Articles*, (Jan. 14), 2–5.
- Hamel, G. (2007). *The future of management*. Boston, MA, Harvard Business School Press.
- McKinsey Global Institute (2021). The future of work after Covid-19. Available from: https://www.mckinsey.com/~/media/mckinsey/featured%20insights/future%20of%20organizations/the%20future%20of%20work%20after%20covid%2019/the-future-of-work-after-covid-19-report-vf.pdf?shouldIndex=false [Accessed 19th September, 2021].

40   Chesbrough, H. W. (2006) *Open business models: How to thrive in the new innovation landscape*. Boston, USA, Harvard Business School Press.

41   See:
- Weiblen, T. & Chesbrough, H. W. (2015) Engaging with startups to enhance corporate innovation, *California Management Review*, 5 (2), 66–90.
- CBInsights (2019) Why 60% of corporate accelerators fail after 2 years. Available from: https://www.cbinsights.com/research/corporate-accelerator-failure/ [Accessed 15th August 2021].

42   See:
- Department for Business, Energy &Industrial Strategy (BEIS) (20187) The innovative firm's journey to finance. *BEIS Research Paper No. 23*. Available from: https://assets.publishing.service.gov.uk/government/uploads/system/uploads/attachment_data/file/666878/BEIS_format_Innovative_Firms_Journey_to_Finance_BMG_CEEDR.pdf [Accessed 15th August 2021].
- Innovate Programme, *IDA Ireland*. Available from: https://www.idaireland.com/newsroom/publications/ida_innovate_programme#:~:text=Innovate%20Start%20is%20designed%20to,on%20their%20Innovation%20Maturity%20Pathway. [Accessed 15th August 2021].
- Government of Ireland (2020) Report of the Grand Canal Innovation District Advisory Group. Available from: https://www.tcd.ie/innovation-district/Report-of-GCID-Advisory-Group.pdf [Accessed 1st February 2022].

43   Viki, T., Toma, D., & Gons, E. (2017) *The corporate startup how established companies can develop successful innovation ecosystems*. Zeist, Netherlands Vakmedianet Management.

44   Pauwels, C., Clarysse, B., Wright, M. & Van Hove, J. (2016) Understanding a new generation incubation model: The accelerator, *Technovation*, 50–51, 13–24.

45   Chesbrough, H. W. (2006) *Open business models: How to thrive in the new innovation landscape*. Boston, USA, Harvard Business School Press.

46   Case based on:
- An interview with Dariusz Dziuba on Thursday 2nd November 2021.
- http://www.cfoundry.com/eng.

47   See:
- Moonshot thinking. Available from: https://x.company/moonshot/ [Accessed 20th August 2021].
- Google X Head on Moonshots: 10X is easier than 10 percent. https://www.wired.com/2013/02/moonshots-matter-heres-how-to-make-them-happen/ [Accessed 20th August 2021].

48   Michaelis, T. L. and Markham, S. K. (2017) Innovation training: Making innovation a core competency. *Research Technology Management*, 60 (2), 36–42.

49   See:
- Cousens, A. Goffin, K., Mitchell, R., Van Der Hoven, C. & Szwejczewski, M. (2009) Teaching new product development using the CityCar simulation. *Creativity and Innovation Management*, 18 (3), 176–189.

- Goffin, K., Essen, A., Nordqvist, M. & Krakowski, S. (2021) Bringing NPD into the virtual classroom: The WORLDSPORT simulation. European Conference of Innovation and Entrepreneurship (ECIE).

50 Case based on:
  - Alltech website See https://www.alltech.com/about/our-story [Accessed 18th October 2021].
  - Interviews with Ciaran Black, an independent strategy and innovation consultant who has helped develop Alltech's innovation system since 2018. He was formerly Innovation Director at Coillte (Case 1-2) and has worked with the authors on several innovation projects and research.
  - Bell, D. E., and Kindred, N. (2017) Alltech. Harvard Business School Case 518-001.
  - Connolly, A. J., Turner, J. and Potocki, A. (2018). IGNITE your corporate innovation: Insights from setting up an Ag-tech start-up accelerator. *International Food and Agribusiness Management Review*, 21 (6), 833–846.
  - Henderson, L. (2008) Alltech: Making of a champion. *Agri Marketing*, 46 (1), 64–67.

INDEX

A

ABI Inform 162
AB Ludvig Svensson
     case study 10, 162
access, gaining 144
acquisition (code) 173
Action learning cycle 281
adaptive learning 290
Adoption life cycle 266ff
adrenaline 89
Aguilar, Francis 323
AI (artificial intelligence) 44, 68, 217, 242
AirBnB 298
Alibakhsh, Massoud 259
All Nippon Airways (ANA) 137
Alltech case study 313
Alphabet 283
Altro Ltd. case study 141
Amazon 162, 283
ambidextrous innovation 43
Amefa Group 201
ANA (All Nippon Airways) 131
Analysis Workshop
     (Phase 3) 163ff, 191
anchoring 204
anger 88
Angrisano, Carlos 139
Ansoff, Igor 39
Apple 42, 136, 247, 284, 293

Armstrong, Paul 73
artificial intelligence (AI) 44, 68, 217, 242
assessing breakthrough
     projects 207
assessing capability gaps 69
assessing incremental
     projects 213
assessing radical projects 207
AT&T 240
attractiveness-feasibility 76,
attributes of innovation
     teams 116

B

B2B (business-to-
     business) 7, 57, 144, 299
B2C (business-to-
     consumer) 7, 144, 299
Baileys 71
Bank of Ireland case study 121
Bankrate.com 94, 138
Barney, Jay 42
BASF 118, 183ff
basic features 188
B-Corporation
     accreditation 287
behaviour 89
Behavioural Economics 203
bias in gathering
     information 203
bias, types of
     confirmation 203
     conservatism 204
     inconsistency 204
     information avoidance 205
     law of small numbers 204
     procrastination 204
     salient information 203
     sunk costs fallacy 204
Black and Decker
     dustbuster 173
Black, Ciaran 315
black-space 15, 17, 75
Blue Ocean Strategy
     (BOS) 5, 190
BMI (Business Model
     Innovation) 44ff, 46
BMW 247
Booth, Charles 133
BOS (Blue Ocean
     Strategy) 5, 190
Boston Matrix 40
bottlenecks 262
brain 90
brainstorming 64
brainwriting technique 65ff, 185, 188, 291
breakthrough projects 208, 251ff

Broussaudier, Charles 218
Bubble Diagram 214ff
Bureaucratic Theory 87
Business growth categories
    core 13, 15, 17ff
    emerging 15, 17ff, 75
    new 16, 17ff, 75
Business Life Cycle 12ff
    start up 13
    scale 13
    renewal 15
    success and decline 14
Business Model Canvas 44ff
business model, customer relationship 45
business model, customer segments 45
Business Model Innovation (BMI) 44ff
business model, channels 45
business model, key collaborators 45
business model, cost structure 45
business model, revenue streams 45
business model, value proposition 45
Business-to-business (B2B) 7, 57, 144, 299
Business-to-consumer (B2C) 7, 144, 299
business-wide innovation 1, 35, 72, 108ff

C

Caldwell, Tommy 186
Canon 42
canvas, see Business Model Canvas 45ff, 306
capabilities, innovation 69, 289ff
capability gaps 69, 289ff
category goals 74
cell therapy 64
Chandler, Alfred 87
chasm, crossing the 267
choosing criteria 208ff
Chouinard, Yves 286
Christensen, Clayton 43
Cicle Pinarello case study 303ff
CISCO 283
CitiGroup 283
claims of idiosyncrasy (code) 175
Clarks Shoes 176
climbOn! Products 186
CNET 94, 138
codes
    acquisition 173
    contradictions 175
    culture 175
    emotions 173
    environment 173
    humour 173
    misuses 172
    problems 172
    processes 172
    triggers 173
    uses 172
    workarounds 172
coding 172ff
Coillte 54ff, 77, 161, 265, 291
comfort zone 9, 14, 17ff, 90, 199, 204
commercial goals 74
commercialization 102, 115
communication 101
Company X case study 49
competitive advantage 40
complexity (diffusion) 267
concurrent engineering 242
construct cards 167
construct categories 167ff
constructs 147ff, 166
contextual interviews 156
contradictions (code) 175
Cooper, Bob 242
core business 17
Cornetta, Hallie 95
Corporate social responsibility (CSR) 285
cost-plus pricing 270
cost structure 45
Couture, Grégory 11
Cranfield Foundry case study 308
creative destruction 241
critical paths 262
CSR (Corporate social responsibility) 285
culture (code) 175
culture of innovation 94ff
customer insights 129ff
customer relationships 45
customer segments 45

D

D2C (direct-to-customer) 301
DaMIS 310
data analysis of
    ethnographic data 172ff
    lead user data 178
    repertory grid data 166ff
    secondary data 180
data collection 145ff
Data Wall 164, 180ff
DCC case study 103
DCV (Dynamic Capabilities View) 42, 289
Decision Making Unit (DMU) 144
declaring innovation intent 73
deep insights 131
defining vision 38
Design-driven Innovation 140
designing innovation structure 108
designing innovation teams 117ff
design thinking 140
Deutsche Bahn 158
Diagio case study 71
Diffusion 257, 265ff
Diffusion, factors impacting 268

digital business models 298ff
   ecosystem driver 300
   modular 300
   omnichannel 299
   optimizing 302
   supplier 299
direct-to-customer) (D2C) 301
disgust 88
disjunctures (code) 175
disruptive innovation 43ff, 242
division of labour 86
DMU (Decision Making Unit) 144
DNA 91
domain-specific capabilities 69
Double Diamond Model 140
Doyle, Evelyn 286
Drucker, Peter 38, 284
duct tape 172
Dugier, Romain 18
Dynamic Capabilities 42, 47, 289
Dynamic Capabilities View (DCV) 42, 289
Dynamic innovation capability 289
Dziuba, Dariusz 309

E

early adopters 266, 272
early majority 266, 272
Easy Jet 41
EBS (European Beer Supply) 71ff, 78
EBSCO 162
ecosystem driver digital business model 301
ecosystems 43, 300ff
element ratings 147
emerging business 15
emotions (code) 173
emotions
   anger 88
   disgust 88
   excitement 89
   fear 88
   sadness 88
   shame 88
   surprise 89
   trust 89
Empathy Map 177
employment 4
environment (code) 173
Environmental, social and governance (ESG) 285
ESG (Environmental, social and governance) 285
espoused values 99
ethnographic insights 176ff
Ethnographic market research 135, 156ff
ethnography 135, 156, 159
EuroCaps case study 253
European Beer Supply (EBS) 71
European Union (EU) 3
Evans-Prichard, E.E. 135
excitement 89
excitement features 188
exploit 8
exploratory sample 144
explore 8
ExxonMobil 283

F

Fabo, Thomas 243
Facebook 283
family business 4, 7, 10, 22, 57
Famorzadeh, Shahram 260
Fashion Power case study 57ff
fear 88
feasibility criteria 209
features 188
Features, performance, excitement, basic 189
Fexco 301
financial goals 54, 74
financial growth goals 54ff
fixed mindset 90
Flanagan, Rob 104
Flavin, Jim 103
focus groups 134
Ford, Henry 87, 131, 204
Frederick the Great 87
Freud, Sigmund 134
Friedman, Milton 284
Frost and Sullivan 161
Fulton Suri, Jane 136
future of work 306

G

Gallop Poll 134
GE 240, 283
Gellert, Ryan 288
generalizations (code) 175
generating
   deep insights 129, 143, 163ff
   novel solutions 185ff
generative learning 290
Gerard, Lucas 18
Glasse, Polly 186
gloss (code) 175
GlaxoSmithKline 237
grey-space 15, 17ff, 75
Great Pyramid 239
Griveau, Yannick 183
growth 12
growth mindset 90
Guinness 71ff
Gunning, David 55

H

Hackathons 5
Hamel, Gary 42
Harvard Business Review 241
Heitkamp & Thumann Group 23
Hidden champions 3
high-performing teams 114ff
history of
   market research 133
   product innovation 239
   strategic management 37
Holgerson, Per 11
human artefacts 239

Human factor analysis 135
humour (code) 173

I

ideation 185
IDEO 136, 140
incident board 181
incremental projects
    assessing 213
    managing 245
Industrial Revolution
    first 239, 282
    second 240, 282
    third 241, 282
    fourth 242, 283
Industry 4.0 242, 283
Innovation
    capabilities ('C') 7, 279ff, 289
    Capability Audit 70
    capability goals 77
    categories 75
    governance 93, 98ff
    intent 73, 93
    journey 6, 24ff, 26
    journey mechanisms 98
    landscape 52ff
    Landscape Boundary
        Check 56, 60
    management capabilities
        ('C') 69
    Manager 8, 36, 86, 111, 132, 200, 236, 281
    mindset 9, 93
    performance measures 106
    strategy 33ff, 50
    Strategy Matrix 75
    Strategic Options
        (ISOs) 52ff, 76, 144, 197
    structure 108
    Team Charter 120
    Team Design Matrix 117ff
    team learning 113
    Values Map 48, 100
Innovation Strategic Options
    (ISOs) 52ff, 76, 144

innovative growth 12
innovators 265
inside view 90
insight generation 143ff
instant coffee 134
intended audience 28
internal view 90
interviewee 148
interviewer 148
interviews 8, 134, 148
ISO 56000 7
ISOs (Innovation Strategic
    Options) 52ff, 76, 144, 197

J

jobs to be done 156, 172, 270
Johnny Walker 71
Johnson & Johnson 160
journey 6, 24
Journey Diagnosis Tool 293ff

K

Kano analysis 188
Kano Model 189
Kano, Noriaki 188
Kärcher 274, 293
key activities 45
key collaborators 45
key resources 45
key success factors 41
Kick-off meetings 257
Kleinkes, Michael 226
knee-jerk decisions 16
Kodak 240
Kromer, Karl 135

L

Laggards (diffusion) 267
Lagrue, Edouard 218
Late majority (diffusion) 267
Launch, market 248, 271
Le Corre, Tristan 18
Lead User Technique
    advantages 161
    analysis 178

    history 136
    preparing 159
    learning 112
        adaptive 290
        digital business models 298
        from outside 296
        from purpose-led
            businesses 284
        generative 290
learning curve 112ff
Levitt, Theodore 38
Literary Digest 134
Lonely Planet 94, 138
Lourenco, Antonio 142
Ludvig Svensson 10, 245
Ludvigson, Anders 11
Lynch, Laura 122
Lyons, Mark 314
Lyons, Pearse 313

M

macro context 39, 66
Malinowski, Bronislaw 135
March, James 39
Market Based View (MBV) 40
market context 65
market launch 248, 271
market planning 271
market research 133ff
Mauro, Chuck 135
Mayo, Elton 87
MBV (Market Based View) 40
McBride, Barry 244
McDonagh, Francesca 122
McKinesey-GE Matrix 40
mechanistic structures 87
Merton, Robert K. 135
Microsoft 283
Mid-sized businesses
    (MSBs) 1, 3
Miele 173
mindset 28, 88
mindset matters 28, 77, 88, 121, 191, 227, 273, 317
Mintzberg, Henry 43

misuse (code) 172
Model T Ford 87, 240
modular digital business model 300
Mölnlycke Health Care 192, 243ff, 245, 273
mountain bikes 136
MSBs (Mid-sized businesses) 1, 3
MyMove.com 138

N

NASA Control Room 135
Nelemans, Jan 57
Nelemans, Maxim 57
Nelemans, Reg 57
Nelemans, Ronald 57
Net Present Value (NPV) 206
Netflix 92
network effects 298
neurons 90
new business 17
new market development 27, 269ff
new product development (NPD) 235, 242, 245ff, 258
New York Stock Exchange 135
Next Advisor 138
Nolan, Eoghan 95
North Face 159
novel solutions 129, 185ff
NPD (new product development) 235, 242, 245ff, 258
NPV (Net Present Value) 206
Nuer 135
Nuesoft case study 259
Nugent, John 122

O

Ó Murchú, Seán 122
O'Leary, Michael 47
O'Reilly III, Charles 43, 88
observability (diffusion) 269
omnichannel digital business model 299
open innovation 307
opportunity criteria 207, 209
Opportunity-Investment Diagram 215
organic structures 87
organizational learning 290
organizational
  artifacts 92
  culture 91
  inertia 88
  structures 87, 108
organizing the journey 83
Osterwalder, Alexander 44
outside view 90

P

pain points 158
Pareto 5
Patagonia case study 286
PayPal 91
Pentathlon Framework 21
perceived risk (diffusion) 269
performance features 188
performance measures 105
personas 177, 183
PESTEL Analysis 39, 49
Pfizer 283
Phases of the innovation journey 24
  Phase 1 33ff
  Phase 2 83ff
  Phase 3 129ff
  Phase 4 197ff
  Phase 5 233ff
  Phase 6 279ff
physical sensations 88
Pigneur, Yves 44
Pinarello case study 303
Pinarello, Fausto 303
Pinarello, Giovanni 303
pivoting 14, 18, 210
pivots 14, 18, 210
Point 'A' 6, 24
Point 'B' 6, 24
Polyn brand 188
Porter, Michael 40
Porter's Five Forces 41
Portfolio Dashboard 219
Portfolio decision checklist 244
Portfolio management
  aims of 202
  bias 204
  impact of 203
Portfolio meetings agenda 223
Post-project review (PPR) 290
Post-project review, template 292
PPR (post-project review) 290
Prahalad, C.K. 42
Prior, Donald 72
problem definition 141
problems (code) 172
process innovation 16, 308
processes (code) 172
Proctor and Gamble 134
project comparisons 221
projection 134
project team 233, 257
project team, kick-off meetings 257
prototype testing 264
proxy measure 207
purpose-led business 284

Q

qualitative market research 114, 163
quantitative market research 145

R

radical projects 207, 210, 251
Rank Xerox 42, 136
RBV (Resource Based View) 42
Rech, Jennifer 183
Redmax brand 58

red pen mentality 14
Red Ventures case
    studies 94, 137
relative advantage
    (diffusion) 269
renewal stage 15
Repertory Grid
    Technique 134, 146ff
Repertory grid
    advantages 155
    constructs 147, 166ff
    data analysis 166ff
    elements 146, 150, 154ff
    interviews 146
    triad 147
resource allocation 102, 144
Resource Based View
    (RBV) 42
Return on investment
    (ROI) 206
Revolut 283
Richardson Sheffield 201
Risk
    assessment 210
    commercial 212
    technical 212
ROI (Return on
    Investment) 206
Rolls-Royce 46, 240
Roosevelt, Franklin D. 134
Royce, Henry 240
Ryanair 41, 46ff
RWW screening
    questions 257, 263ff

S

sadness 88
sample, choosing 144
Sanders, Liz 135
SBUs (Strategic Business
    Units) 4
Schein, Edgar 92
Schumpeter, Joseph 241
Scientific management 87
scouting teams 114

S-curves 63
Sears, Ron 135
secondary data
    advantages 163
    analysis 180
    collection 161
selecting an innovation
    manager 111
selecting innovation teams 117
selecting projects 197ff
selection criteria
    defining 205
    types of 206
Senior Management Team
    (SMT) 5, 28, 36, 200, 281
service products 250
shame 88
Shotgun case study 18
Simon, Herbert 239
six-sigma 93
SKINourishment case
    study 186
Smith, Adam 86, 136
SMT (Senior Management
    Team) 5, 28, 36, 200, 281
sociology 135
soft issues 94, 98
Softbank Robotics case
    study 217
Spiral Development, gates 257
Spiral Development,
    process 256
Stage-Gate™
    enhancing 247ff
    process 245ff
Stalker, G.M. 87
Start-up 12, 18
Stena Line 101, 111
Strategic Business Units
    (SBUs) 4
strategic intent 42
Strategic Roadmap 61ff
Strategic Roadmap example 64
Strategic roadmapping
    teams 64
Strategy process 53

Strategy
    Building blocks of 38
street corner society 135
structure 108
Success and failure in NPD 237
Suchman, Lucy 136
Sun Tzu 37
supplier digital business
    model 299
surprise 88
Svensson (Sweden) 10, 245
swim lanes 61
SWOT Analysis (strengths,
    weaknesses,
    opportunities and
    threats) 39, 49

T

Taylor, Frederick 87
team learning 113
Technology s-curves 63
technology swimlane 61
TechProdLine case study 214
Teece, David 42
The Points Guy 94
Theory of a firm 284
Theory of sociotechnical
    systems 87
Thiel, Peter 91
thoughts, feelings and
    emotions 88
Three Horizons 74ff, 219
Time Magazine 94
time-to-market 107, 219
Tomlin, Brett 254
trialability (diffusion) 268
triggers (code) 173
trust 88
T-shaped 112
Tushman, Michael 43, 88
TVGuide 94, 138

U

UI (user interface) 173, 246
UK Design Council 140

underlying assumptions 92
unicorns 283
usability 246
User experience (UX) 173, 246
User interface (UI) 173, 246
uses (code) 171
UX (user experience) 173, 246

V

value chain 41
value ecosystems 43
value proposition 13, 45, 60, 66
Value-based pricing 235, 270
Values map 98
VMT Vision Power case
    study 225
VOC (Voice of the
    Customer) 7, 131, 149, 242
Voice of the Customer
    (VOC) 7, 131, 149, 242
volatile markets 44
von Hippel, Eric 136
VRIO Analysis 42, 49, 63
VUCA 44

W

Walk the Data Wall 181ff, 185,
    190
Weber, Max 87
Wedgwood, Josiah 239
well-being products 145, 146,
    154, 156, 168
white-space 15, 17ff, 75
William the Conqueror 133
Williams, David 201
willingness to pay,
    questions 264
workarounds (code) 172
Workshop 1 (Phase 1) 54, 69
Workshop 2 (Phase 1) 73, 77

"The management of innovation is essential to sustainable growth. ... This insightful book provides a valuable map to complete it successfully. Leaders and teams will be better equipped after reading it."

Paschal Donohoe
Minister for Finance, Ireland
President of the Eurogroup

"Illustrates that behind great innovations are diverse people who collaborate brilliantly and that behind great businesses are innovative cultures."

Tara Foley
CEO
AXA Retail, UK

"Developing disruptive, digital business models requires managing many moving parts. The lessons here are imperative for senior teams seeking to rapidly scale and sustain performance."

Dr Shahram Famorzadeh
Senior VP Engineering
Dr Chrono, USA

Business-wide innovation is the definitive way to grow. Yet, how to achieve this remains elusive for so many businesses.

This authoritative, no-nonsense book will guide your business on its innovation journey from Point 'A' where it currently is, to Point 'B', the performance you want. It cuts through the clutter of innovation tools, to focus on the essential capabilities 'C' that drive growth.

Five integrated phases that lead to Innovative Growth are clearly mapped out: Shaping innovation strategy; Organizing for the journey; Developing deep insights and novel solutions; Selecting projects to implement; and Getting innovations to market. At each phase the processes that make innovation possible and, crucially, the mindsets needed to make it happen are brought to light.

Includes 24 international case studies—such as Red Ventures (USA), Patagonia (USA), Svensson (Sweden), Pinarello (Italy), Diageo (EU), SoftBank Robotics (France) and DCC (Ireland). These insightful cases demonstrate how innovative growth really happens.

BUSINESS   ALSO AVAILABLE AS AN E-BOOK

ISBN-13: 978-91-87791-32-1

COVER DESIGN: VICTOR MINGOVITS